문제로 쉬워지는 중학영문법

그래머 클라우드

3000제

LEVEL 1

그래머 클라우드 3000제
문제를 풀며 중학영문법의 개념을 잡는다!

- **한눈에 이해되는!** 문장 구조를 시각화한 문법 포인트별 개념 정리
- **단계별로 학습하는!** 개념확인 문제와 기본연습 문제로 이해하고, 실전 문제로 마무리
- **학교 시험 만점 맞는!** 틀리기 쉬운 내신포인트를 확인하며 정답 적중률 높이기

학습자의 마음을 읽는 동아영어콘텐츠연구팀

동아영어콘텐츠연구팀은 동아출판의 영어 개발 연구원, 현장 선생님.
그리고 전문 원고 집필자들이 공동연구를 통해 최적의 콘텐츠를 개발하는 연구조직입니다.

원고 개발에 참여하신 분들

고미라 박현숙 원혜진 윤희진 이정아 정혜진

교재 기획에 도움을 주신 분들

김기성 김나영 김설하 김효성 박정미 이루다 이지혜

문제로 쉬워지는 중학영문법

그래머 클라우드

3000제

LEVEL 1

구성과 특징

POINT별 문법 개념 이해하기

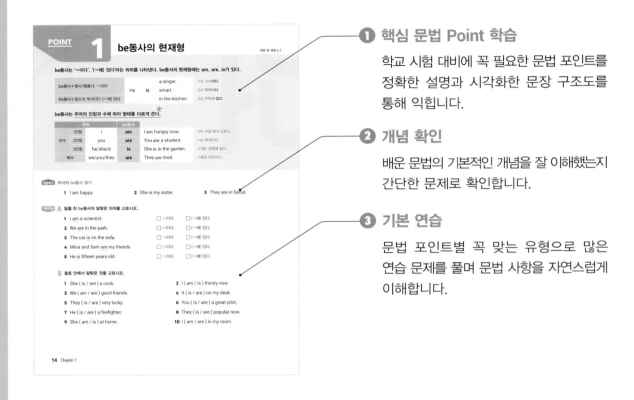

1 핵심 문법 Point 학습

학교 시험 대비에 꼭 필요한 문법 포인트를 정확한 설명과 시각화한 문장 구조도를 통해 익힙니다.

2 개념 확인

배운 문법의 기본적인 개념을 잘 이해했는지 간단한 문제로 확인합니다.

3 기본 연습

문법 포인트별 꼭 맞는 유형으로 많은 연습 문제를 풀며 문법 사항을 자연스럽게 이해합니다.

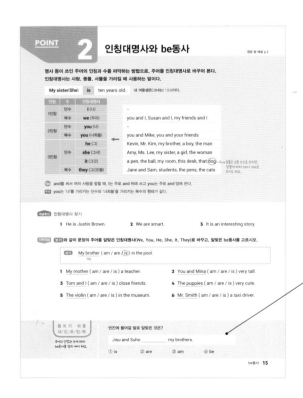

4 틀리기 쉬운 내신 포인트

시험에 꼭 나오는 틀리기 쉬운 내신 포인트를 확인함으로써 실제 학교 시험에서 정답 적중률을 높입니다.

2 ─ 통합하여 개념 완성하기

[개념완성 TEST]

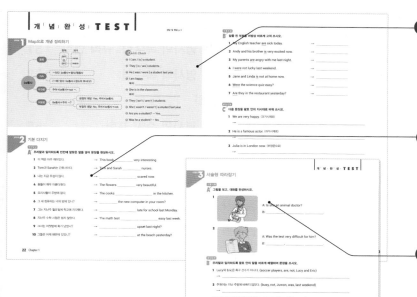

① STEP 1 Map으로 개념 정리하기

해당 Chapter의 문법 내용을 이해하기 쉽게 시각화한 Map을 통해 문법 개념을 정리합니다.

② STEP 2 기본 다지기

해당 Chapter의 문법 내용을 통합하여 연습 문제를 풀며 실력을 다집니다.
(빈칸 완성, 오류 수정, 문장 전환 등)

③ STEP 3 서술형 따라잡기

해당 Chapter의 문법 내용을 통합하여 서술형에 많이 나오는 유형을 집중적으로 훈련합니다.
(그림 이해, 영작 완성, 문장 영작 등)

3 ─ 실제 학교 시험 유형으로 내신 대비하기

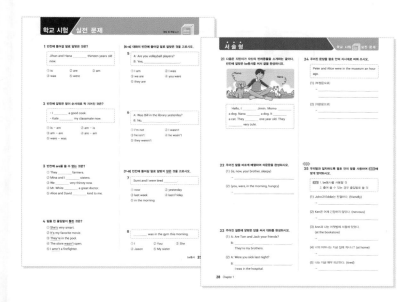

[학교 시험 실전 문제]

해당 Chapter의 문법 내용을 바탕으로 학교 시험에서 자주 출제되는 객관식과 서술형 문제를 풀며 내신 시험에 완벽하게 대비합니다.

차례

차례

문법 기초 다지기

8품사

품사는 각각의 단어를 기능에 따라 나눈 것으로, 영어에는 다음과 같이 8개의 품사가 있다.

| 명사 | 대명사 | 동사 | 형용사 | 부사 | 전치사 | 접속사 | 감탄사 |

명사

명사는 사람이나 사물, 장소 등, **모든 것에 붙여진 이름**이다.

예시 book, pencil, dog, flower, desk, student, James, Korea 등

James is an **actor**. James는 배우이다.

I live in **Seoul**. 나는 서울에 산다.

대명사

대명사는 앞에 나온 명사를 반복해서 쓰지 않기 위해 **명사를 대신해서 쓰는 말**이다.

예시 I, you, he, she, they, your, us, theirs, myself, it, this, that 등

Emily has a dog. **She** loves **it**. Emily는 개를 키운다. 그녀는 그것을 사랑한다.

Tony and **his** friends like soccer. Tony와 그의 친구들은 축구를 좋아한다.

동사

동사는 사람, 동물, 사물의 **동작이나 상태를 나타내는 말**이다.

예시 be, play, eat, study, walk, have, like, watch, make 등

They **are** in the classroom. 그들은 교실에 있다.

We **play** basketball every day. 우리는 매일 농구를 한다.

형용사

형용사는 **명사의 색깔이나 모양, 크기, 성질 등을 나타내는 말**로, 명사나 대명사를 꾸미거나 보충 설명한다.

예시 tall, short, beautiful, cute, large, small 등

I have a **beautiful** dress. 나는 아름다운 드레스를 가지고 있다.

He is **tall** and **handsome**. 그는 키가 크고 잘생겼다.

부사

부사는 **시간, 장소, 방법, 정도, 빈도 등을 나타내는 말**로, 동사, 형용사, 다른 부사를 꾸며 준다.

예시 very, really, slowly, fast, late, early, carefully 등

He usually walks **slowly**. 그는 대개 천천히 걷는다.

I am **very** happy. 나는 매우 행복하다.

전치사

전치사는 **명사나 대명사 앞에서 시간, 장소, 수단 등의 뜻을 더해 주는 말**이다.

예시 at, on, in, under, for, during, by, from, to, with 등

I go **to** school **by** bus. 나는 버스를 타고 학교에 간다.

We met **at** the theater **at** two o'clock. 우리는 2시에 극장에서 만났다.

접속사

접속사는 **단어와 단어, 구와 구, 절과 절을 연결해 주는 말**이다.

예시 and, but, or, so, that, because, if 등

She ordered pizza **and** a salad. 〈단어+단어〉 그녀는 피자와 샐러드를 주문했다.

He will play the piano **or** sing a song. 〈구+구〉 그는 피아노를 연주하거나 노래를 부를 것이다.

I got up late, **but** I wasn't late for school. 〈절+절〉 나는 늦게 일어났지만, 학교에 늦지 않았다.

감탄사

감탄사는 말하는 사람의 기쁨, 슬픔, 놀람 등의 **감정을 표현하는 말**이다.

예시 oh, wow, oops, hooray 등

Wow, it's very tall! 와, 정말 높다!

Oh, she is beautiful! 오, 그녀는 아름답다!

Quiz

다음 단어들의 품사를 쓰시오.

1 pencil ( )   **2** and ( )

3 learn ( )   **4** wow ( )

5 in ( )   **6** very ( )

7 short ( )   **8** they ( )

| 정답 | 1. 명사 2. 접속사 3. 동사 4. 감탄사 5. 전치사 6. 부사 7. 형용사 8. 대명사

문장의 구성 요소

문장은 단어를 조합하여 내용을 표현한 것이다. 문장을 이루는 구성 요소에는 주어, 동사, 목적어, 보어가 있다.

주어	동사	목적어	보어

주어

주어는 **동작이나 상태의 주체가 되는 말**로, 우리말의 '누가, 무엇이'에 해당한다.
주로 문장의 맨 앞에 온다.

Mina speaks English very well. 미나는 영어를 매우 잘한다.

The book is interesting. 그 책은 재미있다.

동사

동사는 **주어의 동작이나 상태를 나타내는 말**로, 우리말의 '~이다, ~하다'에 해당한다.
주로 주어 뒤에 온다.

You **are** very kind. 너는 매우 친절하다.

She **watched** a movie last night. 그녀는 어젯밤에 영화를 봤다.

목적어

목적어는 **동사의 대상이 되는 말**로, 우리말의 '누구를, 무엇을'에 해당한다.
주로 동사 뒤에 온다.

I bought **a cap**. 나는 모자를 샀다.

Ms. Han teaches **science**. 한 선생님은 과학을 가르친다.

보어

보어는 **주어나 목적어를 보충 설명해 주는 말**로, 주로 동사 뒤에 온다.

We are **students**. 우리는 학생이다.

She made me **happy**. 그녀는 나를 행복하게 만들었다.

Quiz

밑줄 친 부분이 문장의 구성 요소 중 무엇에 해당하는지 쓰시오.

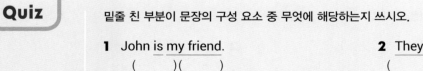

1 John is my friend.
(　　　)(　　　)

2 They are busy.
(　　　) (　　　)

3 She plays the violin.
(　　　) (　　　)

4 The movie made us sad.
(　　　)

| 정답 | 1. 동사, 보어　2. 주어, 보어　3. 동사, 목적어　4. 보어

문장의 종류

문장에는 평서문, 의문문, 감탄문, 명령문이 있다.

| 평서문 | 의문문 | 감탄문 | 명령문 |

평서문

'~은 …하다'와 같은 문장을 평서문이라고 한다. 평서문에는 긍정문과 부정문이 있다.

I **go** to school at 8 o'clock. 〈긍정문〉 나는 8시에 학교에 간다.

I **don't go** to school on Sundays. 〈부정문〉 나는 일요일에 학교에 가지 않는다.

의문문

'~은 …이니?'라고 물어보는 문장을 의문문이라고 한다.

Is he your brother? 그는 너의 남동생이니?

Do you speak English? 너는 영어를 말하니?

감탄문

'오, 아름다워라!'처럼 강한 느낌을 나타내는 문장을 감탄문이라고 한다.

How beautiful! 정말 아름답구나!

What a big house! 정말 큰 집이구나!

명령문

'~해라'라고 어떤 일을 지시할 때 사용하는 문장을 명령문이라고 한다.

Be careful! 조심해!

Get up early! 일찍 일어나라!

Quiz

다음 문장의 종류를 쓰시오.

1 What a tall tower!   (   )

2 Please close the window.   (   )

3 Do you have a pencil?   (   )

4 Sam likes swimming.   (   )

ㅣ정답ㅣ 1. 감탄문   2. 명령문   3. 의문문   4. 평서문

Nothing is stronger than habit.
— Publius Naso Ovidius

1 be동사

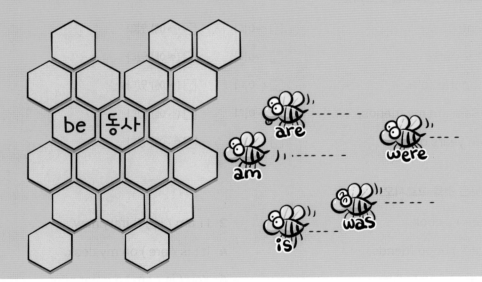

be동사는 주어의 상태나 특징을 설명할 때 쓰는 동사로
am, are, is, was, were를 묶어 부르는 말이다.

be동사의 현재형

정답 및 해설 p.2

be동사는 '~이다', '(~에) 있다'라는 의미를 나타낸다. be동사의 현재형에는 **am, are, is**가 있다.

be동사+명사/형용사: ~이다	He	is	a singer.
			smart.
be동사+장소의 부사(구): (~에) 있다			in the kitchen.

그는 가수**이다**.
그는 똑똑하**다**.
그는 부엌에 **있다**.

be동사는 주어의 인칭과 수에 따라 형태를 다르게 쓴다. ☆

		주어	be동사		
단수	1인칭	I	**am**	I **am** hungry now.	나는 지금 배가 고프다.
	2인칭	you	**are**	You **are** a student.	너는 학생이다.
	3인칭	he/she/it	**is**	She **is** in the garden.	그녀는 정원에 있다.
복수		we/you/they	**are**	They **are** tired.	그들은 피곤하다.

개념확인 주어와 be동사 찾기

1 I am happy.   **2** She is my sister.   **3** They are in Seoul.

기본연습 **A** 밑줄 친 be동사의 알맞은 의미를 고르시오.

1 I am a scientist.   ☐ ~이다   ☐ (~에) 있다

2 We are in the park.   ☐ ~이다   ☐ (~에) 있다

3 The cat is on the sofa.   ☐ ~이다   ☐ (~에) 있다

4 Mina and Sam are my friends.   ☐ ~이다   ☐ (~에) 있다

5 He is fifteen years old.   ☐ ~이다   ☐ (~에) 있다

B 괄호 안에서 알맞은 것을 고르시오.

1 She (is / are) a cook.   **2** I (am / is) thirsty now.

3 We (am / are) good friends.   **4** It (is / are) on my desk.

5 They (is / are) very lucky.   **6** You (is / are) a great pilot.

7 He (is / are) a firefighter.   **8** They (is / are) popular now.

9 She (am / is) at home.   **10** I (am / are) in my room.

인칭대명사와 be동사

명사 등이 쓰인 주어의 인칭과 수를 파악하는 방법으로, 주어를 인칭대명사로 바꾸어 본다.
인칭대명사는 사람, 동물, 사물 등을 가리킬 때 사용하는 말이다.

| My sister(She) | **is** | ten years old. | 내 여동생은(그녀는) 10살이다. |

인칭	수	인칭대명사	
1인칭	단수	**I** (나)	-
	복수	**we** (우리)	you and I, Susan and I, my friends and I
2인칭	단수	**you** (너)	-
	복수	**you** (너희들)	you and Mike, you and your friends
3인칭	단수	**he** (그)	Kevin, Mr. Kim, my brother, a boy, the man
		she (그녀)	Amy, Ms. Lee, my sister, a girl, the woman
		it (그것)	a pen, the ball, my room, this desk, that dog
	복수	**they** (그(것)들)	Jane and Sam, students, the pens, the cats

→ 동물은 보통 it으로 쓰지만, 성별에 따라 he나 she로 쓰기도 해요.

Tips and를 써서 여러 사람을 말할 때, I는 주로 and 뒤에 쓰고 you는 주로 and 앞에 쓴다.

주의 you는 '너'를 가리키는 단수와 '너희들'을 가리키는 복수의 형태가 같다.

 인칭대명사 찾기

1 He is Justin Brown.　　　**2** We are smart.　　　**3** It is an interesting story.

 보기와 같이 문장의 주어를 알맞은 인칭대명사(We, You, He, She, It, They)로 바꾸고, 알맞은 be동사를 고르시오.

> **보기** My brother (am / are /(is)) in the pool.
> 　　　 He

1 My mother (am / are / is) a teacher.　　**2** You and Mina (am / are / is) very tall.

3 Tom and I (am / are / is) close friends.　　**4** The puppies (am / are / is) very cute.

5 The violin (am / are / is) in the museum.　　**6** Mr. Smith (am / are / is) a taxi driver.

틀 리 기 쉬 운
내 / 신 / 포 / 인 / 트

주어의 인칭과 수에 따라
be동사를 달리 써야 해요.

빈칸에 들어갈 말로 알맞은 것은?

Jisu and Suho _____ my brothers.

① is　　　　② are　　　　③ am　　　　④ be

3 be동사 현재형의 줄임말

정답 및 해설 p.2

「주어+be동사」는 줄여 쓸 수 있다.

주어	be동사		줄임말		
I	am		**I'm**	**I'm** happy now.	나는 지금 행복하다
We			**We're**	**We're** thirsty.	우리는 목이 마르다.
You	are		**You're**	**You're** students.	너희들은 학생이다.
They		→	**They're**	**They're** famous.	그들은 유명하다.
He			**He's**	**He's** very tall.	그는 매우 키가 크다.
She	is		**She's**	**She's** my cousin.	그녀는 나의 사촌이다.
It			(It's)	**It's** in the living room.	그것은 거실에 있다.

→ '그것의'라는 뜻의 its와 헷갈리지 않도록 해요.

궁금해요!
'는 뭐라고 읽나요?

줄임말에 사용하는 '는
아포스트로피(apostrophe)라고 해요.

Tips that is는 that's로 줄여 쓴다. this is는 this's로 줄여 쓰지 않는다.

개념확인 줄여 쓸 수 있는 말 찾기

1 He is very cute.　　　　**2** They are my earrings.　　　　**3** We are at the market.

기본연습 **A** 다음 말을 줄임말로 바꿔 쓰시오.

1 I am → _____　　　　**2** It is → _____

3 You are → _____　　　　**4** We are → _____

5 She is → _____　　　　**6** They are → _____

7 He is → _____　　　　**8** That is → _____

B 우리말과 일치하도록 빈칸에 알맞은 말을 줄임말로 넣어 문장을 완성하시오.

1 나는 키가 아주 작다.　　→ _____ very short.

2 그것은 상자 안에 있다.　　→ _____ in the box.

3 우리는 지금 졸리다.　　→ _____ sleepy now.

4 그는 음악 선생님이다.　　→ _____ a music teacher.

5 그녀는 사무실에 있다.　　→ _____ in the office.

6 그들은 매우 무례하다.　　→ _____ very rude.

7 너는 중학생이다.　　→ _____ a middle school student.

be동사의 과거형

정답 및 해설 p.2

be동사의 과거형은 was나 were를 쓰며, '〜이었다', '(〜에) 있었다'라고 해석한다.

현재형	과거형	
am, is	**was**	→ 주어와 be동사의 과거형은 줄여 쓰지 않아요.
		I **was** busy last weekend. 나는 지난 주말에 바빴다.
are	**were**	We **were** middle school students. 우리는 중학생이었다.

Tips 과거형은 yesterday, last week, in 2012, two days ago, at that time 등의 과거를 나타내는 부사(구)와 함께 자주 쓰인다.
My father **was** in Tokyo **last month**. 우리 아버지는 지난달에 도쿄에 계셨다.

개념확인 be동사와 과거를 나타내는 말 찾기

1 He was sad yesterday.   **2** I was sick last night.   **3** They were in L.A. in 2020.

기본연습 **A** 괄호 안에서 알맞은 것을 고르시오.

1 I (am / was) tired last Monday.

2 Jimin (is / was) my classmate now.

3 My brother (is / was) upset last night.

4 Ann and I (are / were) 13 years old this year.

5 My sisters (was / were) in Seoul two days ago.

6 Ken and Sally (was / were) in the gym yesterday.

B 밑줄 친 부분을 어법상 바르게 고쳐 쓰시오.

1 I <u>were</u> a student in 2015.   → _____

2 My mother <u>is</u> unhappy at that time.   → _____

3 Erica and I <u>is</u> in Rome last week.   → _____

4 We <u>was</u> late for school yesterday.   → _____

5 My hands <u>were</u> cold now.   → _____

틀리기 쉬운 내/신/포/인/트

시간을 나타내는 부사(구)를 확인하여 시제에 맞게 be동사를 써야 해요.

빈칸에 들어갈 말로 알맞은 것은?

My sister _____ absent from school yesterday.

① is   ② are   ③ was   ④ were

be동사의 부정문

정답 및 해설 p.2

be동사의 부정문은 **be동사 뒤에 not을 써서 나타내며**, 현재형은 '~이 아니다', '(~에) 없다'라고 해석하고 과거형은 '~이 아니었다', '(~에) 없었다'라고 해석한다.

		be동사	not		
현재	I	**am**		a cook.	나는 요리사가 아니다.
	You	**are**	not	tall.	너는 키가 크지 않다.
	She	**is**		in the gym.	그녀는 체육관에 없다.
과거	I	**was**	not	hungry.	나는 배고프지 않았다.
	We	**were**		at home.	우리는 집에 없었다.

줄임말
I'm **not** → am not은 줄여 쓰지 않아요.
We/You/They **aren't**
He/She/It **isn't**
I/He/She/It **wasn't**
We/You/They **weren't**

주의 「주어+was/were」는 줄여 쓰지 않지만, was not은 wasn't로, were not은 weren't로 줄여 쓸 수 있다.
He **wasn't** a singer. 그는 가수가 아니었다.
They **weren't** friends at that time. 그들은 그 당시에 친구가 아니었다.

궁금해요!
You're not이 맞나요,
You aren't가 맞나요?

둘 다 맞는 표현이에요.
I am not만 I amn't로 쓰지 않고,
I'm not으로 줄여 써요.

개념확인 not이 들어갈 위치 찾기

1 I am bored. **2** He was late yesterday. **3** They are in the mall.

기본연습 **A** 괄호 안에서 알맞은 것을 고르시오.

1 It (isn't / aren't) my toothbrush.

2 I (am not / not am) thirsty now.

3 Ted (is not / not is) my classmate.

4 I (amn't / am not) in the hospital.

5 Kevin and I (isn't / aren't) cousins.

6 The sky (am not / is not) clear now.

7 You (is not / are not) a good dancer.

8 Tony (is not / are not) in the art club.

9 I (wasn't / weren't) busy last weekend.

10 Sora (wasn't / weren't) in the theater last night.

11 We (wasn't / weren't) very tired an hour ago.

12 The food at the restaurant (wasn't / weren't) expensive.

13 These toys (was not / were not) cheap at that time.

14 The keys (wasn't / weren't) in my bag this morning.

B 다음 문장을 부정문으로 바꿀 때 빈칸에 알맞은 말을 쓰시오.

1 Harry was a movie star. → _____ _____ a movie star.

2 They are in the music room. → _____ _____ in the music room.

3 I am from New Zealand. → _____ _____ from New Zealand.

4 Tina is fourteen years old. → _____ _____ fourteen years old.

5 I was at home in the morning. → _____ _____ at home in the morning.

6 We were in Busan last Saturday. → _____ _____ in Busan last Saturday.

7 The cookies were sweet. → _____ _____ _____ sweet.

C 우리말과 일치하도록 빈칸에 알맞은 말을 넣어 문장을 완성하시오.

1 나는 걱정되지 않는다. → _____ _____ worried.

2 그 영화는 인기 있지 않았다. → The movie _____ popular.

3 그녀는 게으르지 않다. → _____ _____ lazy.

4 Sam은 친절하지 않다. → Sam _____ _____ kind.

5 우리는 지금 졸리지 않다. → _____ _____ sleepy now.

6 그 상자들은 무겁지 않았다. → The boxes _____ _____ heavy.

7 나는 어젯밤에 슬프지 않았다. → I _____ _____ sad last night.

8 White 씨는 작가가 아니었다. → Ms. White _____ _____ a writer.

9 그 책들은 상자 안에 없다. → The books _____ _____ in the box.

10 너희들은 중학생이 아니다. → You _____ _____ middle school students.

11 너희들은 지난 금요일에 도서관에 없었다. → You _____ _____ in the library last Friday.

12 유미와 나는 작년에 같은 반이 아니었다. → Yumi and I _____ in the same class last year.

밑줄 친 줄임말이 틀린 것은?

① She's not pretty.
② I amn't angry.
③ It's not my book.
④ They aren't in the classroom.

POINT 6 be동사의 의문문

be동사 현재형의 의문문은 「Am/Are/Is＋주어 ~?」의 형태로 쓰며, '~이니?', '(~에) 있니?'라고 해석한다.

의문문		긍정의 대답	부정의 대답
Am	I ~?	Yes, you are.	No, you aren't.
Are	we ~?	Yes, we/you are.	No, we/you aren't.
	you ~?	Yes, I am. / Yes, we are.	No, I'm not. / No, we aren't.
	they ~?	Yes, they are.	No, they aren't.
Is	he/she/it ~?	Yes, he/she/it is.	No, he/she/it isn't.

> 부정의 대답에서 be동사와 not은 주로 줄여 써요.

> Yes로 시작하는 짧은 대답에서는 주어와 be동사를 줄여 쓰지 않아요.

A: **Are you** sad? 너는 슬프니?
B: Yes, I am. / No, I'm not. 응, 그래. / 아니, 그렇지 않아.

be동사 과거형의 의문문은 「Was/Were＋주어 ~?」의 형태로 쓰며, '~이었니?', '(~에) 있었니?'라고 해석한다.

의문문	긍정의 대답	부정의 대답
Was/Were＋주어 ~?	Yes, 주어＋was/were.	No, 주어＋wasn't/weren't.

A: **Were they** happy? 그들은 행복했니?
B: Yes, they were. / No, they weren't. 응, 그랬어. / 아니, 그렇지 않았어.

주의 의문문에 대답을 할 때에는 주어의 인칭과 수에 유의하고, 성별에 따라 알맞은 대명사로 바꿔서 답해야 한다.
A: Is **Mr. Brown** an actor? Brown 씨는 배우니?
B: Yes, **he** is. / No, **he** isn't. 응, 그래. / 아니, 그렇지 않아.

주의 Are you ~?로 질문하면 뒤에 나오는 명사가 단수인지 복수인지 확인한다.
A: **Are you** a singer? 너는 가수니?   A: **Are you** singers? 너희들은 가수니?
B: Yes, **I** am. 응, 그래.   B: No, **we** aren't. 아니, 그렇지 않아.

개념확인 be동사와 주어 찾기

1 Are you angry?   **2** Was John in his car?   **3** Am I on Main Street?

기본연습 **A** 괄호 안에서 알맞은 것을 고르시오.

1 (It is / Is it) your key?

2 (Am / Are) I late again?

3 (Is / Are) Kevin nervous?

4 (Is / Are) Eva and Jane from Canada?

5 (Is / Was) the weather nice yesterday?

6 (Was / Were) you in the school cafeteria at that time?

B 빈칸에 알맞은 말을 넣어 의문문에 대한 답을 완성하시오.

1 A: Is your room dirty?

    B: Yes, _____ _____.

2 A: Is your mother a doctor?

    B: No, _____ _____.

3 A: Was she at the zoo?

    B: No, _____ _____.

4 A: Are you pianists?

    B: No, _____ _____.

5 A: Are you Tom Smith?

    B: No, _____ _____.

6 A: Are you a student at this school?

    B: Yes, _____ _____.

7 A: Are the students in the playground?

    B: Yes, _____ _____.

8 A: Was the book boring?

    B: No, _____ _____.

9 A: Were they busy last weekend?

    B: Yes, _____ _____.

10 A: Was Mike your classmate last year?

    B: Yes, _____ _____.

11 A: Were Joe and Bill in Boston last month?

    B: No, _____ _____.

12 A: Were you hungry in the morning?

    B: Yes, _____ _____.

C 우리말과 일치하도록 빈칸에 알맞은 말을 넣어 문장을 완성하시오.

1 그것은 그녀의 책이니?
→ _____ _____ her book?

2 Jessica는 어젯밤에 아팠니?
→ _____ _____ sick last night?

3 그는 지금 과학 실험실에 있니?
→ _____ _____ in the science lab now?

4 그들은 2년 전에 키가 컸니?
→ _____ _____ tall two years ago?

5 너는 작년에 반장이었니?
→ _____ _____ the class president last year?

6 당신들은 이곳의 손님인가요?
→ _____ _____ guests here?

7 내가 너무 시끄럽니?
→ _____ _____ too noisy?

대화의 빈칸에 들어갈 말로 알맞은 것은?

A: Is Kate from Sydney?

B: _____

① Yes, I am.
② No, it is.
③ Yes, she is.
④ No, you aren't.

개 념 완 성 TEST

STEP 1 Map으로 개념 정리하기

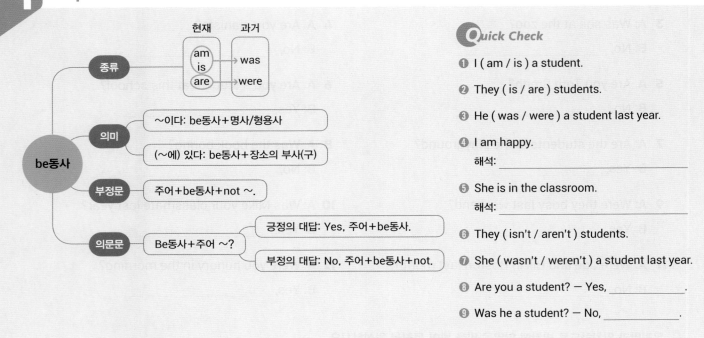

Quick Check

❶ I (am / is) a student.

❷ They (is / are) students.

❸ He (was / were) a student last year.

❹ I am happy.

　해석: _____

❺ She is in the classroom.

　해석: _____

❻ They (isn't / aren't) students.

❼ She (wasn't / weren't) a student last year.

❽ Are you a student? — Yes, _____.

❾ Was he a student? — No, _____.

STEP 2 기본 다지기

빈칸완성

A 우리말과 일치하도록 빈칸에 알맞은 말을 넣어 문장을 완성하시오.

1 이 책은 아주 재미있다.　→　This book _____ very interesting.

2 Tom과 Sarah는 간호사이다.　→　Tom and Sarah _____ nurses.

3 나는 지금 무섭지 않다.　→　_____ _____ scared now.

4 꽃들이 매우 아름다웠다.　→　The flowers _____ very beautiful.

5 요리사들이 주방에 없다.　→　The cooks _____ _____ in the kitchen.

6 그 새 컴퓨터는 너의 방에 있니?　→　_____ the new computer in your room?

7 그는 지난주 월요일에 학교에 지각했다.　→　_____ _____ late for school last Monday.

8 지난주 수학 시험은 쉽지 않았다.　→　The math test _____ _____ easy last week.

9 그녀는 어젯밤에 화가 났었니?　→　_____ _____ upset last night?

10 그들은 어제 해변에 있었니?　→　_____ _____ at the beach yesterday?

B 밑줄 친 부분을 어법상 바르게 고쳐 쓰시오.

1 My English teacher <u>are</u> sick today. → _____

2 Andy and his brother <u>is</u> very excited now. → _____

3 My parents <u>are</u> angry with me last night. → _____

4 <u>I were</u> not lucky last weekend. → _____

5 Jane and Linda <u>is</u> not at home now. → _____

6 <u>Were</u> the science quiz easy? → _____

7 <u>Are</u> they in the restaurant yesterday? → _____

C 다음 문장을 괄호 안의 지시대로 바꿔 쓰시오.

1 We are very happy. (과거시제로)

→ _____

2 He is a famous actor. (과거시제로)

→ _____

3 Julia is in London now. (부정문으로)

→ _____

4 They were in the office yesterday. (의문문으로)

→ _____

5 James and I are good singers. (부정문으로)

→ _____

6 Yujin and Sumi are best friends now. (의문문으로)

→ _____

7 Her voice was clear this morning. (부정문으로)

→ _____

8 The children were in the playground. (부정문으로)

→ _____

9 Your room was very clean. (의문문으로)

→ _____

그림이해

A 그림을 보고, 대화를 완성하시오.

1

A: Is she an animal doctor?

B: _____, _____ _____.

2

A: Was the test very difficult for him?

B: _____, _____ _____.

영작완성

B 우리말과 일치하도록 괄호 안의 말을 바르게 배열하여 문장을 쓰시오.

1 Lucy와 Eric은 축구 선수가 아니다. (soccer players, are, not, Lucy and Eric)

→ _____

2 주원이는 지난 주말에 바쁘지 않았다. (busy, not, Juwon, was, last weekend)

→ _____

3 네 아버지는 지금 차고에 계시니? (now, is, your father, in the garage)

→ _____

4 남동생과 나는 어제 공원에 있었다. (in the park, were, my brother and I, yesterday)

→ _____

문장영작

C 우리말과 일치하도록 괄호 안의 말을 이용하여 영작하시오.

1 Sally는 작년에 키가 작았니? (short)

→ _____

2 나는 고등학생이 아니다. (a high school student)

→ _____

3 너와 Lisa는 도서관에 있었니? (in the library)

→ _____

4 우리는 지금 매우 배가 고프다. (very hungry)

→ _____

1 빈칸에 들어갈 말로 알맞은 것은?

> Jihun and Hana _____ thirteen years old now.

① is
② are
③ am
④ was
⑤ were

2 빈칸에 알맞은 말이 순서대로 짝 지어진 것은?

> • I _____ a good cook.
> • Kate _____ my classmate now.

① is – am
② am – is
③ am – are
④ are – am
⑤ were – was

3 빈칸에 **are**를 쓸 수 **없는** 것은?

① They _____ farmers.
② Mina and I _____ sisters.
③ We _____ very thirsty now.
④ Mr. White _____ a great doctor.
⑤ Alice and David _____ kind to me.

4 밑줄 친 줄임말이 **틀린** 것은?

① She's very smart.
② It's my favorite movie.
③ They're in the pool.
④ The store wasn't open.
⑤ I amn't a firefighter.

[5-6] 대화의 빈칸에 들어갈 말로 알맞은 것을 고르시오.

5

> A: Are you volleyball players?
> B: Yes, _____.

① I am
② I was
③ we are
④ you were
⑤ they are

6

> A: Was Bill in the library yesterday?
> B: No, _____.

① I'm not
② I wasn't
③ he isn't
④ he wasn't
⑤ they weren't

[7-8] 빈칸에 들어갈 말로 알맞지 **않은** 것을 고르시오.

7

> Sumi and I were tired _____.

① now
② yesterday
③ last week
④ last Friday
⑤ in the morning

8

> _____ was in the gym this morning.

① I
② You
③ She
④ Jason
⑤ My sister

9 밑줄 친 부분의 의미가 나머지와 다른 하나는?

① The box <u>is</u> very heavy.
② Tennis <u>is</u> my favorite sport.
③ My parents <u>are</u> good dancers.
④ Jenny <u>is</u> my best friend.
⑤ My brother <u>is</u> in his room.

10 ①~⑤ 중 not이 들어갈 위치로 알맞은 곳은?

(①) Judy (②) and (③) Minho (④) were (⑤) in the same class last year.

11 빈칸에 들어갈 be동사가 보기 와 같은 것은?

보기 They _____ at the beach last weekend.

① I'm sorry. I _____ so rude last time.
② Julia _____ ten years old last year.
③ Eric and Sam _____ at school now.
④ Mike _____ not at the museum yesterday.
⑤ The pictures _____ on the wall two days ago.

12 다음 문장을 부정문으로 바르게 바꾼 것은?

He is my English teacher.

① He isn't my English teacher.
② He is no my English teacher.
③ He not is my English teacher.
④ He aren't my English teacher.
⑤ He was not my English teacher.

13 밑줄 친 부분이 어법상 올바른 것은?

① Bomi <u>not was</u> kind.
② Harry <u>are</u> my brother.
③ I <u>was</u> very bored yesterday.
④ My aunt <u>was</u> in the kitchen now.
⑤ Sue and Tom <u>are</u> in the bank yesterday.

고난도
14 밑줄 친 부분이 어법상 틀린 문장의 개수는?

ⓐ I <u>was</u> not happy now.
ⓑ It <u>is</u> my favorite doll.
ⓒ <u>Is</u> Mr. Lee your uncle?
ⓓ We <u>were</u> in the same club last year.

① 0개   ② 1개   ③ 2개
④ 3개   ⑤ 4개

15 대화가 자연스럽지 않은 것은?

① A: Are you full now?

   B: Yes, I am.

② A: Am I late for the concert?

   B: No, you aren't.

③ A: Is your mother a police officer?

   B: Yes, she is.

④ A: Were they in the science lab yesterday?

   B: No, they aren't.

⑤ A: Was Mike surprised yesterday?

   B: Yes, he was.

16 어법상 틀린 부분을 바르게 고친 것은?

> Wendy and I was not upset about the news yesterday.

① was → are

② was → were

③ was not → not was

④ not → no

⑤ yesterday → today

17 빈칸에 들어갈 be동사가 나머지와 다른 하나는?

① We _____ very sad yesterday.

② You _____ very strong two years ago.

③ They _____ at the party last night.

④ Minho and Jinho _____ on the soccer team now.

⑤ My brother and I _____ in the park last Sunday.

18 빈칸에 들어갈 질문으로 알맞은 것은?

> A: _____
>
> B: Yes, it was.

① Is the apple fresh?

② Were the books heavy?

③ Was Sam in the garden?

④ Was the musical interesting?

⑤ Were you sixteen years old last year?

19 밑줄 친 부분이 어법상 틀린 것은?

① They are from Taiwan.

② We weren't busy last week.

③ James and I are in the zoo now.

④ She is absent from school yesterday.

⑤ Michael wasn't a musician five years ago.

고난도

20 어법상 올바른 문장의 개수는?

> ⓐ They are not from New Zealand.
>
> ⓑ The books is on the desk.
>
> ⓒ Andy and Ben are in the airport.
>
> ⓓ Molly and I are in the same club.
>
> ⓔ Was you at the concert last night?

① 0개   ② 1개   ③ 2개

④ 3개   ⑤ 4개

21 다음은 지민이가 자신의 반려동물을 소개하는 글이다. 빈칸에 알맞은 be동사를 써서 글을 완성하시오.

Momo   Nana

Hello, I _____ Jimin. Momo _____ a dog. Nana _____ a dog. It _____ a cat. They _____ one year old. They _____ very cute.

22 주어진 말을 바르게 배열하여 의문문을 완성하시오.

(1) (is, now, your brother, sleepy)

→ _____

(2) (you, were, in the morning, hungry)

→ _____

23 주어진 질문에 알맞은 답을 써서 대화를 완성하시오.

(1) A: Are Tom and Jack your friends?

B: _____, _____ _____.
They're my brothers.

(2) A: Were you sick last night?

B: _____, _____ _____.
I was in the hospital.

24 주어진 문장을 괄호 안의 지시대로 바꿔 쓰시오.

Peter and Alice were in the museum an hour ago.

(1) (부정문으로)

→ _____

(2) (의문문으로)

→ _____

고난도
25 우리말과 일치하도록 괄호 안의 말을 사용하여 조건에 맞게 영작하시오.

조건 1. be동사를 사용할 것
2. 줄여 쓸 수 있는 경우 줄임말로 쓸 것

(1) John과 Eddie는 친절하다. (friendly)

→ _____

(2) Ken은 어제 긴장하지 않았다. (nervous)

→ _____

(3) Ann과 나는 어젯밤에 서점에 있었다.
(at the bookstore)

→ _____

(4) 너의 어머니는 지금 집에 계시니? (at home)

→ _____

(5) 나는 지금 매우 피곤하다. (tired)

→ _____

CHAPTER

2 일반동사

일반동사는 주어의 동작이나 상태를 설명할 때 쓰는 동사를 말한다.

일반동사의 현재형

정답 및 해설 p.4

일반동사는 주어의 동작이나 상태 등을 나타낼 때 쓴다. 일반동사의 현재형은 현재의 상태나 반복되는 습관 등을 나타낼 때 쓰며, 주어가 3인칭 단수일 때는 -(e)s를 붙여 쓴다.

1인칭, 2인칭, 복수 주어 + 동사원형 (I, You, We, They 등)	I	like	comic books.	나는 만화책을 좋아한다.
	We	eat	breakfast at 7 a.m.	우리는 7시에 아침을 먹는다.
3인칭 단수 주어 + 동사원형+-(e)s (He, She, It 등)	He	likes	comic books.	그는 만화책을 좋아한다.
	She	eats	breakfast at 7 a.m.	그녀는 7시에 아침을 먹는다.

↳ John, my sister, a boy, Ms. Kim 등도 3인칭 단수 주어예요.

Tips 현재형과 함께 주로 쓰이는 부사(구)에는 always, usually, every day, every Sunday, on Sundays 등이 있다.
They play baseball **every day**. 그들은 매일 야구를 한다.

궁금해요!
동사에는
어떤 것들이 있나요?

be동사, 일반동사, 조동사가 있어요.
be동사는 Chapter 1에서 배웠어요.
조동사는 Chapter 6에서
알아보기로 해요.

개념확인 be동사와 일반동사 구별하기

1 It <u>is</u> a tomato.

☐ be동사 ☐ 일반동사

2 They <u>know</u> my brother.

☐ be동사 ☐ 일반동사

3 I <u>go</u> to school every weekday.

☐ be동사 ☐ 일반동사

기본연습 **A** 각 문장에 알맞은 우리말 뜻을 찾아 연결하시오.

1 We are Italian. •

2 We are in the hospital. •

3 We study English every day. •

4 We live in Seoul. •

5 We love action movies. •

• ⓐ 우리는 병원에 있다.

• ⓑ 우리는 서울에 산다.

• ⓒ 우리는 액션 영화를 정말 좋아한다.

• ⓓ 우리는 이탈리아인이다.

• ⓔ 우리는 매일 영어를 공부한다.

B 괄호 안에서 알맞은 것을 고르시오.

1 I (want / wants) a smartphone.

2 We often (watch / watches) TV at home.

3 My brother (sing / sings) very well.

4 They usually (walk / walks) to school.

5 You and Judy (know / knows) his name.

6 Erica (drink / drinks) milk every morning.

7 My sister and I (play / plays) tennis every day.

8 She (ride / rides) her bike in the park every afternoon.

주어가 3인칭 단수일 때 일반동사의 현재형은 동사원형에 **-s**나 **-es**를 붙인다.

대부분의 동사	동사원형+-s	runs	wants	needs	gives
-o, -s, -x, -ch, -sh로 끝나는 동사	동사원형+-es	goes fixes	does watches	passes washes	misses finishes
「자음+y」로 끝나는 동사	y를 i로 바꾸고+-es	study – studies		fly – flies	
불규칙하게 변하는 동사		have – **has**			

Lisa **runs** very fast. Lisa는 매우 빨리 달린다.

Tom **watches** TV every night. Tom은 매일 밤 TV를 본다.

주의 「모음+y」로 끝나는 동사는 -s를 붙인다.
　　play – plays　　　enjoy – enjoys　　　stay – stays

개념확인 주어와 동사 찾기

1 Jane dances very well.　　**2** Tony speaks Chinese.　　**3** Mina studies Italian every day.

기본연습 A 다음 동사의 3인칭 단수형을 쓰시오.

1 smell　→ _____　　**2** do　→ _____

3 need　→ _____　　**4** close　→ _____

5 fix　→ _____　　**6** want　→ _____

7 stay　→ _____　　**8** take　→ _____

9 sleep　→ _____　　**10** finish　→ _____

11 see　→ _____　　**12** tell　→ _____

13 hurry　→ _____　　**14** wash　→ _____

15 learn　→ _____　　**16** catch　→ _____

17 ask　→ _____　　**18** run　→ _____

19 make　→ _____　　**20** try　→ _____

21 pass　→ _____　　**22** work　→ _____

23 enjoy　→ _____　　**24** fly　→ _____

25 cry　→ _____　　**26** have　→ _____

B 괄호 안에서 알맞은 것을 고르시오.

1 Jane (miss / misses) her grandmother.

2 He always (wear / wears) a hat outside.

3 Alice and Paul (like / likes) comedy movies.

4 Her parents (drink / drinks) coffee every morning.

5 She (come / comes) home at six o'clock.

6 My mother (write / writes) a letter to her friend every week.

7 My brother (exercise / exercises) in the evening.

8 Ms. Yun (has / haves) an umbrella.

9 My sister (studys / studies) math every day.

10 Mr. Green (teachs / teaches) English at a middle school.

C 빈칸에 알맞은 말을 보기 에서 골라 올바른 형태로 쓰시오.

보기	have	go	wash	live	play	listen	speak	read

1 Helen ＿＿＿＿＿＿ blue eyes.

2 She ＿＿＿＿＿＿ Korean well.

3 My father always ＿＿＿＿＿＿ the dishes.

4 The boys ＿＿＿＿＿＿ basketball every day.

5 Sandy and Tom ＿＿＿＿＿＿ to the radio in the evening.

6 David ＿＿＿＿＿＿ in Paris with his parents.

7 My brother ＿＿＿＿＿＿ a book every night.

8 Mr. Park ＿＿＿＿＿＿ to the gym every day.

틀 리 기 쉬 운
내/신/포/인/트

주어의 인칭과 수에 따라
알맞은 형태의 일반동사를
써야 해요.

빈칸에 알맞은 말이 순서대로 짝 지어진 것은?

• Yujin ＿＿＿＿＿ her teeth after meals.

• My mother ＿＿＿＿＿ French at a high school.

① brush – teach   ② brush – teaches

③ brushes – teach   ④ brushes – teaches

POINT 3 일반동사 현재형의 부정문

정답 및 해설 p.5

일반동사 현재형의 부정문은 「do/does＋not＋동사원형」의 형태로 쓴다. do not은 don't로, does not은 doesn't로 줄여 쓸 수 있다.

1인칭, 2인칭, 복수 주어＋ don't(do not)＋동사원형	I	don't	like	tomatoes.	나는 토마토를 좋아하지 않는다.
	We	do not	use	paper cups.	우리는 종이컵을 사용하지 않는다.
3인칭 단수 주어＋ doesn't(does not)＋동사원형	He	doesn't	like	tomatoes.	그는 토마토를 좋아하지 않는다.
	She	does not	use	paper cups.	그녀는 종이컵을 사용하지 않는다.

↳ 이때 do/does는 '~하다'라는 뜻의 일반동사가 아니라 뒤에 오는 일반동사를 도와주는 역할을 해요.
not과 함께 부정문을 만들고 주어와 자리를 바꿔 의문문을 만들어요.

주의 doesn't 뒤에 나오는 동사는 주어가 3인칭 단수여도 -(e)s를 붙이지 않고 동사원형을 쓴다.
Mike **doesn't drink** coffee. Mike는 커피를 마시지 않는다.

> be동사의 부정문은
> I am not tall.과 같이
> be동사 뒤에 not을 써요.

개념확인 주어와 동사원형 찾기

1 Ann doesn't have a sister.　　**2** They don't eat junk food.　　**3** Eric doesn't want a bike.

기본연습 A 괄호 안에서 알맞은 것을 고르시오.

1 I (don't / doesn't) eat breakfast these days.

2 Jina (don't / doesn't) work in the library.

3 We (don't / doesn't) know his phone number.

4 Jason (don't / doesn't) wash his hair every day.

5 They (don't / doesn't) listen to hip hop music.

6 My sister doesn't (like / likes) insects.

7 My brother doesn't (have / has) a music class today.

B 다음 문장을 부정문으로 바꿀 때 빈칸에 알맞은 말을 쓰시오.

1 The bus stops here.　　→　The bus ＿＿＿＿＿ ＿＿＿＿＿ here.

2 I get up early in the morning.　　→　I ＿＿＿＿＿ ＿＿＿＿＿ up early in the morning.

3 Alex takes a yoga class on Fridays.　　→　Alex ＿＿＿＿＿ ＿＿＿＿＿ a yoga class on Fridays.

4 Ted and Ben live in New York.　　→　Ted and Ben ＿＿＿＿＿ ＿＿＿＿＿ in New York.

5 They play soccer every Sunday.　　→　They ＿＿＿＿＿ ＿＿＿＿＿ soccer every Sunday.

6 She teaches at my school.　　→　She ＿＿＿＿＿ ＿＿＿＿＿ at my school.

일반동사 **33**

일반동사 현재형의 의문문은 「Do/Does＋주어＋동사원형 ~?」의 형태로 쓴다.

| 1인칭, 2인칭, 복수 주어 | **Do**＋주어＋**동사원형** ~? | **Do** | you | **like** | flowers? | 너는 꽃을 좋아하니? |
| 3인칭 단수 주어 | **Does**＋주어＋**동사원형** ~? | **Does** | he | **like** | flowers? | 그는 꽃을 좋아하니? |

의문문에 대한 긍정의 대답은 「Yes, 주어＋do/does.」, 부정의 대답은 「No, 주어＋don't/doesn't.」로 한다.

의문문	긍정의 대답	부정의 대답
Do＋주어＋동사원형 ~?	Yes, 주어＋do.	No, 주어＋don't.
Does＋주어＋동사원형 ~?	Yes, 주어＋does.	No, 주어＋doesn't.

A: **Do** you always **wear** glasses? 너는 항상 안경을 쓰니?
B: **Yes**, I **do**. / **No**, I **don't**. 응, 써. / 아니, 쓰지 않아.

A: **Does** Jessica **have** a dog? Jessica는 개를 키우니?
B: **Yes**, she **does**. / **No**, she **doesn't**. 응, 키워. / 아니, 키우지 않아.

주의 의문문의 주어가 1인칭 I일 경우 2인칭 you로 대답하고, 주어가 2인칭 you일 경우 1인칭 I나 we로 대답한다.
A: Do **I** know your sister?　　　　　　　A: Do **you** have time? you가 '너'라는 뜻이면 I로 답하고,
B: Yes, **you** do.　　　　　　　　　　　　B: Yes, **I** do. / Yes, **we** do. '너희들'이라는 뜻이면 we로 답해요.

주의 do가 '하다'라는 뜻의 일반동사로 쓰일 때, 부정문이나 의문문에서 do를 빠뜨리지 않아야 한다.
〈긍정문〉 He always **does** his homework. 그는 항상 숙제를 한다.
〈부정문〉 He **doesn't** always **do** his homework. 그는 항상 숙제를 하지는 않는다.
〈의문문〉 **Does** he always **do** his homework? 그는 항상 숙제를 하니?

개념확인 주어와 동사원형 찾기

1 Do you play golf?　　　　**2** Does she like green?　　　　**3** Do they use email?

기본연습 A 괄호 안에서 알맞은 것을 고르시오.

1 (Do / Does) they learn English in school?

2 (Do / Does) Ted speak French to you?

3 (Do / Does) you eat breakfast every morning?

4 (Do / Does) she read comic books in her free time?

5 Do they (like / likes) this picture?

6 Does the store (close / closes) at 9 p.m.?

7 Does Mr. Williams always (make / makes) his lunch?

8 Do James and Lisa (study / studies) in the same class?

B 다음 문장을 의문문으로 바꿀 때 빈칸에 알맞은 말을 쓰시오.

1 You like hamburgers. → _____ _____ _____ hamburgers?

2 She knows Kevin. → _____ _____ _____ Kevin?

3 They need our help. → _____ _____ _____ our help?

4 He remembers my birthday. → _____ _____ _____ my birthday?

5 Jessy plays soccer on Sundays. → _____ _____ _____ soccer on Sundays?

6 Jimin makes gimbap well. → _____ _____ _____ gimbap well?

7 Peter loves his curly hair. → _____ _____ _____ his curly hair?

8 His dogs have short tails. → _____ _____ _____ short tails?

9 The baby cries every night. → _____ _____ _____ every night?

10 Her parents sell cars. → _____ _____ _____ cars?

C 빈칸에 알맞은 말을 넣어 의문문에 대한 답을 완성하시오.

1 A: Does he teach English?
   B: Yes, _____ _____ .

2 A: Does Jake go to school by subway?
   B: No, _____ _____ .

3 A: Do you have a brother?
   B: Yes, _____ _____ .

4 A: Does the bookstore open at 10 a.m.?
   B: Yes, _____ _____ .

5 A: Does she ride her bicycle to school?
   B: No, _____ _____ .

6 A: Do Lucy and Harry work at the bank?
   B: No, _____ _____ .

7 A: Do they live in Busan?
   B: Yes, _____ _____ .

8 A: Does your grandmother miss your family?
   B: Yes, _____ _____ .

9 A: Do you like winter?
   B: No, _____ _____ .

10 A: Do we have time for lunch?
   B: No, _____ _____ .

틀리기 쉬운 내/신/포/인/트

의문문에 대답을 할 때에는 질문에 쓰인 주어를 알맞은 대명사로 바꿔 써야 해요.

대화의 빈칸에 들어갈 말로 알맞은 것은?

A: Does the show start at 4 p.m.?
B: _____ It starts at 7 p.m.

① Yes, I do.   ② Yes, it does.
③ No, it don't.   ④ No, it doesn't.

일반동사 과거형의 규칙 변화

정답 및 해설 p.5

일반동사의 과거형은 과거에 이미 끝난 동작이나 상태 등을 나타낼 때 쓰며, 주어의 인칭이나 수에 상관없이 동일한 형태를 쓴다.☆

| 현재 | We | live | in Seoul | now. | 우리는 지금 서울에 **산다**. |
| 과거 | | lived | | last year. | 우리는 작년에 서울에 **살았다**. |

일반동사의 과거형은 규칙 변화와 불규칙 변화가 있는데, 규칙 변화는 다음과 같다.

대부분의 동사	동사원형+-ed	called cooked	finished watched
-e로 끝나는 동사	동사원형+-d	liked lived	loved closed
「자음+y」로 끝나는 동사	y를 i로 바꾸고+-ed	try – tried cry – cried	study – studied carry – carried
「단모음+단자음」으로 끝나는 동사	자음을 한 번 더 쓰고+-ed	stop – stopped drop – dropped	plan – planned occur – occurred

주의 「모음+y」로 끝나는 동사는 -ed를 붙인다.
play – played   enjoy – enjoyed   stay – stayed

Tips 과거형과 함께 주로 쓰이는 부사(구)에는 yesterday, last night, last year, ~ ago 등이 있다.
I listened to the radio **yesterday**. 나는 어제 라디오를 들었다.

개념확인 동사 찾기

1 I studied science yesterday.   **2** The rain stopped.   **3** Sam played tennis after school.

기본연습 A 다음 동사의 과거형을 쓰시오.

1 clean   → _____   **2** like   → _____

3 walk   → _____   **4** show   → _____

5 love   → _____   **6** want   → _____

7 try   → _____   **8** help   → _____

9 carry   → _____   **10** visit   → _____

11 look   → _____   **12** talk   → _____

13 start   → _____   **14** cry   → _____

15 drop   → _____   **16** dance   → _____

17 fail   → _____   **18** enjoy   → _____

19 open → _____ **20** stop → _____

21 need → _____ **22** close → _____

23 use → _____ **24** wash → _____

25 worry → _____ **26** exercise → _____

27 travel → _____ **28** ask → _____

29 finish → _____ **30** pass → _____

31 arrive → _____ **32** wish → _____

33 practice → _____ **34** hurry → _____

B 괄호 안에서 알맞은 것을 고르시오.

1 Brian (stays / stayed) with us last week.

2 We (miss / missed) the school bus a minute ago.

3 Jenny (played / plaied) the guitar.

4 My little sister (cryed / cried) a lot last night.

5 My parents (worked / workked) last Saturday.

6 They (planed / planned) a birthday party for Amy.

C 빈칸에 알맞은 말을 보기 에서 골라 올바른 형태로 쓰시오.

보기	turn	invite	watch	cook	move	study

1 Ms. Jones _____ the movie two days ago.

2 We _____ English after school yesterday.

3 I _____ my friends to my house last weekend.

4 Peter _____ spaghetti for dinner last night.

5 My family _____ to New York last summer.

6 Mina _____ off the TV a minute ago.

틀리기 쉬운
내/신/포/인/트

일반동사 과거형의 형태를
기억해요.

동사의 현재형과 과거형이 잘못 짝 지어진 것은?

① marry – married ② call – called
③ enjoy – enjoyed ④ stop – stoped

일반동사 과거형의 불규칙 변화

현재형은 [ri:d], 과거형은 [red]로 발음해요.

형태가 같은 동사	put 놓다 – **put**	cut 자르다 – **cut**	read 읽다 – **read**
	hit 때리다 – **hit**	hurt 다치게 하다 – **hurt**	set 놓다, 차리다 – **set**
모음이 바뀌는 동사	begin 시작하다 – **began**	become ~이 되다 – **became**	come 오다 – **came**
	draw 그리다 – **drew**	drink 마시다 – **drank**	fall 떨어지다 – **fell**
	fight 싸우다 – **fought**	get 얻다 – **got**	give 주다 – **gave**
	grow 자라다 – **grew**	know 알다 – **knew**	ride 타다 – **rode**
	run 달리다 – **ran**	sing 노래하다 – **sang**	sit 앉다 – **sat**
	swim 수영하다 – **swam**	win 이기다 – **won**	write 쓰다 – **wrote**
형태가 완전히 다른 동사	break 깨다 – **broke**	bring 가져오다 – **brought**	buy 사다 – **bought**
	catch 잡다 – **caught**	do 하다 – **did**	eat 먹다 – **ate**
	feel 느끼다 – **felt**	find 찾다, 발견하다 – **found**	fly 날다 – **flew**
	go 가다 – **went**	have 먹다, 가지다 – **had**	hear 듣다 – **heard**
	hide 숨다 – **hid**	keep 유지하다 – **kept**	leave 떠나다 – **left**
	lose 잃어버리다 – **lost**	make 만들다 – **made**	meet 만나다 – **met**
	pay 지불하다 – **paid**	say 말하다 – **said**	see 보다 – **saw**
	sell 팔다 – **sold**	send 보내다 – **sent**	sleep 자다 – **slept**
	speak 말하다 – **spoke**	spend (돈을) 쓰다, (시간을) 보내다 – **spent**	
	stand 서다 – **stood**	take 잡다 – **took**	teach 가르치다 – **taught**
	tell 말하다 – **told**	think 생각하다 – **thought**	wear 입다 – **wore**
	understand 이해하다 – **understood**		

주의 일반동사의 과거형은 주어의 인칭이나 수에 상관없이 동일한 형태를 쓴다.
She **came** home late last night. 그녀는 어젯밤에 늦게 집에 왔다.

개념확인 동사 찾기

1 I went to the museum.   **2** We swam in the sea.   **3** He hurt his leg yesterday.

기본연습 **A** 다음 동사의 과거형을 쓰시오.

1 come   → _____   **2** eat   → _____

3 catch   → _____   **4** feel   → _____

5 do   → _____   **6** make   → _____

7 see   → _____   **8** sleep   → _____

9 write   → _____   **10** set   → _____

11 break   → _____   **12** grow   → _____

13 lose   → _____   **14** have   → _____

15 read	→ _____	**16** tell	→ _____

15 read → _____ **16** tell → _____

17 run → _____ **18** teach → _____

19 ride → _____ **20** find → _____

21 put → _____ **22** sing → _____

23 sit → _____ **24** speak → _____

25 send → _____ **26** take → _____

27 get → _____ **28** think → _____

29 fight → _____ **30** say → _____

31 wear → _____ **32** give → _____

33 sell → _____ **34** stand → _____

35 drink → _____ **36** fly → _____

37 know → _____ **38** leave → _____

39 hear → _____ **40** bring → _____

B 빈칸에 알맞은 말을 보기 에서 골라 올바른 형태로 쓰시오.

보기	spend	fall	win	buy	meet

1 James _____ a movie star yesterday.

2 Many leaves _____ from the tree yesterday.

3 They _____ the soccer game last Sunday.

4 He _____ a cake for me last night.

5 I _____ last weekend with my aunt.

**틀 리 기 쉬 운
내/신/포/인/트**

과거형이 불규칙하게 변하는
동사들은 모두 암기하도록 해요.

밑줄 친 동사의 과거형이 틀린 것은?

① We knew the answer.
② She made a paper airplane.
③ I did my history homework.
④ Mark readed the comic books.

일반동사 과거형의 부정문

정답 및 해설 p.6

일반동사 과거형의 부정문은 「did not + 동사원형」의 형태로 쓴다. did not은 didn't로 줄여 쓸 수 있다.

주어 + didn't(did not) + 동사원형	We	didn't	take	the subway.	우리는 지하철을 **타지 않았다**.
	He	did not	go	to the zoo.	그는 동물원에 **가지 않았다**.

주의 did not(didn't) 뒤에는 항상 동사원형을 써야 하며, 동사의 과거형을 쓰지 않도록 주의한다.
She **didn't study** English yesterday. 그녀는 어제 영어를 공부하지 않았다.

개념확인 **주어와 동사원형 찾기**

1 I didn't watch TV yesterday.　　**2** He didn't like the hot dog.　　**3** They didn't study hard.

기본연습 **A** 괄호 안에서 알맞은 것을 고르시오.

1 I (did not / not did) clean my room last night.

2 We (don't / didn't) go to school yesterday.

3 Mina (doesn't / didn't) play outside last weekend.

4 They didn't (enjoy / enjoyed) the movie.

5 Sally didn't (have / had) lunch yesterday.

6 My brother and I didn't (turn / turned) on the TV last night.

7 My sister didn't (writes / write) the letter.

8 Mr. Han didn't (speaks / speak) Chinese very well.

B 다음 문장을 부정문으로 바꿀 때 빈칸에 알맞은 말을 쓰시오.

1 I ran in the park.　　　　　　　→ I _____ _____ in the park.

2 Jiho agreed with my plan.　　　　→ Jiho _____ _____ with my plan.

3 They did their homework.　　　　→ They _____ _____ their homework.

4 She went to the bookstore yesterday.　→ She _____ _____ to the bookstore yesterday.

5 Ms. Lopez brought an umbrella.　　→ Ms. Lopez _____ _____ an umbrella.

6 Kate lost her wallet on the street.　　→ Kate _____ _____ her wallet on the street.

7 He read the newspaper last night.　　→ He _____ _____ the newspaper last night.

8 The train stopped at the station.　　→ The train _____ _____ at the station.

POINT 8 일반동사 과거형의 의문문

일반동사 과거형의 의문문은 「Did+주어+동사원형 ~?」의 형태로 쓰며, 긍정의 대답은 「Yes, 주어+did.」, 부정의 대답은 「No, 주어+didn't.」로 한다.

의문문	긍정의 대답	부정의 대답
Did+주어+동사원형 ~?	Yes, 주어+did.	No, 주어+didn't.

A: **Did** you **have** a good day? 너는 즐거운 하루를 보냈니?
B: **Yes**, I **did**. / **No**, I **didn't**. 응, 즐거웠어. / 아니, 즐겁지 않았어.

A: **Did** she **watch** the movie last night? 그녀는 어젯밤에 그 영화를 보았니?
B: **Yes**, she **did**. / **No**, she **didn't**. 응, 봤어. / 아니, 보지 않았어.

주의 「Did+주어」 뒤에 오는 동사는 항상 동사원형을 써야 하며, 과거형을 쓰지 않도록 주의한다.
Did he **play** soccer yesterday? 그는 어제 축구를 했니?

개념확인 주어와 동사원형 찾기

1 Did you call her yesterday?　　**2** Did he meet Bob last week?　　**3** Did they sing at the festival?

기본연습 **A** 우리말과 일치하도록 **보기** 에서 알맞은 말을 골라 문장을 완성하시오.

보기	use	know	join	live	play	listen

1 Sam은 컴퓨터 게임을 자주 하니?　　→　_____ Sam often _____ computer games?

2 보라와 지민이는 Brown 씨를 아니?　　→　_____ Bora and Jimin _____ Mr. Brown?

3 그녀는 작년에 제주도에 살았니?　　→　_____ she _____ in Jeju-do last year?

4 그들은 어젯밤에 라디오를 들었니?　　→　_____ they _____ to the radio last night?

5 너는 어제 미술 동아리에 가입했니?　　→　_____ you _____ the art club yesterday?

6 Amy가 오늘 아침에 네 컴퓨터를 사용했니?　→　_____ Amy _____ your computer this morning?

B 빈칸에 알맞은 말을 넣어 의문문에 대한 답을 완성하시오.

1 A: Did they finish their work last week?
　　B: No, _____ _____.

2 A: Did Ann have a smartphone in her bag?
　　B: Yes, _____ _____.

3 A: Did Sue and you hear about Jim's party?
　　B: Yes, _____ _____.

4 A: Did your uncle go to Canada last year?
　　B: No, _____ _____.

개 념 완 성 T E S T

STEP 1 Map으로 개념 정리하기

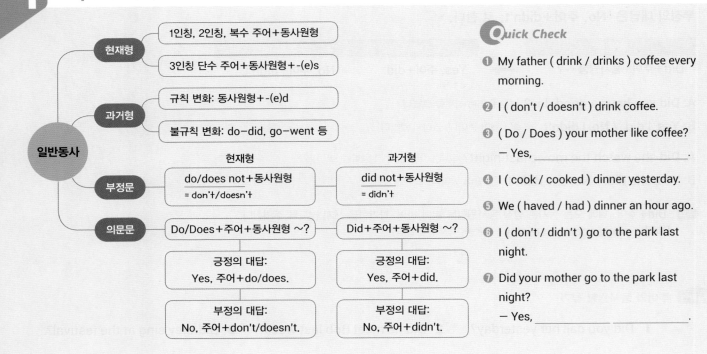

Quick Check

1 My father (drink / drinks) coffee every morning.

2 I (don't / doesn't) drink coffee.

3 (Do / Does) your mother like coffee?
— Yes, _____.

4 I (cook / cooked) dinner yesterday.

5 We (haved / had) dinner an hour ago.

6 I (don't / didn't) go to the park last night.

7 Did your mother go to the park last night?
— Yes, _____.

STEP 2 기본 다지기

빈칸완성

A 우리말과 일치하도록 빈칸에 알맞은 말을 넣어 문장을 완성하시오.

1 나의 여동생은 8시에 학교에 간다. → My sister _____ to school at 8 a.m.

2 그들은 매일 아침 운동한다. → They _____ every morning.

3 그는 과학을 가르치지 않는다. → He _____ _____ science.

4 나는 피아노를 매일 연습하지는 않는다. → I _____ _____ the piano every day.

5 그녀는 큰 도시에 사니? → _____ she _____ in a big city?

6 수호와 유나는 영어를 잘 말하니? → _____ Suho and Yuna _____ English well?

7 그들은 콘서트에서 함께 노래를 불렀다. → They _____ songs together in the concert.

8 Karen은 오늘 아침에 공항에 도착했다. → Karen _____ at the airport this morning.

9 그 아기는 어젯밤에 울지 않았다. → The baby _____ _____ last night.

10 네가 정원에서 반지를 찾았니? → _____ you _____ the ring in the garden?

B 밑줄 친 부분을 어법상 바르게 고쳐 쓰시오.

1 The music <u>stoped</u> one hour ago.　　→ _____

2 I didn't <u>had</u> a good time yesterday.　　→ _____

3 My brother <u>wash</u> his hair every day.　　→ _____

4 David <u>don't</u> play soccer on weekends.　　→ _____

5 <u>Do</u> you enjoy the magic show last week?　　→ _____

6 Do Kate and Mary <u>watches</u> movies on Sundays?　　→ _____

C 다음 문장을 괄호 안의 지시대로 바꿔 쓰시오.

1 I have a headache. (주어를 he로)
→ _____

2 My sister rides her bike every day. (부정문으로)
→ _____

3 They go to the movies on Saturdays. (의문문으로)
→ _____

4 Fred doesn't study English in the library. (긍정문으로)
→ _____

5 Sarah remembers her first day at school. (의문문으로)
→ _____

6 He writes a letter to Yumi. (동사를 과거형으로)
→ _____

7 My parents work at a hospital. (동사를 과거형으로)
→ _____

8 Tom brought his lunch to school. (의문문으로)
→ _____

9 Minho and Gisu did their homework last night. (부정문으로)
→ _____

10 My brother didn't eat noodles for lunch yesterday. (긍정문으로)
→ _____

STEP 3 서술형 따라잡기

그림이해

A 그림을 보고, 대화를 완성하시오.

1

A: Does Kate like dogs?

B: _____, _____ _____.

2

A: Did Rick go to bed early last night?

B: _____, _____ _____.

영작완성

B 우리말과 일치하도록 괄호 안의 말을 바르게 배열하여 문장을 쓰시오.

1 그는 오늘 좋아 보이지 않는다. (doesn't, he, well, look, today)

→ _____

2 너는 지하철을 탔니? (take, did, you, the subway)

→ _____

3 그들은 그 수학 문제를 이해하지 못했다. (understand, they, didn't, the math problem)

→ _____

4 그의 고양이는 작은 코를 가지고 있니? (have, a small nose, his cat, does)

→ _____

문장영작

C 우리말과 일치하도록 괄호 안의 말을 이용하여 영작하시오.

1 그는 아침으로 사과 두 개를 먹는다. (eat, for breakfast)

→ _____

2 그녀는 어제 그녀의 안경을 떨어뜨렸다. (drop, her glasses)

→ _____

3 내 친구들과 나는 어제 박물관에 갔다. (go, to the museum)

→ _____

4 Mark는 그의 책상을 매일 닦는다. (clean, his desk)

→ _____

1 동사의 현재형과 과거형이 잘못 짝 지어진 것은?

① put – put   ② keep – kept

③ fail – failed   ④ plan – planed

⑤ carry – carried

2 빈칸에 알맞은 말이 순서대로 짝 지어진 것은?

> • Steve _____ my brother well.
>
> • Does Kate _____ the answer?

① know – know   ② knows – knew

③ know – knows   ④ knows – know

⑤ knows – knows

3 빈칸에 공통으로 들어갈 말로 알맞은 것은?

> • _____ you read a book last night?
>
> • He _____ not go to church yesterday.

① Do(do)   ② Does(does)

③ Don't(don't)   ④ Doesn't(doesn't)

⑤ Did(did)

[4-5] 빈칸에 들어갈 말로 알맞지 <u>않은</u> 것을 고르시오.

4

> _____ plays the piano very well.

① She   ② Ms. White

③ Paul   ④ My brother

⑤ Ann and Tim

5

> Bill _____ to music in the evening.

① listens   ② doesn't listen

③ don't listen   ④ listened

⑤ didn't listen

[6-7] 대화의 빈칸에 들어갈 말로 알맞은 것을 고르시오.

6

> A: Did you enjoy the concert?
>
> B: _____ It was great.

① Yes, I do.   ② No, I don't.

③ Yes, I did.   ④ No, I didn't.

⑤ No, I did.

7

> A: Does she drink milk every morning?
>
> B: _____ She doesn't like milk.

① Yes, she does.   ② No, she doesn't.

③ Yes, she did.   ④ No, she didn't.

⑤ No, she does.

8 밑줄 친 부분이 어법상 올바른 것은?

① Do you <u>liked</u> summer?

② Did you <u>opened</u> the window?

③ We <u>have</u> an art class yesterday.

④ She <u>made</u> some cookies last night.

⑤ They didn't <u>lived</u> in London last year.

9 빈칸에 don't나 doesn't를 쓸 때 나머지와 <u>다른</u> 하나는?

① Andrew _____ smoke.

② She _____ read comic books.

③ The DVD player _____ work.

④ Minho and I _____ eat cucumbers.

⑤ My mother _____ believe the rumor.

10 밑줄 친 부분의 쓰임이 나머지와 <u>다른</u> 하나는?

① <u>Did</u> they stay home?

② We <u>did</u> not have breakfast.

③ I <u>did</u> the dishes after lunch.

④ <u>Did</u> your brother win the game?

⑤ Mr. Kim <u>did</u> not teach history at school.

11 대화가 자연스럽지 <u>않은</u> 것은?

① A: Do you have a dog?

   B: Yes, I do.

② A: Does John exercise in the morning?

   B: Yes, he does.

③ A: Does Yujin sing well?

   B: No, she doesn't.

④ A: Do you and your sister love ice cream?

   B: Yes, we do.

⑤ A: Did Kevin and Aron play tennis last Friday?

   B: No, they don't.

12 어법상 틀린 문장은?

① Julia has a blue bag.

② Do you run every morning?

③ I wrote a letter to my friend.

④ Does Hana spoke English?

⑤ They didn't tell me about the news.

13 우리말을 영어로 바르게 옮긴 것은?

그는 어제 스마트폰을 사지 않았다.

① He buys not a smartphone yesterday.

② He don't buy a smartphone yesterday.

③ He doesn't buy a smartphone yesterday.

④ He bought not a smartphone yesterday.

⑤ He didn't buy a smartphone yesterday.

14 다음 문장을 의문문으로 바르게 바꾼 것은?

He caught a big fish.

① Does he caught a big fish?

② Does he catch a big fish?

③ Do he catch a big fish?

④ Did he caught a big fish?

⑤ Did he catch a big fish?

15 다음 문장을 부정문으로 바르게 바꾼 것은?

> My uncle enjoys Italian food.

① My uncle don't enjoys Italian food.
② My uncle don't enjoy Italian food.
③ My uncle doesn't enjoys Italian food.
④ My uncle doesn't enjoy Italian food.
⑤ My uncle didn't enjoy Italian food.

16 빈칸에 **didn't**를 쓸 수 있는 것은?

① He _____ turns on TV every night.
② I _____ wear my glasses yesterday.
③ The students _____ came on time.
④ The man _____ collected the stamps.
⑤ The bus _____ left ten minutes ago.

고난도
17 빈칸 (A)~(C)에 들어갈 말이 바르게 짝 지어진 것은?

> • I ___(A)___ my bike a week ago.
> • Does he ___(B)___ to school every day?
> • Amy ___(C)___ the piano last night.

	(A)	(B)	(C)
①	lost	– walk	– doesn't practice
②	lost	– walk	– didn't practice
③	lost	– walks	– didn't practice
④	losed	– walk	– doesn't practice
⑤	losed	– walks	– didn't practice

18 우리말과 일치하도록 주어진 말을 배열할 때, 세 번째로 오는 단어는?

> 너는 오늘 아침에 이를 닦았니?
> (your, brush, this morning, teeth, did, you)

① teeth   ② brush   ③ did
④ your   ⑤ you

19 빈칸에 들어갈 질문으로 알맞은 것은?

> A: _____
> B: Yes, she did.

① Does your aunt work in the library?
② Do your aunt work in the library?
③ Does your aunt worked in the library?
④ Did your aunt work in the library last year?
⑤ Did your aunt worked in the library last year?

고난도
20 어법상 올바른 문장의 개수는?

> ⓐ Does he need a doctor?
> ⓑ Alice didn't called me last night.
> ⓒ She cuted a carrot with a knife.
> ⓓ Did she finished her project?
> ⓔ John and I had dinner in the restaurant.

① 0개   ② 1개   ③ 2개
④ 3개   ⑤ 4개

21 지호의 메모를 보고, 어제 한 일(✓)과 하지 않은 일(✗)을 나타내는 문장을 완성하시오.

> • morning – bake cookies ✓
> • afternoon – clean the living room ✗
> • evening – go to Mina's birthday party ✓

(1) Jiho _____

in the morning.

(2) He _____

in the afternoon.

(3) He _____

in the evening.

22 주어진 질문에 알맞은 답을 써서 대화를 완성하시오.

(1) **A:** Does Taeho usually wear a blue shirt?

B: _____, _____ _____.

He usually wears a green shirt.

(2) **A:** Did Jenny meet Sam at school last week?

B: _____, _____ _____.

They played soccer together.

23 주어진 문장을 괄호 안의 지시대로 바꿔 쓰시오.

> He dropped the cup.

(1) (부정문으로 바꿀 것)

→ _____

(2) (의문문으로 바꿀 것)

→ _____

24 다음 글을 읽고, Tom을 다른 사람에게 소개하는 글을 완성하시오.

> My name is Tom. I live in Seoul. I have a brother. I go to Dream Middle School. I like movies. I watch movies every weekend. I don't like sports.

⬇

> Tom _____ in Seoul. He _____ a brother. He _____ to Dream Middle School. He _____ movies. He _____ movies every weekend. He _____ _____ sports.

고난도

25 우리말과 일치하도록 조건 에 맞게 영작하시오.

> 조건 1. 괄호 안의 말을 이용할 것
> 2. 줄여 쓸 수 있는 경우 줄임말로 쓸 것

(1) Paul은 매일 아침을 먹는다. (eat, breakfast)

→ _____

(2) Peter는 지난달에 서울로 이사를 갔다. (move, to)

→ _____

(3) 우리 아버지는 운전을 하지 않으신다. (drive, a car)

→ _____

(4) 너는 지금 펜을 가지고 있니? (have, a pen)

→ _____

(5) 나는 어제 나의 시계를 가지고 가지 않았다.
(bring, my watch)

→ _____

명사와 관사

명사는 '학생', '고양이', '나무'처럼 사람이나 동물, 사물 등의 이름을 나타내는 말이다.
관사는 명사 앞에 사용하며 명사의 수나 성격을 나타낸다.

셀 수 있는 명사와 셀 수 없는 명사 정답 및 해설 p.8

- **셀 수 있는 명사**: 구체적으로 셀 수 있는 사람이나 동물, 사물 등을 나타내는 명사이다.
  하나일 때는 명사 앞에 **a/an**을 쓰고, 둘 이상일 때는 복수형으로 쓴다.

I have	**a ticket**.	단수	나는 표 한 장이 있다.
	two **tickets**.	복수	나는 표 두 장이 있다.

- **셀 수 없는 명사**: 항상 단수형으로 쓰고, 명사 앞에 **a/an**을 쓰지 않는다.

물질명사	일정한 형태가 없는 물질	water, salt, paper, money, cheese, bread, air …
추상명사	눈에 보이지 않는 추상적인 개념	love, hope, luck, health, homework, music …
고유명사	사람이나 지역 등의 고유한 이름	Jenny, Paris, Korea, April, Friday …

↳ 첫 글자는 항상 대문자로 써요.

> 궁금해요!
> salt는 셀 수 있지 않나요?

> salt처럼 너무 작거나 cheese처럼 형태가 다양한 것은 셀 수 없다고 봐요.

개념확인 명사 찾기

1 The students are busy.　　**2** He joined a club.　　**3** Would you like some tea?

기본연습 **A** 셀 수 있는 명사에는 ○표, 셀 수 없는 명사에는 ×표 하시오.

1 girl _____　　**2** sugar _____　　**3** peace _____

4 group _____　　**5** milk _____　　**6** elephant _____

7 class _____　　**8** money _____　　**9** information _____

10 Seoul _____　　**11** horse _____　　**12** fork _____

B 괄호 안에서 알맞은 것을 고르시오.

1 James lives in (a Poland / Poland).

2 (A love / Love) is very important to us.

3 The two (team / teams) met in the final.

4 Do your three (boy / boys) go to the same school?

틀 리 기 쉬 운
내/신/포/인/트

a나 an 뒤에는 셀 수 있는 명사가 와요.

빈칸에 들어갈 말로 알맞은 것은?

Daniel wants a _____.

① bread　　② new bag　　③ happiness　　④ health

POINT 2 셀 수 있는 명사의 복수형: 규칙 변화

정답 및 해설 p.8

셀 수 있는 명사의 개수가 하나일 때는 앞에 a나 an을 쓰고, 둘 이상일 때는 다음과 같이 복수형으로 쓴다.

대부분의 명사	명사+-s	books dogs pens cats toys schools
-s, -x, -sh, -ss, -ch, -o로 끝나는 명사	명사+-es	buses boxes dishes classes benches potatoes 〈예외〉 pianos, photos, videos
「자음+y」로 끝나는 명사	y를 i로 바꾸고 +-es	baby – babies city – cities lady – ladies
-f, -fe로 끝나는 명사	f, fe를 v로 바꾸고 +-es	leaf – leaves wolf – wolves knife – knives 〈예외〉 roofs, chefs

주의 scissors(가위), pants(바지), glasses(안경), shoes(신발)와 같이 두 개가 짝을 이루어 하나가 되는 옷이나 기구 등은 항상 복수형으로 쓰고, a pair of ~나 two pairs of ~ 등을 사용하여 수량을 표현한다.
I bought **a pair of scissors**. 나는 가위 한 자루를 샀다.
I want **two pairs of pants**. 나는 바지 두 벌을 원한다.

개념확인 셀 수 있는 명사 찾기

1 ☐ pencil ☐ milk   **2** ☐ water ☐ tomato   **3** ☐ song ☐ music

기본연습 A 다음 단어의 복수형을 쓰시오.

1 bus → _____   **2** bag → _____

3 fox → _____   **4** brush → _____

5 glass → _____   **6** watch → _____

7 puppy → _____   **8** story → _____

9 wife → _____   **10** shelf → _____

11 glove → _____   **12** box → _____

13 dish → _____   **14** kiss → _____

15 church → _____   **16** crayon → _____

17 fly → _____   **18** wolf → _____

19 knife → _____   **20** party → _____

21 piano → _____   **22** roof → _____

23 beach → _____   **24** diary → _____

B 괄호 안에서 알맞은 것을 고르시오.

1 (Cow / Cows) make milk.

2 We need two (potatos / potatoes).

3 Sam put the (coins / coines) in his pocket.

4 (Monkey / Monkeys) play in the trees.

5 My mother doesn't like (meat / meats).

6 Annie has ten (candys / candies) in her hands.

7 Spread the (butter / butters) on the bread.

8 Ms. Wilson has three (son / sons) and one daughter.

9 (Leafes / Leaves) fall from the trees in autumn.

10 Kate saves (money / moneys) in her piggy bank.

C 괄호 안의 말을 이용하여 문장을 완성하시오.

1 An octopus has eight _____. (leg)

2 We have lots of _____ every winter. (snow)

3 Add some _____ to your coffee. (sugar)

4 Sixty _____ live in this village. (family)

5 My father fried five _____. (tomato)

6 Tom saw some _____ on the wall in the room. (photo)

7 The _____ in the playground are clean. (bench)

8 I have three _____ in my room. (bookshelf)

9 I made some _____ for the field trip. (sandwich)

10 France and Hungary are _____ in Europe. (country)

틀 리 기   쉬 운
내/신/포/인/트

명사의 복수형은 명사에
-s나 -es를 붙여서 만들어요.

명사의 단수형과 복수형이 잘못 짝 지어진 것은?

① fox − foxes
② wife − wives
③ potato − potatos
④ watch − watches

3 셀 수 있는 명사의 복수형: 불규칙 변화 정답 및 해설 p.8

일부 명사는 일정한 규칙 없이 복수형으로 변화한다.

| man – **men** | woman – **women** | goose – **geese** | mouse – **mice** |
| foot – **feet** | tooth – **teeth** | child – **children** | |

일부 명사는 단수형과 복수형의 형태가 같다.

| fish | sheep | deer |

> **주의** news(뉴스), mathematics(수학)는 복수형처럼 보이지만 단수로 취급하는 셀 수 없는 명사이다.
> The **news** is on TV now. 지금 TV에서 뉴스가 나오고 있다.

개념확인 셀 수 있는 명사 찾기

1 ☐ man ☐ money 2 ☐ rice ☐ fish 3 ☐ child ☐ health

기본연습 A 다음 단어의 복수형을 쓰시오.

1 man → _____ 2 deer → _____

3 child → _____ 4 mouse → _____

5 goose → _____ 6 tooth → _____

7 fish → _____ 8 match → _____

9 foot → _____ 10 sheep → _____

11 boy → _____ 12 dress → _____

B 괄호 안에서 알맞은 것을 고르시오.

1 My (feet / foots) are very long.

2 Helen has four (childs / children).

3 He has ten (deer / deers) on his farm.

4 Tina brushed her (teeth / toothes) again.

5 I found two (mouses / mice) in the picture.

6 (Mathematics / Mathematicses) is very difficult for me.

7 My grandmother knows many interesting (storys / stories).

8 353 (women / womans) passed the exam last year.

C 우리말과 일치하도록 빈칸에 알맞은 말을 넣어 문장을 완성하시오.

1 거위들은 겨울에 남쪽으로 날아간다.

→ _____ fly south in winter.

2 그는 양발에 부츠를 신었다.

→ He wore boots on his _____.

3 서울과 도쿄는 큰 도시들이다.

→ Seoul and Tokyo are large _____.

4 악어들은 매우 날카로운 이빨을 가졌다.

→ Alligators have very sharp _____.

5 아이들은 모래사장에서 놀았다.

→ The _____ played on the sand.

6 우리 어머니는 우리 농장에서 양들에게 먹이를 주신다.

→ My mother feeds _____ on our farm.

7 그 두 명의 여자는 프랑스 출신이다.

→ The two _____ are from France.

8 그 물고기들은 정말 위험하다.

→ The _____ are very dangerous.

9 세 명의 남자가 건물에 들어갔다.

→ Three _____ entered the building.

10 그 뉴스는 우리 학교에 관한 것이다.

→ The _____ is about our school.

11 우리 고양이는 오늘 쥐 네 마리를 잡았다.

→ My cat caught four _____ today.

대화의 빈칸에 알맞은 말이 순서대로 짝 지어진 것은?

A: Do you have a _____ on your farm?

B: No, but I have two _____.

① duck – gooses   ② duck – geese
③ ducks – gooses   ④ ducks – geese

셀 수 없는 명사의 수량은 용기나 단위를 사용하여 나타낸다.

a cup of	coffee, tea, water …	한 컵의 ~		a slice of	cheese, cake, pizza …	한 조각의 ~
a glass of	water, milk, juice …	한 잔의 ~		a piece of	cheese, cake, paper …	한 조각(장)의 ~
a bottle of	water, ink, oil …	한 병의 ~		a loaf of	bread	한 덩어리의 ~
a bowl of	soup, rice, cereal …	한 그릇의 ~		a spoonful of	sugar, salt, honey …	한 숟가락의 ~

주의 셀 수 없는 명사의 복수는 용기나 단위를 복수형으로 만들어 표현한다.

I bought **two loaves of bread**. 나는 빵 두 덩어리를 샀다.

빵 한 덩어리는
a loaf of bread라고 하고,
빵 한 조각은
a slice(piece) of bread라고 해요.

개념확인 용기나 단위를 나타내는 표현 찾기

1 a piece of pizza　　　　**2** a bottle of water　　　　**3** a glass of juice

기본연습 **A** 그림을 보고, 빈칸에 알맞은 말을 쓰시오.

1

a _____ of coffee

2

a _____ of paper

3

a _____ of sugar

4

a _____ of juice

5

a _____ of bread

6

a _____ of cake

7

a _____ of water

8

a _____ of cereal

9

a _____ of bread

B 다음을 복수의 수량 표현으로 다시 쓰시오.

1 a cup of tea　　　　→ two _____

2 a piece of cheese　　→ three _____

3 a bowl of fruit　　　→ four _____

4 a spoonful of salt　　→ five _____

C 우리말과 일치하도록 **보기** 에서 알맞은 말을 골라 빈칸에 올바른 형태로 쓰시오. (중복 사용 가능)

| **보기** | cup | glass | bottle | bowl | piece | loaf | spoonful |

1 우유 여섯 컵 → six _____ of milk

2 와인 네 병 → four _____ of wine

3 기름 한 병 → a _____ of oil

4 샐러드 한 그릇 → a _____ of salad

5 피자 한 조각 → a _____ of pizza

6 주스 다섯 잔 → five _____ of juice

7 빵 한 덩어리 → a _____ of bread

8 꿀 한 숟가락 → a _____ of honey

9 종이 두 장 → two _____ of paper

10 밥 두 그릇 → two _____ of rice

D 우리말과 일치하도록 빈칸에 알맞은 말을 넣어 문장을 완성하시오.

1 나는 저녁 식사 후에 물 한 컵을 마셨다.

→ I drank _____ after dinner.

2 나는 식당에서 수프 한 그릇을 주문했다.

→ I ordered _____ at the restaurant.

3 Nancy는 케이크 두 조각과 사과 하나를 먹었다.

→ Nancy ate _____ and an apple.

4 Cathy는 가게에서 잉크 세 병을 샀다.

→ Cathy bought _____ at the store.

5 너의 차에 설탕 두 숟가락을 넣어라.

→ Put _____ in your tea.

6 Daniel은 매일 아침 우유 한 잔을 마신다.

→ Daniel drinks _____ every morning.

7 종이 한 장을 꺼내서 그 위에 당신의 이름을 쓰세요.

→ Take out _____ and write your name on it.

8 우리는 바구니에 빵 세 덩어리가 있다.

→ We have _____ in the basket.

틀리기 쉬운
내/신/포/인/트

셀 수 없는 명사의 수량을
나타내는 방법을 기억해요.

빈칸에 들어갈 말로 알맞지 <u>않은</u> 것은?

Mike wants a piece of _____.

① cake　　　② cheese　　　③ bread　　　④ coffee

POINT 5 명사의 소유격

소유격은 '~의'라는 의미로, 소유 관계를 나타낸다. 명사의 소유격은 명사에 -'s를 붙이거나 of를 써서 나타낸다.

사람이나 동물의 소유격	명사+-'s	Olivia's new skirt is short.	Olivia의 새 치마는 짧다.
		My cat's fur is long and soft.	우리 고양이의 털은 길고 부드럽다.
무생물의 소유격	of+명사	The roof of the house is red.	그 집의 지붕은 빨간색이다.
		The leg of the chair is broken.	의자의 다리가 부러졌다.

주의 -s로 끝나는 고유명사의 소유격은 '(아포스트로피) 뒤의 s를 생략하기도 한다.
This is **Jess's/Jess'** watch. 이것은 Jess의 시계이다.

Tips -s로 끝나는 복수 명사의 소유격은 '(아포스트로피) 뒤의 s를 생략한다.
Her **sons'** names are Ian and Ethan. 그녀의 아들들의 이름은 Ian과 Ethan이다.

개념확인 소유한 사람이나 사물 찾기

1 Sam's coat **2** my sister's books **3** the door of the car

기본연습 **A** 우리말과 일치하도록 괄호 안의 말과 아포스트로피(')를 이용하여 쓰시오.

1 토끼의 꼬리 (the rabbit, tail) → _____

2 여성복 (women, clothes) → _____

3 Daniel의 삼촌 (Daniel, uncle) → _____

4 백조의 깃털 (the swan, feather) → _____

5 우리 부모님의 집 (my parents, house) → _____

6 Dickens의 소설들 (Dickens, novels) → _____

B 우리말과 일치하도록 괄호 안의 말과 of를 이용하여 쓰시오.

1 집의 벽 (the wall, the house) → _____

2 책의 표지 (the cover, the book) → _____

3 페이지의 상단 (the top, the page) → _____

4 거리의 이름 (the name, the street) → _____

5 건물의 지붕 (the roof, the building) → _____

6 신발의 색 (the color, the shoes) → _____

부정관사 a/an

정답 및 해설 p.9

부정관사 a나 an은 셀 수 있는 명사의 단수형 앞에 쓴다. 정해지지 않은 '(막연한) 하나의'를 의미한다.

a + 첫소리가 자음으로 발음되는 단어	a son, a book, a reporter, a cute rabbit, a tall man ... uniform, university는 모음인 u로 시작하지만, 자음으로 소리가 나므로 a를 써요.
an + 첫소리가 모음으로 발음되는 단어	an egg, an apple, an engineer, an interesting book ... hour는 자음인 h로 시작하지만, 모음으로 소리가 나므로 an을 써요.

My brother has **a** camera. 내 남동생은 카메라 한 대가 있다.

Sam bought **an** egg and **an** orange. Sam은 달걀 한 개와 오렌지 한 개를 샀다.

주의 부정관사 a나 an이 시간을 나타내는 말과 함께 쓰일 때는 '~당, ~마다'의 뜻을 나타낸다.
three times **a** day 하루에 세 번　　　once **an** hour 한 시간에 한 번

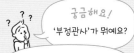

궁금해요!
'부정관사'가 뭐예요?

명사 앞에 붙어서 명사에 대한 정보를 주는 말이 '관사'예요. '부정관사'는 불특정한 막연한 것을 나타내는 관사예요.

개념확인 부정관사와 명사 찾기

1 She has a daughter.　　　**2** I bought an oven.　　　**3** I saw an iguana.

기본연습 **A** 괄호 안에서 알맞은 것을 고르시오.

1 (a / an) table　　　　　　　　**2** (a / an) album

3 (a / an) watch　　　　　　　　**4** (a / an) basket

5 (a / an) airplane　　　　　　　**6** (a / an) idea

B 빈칸에 a나 an 중 알맞은 것을 넣어 문장을 완성하시오.

1 We live in _____ apartment.　　　**2** I'm not _____ elementary school student.

3 Chris needs _____ umbrella.　　　**4** My father drives _____ taxi in Seoul.

5 Kate ate _____ sandwich for lunch.　　**6** I made _____ apple pie this morning.

7 Mr. Brown is _____ good cook.　　**8** Emily takes a lesson once _____ week.

9 I don't wear _____ uniform.　　　**10** Take the medicine two times _____ day.

11 I waited for _____ hour.　　　　**12** Dad, you're _____ angel.

틀 리 기　쉬 운
내/신/포/인/트

부정관사 a나 an은 뒤에 오는 단어의 첫소리에 따라 달리 쓰여요.

빈칸에 들어갈 말로 알맞은 것은?

My father is an _____ .

① pilot　　　② actor　　　③ teacher　　　④ doctor

POINT 7 정관사 the

정관사 the는 특정하거나 명확한 대상 앞에 쓴다.

앞에 나온 명사를 다시 말할 때	I have a dog. **The** dog is cute.	나에게 개가 한 마리 있다. 그 개는 귀엽다.
서로 알고 있는 대상을 말할 때	Close **the** window, please.	창문 좀 닫아 주세요.
세상에서 유일한 것을 말할 때	**The** Earth goes around **the** sun.	지구는 태양 주위를 돈다.
악기 이름 앞에	Jenny plays **the** cello very well.	Jenny는 첼로를 매우 잘 연주한다.
수식어구가 명사를 뒤에서 꾸며줄 때	I like **the** wallet *on your left*.	나는 네 왼쪽의 그 지갑이 마음에 든다.

↳ on your left가 명사 the wallet을 뒤에서 수식하고 있어요.

주의 서수 앞에도 정관사 the를 쓴다.
Sumin is in **the** first grade. 수민이는 1학년이다.

궁금해요! '정관사'가 뭐예요?

'정관사'는 명사 앞에 붙어서 특정한 것임을 나타내는 관사예요.

개념확인 정관사와 명사 찾기

1 The sun is shining. **2** She plays the violin. **3** Open the door, please.

기본연습 괄호 안에서 알맞은 것을 고르시오.

1 Mina plays (a / an / the) drums.

2 Jimin is in (a / an / the) second grade.

3 (A / An / The) sun rises in the east.

4 (A / An / The) moon isn't out tonight.

5 It's too noisy outside. Close (a / an / the) door, please.

6 (A / An / The) hat with a ribbon is not Camila's.

7 Please don't play (a / an / the) guitar late at night.

8 I really like (a / an / the) bag with two pockets.

9 Jimmy has (a / an / the) bike. (A / An / The) bike is blue.

10 Mike has (a / an / the) MP3 player. He brings (a / an / the) MP3 player every day.

틀리기 쉬운 내/신/포/인/트

특정한 것을 가리킬 때는 정관사 the를 써요.

빈칸에 공통으로 들어갈 말로 알맞은 것은?

· _____ boy on the bench is my brother.
· I bought a jacket. _____ jacket is nice.

① A ② An ③ The ④ Two

관사는 다음과 같은 경우에는 쓰지 않는다.

식사, 운동 경기, 과목 이름 앞에	Sophia had **dinner** at seven.	Sophia는 7시에 저녁을 먹었다.
	The kids played **tennis** together.	아이들이 함께 테니스를 쳤다.
	Henry likes **math** and **science**.	Henry는 수학과 과학을 좋아한다.
「by+교통수단」으로 말할 때	Michael went home **by subway**.	Michael은 지하철을 타고 집에 갔다.
장소가 원래 목적으로 쓰일 때	Ann went to **bed** at ten o'clock.	Ann은 10시에 잠자리에 들었다.
	Bob ran in the park after **school**.	Bob은 방과 후에 공원에서 달렸다.

주의 장소가 원래 목적으로 쓰이지 않을 때는 관사를 쓴다.
The bank is next to **the school**. 그 은행은 학교 옆에 있다.

개념확인 관사를 쓰지 않는 명사 찾기

1 I didn't have lunch.　　　**2** He went to school.　　　**3** They played soccer together.

기본연습 빈칸에 a나 an, the 중 알맞은 것을 넣거나 필요 없으면 ×표 하여 문장을 완성하시오.

1 I always skip _____ breakfast.

2 Tom and I meet once _____ month.

3 I went to Seattle by _____ plane.

4 My sister goes to _____ bed early every day.

5 I usually eat _____ egg for lunch.

6 My father plays _____ piano every morning.

7 My mother teaches _____ history in high school.

8 My friends and I played _____ basketball after _____ school.

틀 리 기 쉬 운
내/신/포/인/트

관사를 사용하지 않는 경우를
기억해요.

빈칸에 the를 쓸 수 <u>없는</u> 것은?

① Don't open _____ door.
② Jenny plays _____ flute very well.
③ Maria is in _____ fourth grade.
④ They study _____ math every Monday.

POINT 9 동격

명사 뒤에 콤마(,)를 써서 부연 설명을 덧붙일 수 있다. 이때 콤마(,) 앞뒤의 명사(구)는 동일한 대상을 가리킨다.

This is **Dylan**, **my friend**. 이 아이는 내 친구인 Dylan이다.
____ = ____

Adam, **my English teacher**, is very kind. 우리 영어 선생님인 Adam은 정말 친절하다.
____ = ____

개념확인 밑줄 친 말과 같은 대상 찾기

1 She is <u>J.K. Rowling</u>, a famous writer.　　**2** <u>Minsu</u>, my best friend, left for London.

기본연습 다음 두 문장을 한 문장으로 고쳐 쓰시오.

1 This is Paul Gauguin. He is a famous painter.

→ This is ＿＿＿＿＿＿＿, ＿＿＿＿＿＿＿＿＿＿＿.

2 Mr. Kim is my math teacher. He is very gentle.

→ ＿＿＿＿＿＿＿, ＿＿＿＿＿＿＿＿＿＿＿, is very gentle.

3 My role model is Jane Goodall. She is an animal scientist.

→ My role model is ＿＿＿＿＿＿＿, ＿＿＿＿＿＿＿＿＿＿＿.

4 That's Justin Bieber. He is a good singer.

→ That's ＿＿＿＿＿＿＿, ＿＿＿＿＿＿＿＿＿＿.

5 Jude Law is his uncle. He is a very popular actor.

→ His uncle is ＿＿＿＿＿＿＿, ＿＿＿＿＿＿＿＿＿＿.

6 This is *Avatar*. It is my favorite movie.

→ This is ＿＿＿＿＿＿＿, ＿＿＿＿＿＿＿＿＿＿.

틀리기 쉬운 내/신/포/인/트

콤마(,)를 사용하여 앞뒤의 명사(구)가 같음을 나타낼 수 있어요.

빈칸에 들어갈 말로 알맞지 <u>않은</u> 것은?

＿＿＿＿＿, my favorite subject, is very interesting.

① Math　　　　② Science
③ Art　　　　④ School

개 념 완 성 TEST

정답 및 해설 p.10

STEP 1 Map으로 개념 정리하기

- 명사
  - 셀 수 있는 명사
    - 한 개: a/an+명사
    - 여러 개: 명사+-s/-es
  - 셀 수 없는 명사
    - 물질명사 (water)
    - 추상명사 (love)
    - 고유명사 (Japan)
  - 소유격
    - 사람, 동물+-'s
    - 무생물: of 사용
  - 동격
    - 콤마(,) 사용
- 관사
  - a/an
    - +셀 수 있는 명사의 단수형
  - the
    - +특정하거나 명확한 대상

Quick Check

❶ I saw (a / an) elephant and (a / an) tiger in the zoo.

❷ I saw four _____(fox) and six _____(goose) in the zoo.

❸ The monkey's name is Mikey. [○ / ×]

❹ The name of the zoo is Animals' Friends.
   해석: _____

❺ He ordered a (loaf / bottle) of coke.

❻ He ordered two (bowl / bowls) of soup.

❼ He plays the piano every morning. [○ / ×]

❽ He plays the soccer every morning. [○ / ×]

STEP 2 기본 다지기

빈칸완성

A 우리말과 일치하도록 빈칸에 알맞은 말을 넣어 문장을 완성하시오.

1 Andy는 매일 사과 한 개를 먹는다. → Andy eats _____ _____ every day.

2 그는 어제 생선 다섯 마리를 잡았다. → He caught _____ _____ yesterday.

3 Tom은 버스를 타고 바다에 갔다. → Tom went to the sea _____ _____.

4 Jenny는 첼로를 매우 잘 연주한다. → Jenny plays _____ _____ very well.

5 달은 지구 주위를 돈다. → _____ _____ goes around the Earth.

6 Maria는 올해 3학년이다. → Maria is in _____ _____ grade this year.

7 지나는 주스 한 잔을 마셨다. → Jina drank _____ _____.

8 민호는 피자 두 조각을 먹었다. → Minho ate _____ _____ _____.

9 저 사람은 내 삼촌인 Mike이다. → That man is _____, _____.

10 Emily의 어머니는 택시 운전사이시다. → _____ _____ is a taxi driver.

B 밑줄 친 부분이 어법상 바르면 ○라고 쓰고, 틀리면 바르게 고쳐 쓰시오.

1 Two <u>man</u> helped the woman. → _____

2 The five <u>deers</u> live in that wood. → _____

3 Mathematics <u>are</u> my favorite subject. → _____

4 My brother bought two pairs of <u>pant</u> today. → _____

5 Alice played <u>the guitar</u> in the living room. → _____

6 I put three slices of <u>cheeses</u> on my bread. → _____

7 Do you want a <u>piece</u> of coffee? → _____

8 My father goes to work <u>by the car</u> every day. → _____

9 John fixed <u>the roof</u> of the house. → _____

C 다음 문장을 괄호 안의 지시대로 바꿔 쓰시오.

1 The girls ate <u>a cotton candy</u>. (a cotton candy를 복수형으로)
→ _____

2 Look at the <u>monkey</u> in this picture. (monkey를 복수형으로)
→ _____

3 <u>A</u> child played in the playground. (a를 five로)
→ _____

4 My baby brother has <u>two</u> teeth. (two를 one으로)
→ _____

5 Rachel has <u>three</u> cute puppies. (three를 a로)
→ _____

6 William drank <u>a</u> glass of water. (a를 two로)
→ _____

7 <u>Kate</u> answered the phone. (Kate를 Kate의 어머니로)
→ _____

8 Ms. Brown loves her students. (Ms. Brown이 my history teacher라는 설명을 추가하여)
→ _____

그림이해

A 그림을 보고, 쇼핑 목록을 완성하시오.

My shopping list

☑ a piece of cake

☑ _____

☑ _____

☑ _____

☑ _____

영작완성

B 우리말과 일치하도록 괄호 안의 말을 바르게 배열하여 문장을 쓰시오.

1 우리는 매일 7시에 아침을 먹는다. (we, every day, at 7, have, breakfast)

→ _____

2 책의 표지가 두껍다. (is, the book, thick, the cover, of)

→ _____

3 나의 소망은 우리 가족의 행복이다. (happiness, my wish, is, my family's)

→ _____

4 Jane은 고기와 토마토를 먹지 않는다. (meat, tomatoes, and, Jane, doesn't, eat)

→ _____

문장영작

C 우리말과 일치하도록 괄호 안의 말을 이용하여 영작하시오.

1 나는 지하철을 타고 학교에 간다. (go to, school, by, subway)

→ _____

2 우리는 농장에 돼지 두 마리와 양 세 마리가 있다. (have, pig, sheep, on our farm)

→ _____

3 손잡이가 있는 그 꽃병은 내 것이다. (vase, with a handle)

→ _____

4 그의 이모인 Anne Hathaway는 아주 유명한 여배우이다. (his aunt, a very famous actress)

→ _____

1 명사의 단수형과 복수형이 <u>잘못</u> 짝 지어진 것은?

① dish – dishes   ② toy – toys

③ mouse – mice   ④ foot – foots

⑤ child – children

2 명사의 성격이 나머지와 <u>다른</u> 하나는?

① air   ② rice   ③ luck

④ Beijing   ⑤ bag

[3-5] 빈칸에 들어갈 말로 알맞은 것을 고르시오.

3
> He painted two _____ in his sketchbook.

① ant   ② bird   ③ leafs

④ geese   ⑤ woman

4
> Mary ate an _____ last night.

① salad   ② cherry   ③ apple

④ yogurt   ⑤ bread

5
> Robin wants a piece of _____.

① rice   ② paper   ③ soup

④ water   ⑤ coffee

6 세는 단위와 셀 수 없는 명사가 <u>잘못</u> 짝 지어진 것은?

① a cup of – tea   ② a bottle of – water

③ a glass of – milk   ④ a slice of – cheese

⑤ a bowl of – bread

7 빈칸에 알맞은 말이 순서대로 짝 지어진 것은?

> Tom has _____ digital camera. _____
> camera is very nice.

① a – A   ② a – The   ③ an – The

④ the – A   ⑤ the – The

8 밑줄 친 부분의 쓰임이 나머지와 <u>다른</u> 하나는?

① My dog<u>'s</u> nose is very soft.
② He<u>'s</u> in the school cafeteria.
③ Eric<u>'s</u> new bike is really expensive.
④ Wendy<u>'s</u> aunt lives in New York.
⑤ My father<u>'s</u> car broke down again.

9 다음 두 문장을 한 문장으로 바르게 쓴 것은?

> • Mr. Lee is my music teacher.
> • He has a great sense of humor.

① Mr. Lee has my music teacher, a great sense of humor.
② Mr. Lee has a great sense of humor, my music teacher.
③ Mr. Lee, my music teacher, has a great sense of humor.
④ Mr. Lee, he, has my music teacher, a great sense of humor.
⑤ He, Mr. Lee, my music teacher, has a great sense of humor.

10 빈칸에 **the**를 쓸 수 <u>없는</u> 것은?

① Please open _____ window.
② The store is on _____ first floor.
③ We played _____ baseball after dinner.
④ Jenny played _____ flute in the concert.
⑤ Sally wants _____ cap on the top shelf.

11 빈칸에 **a**나 **an**을 쓸 때 나머지와 <u>다른</u> 하나는?

① I have _____ question.
② Peter is _____ very honest boy.
③ Alice is _____ elementary school student.
④ Yesterday was _____ terrible day for me.
⑤ James plays tennis twice _____ week.

[12-13] 빈칸에 들어갈 말로 알맞지 <u>않은</u> 것을 고르시오.

12
> William has four _____.

① teeth   ② boxes   ③ children
④ salts   ⑤ houses

13
> Jake bought a pair of _____.

① socks   ② skates   ③ pants
④ jackets   ⑤ sunglasses

14 우리말을 영어로 바르게 옮긴 것은?

> 양들은 훌륭한 기억력을 가지고 있다.

① Sheep has great memories.
② Sheeps has great memories.
③ Sheep have great memories.
④ Sheeps have great memories.
⑤ Sheepes have great memories.

15 밑줄 친 명사의 성격이 나머지와 **다른** 하나는?

① Everyone wants peace.
② Jenny is a good cellist.
③ I have good news for you!
④ Daniel has enough money for the game.
⑤ Samuel caught a lot of fish last weekend.

고난도
16 빈칸에 a나 an을 쓸 때 들어갈 말이 같은 것끼리 짝 지어진 것은?

ⓐ I have _____ 8-year-old brother.
ⓑ It's _____ very beautiful painting.
ⓒ Frida Kahlo was _____ artist from Mexico.
ⓓ She wears _____ white blouse every day.
ⓔ Mr. Smith was _____ engineer.

① ⓐ, ⓑ   ② ⓐ, ⓑ, ⓒ
③ ⓐ, ⓒ, ⓔ   ④ ⓑ, ⓒ, ⓓ
⑤ ⓑ, ⓓ, ⓔ

[17-18] 밑줄 친 부분이 어법상 틀린 것을 고르시오.

17 ① I want a bowl of cereal.
② Do you want two bottles of milks?
③ Add three slices of cheese there.
④ He drinks a cup of coffee in the morning.
⑤ She put two spoonfuls of salt in her soup.

18 ① The Earth is a beautiful planet.
② I usually go to the bed at 10 p.m.
③ Someone knocked on the door.
④ The pencil with an eraser is mine.
⑤ My sister plays the violin very well.

19 밑줄 친 부분을 고친 것 중 틀린 것은?

① Susan visited the Amsterdam.
    → a Amsterdam.
② Aunt Mary has a three sons.
    → three sons
③ A penguin' legs are short.
    → penguin's legs
④ I boiled some potatos.
    → potatoes
⑤ Did you eat the breakfast?
    → breakfast

고난도
20 어법상 올바른 문장의 개수는?

ⓐ The men' restroom is on the second floor.
ⓑ She ate two slice of bread for lunch.
ⓒ The bird's feathers are colorful.
ⓓ I ordered three cups of coffee.
ⓔ Sarah is in the teachers' office.

① 0개   ② 1개   ③ 2개
④ 3개   ⑤ 4개

21 그림을 보고, 빈칸에 a, an, the 중 알맞은 것을 쓰시오.
(필요 없을 시 X표 할 것)

I live in (1) _____ Africa. I have
(2) _____ long nose. I have two big
ears. I'm (3) _____ elephant. Look at
(4) _____ elephant under the tree. She
is my mother.

22 어법상 틀린 부분을 바르게 고친 후, 틀린 이유를 쓰시오.

(1) I counted the moneys carefully.

_____ → _____

틀린 이유: _____

(2) The robot walked on its two foots.

_____ → _____

틀린 이유: _____

23 그림을 보고, 조건 에 맞게 글을 완성하시오.

조건 1. 괄호 안의 말을 이용할 것
　　　2. 수량을 표현할 것

The man is wearing (1) _____
(glove). He has (2) _____
(mouse) on his left hand. On his right hand,
he has (3) _____ (candy).

24 그림을 보고, 보기 에서 알맞은 말을 골라 글을 완성하시오.

| 보기 | bowl | glass | piece |

Andy set the table for dinner. He put
(1) _____ on the table.
He put (2) _____ on the
plate. He made (3) _____.

고난도
25 우리말과 일치하도록 괄호 안의 말을 이용하여 영작하시오.

(1) 내 개의 다리들은 매우 길다. (are, very long)

→ _____

(2) 해는 동쪽에서 뜬다. (rise, in the east)

→ _____

(3) Jess는 매일 피아노를 친다. (play, piano)

→ _____

(4) Emily는 일주일에 한 번 테니스를 친다.
(play, tennis, once)

→ _____

4

대명사

대명사는 명사를 대신해서 사용하는 말이다.

POINT 1 인칭대명사

인칭대명사는 사람이나 동물, 사물을 대신하여 가리키는 말로, 인칭과 수, 격에 따라 형태가 달라진다.

인칭	수	주격(~은)	소유격(~의)	목적격(~을)	소유대명사(~의 것)
1인칭	단수	I	my	me	mine
	복수	we	our	us	ours
2인칭	단수	you (너)	your	you	yours
	복수	you (너희들)	your	you	yours
3인칭	단수	he	his	him	his
		she	her	her	hers
		it	its	it	없음
	복수	they	their	them	theirs

→ 2인칭은 단수와 복수의 형태가 같아요.

→ he는 소유격과 소유대명사의 형태가 his로 같아요.

(1) 주격과 목적격: 문장 안에서 주격은 주어 역할을 하고, 목적격은 목적어 역할을 한다.

You are a good dancer. 〈주격〉 너는 춤을 잘 춘다.
Jack met **them** yesterday. 〈목적격〉 Jack은 어제 그들을 만났다.

(2) 소유격과 소유대명사: 소유격은 '~의'라는 뜻으로 뒤에 명사가 오고, 소유대명사는 '~의 것'이라는 뜻으로
「소유격＋명사」를 대신한다.

Mina took **my** scarf. 〈소유격〉 미나가 나의 스카프를 가져갔다.
The coat on the chair is **hers**. 〈소유대명사〉 의자에 있는 코트는 그녀의 것이다.

Tips 명사의 소유격은 명사에 -'s를 붙이거나 of를 써서 나타낸다.
It is my **mother's** hat. 그것은 우리 엄마의 모자이다.
The leg **of** the chair is loose. 의자의 다리가 헐겁다.

개념확인 격 구분하기

1 We invited him.
☐ 주격 ☐ 목적격

2 He washed his dog.
☐ 주격 ☐ 소유격

3 Sally knows me.
☐ 소유격 ☐ 목적격

기본연습 **A** 괄호 안에서 알맞은 것을 고르시오.

1 Do (you / your) know this movie?

2 (They / Their) hands were really dirty.

3 Everybody likes (she / her) beautiful voice.

4 This English dictionary is (my / mine).

5 My father and mother love (us / our).

6 Look at that rabbit. (Its / It) tail is too short.

B 밑줄 친 부분을 알맞은 인칭대명사로 바꿔 쓰시오.

1 Jenny and Daniel went to the gym. → _____

2 Mike doesn't know Ms. Kim's address. → _____

3 Rick and I helped the old lady. → _____

4 My father bought a pair of glasses. → _____

5 I always tell my secrets to my brother. → _____

6 Basketball is my favorite sport. → _____

7 You and Tom came home late today. → _____

8 A police officer stopped Sam and me. → _____

C 우리말과 일치하도록 빈칸에 알맞은 말을 넣어 문장을 완성하시오.

1 나는 어제 너의 사진들을 봤다. → I saw _____ pictures yesterday.

2 그들의 집은 우리 학교와 가깝다. → _____ house is near my school.

3 그 장화들은 그녀의 것이다. → The rainboots are _____.

4 나의 농구공은 비싸다. → _____ basketball is expensive.

5 나는 어제 그녀를 만나지 않았다. → I didn't meet _____ yesterday.

6 그녀는 도서관에서 책을 읽었다. → _____ read books in the library.

7 이 선물은 너를 위한 거야. → This present is for _____.

8 저를 병원에 데려가 주세요. → Please take _____ to the hospital.

9 나는 고양이와 개를 키운다. 그들은 귀엽다. → I have a cat and a dog. _____ are cute.

10 내 머리는 검은색이고, 그의 것은 붉은색이다. → My hair is black, and _____ is red.

틀리기 쉬운
내/신/포/인/트

인칭대명사의 인칭과 수,
격에 따라 달라지는 형태를
기억해요.

대화의 빈칸에 알맞은 말이 순서대로 짝 지어진 것은?

A: Is _____ friend from Mexico?
B: No, _____ isn't. She's from France.

① you – she   ② you – her
③ your – she   ④ your – hers

비인칭 주어 it

정답 및 해설 p.11

시간, 요일, 날짜, 날씨, 계절, 거리 등을 나타낼 때 주어로 사용하는 **it**을 비인칭 주어라고 한다.
이때 **it**은 해석하지 않는다.

시간	**A:** What time is **it** now? **B:** **It**'s seven thirty.	지금 몇 시죠? 7시 30분이에요.
요일	**A:** What day is **it** today? **B:** **It**'s Saturday.	오늘이 무슨 요일이죠? 토요일이에요.
날짜	**A:** What date is **it** today? **B:** **It**'s June 5th.	오늘이 며칠이죠? 6월 5일이에요.
날씨	**A:** How is the weather today? **B:** **It**'s sunny.	오늘 날씨가 어떻죠? 맑아요.
계절	**It**'s spring.	봄이에요.
거리	**A:** How far is **it** from here? **B:** **It**'s 1 km from here.	여기서부터 얼마나 먼가요? 여기서부터 1km 떨어져 있어요.

주의 인칭대명사 it은 사물이나 동물을 대신하는 말로 '그것'이라고 해석한다.
It is my favorite book. 그것은 내가 가장 좋아하는 책이다.

궁금해요!
비인칭 주어 it과
인칭대명사 it은
어떻게 구별하나요?

'그것'으로 해석되지 않을 때는
비인칭 주어이고,
'그것'으로 해석되면 인칭대명사예요.

개념확인 **비인칭 주어 찾기**

1 It is windy now.   **2** It is January 1st.   **3** It is six forty.

기본연습 **A** 질문에 알맞은 대답을 골라 연결하시오.

1 A: What time is it now?   ·   · ⓐ B: It's Sunday.

2 A: What day is it today?   ·   · ⓑ B: It's December 25th.

3 A: What date is it today?   ·   · ⓒ B: It's rainy.

4 A: How is the weather today?   ·   · ⓓ B: It's about 2 km from here.

5 A: How far is it from here?   ·   · ⓔ B: It's 9 o'clock.

B 밑줄 친 It의 쓰임으로 알맞은 것을 고르시오.

1 It is autumn already.   ☐ 비인칭 주어   ☐ 인칭대명사

2 It takes an hour by bus.   ☐ 비인칭 주어   ☐ 인칭대명사

3 It is my mother's ring.   ☐ 비인칭 주어   ☐ 인칭대명사

4 It was a very exciting game.   ☐ 비인칭 주어   ☐ 인칭대명사

5 It was cold yesterday.   ☐ 비인칭 주어   ☐ 인칭대명사

C 그림을 보고, 대화를 완성하시오.

10:00
Monday, February 2nd

23°C
△ 55%

cloudy

1 A: How's the weather today?

B: _____ _____ _____ today.

2 A: What time is it now?

B: _____ _____ _____ o'clock.

3 A: What date is it today?

B: _____ _____ _____ _____.

4 A: What day is it today?

B: _____ _____ _____.

D 우리말과 일치하도록 괄호 안의 말을 이용하여 문장을 완성하시오.

1 이곳에서 3 km 떨어져 있다. (3 km) → _____ from here.

2 밖에 눈이 내린다. (snowy) → _____ outside.

3 오늘은 수요일이다. (Wednesday) → _____ today.

4 오늘은 덥다. (hot) → _____ today.

5 북극은 매우 춥다. (very cold) → _____ at the North Pole.

6 뉴질랜드는 겨울이다. (winter) → _____ in New Zealand.

7 지금은 여름이다. (summer) → _____ now.

8 지금은 12시 5분이다. (twelve five) → _____ now.

9 오늘이 5월 17일인가요? (May 17th) → _____ today?

10 역까지 200 m이다. (200 meters) → _____ to the station.

틀 리 기 쉬 운
내/신/포/인/트

비인칭 주어 it과 인칭대명사
it을 구별해요.

밑줄 친 It의 쓰임이 나머지와 <u>다른</u> 하나는?

① <u>It</u> is April 20th.
② <u>It</u> has eight legs.
③ <u>It</u> is very hot and sunny.
④ <u>It</u> is eleven twenty now.

지시대명사는 특정한 사물이나 사람을 가리킬 때 사용한다.

가까이에 있는 대상	**this** (이것, 이 사람)	**This** is my father's car.	이것은 우리 아버지의 차이다.
	these (이것들, 이 사람들)	**These** are my friends.	이 사람들은 내 친구들이다.
멀리 떨어져 있는 대상	**that** (저것, 저 사람)	**That** is my grandfather.	저분은 우리 할아버지시다.
	those (저것들, 저 사람들)	**Those** are my pencils.	저것들은 내 연필들이다.

주의 this/these와 that/those는 명사 앞에서 형용사로도 쓰인다.
This book is very interesting. 이 책은 매우 재미있다.

Those baseball caps are dirty. 저 야구 모자들은 더럽다.

Tips 전화 통화 시 자신이 누구인지 밝힐 때도 this를 쓴다.
Hello. **This** is Grace, Jenny's friend. 여보세요. 저는 Jenny의 친구인 Grace예요.

궁금해요!
Is this your pen?이라고 물으면
Yes, this is.라고 답하나요?

아니에요. this/that으로 물으면
it으로 답해요. Yes, it is.가 되는 거죠.
these/those로 물으면
they로 답하세요.

개념확인 **지시대명사 찾기**

1 These are not my earrings. **2** Those are my friends. **3** Is this your book?

기본연습 **A** 괄호 안에서 알맞은 것을 고르시오.

1 (That / Those) are my grandparents. **2** (This / These) is too small for me.

3 I solved (this / these) questions. **4** Jihun likes (that / those) robots.

5 (That / Those) watch is too expensive. **6** I like (this / these) new computer.

7 (That / Those) is my brother's room. **8** Hello. (This / That) is Alice.

B 우리말과 일치하도록 빈칸에 알맞은 말을 넣어 문장을 완성하시오.

1 이 사람들은 우리 반 친구들이다. → _____ are my classmates.

2 저 병아리들을 봐. 그들은 정말 귀여워. → Look at _____ chicks. They are so cute.

3 저 학생들은 키가 정말 크다. → _____ students are very tall.

4 저것은 나의 새 배낭이다. → _____ is my new backpack.

5 그녀는 친구에게 이 카드를 썼다. → She wrote _____ card to her friend.

6 나는 이 신발이 마음에 든다. 그것들은 싸다. → I like _____ shoes. They are cheap.

7 이것은 내가 가장 좋아하는 그림이다. → _____ is my favorite painting.

재귀대명사는 인칭대명사의 소유격이나 목적격에 **-self**나 **-selves**를 붙인 것으로, '〜 자신'이라는 뜻을 나타낸다.

	단수	복수		
1인칭	myself	ourselves	I introduced **myself**.	나는 내 **자신**을 소개했다.
2인칭	yourself	yourselves	Introduce **yourself** to the class.	너 **자신**을 반에 소개해.
3인칭	himself, herself, itself	themselves	Tim introduced **himself** to us.	Tim은 우리에게 **자신**을 소개했다.

재귀대명사는 재귀 용법이나 강조 용법으로 쓰인다.

재귀 용법 (〜 자신)	목적어가 주어와 같은 대상일 때 목적어로 재귀대명사를 쓴다.	Susan talked about **herself**.	Susan은 **그녀 자신**에 대해 이야기했다. 〈Susan = herself〉
강조 용법 (〜 자체, 직접)	주어나 목적어를 강조하기 위해 강조하는 말 바로 뒤나 문장 끝에 재귀대명사를 쓸 수 있다.	Bob **himself** cooked dinner.	Bob은 **직접** 저녁을 요리했다. 〈주어 강조〉
		I saw the elephant **myself**.	내가 **직접** 그 코끼리를 봤다. 〈주어 강조〉
		I don't like the picture **itself**.	나는 그 그림 **자체**를 좋아하지 않는다. 〈목적어 강조〉

↪ 강조 용법으로 쓰인 재귀대명사는 생략해도 완전한 문장이에요.

개념확인 재귀대명사 찾기

1 We love ourselves.   **2** He talked to himself.   **3** I made dinner myself.

기본연습 A 우리말과 일치하도록 보기 에서 알맞은 말을 골라 문장을 완성하시오.

> 보기   myself   himself   herself   itself   themselves

1 그 새는 직접 둥지를 지었다.   → The bird built a nest ＿＿＿＿＿＿.

2 그들은 자신들을 무척 좋아한다.   → They love ＿＿＿＿＿＿ very much.

3 나는 나 자신을 위해 코코아를 만들었다.   → I made hot chocolate for ＿＿＿＿＿＿.

4 Morris 씨가 직접 전화를 받았다.   → Mr. Morris answered the phone ＿＿＿＿＿＿.

5 Amy는 거울 속의 자신의 모습을 보았다.   → Amy looked at ＿＿＿＿＿＿ in the mirror.

B 밑줄 친 단어의 쓰임으로 알맞은 것을 고르시오.

1 We washed the dishes <u>ourselves</u>.   ☐ 재귀 용법   ☐ 강조 용법

2 Did you play the piano <u>yourself</u>?   ☐ 재귀 용법   ☐ 강조 용법

3 I wrote a story about <u>myself</u>.   ☐ 재귀 용법   ☐ 강조 용법

4 My cat always cleans <u>itself</u>.   ☐ 재귀 용법   ☐ 강조 용법

C 괄호 안에서 알맞은 것을 고르시오.

1 (1) Did Alex hurt (you / yourself)?

(2) Did you hurt (you / yourself)?

2 (1) I baked the bread (me / myself).

(2) My mom baked the bread for (me / myself).

3 (1) We painted the house (us / ourselves).

(2) Daniel painted (our / ourselves) house.

4 (1) They did well in (their / themselves) exams.

(2) The exams (them / themselves) were not easy.

5 (1) Will you introduce (you / yourself)?

(2) Emily will introduce (you / yourself) to her friends.

D 빈칸에 알맞은 재귀대명사를 쓰시오.

1 Mr. Smith drew _____.

2 I _____ wrote these poems.

3 Some people don't love _____.

4 I bought a new cap for _____.

5 He only thought about _____.

6 The girl always talks about _____.

7 "You can do it!" I said to _____.

8 The little bird washes _____ every morning.

9 My brother _____ fixed the computer.

10 We _____ made the huge kite.

밑줄 친 부분이 어법상 **틀린** 것은?

① I designed the skirt <u>myself</u>.

② I walked the dog <u>myself</u>.

③ I'm really angry with <u>me</u>.

④ Ms. Jones looked at <u>me</u> sadly.

부정대명사 one은 정해지지 않은 불특정한 것을 가리킬 때 사용하며, 복수형은 ones로 쓴다.

one (하나)	Do you need an umbrella? I have **one**. an umbrella, 즉 정해지지 않은 '우산'을 말해요.	너는 우산이 필요하니? 나에게 **하나**가 있어.
(관사)+형용사+one (~것)	My phone is broken. I need a new **one**. a new phone, 즉 one은 정해지지 않은 '전화기'를 말해요.	내 전화기가 부서졌다. 나는 새 **것**이 필요하다.

주의 앞에서 언급한 특정한 것을 가리킬 때는 인칭대명사 it이나 they/them을 쓴다.
I bought this umbrella. I love **it**.
↳ 앞에서 언급한 this umbrella를 가리켜요.

개념확인 가리키는 대상 고르기

1 I lost my pencil. I need a new <u>one</u>.

☐ 불특정한 연필 ☐ 내가 가지고 있던 연필

2 I don't have a cap. I need <u>one</u>.

☐ 불특정한 모자 ☐ 내가 보고 있는 모자

기본연습 **A** 괄호 안에서 알맞은 것을 고르시오.

1 I need an eraser. Do you have (it / one)?

2 Daniel wrote a card for me. I like (it / one) very much.

3 Amy lost her calculator. She bought a new (it / one).

4 I don't like the color. Do you have a red (it / one)?

5 This cup is dirty. Do you have a clean (it / one)?

6 I bought a blue shirt and two green (one / ones).

B 빈칸에 one이나 it을 넣어 대화를 완성하시오.

1 A: I need a pen.

B: I have lots of pens. Just take _____.

2 A: I like your new dress.

B: Thanks. My mom bought _____ for me.

3 A: My pencil case is too old.

B: Do you want a new _____?

4 A: Did you get my text message?

B: Yes, I read _____ a few minutes ago.

개 | 념 | 완 | 성 | T E S T

정답 및 해설 p.12

STEP 1 Map으로 개념 정리하기

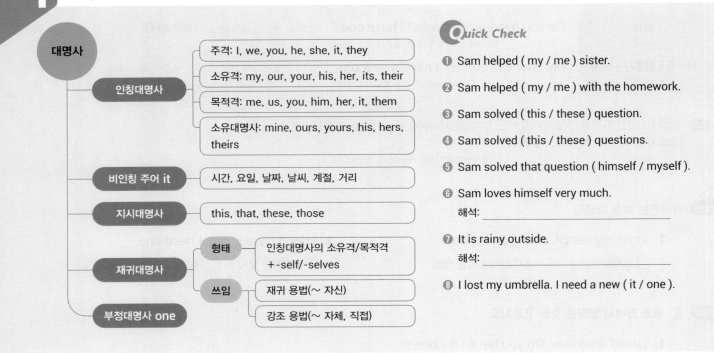

Quick Check

❶ Sam helped (my / me) sister.

❷ Sam helped (my / me) with the homework.

❸ Sam solved (this / these) question.

❹ Sam solved (this / these) questions.

❺ Sam solved that question (himself / myself).

❻ Sam loves himself very much.
해석: _____

❼ It is rainy outside.
해석: _____

❽ I lost my umbrella. I need a new (it / one).

STEP 2 기본 다지기

빈칸완성

A 우리말과 일치하도록 빈칸에 알맞은 말을 넣어 문장을 완성하시오.

1 오늘은 따뜻하다.　　　　　　　→ _____ is warm today.

2 저것은 내 자동차 열쇠가 아니다.　→ _____ is not my car key.

3 Emma가 이 쿠키들을 샀다.　　　→ Emma bought _____ cookies.

4 Julie는 그녀 자신을 너무 자주 씻는다.　→ Julie washes _____ too often.

5 너는 자신을 다치게 했니?　　　→ Did you hurt _____?

6 그곳은 맑나요?　　　　　　　→ Is _____ sunny there?

7 제 포크가 더러워요. 깨끗한 것이 있나요?　→ My fork is dirty. Do you have a clean _____?

8 새들을 봐. 그들은 정말 아름다워.　→ Look at the birds. _____ are so beautiful.

9 이 가방은 내 거야. 저 가방이 네 거야.　→ This bag is _____. That bag is _____.

10 나는 그의 춤이 좋다. 그는 훌륭한 춤꾼이다.　→ I like _____ dance. _____ is a good dancer.

B 밑줄 친 부분을 어법상 바르게 고쳐 쓰시오.

1 I introduced <u>me</u> to the class. → _____

2 <u>This</u> was snowy yesterday. → _____

3 This car is not his. It's <u>her's</u>. → _____

4 Sumi has a doll. <u>They</u> is very pretty. → _____

5 Angela doesn't have a piano. She needs <u>it</u>. → _____

6 <u>This</u> are my grandparents. → _____

7 <u>This</u> is September 4th today. → _____

C 다음 문장을 괄호 안의 지시대로 바꿔 쓰시오.

1 <u>The T-shirts</u> are in the closet. (밑줄 친 부분을 인칭대명사로)

→ _____

2 Did <u>you and Kate</u> help <u>the kids</u>? (밑줄 친 부분을 인칭대명사로)

→ _____

3 <u>Elly's mom</u> gave some fruit to <u>Jenny and me</u>. (밑줄 친 부분을 인칭대명사로)

→ _____

4 My mom bought a new purse. I don't like <u>that purse</u>. (밑줄 친 부분을 인칭대명사로)

→ _____

5 <u>Susie</u> looked at <u>her</u> in the mirror. (Susie와 her를 동일한 사람으로)

→ _____

6 Simon always makes his own clothes. (Simon을 강조하는 재귀대명사를 추가하여)

→ _____

7 Today is Monday. (비인칭 주어 it을 사용하여)

→ _____

8 Today is July 10th. (비인칭 주어 it을 사용하여)

→ _____

9 He broke his smartphone. He bought a new smartphone. (부정대명사 one을 사용하여)

→ _____

STEP 3 서술형 따라잡기

그림이해

A 그림을 보고, 빈칸에 알맞은 말을 넣어 대화를 완성하시오.

1

A: Helen is in the hospital now.

B: I know. She hurt _____ on the street.

2

A: Jiho, did you buy those cookies?

B: No. I made them _____.

영작완성

B 우리말과 일치하도록 괄호 안의 말을 바르게 배열하여 문장을 쓰시오.

1 오늘은 일요일이니? (it, is, today, Sunday)

→ _____

2 나는 나 자신을 위해 멋진 선물을 샀다. (bought, I, for, a nice present, myself)

→ _____

3 Andy는 그의 형과 다르다. (is, Andy, his, different, brother, from)

→ _____

4 저 사람들이 나의 가장 친한 친구들이다. (are, those, best friends, my)

→ _____

문장영작

C 우리말과 일치하도록 괄호 안의 말을 이용하여 영작하시오.

1 저 재킷은 그의 것이 아니다. (jacket)

→ _____

2 나는 이 영화 장르를 좋아하지 않는다. (like, movie genre)

→ _____

3 내가 직접 이 토마토들을 키웠다. (grow, tomatoes)

→ _____

4 버스 정류장까지 100미터이다. (100 meters, to the bus stop)

→ _____

[1-2] 빈칸에 들어갈 말로 알맞은 것을 고르시오.

1

> I like these flowers. _____ are beautiful.

① It   ② Its   ③ They
④ Their   ⑤ We

2

> This is Ms. Kim. She is _____ English teacher.

① we   ② our   ③ it
④ ours   ⑤ its

[3-4] 빈칸에 알맞은 말이 순서대로 짝 지어진 것을 고르시오.

3

> • This is Andy. Everybody likes _____.
> • I brought this ball. This ball is _____.

① his – my   ② his – mine
③ him – my   ④ him – mine
⑤ him – me

4

> • I have lots of umbrellas. You can have _____.
> • She wore her new coat. She bought _____ yesterday.

① it – it   ② it – one
③ one – it   ④ one – one
⑤ one – them

5 대화의 빈칸에 들어갈 말로 알맞은 것은?

> A: This room is really clean!
> B: I cleaned it _____.

① myself   ② yourself   ③ himself
④ ourselves   ⑤ themselves

[6-7] 빈칸에 공통으로 들어갈 말로 알맞은 것을 고르시오.

6

> • _____ is October 10th today.
> • _____ rained a lot last night.

① It   ② This   ③ One
④ That   ⑤ They

7

> • _____ is a gift for you.
> • Hello. _____ is Rosa, Mina's friend.

① That   ② This   ③ These
④ Those   ⑤ They

8 빈칸에 That을 쓸 수 <u>없는</u> 것은?

① _____ is my diary.
② _____ night was very windy.
③ _____ cup is mine.
④ _____ is 1,000 km from here.
⑤ _____ is Tony's cat.

9 밑줄 친 It의 쓰임이 나머지와 다른 하나는?

① It's Tuesday today.
② It's already winter.
③ It's ten thirty now.
④ It's Ashely's bike.
⑤ It's cold and windy.

10 주어진 문장을 바르게 고친 사람은?

> These are hers cameras.

① 소라: These를 This로 고쳐야 해.
② 수영: are를 is로 고쳐야 해.
③ 준수: hers를 her로 고쳐야 해.
④ 민재: cameras를 a camera로 고쳐야 해.
⑤ 서윤: cameras 뒤에 themselves를 써야 해.

11 밑줄 친 부분의 쓰임이 〔보기〕와 같은 것은?

> 〔보기〕 He introduced himself in English.

① Yujin often speaks to herself.
② Bill cooked dinner himself.
③ They built the house themselves.
④ I did the homework myself.
⑤ I saw Pablo Picasso's *Guernica* myself.

12 밑줄 친 부분을 복수형으로 바르게 바꿔 쓴 문장은?

> Is this book interesting?

① Is this books interesting?
② Is these book interesting?
③ Are this books interesting?
④ Are these book interesting?
⑤ Are these books interesting?

13 밑줄 친 비인칭 주어 It의 쓰임이 〔보기〕와 같은 것은?

> 〔보기〕 It is five kilometers from here.

① It was very cloudy.
② It is 7:30 in the morning.
③ It is not far from my house.
④ It is summer in Australia now.
⑤ It snowed all day yesterday.

14 밑줄 친 부분을 생략할 수 있는 것은?

① Minsu loves himself.
② Pedro made these cookies himself.
③ Do you know yourself?
④ Alice often looks at herself in the mirror.
⑤ Jenny hurt herself during the game.

15 밑줄 친 부분이 어법상 틀린 것은?

① Are <u>they</u> classmates?

② The coat is not mine. It's <u>her</u>.

③ Pizza is <u>my</u> favorite food.

④ We met <u>him</u> at the train station.

⑤ They are my neighbors. I know <u>them</u>.

16 대화가 자연스럽지 않은 것은?

① A: Is this your watch?
  B: No, it isn't.

② A: Hello.
  B: Hello. This is Sunny.

③ A: Are those your socks?
  B: No, it isn't.

④ A: Did you hurt yourself?
  B: Yes, I did.

⑤ A: How is the weather today?
  B: It's sunny and cool.

17 밑줄 친 부분이 의미하는 것은?

> I brought my notebook, but I didn't bring a pen. Can I borrow <u>one</u>?

① a notebook ② a bag ③ a pen

④ an eraser ⑤ a book

[고난도]
18 밑줄 친 부분이 어법상 틀린 문장의 개수는?

> ⓐ I turned off the TV <u>me</u>.
> ⓑ Did you see the actor <u>himself</u>?
> ⓒ Emily invited <u>them</u> to her birthday party.
> ⓓ I helped him with <u>his</u> homework.

① 0개 ② 1개 ③ 2개

④ 3개 ⑤ 4개

19 우리말을 영어로 바르게 옮긴 것은?

> 나는 이것들을 좋아한다. 나는 저것들을 좋아하지 않는다.

① I like this. I don't like that.

② I like that. I don't like this.

③ I like these. I don't like those.

④ I like these. I don't like these.

⑤ I like those. I don't like those.

[고난도]
20 어법상 올바른 문장의 개수는?

> ⓐ Do you remember myself?
> ⓑ Are these your new pants?
> ⓒ The teacher him gave the book to me.
> ⓓ That's 9 o'clock now.
> ⓔ These textbooks are him.

① 0개 ② 1개 ③ 2개

④ 3개 ⑤ 4개

고난도
21 그림을 보고, 질문에 대한 답을 완전한 문장으로 쓰시오.

(1) What date is it today?

→ _____

(2) What day is it today?

→ _____

(3) What time is it now?

→ _____

(4) How is the weather outside?

→ _____

22 Mike가 친구에게 자신의 가족을 소개하는 말을 완성하시오.

Hi. (1) _____ are my parents.
(2) _____ is my sister. Her name is Ann.
(3) _____ are our dogs.
(4) _____ really love balls.

23 밑줄 친 ①~⑤ 중 어법상 틀린 것을 찾아 바르게 고친 후, 틀린 이유를 쓰시오.

> A: Where is my ① math textbook? I need ② it now.
> B: ③ I don't know. I don't have ④ your book. Let's find ⑤ one together.

→ _____

틀린 이유: _____

24 Peter의 자기소개를 읽고, 그를 다른 사람에게 소개하는 글을 다시 쓰시오.

> My name is Peter. I live in Australia.
> My favorite sport is baseball.
> I have two dogs. They love me a lot.

⬇

> His name is Peter. _____
> _____
> _____

고난도
25 우리말과 일치하도록 괄호 안의 말을 이용하여 조건에 맞게 문장을 쓰시오.

> 조건 1. 재귀대명사를 이용할 것
> 2. 각 문장은 총 5단어로 쓸 것

(1) 우리는 우리 자신을 TV에서 봤다. (see, on TV)

→ _____

(2) 우리 아버지가 직접 저녁을 만들었다.
(make, dinner)

→ _____

5

시제

동사의 형태를 바꿔 동작이 언제 일어났는지를 나타낼 수 있는데, 이것을 시제라고 한다.

현재시제는 현재의 상태나 사실, 반복되는 일이나 습관, 일반적·과학적 사실을 나타낼 때 쓴다.

> be동사의 현재형은 am, are, is로 써요.

현재의 상태나 사실	Andrew **is** my little brother.	Andrew는 나의 남동생**이다**.
	My aunt **lives** in New York.	나의 이모는 뉴욕에 **산다**.
반복되는 일이나 습관	He **plays** soccer on Fridays.	그는 금요일마다 축구를 **한다**.
	She always **eats** breakfast.	그녀는 항상 아침을 **먹는다**.
일반적·과학적 사실	The sun **sets** in the west.	태양은 서쪽으로 **진다**.
	Water **boils** at 100°C.	물은 섭씨 100도에서 **끓는다**.

> 일반동사의 현재형은 동사원형으로 쓰고,
> 주어가 3인칭 단수일 경우에는 동사원형 뒤에 -(e)s를 붙여요.

Tips 현재시제는 격언이나 속담에도 쓰인다.
Time **is** money. 시간이 돈이다.

Tips 현재시제는 every day, on Sundays, always, usually 등과 같이 반복이나 빈도를 나타내는 부사(구)와 주로 함께 쓴다.
I exercise **every day**. 나는 매일 운동한다.

개념확인 동사 찾은 후 옳은 해석 고르기

1 I run every day.

　□ 달렸다　□ 달린다

2 She likes her shoes.

　□ 좋아한다　□ 좋아할 것이다

3 He wants a cute dog.

　□ 원했다　□ 원한다

기본연습 **A** 괄호 안에서 알맞은 것을 고르시오.

1 She (walk / walks) to school every day.

2 My parents (are / were) in London now.

3 A spider (have / has) eight legs.

4 The Han River (flows / flowed) into the West Sea.

B 괄호 안의 동사를 이용하여 현재시제 문장을 완성하시오.

1 Kevin _____ two brothers. (have)

2 He _____ eight hours every day. (sleep)

3 I _____ my room every weekend. (clean)

4 Mr. Brown _____ history at school. (teach)

5 She _____ three books every month. (read)

6 My sister _____ a high school student. (be)

C 밑줄 친 동사를 어법상 바르게 고쳐 쓰시오.

1 We had four seasons in Korea. → _____

2 They lived in Canada now. → _____

3 He wear a baseball cap every day. → _____

4 The moon moved around the Earth. → _____

5 The restaurant open at 10 every morning. → _____

D 우리말과 일치하도록 빈칸에 들어갈 말을 보기 에서 골라 알맞은 형태로 쓰시오.

보기	make	write	have	rise	practice	visit	go

1 그는 10시에 잠자리에 든다.

→ He _____ to bed at 10.

2 태양은 동쪽에서 뜬다.

→ The sun _____ in the east.

3 우리 개는 긴 귀를 가지고 있다.

→ My dog _____ long ears.

4 나는 매일 아침 피아노를 연습한다.

→ I _____ the piano every morning.

5 Peter는 매일 일기를 쓴다.

→ Peter _____ in his diary every day.

6 그녀는 일요일마다 그녀의 할머니를 방문한다.

→ She _____ her grandmother every Sunday.

7 White 씨는 월요일마다 머핀을 만든다.

→ Ms. White _____ muffins on Mondays.

틀 리 기 쉬 운
내/신/포/인/트

현재시제에서는 주어에 따라
동사의 형태가 달라져요.

우리말과 일치하도록 빈칸에 들어갈 말로 알맞은 것은?

My brother _____ his bike every day.
(나의 남동생은 매일 자전거를 탄다.)

① ride   ② rides   ③ is riding   ④ rode

POINT 2 과거시제

과거시제는 과거에 이미 일어난 일이나 상태, 역사적 사실을 나타낼 때 쓴다.

> be동사의 과거형은 was, were로 써요.

과거에 일어난 일이나 상태	They **were** in the same class last year.	그들은 작년에 같은 반**이었다.**
	She **went** on a picnic three days ago.	그녀는 사흘 전에 소풍을 **갔다.**
역사적 사실	King Sejong **invented** Hangeul in 1443.	세종대왕은 1443년에 한글을 **발명했다.**
	Henri Matisse **painted** *Music* in 1939.	Henri Matisse는 1939년에 '음악'을 **그렸다.**

> 일반동사의 과거형은 동사원형에 -(e)d를 붙여요. 불규칙으로 변하는 동사도 있어요.

Tips 과거시제는 yesterday, last night, last weekend, two days ago, in 2020 등과 같이 명백한 과거를 나타내는 부사(구)와 주로 함께 쓴다.
He watched a movie **last weekend**. 그는 지난 주말에 영화를 봤다.

개념확인 동사와 과거를 나타내는 표현 찾기

1 She was angry yesterday. **2** They ate too much last night. **3** I moved to L.A. two days ago.

기본연습 A 괄호 안에서 알맞은 것을 고르시오.

1 He (is / was) busy yesterday.

2 They (live / lived) in Busan now.

3 I (am / was) 13 years old last year.

4 We (enjoy / enjoyed) the concert last night.

5 She (loses / lost) her key this morning.

6 Jane (goes / went) to the museum last Sunday.

7 Tony (visits / visited) his grandfather three days ago.

B 밑줄 친 부분을 어법상 바르게 고쳐 쓰시오.

1 He <u>calls</u> me this morning. → _____

2 We <u>meet</u> Minho last Friday. → _____

3 Water <u>froze</u> at 0℃. → _____

4 Mary <u>cleans</u> her room yesterday. → _____

5 She <u>rides</u> her bike last weekend. → _____

6 Jane <u>buys</u> a backpack last week. → _____

7 They <u>see</u> the magic show last month. → _____

C 우리말과 일치하도록 괄호 안의 동사를 알맞은 형태로 바꿔 쓰시오.

1 나는 어젯밤에 샌드위치를 먹었다. (have)

→ I _____ a sandwich last night.

2 내 여동생은 지난 주말에 아팠다. (be)

→ My sister _____ sick last weekend.

3 우리 아빠는 어제 저녁을 요리하셨다. (cook)

→ My dad _____ dinner yesterday.

4 그 남자는 오늘 아침에 울었다. (cry)

→ The man _____ this morning.

5 그 기차는 11시 30분에 도착했다. (arrive)

→ The train _____ at 11:30.

6 그녀는 일요일마다 만화책을 읽는다. (read)

→ She _____ comic books on Sundays.

7 우리는 이틀 전에 등산을 했다. (climb)

→ We _____ the mountain two days ago.

8 Ann은 지난달에 낚시를 하러 갔다. (go)

→ Ann _____ fishing last month.

9 그들은 2020년에 부산에 있었다. (be)

→ They _____ in Busan in 2020.

10 Brown 씨는 작년에 은행에서 일했다. (work)

→ Mr. Brown _____ at a bank last year.

11 남동생과 나는 주말마다 공원에 간다. (go)

→ My brother and I _____ to the park every weekend.

12 Alfred Nobel은 1867년에 다이너마이트를 발명했다. (invent)

→ Alfred Nobel _____ dynamite in 1867.

틀리기 쉬운 내/신/포/인/트

시간을 나타내는 부사(구)를 보고 어울리는 시제를 파악해요.

빈칸에 알맞은 말이 순서대로 짝 지어진 것은?

• She _____ breakfast at 8 every day.

• They _____ Italian food yesterday.

① has – have ② has – had
③ have – have ④ had – had

미래시제는 앞으로 일어날 일이나 계획을 나타낼 때 쓰며, will 또는 be going to 뒤에 동사원형을 써서 표현한다.

will+동사원형	He	will	leave	tomorrow.
be going to+동사원형		is going to		

그는 내일 떠날 것이다.

주의 will은 주어의 인칭이나 수에 따라 형태가 변하지 않는다.
Suji **will** play soccer this weekend. 수지는 이번 주말에 축구를 할 것이다.

주의 be going to의 be동사는 주어의 인칭과 수에 따라 형태를 맞춰 쓴다.
We **are going to** have a party. 우리는 파티를 할 예정이다.

Tips 미래시제는 tomorrow, this weekend, next week, soon 등과 같이 미래를 나타내는 부사(구)와 주로 함께 쓴다.
Tom is going to visit the museum **this weekend**.
Tom은 이번 주말에 박물관을 방문할 것이다.

> 궁금해요!
> He is를 He's로 줄여 쓰는 것처럼 He will도 줄여 쓸 수 있나요?

> 네, He will은 He'll로 줄여 쓸 수 있어요.
> 주어가 대명사일 때 주어와 will은 I'll, She'll, They'll과 같이 줄여 쓸 수 있어요.

개념확인 미래를 나타내는 표현 찾기

1 I will call her tomorrow.　　**2** He is going to arrive next week.　　**3** They will come back soon.

기본연습 괄호 안에서 알맞은 것을 고르시오.

1 I will (take / taking) the train tomorrow.

2 Sam (lives / will live) with his family now.

3 He will (buy / buys) a present for Amy this weekend.

4 They (be / are) going to play baseball tomorrow.

5 She is going (watch / to watch) a movie tonight.

6 My sister (cooked / is going to cook) dinner yesterday.

7 Minho (is / are) going to join the dance club.

8 We (met / are going to meet) her next week.

**틀 리 기 쉬 운
내/신/포/인/트**

미래시제를 나타내는
두 가지 형태를 구별하여
기억해요.

빈칸에 알맞은 말이 순서대로 짝 지어진 것은?

- He will _____ lunch with Jane.
- He _____ going to visit his uncle next week.

① eats − be　　　　　　② eats − is

③ eat − be　　　　　　④ eat − is

will의 부정문은 「will+not+동사원형」으로 쓴다. will not은 won't로 줄여 쓸 수 있다.

We	will	not	watch	the TV show.

우리는 그 TV 쇼를 보지 않을 것이다.

be going to의 부정문은 「be동사+not+going to+동사원형」으로 쓴다.

He	is	not	going to	buy	the bag.

그는 그 가방을 사지 않을 것이다.

개념확인 not이 들어갈 위치 찾기

1 I will wear the pants.　　**2** We are going to swim.　　**3** He's going to meet Jane.

기본연습 A 다음 문장을 부정문으로 바꿔 쓸 때, 빈칸에 알맞은 말을 쓰시오.

1 She will ride her bike.

　→ She ＿＿＿＿＿ ＿＿＿＿＿ ＿＿＿＿＿ her bike.

2 The movie will start at 6.

　→ The movie ＿＿＿＿＿ ＿＿＿＿＿ at 6.

3 I am going to be an inventor.

　→ I ＿＿＿＿＿ ＿＿＿＿＿ ＿＿＿＿＿ ＿＿＿＿＿ an inventor.

4 They are going to meet Dr. Lee this weekend.

　→ They ＿＿＿＿＿ ＿＿＿＿＿ ＿＿＿＿＿ ＿＿＿＿＿ Dr. Lee this weekend.

B 우리말과 일치하도록 괄호 안의 말을 이용하여 문장을 완성하시오.

1 내일 비가 내리지 않을 것이다. (will, rain)

　→ It ＿＿＿＿＿ ＿＿＿＿＿ ＿＿＿＿＿ tomorrow.

2 나는 내일 아침에 학교에 걸어가지 않을 것이다. (will, walk)

　→ I ＿＿＿＿＿ ＿＿＿＿＿ to school tomorrow morning.

3 우리는 다음 주에 동물원에 가지 않을 것이다. (be going to, go)

　→ We ＿＿＿＿＿ ＿＿＿＿＿ ＿＿＿＿＿ ＿＿＿＿＿ ＿＿＿＿＿ to the zoo next week.

4 그녀는 오늘 오후에 쿠키를 만들지 않을 것이다. (be going to, make)

　→ She ＿＿＿＿＿ ＿＿＿＿＿ ＿＿＿＿＿ ＿＿＿＿＿ cookies this afternoon.

미래시제의 의문문

정답 및 해설 p.14

will의 의문문은 「Will+주어+동사원형 ~?」으로 쓰고, be going to의 의문문은 「Be동사+주어+going to+동사원형 ~?」으로 쓴다.

의문문
Will+주어+동사원형 ~?
Be동사+주어+going to+동사원형 ~?

↳ 주어에 맞게 be동사를 달리 써요.

긍정의 대답	부정의 대답
Yes, 주어+will.	No, 주어+won't.
Yes, 주어+be동사.	No, 주어+be동사+not.

Yes 뒤의 「주어+will」과 「주어+be동사」는 줄여 쓰지 않아요.

A: **Will** you **join** the club? 너는 그 동아리에 가입할 거니?
B: **Yes,** I **will**. / **No,** I **won't**. 응, 가입할 거야. / 아니, 가입하지 않을 거야.

A: **Are** you **going to take** the train? 너는 기차를 탈 거니?
B: **Yes,** I **am**. / **No,** I'm **not**. 응, 탈 거야. / 아니, 타지 않을 거야.

개념확인 주어와 동사원형 찾기

1 Will you call me?　　**2** Is he going to swim?　　**3** Are you going to visit her?

기본연습 A 다음 문장을 의문문으로 바꿔 쓸 때, 빈칸에 알맞은 말을 쓰시오.

1 She will visit us soon.
→ _____ _____ _____ us soon?

2 David will like this present.
→ _____ _____ _____ this present?

3 He is going to play soccer tomorrow.
→ _____ _____ _____ _____ _____ soccer tomorrow?

4 They are going to watch a musical next week.
→ _____ _____ _____ _____ _____ a musical next week?

B 빈칸에 알맞은 말을 넣어 의문문에 대한 답을 완성하시오.

1 A: Will you come to my birthday party?
B: Yes, _____ _____.

2 A: Is she going to study in the library tomorrow?
B: No, _____ _____.

3 A: Will Peter go to the movies with us?
B: No, _____ _____.

4 A: Are they going to go camping this weekend?
B: Yes, _____ _____.

5 A: Will you buy a new computer next week?
B: No, _____ _____.

6 A: Are you going to see a doctor?
B: Yes, _____ _____.

현재진행형

정답 및 해설 p.15

현재진행형은 「am/are/is+동사원형-ing」의 형태로, 현재 하고 있는 일이나 동작을 나타낼 때 쓴다.

| am/are/is+동사원형-ing | He | is | cleaning | his room now. | 그는 지금 그의 방을 청소하고 있다. |
| | We | are | listening | to music now. | 우리는 지금 음악을 듣고 있다. |

동사원형-ing형을 만드는 법은 다음과 같다.

대부분의 동사	동사원형+-ing	watching playing	cleaning going
-e로 끝나는 동사	e를 빼고+-ing	come – coming take – taking 〈예외〉 seeing	make – making write – writing
-ie로 끝나는 동사	ie를 y로 바꾸고+-ing	lie – lying	die – dying
「단모음+단자음」으로 끝나는 동사	자음을 한 번 더 쓰고+-ing	stop – stopping swim – swimming	run – running plan – planning

개념확인 be동사와 동사원형-ing 찾기

1 They are playing the guitar.　　**2** She is singing a song.　　**3** I am doing my homework.

기본연습 A 다음 동사의 -ing형을 쓰시오.

1 move　　→ _____　　　**2** come　　→ _____

3 brush　　→ _____　　　**4** dance　　→ _____

5 tell　　→ _____　　　**6** stand　　→ _____

7 win　　→ _____　　　**8** have　　→ _____

9 send　　→ _____　　　**10** fly　　→ _____

11 stop　　→ _____　　　**12** take　　→ _____

13 draw　　→ _____　　　**14** sit　　→ _____

15 teach　　→ _____　　　**16** try　　→ _____

17 run　　→ _____　　　**18** clean　　→ _____

19 cry　　→ _____　　　**20** plan　　→ _____

21 lie　　→ _____　　　**22** visit　　→ _____

23 walk　　→ _____　　　**24** sleep　　→ _____

B 괄호 안에서 알맞은 것을 고르시오.

1 It (is snowing / snowed) now.

2 She (is / are) taking a picture now.

3 Mike and I (am / are) eating lunch now.

4 They are (makeing / making) a cake now.

5 My brother (is ride / is riding) his bicycle now.

C 밑줄 친 동사를 현재진행형으로 바꿔 쓰시오.

1 I <u>watch</u> TV every day.

→ I _____ _____ TV now.

2 She <u>reads</u> a newspaper every morning.

→ She _____ _____ a newspaper now.

3 They always <u>run</u> in the park.

→ They _____ _____ in the park now.

4 He <u>cooks</u> dinner every Friday.

→ He _____ _____ dinner now.

5 Ann <u>washes</u> her hair every day.

→ Ann _____ _____ her hair now.

6 Sam <u>listens</u> to the radio every night.

→ Sam _____ _____ to the radio now.

7 We <u>study</u> math in the library.

→ We _____ _____ math in the library now.

8 I <u>write</u> a letter to my grandmother every month.

→ I _____ _____ a letter to my grandmother now.

9 My friends <u>swim</u> in the pool.

→ My friends _____ _____ in the pool now.

틀리기 쉬운
내/신/포/인/트

현재진행형의
「am/are/is+동사원형-ing」
형태를 기억해요.

우리말과 일치하도록 빈칸에 들어갈 말로 알맞은 것은?

He _____ a story now.
(그는 지금 이야기를 하고 있다.)

① told   ② will tell   ③ is telling   ④ are telling

POINT 7 과거진행형

과거진행형은 「was/were＋동사원형-ing」의 형태로, 과거의 특정 시점에 진행 중이었던 일이나 동작을 나타낼 때 쓴다.

was/were＋동사원형-ing	He	was	writing	a letter last night.	그는 어젯밤에 편지를 쓰고 있었다.
	We	were	listening	to the radio.	우리는 라디오를 듣고 있었다.

개념확인 옳은 해석 고르기

1 She <u>was running</u>.

☐ 달렸다 ☐ 달리고 있었다

2 They <u>were swimming</u>.

☐ 수영했다 ☐ 수영하고 있었다

3 I <u>was watching</u> TV.

☐ 보고 있다 ☐ 보고 있었다

기본연습 **A** 괄호 안에서 알맞은 것을 고르시오.

1 She (is / was) cleaning her room last night.

2 The girls (are / were) eating chicken soup now.

3 They (are / were) playing baseball yesterday.

4 A boy (was / were) singing a song.

5 Tom and Jane (was / were) studying science.

6 He (was eat / was eating) a sandwich at that time.

B 밑줄 친 동사를 과거진행형으로 바꿔 쓰시오.

1 I <u>washed</u> my hands.

→ I _____ _____ my hands.

2 She <u>watched</u> a movie.

→ She _____ _____ a movie.

3 They <u>made</u> a kite.

→ They _____ _____ a kite.

4 My brother <u>used</u> my computer.

→ My brother _____ _____ my computer.

5 Amy and I <u>did</u> our math homework.

→ Amy and I _____ _____ our math homework.

6 The students <u>looked</u> at the stars.

→ The students _____ _____ at the stars.

정답 및 해설 p.15

진행형의 부정문은 「be동사＋not＋동사원형-ing」의 형태로 쓴다.

현재진행형	am/are/is＋**not**＋동사원형-ing		**is**	**not**	**watching**	TV.	그는 TV를 보고 있지 않다.
과거진행형	was/were＋**not**＋동사원형-ing	He	**was**				그는 TV를 보고 있지 않았다.

진행형의 의문문은 「Be동사＋주어＋동사원형-ing ~?」의 형태로 쓴다.

	의문문	긍정의 대답	부정의 대답
현재진행형	Am/Are/Is＋주어＋동사원형-ing ~?	Yes, 주어＋am/are/is.	No, 주어＋am/are/is＋not.
과거진행형	Was/Were＋주어＋동사원형-ing ~?	Yes, 주어＋was/were.	No, 주어＋was/were＋not.

A: **Are** you **writing** a letter? 너는 편지를 쓰고 있니?
B: **Yes**, I **am**. / **No**, I **am not**. 응, 쓰고 있어. / 아니, 쓰고 있지 않아.

A: **Were** they **swimming**? 그들은 수영을 하고 있었니?
B: **Yes**, they **were**. / **No**, they **weren't**. 응, 수영하고 있었어. / 아니, 수영하고 있지 않았어.

개념확인 옳은 해석 고르기

1 I was not crying.
☐ 나는 울고 있지 않다.
☐ 나는 울고 있지 않았다.

2 Are you running?
☐ 너는 달리고 있니?
☐ 너는 달리고 있었니?

3 They aren't sleeping.
☐ 그들은 자고 있지 않다.
☐ 그들은 자고 있지 않았다.

기본연습 **A** 괄호 안에서 알맞은 것을 고르시오.

1 (Are / Do) you playing the piano now?

2 She (not is / is not) flying a kite now.

3 They (are not / were not) moving the boxes now.

4 Were you (wait / waiting) for her yesterday?

5 (Is / Are) Mina and Jimin reading books?

6 He (wasn't take / wasn't taking) a picture.

7 We were not (have / having) lunch at the restaurant.

8 Is the boy (run / running) in the park now?

9 (Was / Were) your sister sleeping on the sofa?

10 They are not (sit / sitting) on the bench.

11 (Was / Were) Jack and Daniel shopping in the mall?

12 We (were not writing / didn't writing) Christmas cards at that time.

B 우리말과 일치하도록 괄호 안의 말을 이용하여 문장을 완성하시오.

1 우리는 축구를 하고 있지 않다. (play)

→ We _____ _____ _____ soccer.

2 너는 지금 지도를 그리고 있니? (draw)

→ _____ you _____ a map now?

3 그들은 창문을 청소하고 있지 않았다. (clean)

→ They _____ _____ _____ the windows.

4 그는 그때 숙제를 하고 있었니? (do)

→ _____ he _____ his homework at that time?

5 그녀는 지금 이메일을 쓰고 있지 않다. (write)

→ She _____ _____ _____ an email now.

6 너희들은 저녁을 요리하고 있었니? (cook)

→ _____ you _____ dinner?

7 그 아기는 자고 있지 않았다. (sleep)

→ The baby _____ _____ _____.

C 괄호 안의 지시대로 바꿔 쓴 문장을 완성하시오.

1 John and Judy are dancing now. (부정문으로)

→ John and Judy _____ _____ _____ now.

2 She is eating breakfast. (의문문으로)

→ _____ _____ _____ breakfast?

3 He was walking on the street. (부정문으로)

→ He _____ _____ _____ on the street.

4 They were running in the gym. (의문문으로)

→ _____ _____ _____ in the gym?

우리말과 일치하도록 괄호 안의 말을 바르게 배열하여 문장을 완성하시오.

(1) 그녀는 바이올린을 연주하고 있지 않다. (is, playing, she, not)

→ _____ the violin.

(2) 그는 자전거를 타고 있었니? (he, riding, was)

→ _____ his bicycle?

개 념 완 성 TEST

정답 및 해설 p.15

STEP 1 Map으로 개념 정리하기

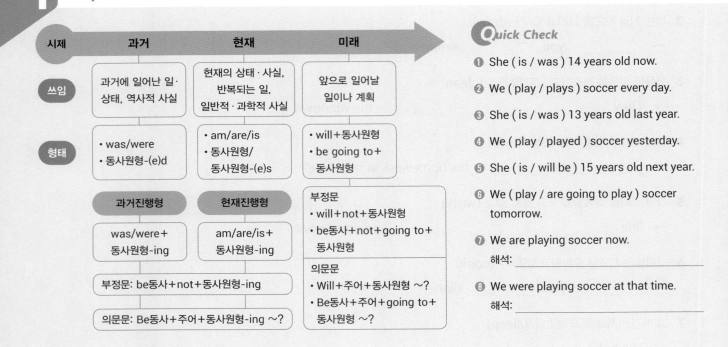

Quick Check

❶ She (is / was) 14 years old now.

❷ We (play / plays) soccer every day.

❸ She (is / was) 13 years old last year.

❹ We (play / played) soccer yesterday.

❺ She (is / will be) 15 years old next year.

❻ We (play / are going to play) soccer
tomorrow.

❼ We are playing soccer now.
해석: _____

❽ We were playing soccer at that time.
해석: _____

STEP 2 기본 다지기

빈칸완성

A 우리말과 일치하도록 빈칸에 알맞은 말을 넣어 문장을 완성하시오.

1 내 남동생은 차고에 있었다.
→ My brother _____ in the garage.

2 그는 아침마다 사과 한 개를 먹는다.
→ He _____ an apple every morning.

3 나의 삼촌은 학교에서 음악을 가르친다.
→ My uncle _____ music at school.

4 하나는 일주일 전에 뉴욕으로 떠났다.
→ Hana _____ for New York a week ago.

5 그녀는 지난 주말에 할머니를 방문했다.
→ She _____ her grandmother last weekend.

6 Kevin은 지금 소파에 누워 있다.
→ Kevin _____ _____ on the sofa now.

7 Jane은 그때 편지를 쓰고 있었다.
→ Jane _____ _____ a letter at that time.

8 그들은 음악을 듣고 있지 않았다.
→ They _____ _____ _____ to music.

9 우리는 이번 주말에 등산을 할 것이다.
→ We _____ _____ the mountain this weekend.

10 나는 이번 주 토요일에 캠핑을 가지 않을 것이다.
→ I _____ _____ _____ camping this
Saturday.

B 밑줄 친 부분을 어법상 바르게 고쳐 쓰시오.

1 We <u>are</u> in the same class last year. → _____

2 The Earth <u>moved</u> around the sun. → _____

3 Jenny <u>goes</u> to the beach last week. → _____

4 Tom and Mina <u>is</u> watching a movie now. → _____

5 Will Mr. Brown <u>comes</u> to my party? → _____

6 They are going to <u>meeting</u> Amy tomorrow. → _____

7 My family <u>will stay</u> home last weekend. → _____

C 다음 문장을 괄호 안의 지시대로 바꿔 쓰시오.

1 The store opens at 10 a.m. (과거시제로)

→ _____

2 My father drinks coffee. (현재진행형으로)

→ _____

3 Mina and Jina ate breakfast together. (과거진행형으로)

→ _____

4 She is washing her hands. (의문문으로)

→ _____

5 They were playing hockey. (부정문으로)

→ _____

6 Sally will cook dinner. (부정문으로)

→ _____

7 He is going to see a musical next week. (의문문으로)

→ _____

8 Sam was brushing his teeth. (의문문으로)

→ _____

9 I will wear a red T-shirt today. (be going to를 이용하여)

→ _____

STEP 3 서술형 따라잡기

그림이해

A 포스터를 보고, 학생들이 Green Week에 할 일과 하지 않을 일을 나타낸 문장을 완성하시오.

Green Week

Monday: walk to school
Tuesday: don't use paper cups
Wednesday: plant trees
Thursday: don't eat meat
Friday: clean up the trash

Next week is "Green Week."

On Monday, we will walk to school.

1 On Tuesday, we _____.

2 On Wednesday, we _____.

3 On Thursday, we _____.

4 On Friday, we _____.

영작완성

B 우리말과 일치하도록 괄호 안의 말을 바르게 배열하여 문장을 쓰시오.

1 그녀는 전화로 이야기하고 있니? (on the phone, is, talking, she)

→ _____

2 너는 내일 Ann을 만날 거니? (meet, you, going to, Ann, are, tomorrow)

→ _____

3 그는 어젯밤에 TV를 보고 있지 않았다. (not, he, TV, last night, was, watching)

→ _____

4 그들은 다음 주에 박물관을 방문할 예정이다. (are, going to, they, the museum, visit, next week)

→ _____

문장영작

C 우리말과 일치하도록 괄호 안의 말을 이용하여 영작하시오.

1 그는 매일 바이올린을 연주한다. (play, the violin)

→ _____

2 그들은 지금 수영장에서 수영하고 있다. (swim, in the pool)

→ _____

3 우리는 어제 도서관에서 공부했다. (study, in the library)

→ _____

4 나는 지난 주말에 그 영화를 보지 않았다. (watch, the movie)

→ _____

1 동사의 -ing형이 바르게 짝 지어진 것은?

① run – runing ② lie – liing
③ write – writing ④ rain – rainning
⑤ study – studing

5

> They're going to go on a trip _____ .

① tomorrow ② next Friday
③ soon ④ next month
⑤ last night

[2-3] 빈칸에 들어갈 말로 알맞은 것을 고르시오.

2

> Minho _____ a song now.

① sang ② is singing
③ singing ④ are singing
⑤ was singing

[6-7] 빈칸에 알맞은 말이 순서대로 짝 지어진 것을 고르시오.

6

> • It _____ a lot yesterday.
> • The moon _____ around the Earth.

① snows – moved ② snows – moves
③ snowed – moved ④ snowed – moves
⑤ will snow – moves

3

> Will he _____ to my birthday party?

① come ② comes
③ came ④ coming
⑤ going to come

7

> • I _____ my friends soon.
> • He was _____ his room at that time.

① invited – clean ② invited – cleaning
③ will invite – clean ④ will invite – cleaned
⑤ will invite – cleaning

[4-5] 빈칸에 들어갈 말로 알맞지 <u>않은</u> 것을 고르시오.

4

> I visited my uncle's house _____ .

① yesterday ② last month
③ two days ago ④ next weekend
⑤ last night

8 밑줄 친 부분이 어법상 틀린 것은?

① <u>Is</u> I talking too fast?
② Jina <u>learned</u> taekwondo last year.
③ They <u>will watch</u> a movie tomorrow.
④ Mr. Green <u>is</u> in Alaska now.
⑤ My brother and I <u>made</u> a kite last weekend.

9 어법상 틀린 문장은?

① He walks to school every day.
② My sister was not sleeping now.
③ She lost her umbrella two days ago.
④ I won't make cookies this weekend.
⑤ Are they going to visit us next week?

12 우리말과 일치하도록 괄호 안의 말을 배열할 때, 네 번째로 오는 단어는?

> 그는 내일 자전거를 타지 않을 것이다.
> (going, is, bike, he, to, ride, his, not, tomorrow)

① to
② is
③ going
④ bike
⑤ ride

10 대화가 자연스럽지 않은 것은?

① A: Is she eating lunch now?
　B: Yes, she is.
② A: Are you going to go swimming tomorrow?
　B: No, I'm not.
③ A: Was he using my computer?
　B: No, he won't.
④ A: Will you come back soon?
　B: Yes, I will.
⑤ A: Is Kate going to travel to Jeju-do?
　B: Yes, she is.

13 빈칸 (A)~(C)에 들어갈 말이 바르게 짝 지어진 것은?

> • ___(A)___ Bill walking his dog now?
> • She ___(B)___ a coat last week.
> • They ___(C)___ visit me tomorrow.

	(A)	(B)	(C)
①	Is	bought	won't
②	Is	bought	didn't
③	Is	will buy	won't
④	Was	bought	didn't
⑤	Was	will buy	won't

11 어법상 올바른 문장의 개수는?

> ⓐ Water boils at 100˚C.
> ⓑ Is the boy reading a book now?
> ⓒ Will they come back last week?
> ⓓ King Sejong invented Hangeul in 1443.

① 0개
② 1개
③ 2개
④ 3개
⑤ 4개

14 빈칸에 들어갈 be동사가 나머지와 다른 하나는?

① The Earth _____ round.
② He _____ not eating noodles now.
③ _____ Ann and Peter going to study math?
④ _____ a boy running in the park now?
⑤ Mr. White _____ going to meet us next month.

15 어법상 올바른 문장은?

① He is not reading a book last night.

② Were they going to the hospital now?

③ We started the project next week.

④ The plane arrives two minutes ago.

⑤ Triangles have three sides and three angles.

16 어법상 <u>틀린</u> 문장의 개수는?

> ⓐ Mina is drawing a map now.
> ⓑ He always eats lunch at 12:30.
> ⓒ Was Danny and Tony doing the dishes?
> ⓓ I won't going to see a doctor tomorrow.

① 0개   ② 1개   ③ 2개

④ 3개   ⑤ 4개

17 대화의 빈칸에 들어갈 말로 알맞은 것은?

> A: Are they watching TV?
> B: _____ They're listening to music.

① Yes, they are.   ② Yes, they do.

③ No, they are.   ④ No, they aren't.

⑤ No, they don't.

18 우리말을 영어로 옮길 때 빈칸에 알맞은 말이 순서대로 짝 지어진 것은?

> 너와 Mike는 로봇을 만들고 있었니?
> → _____ you and Mike _____ a robot?

① Are – make   ② Are – making

③ Were – make   ④ Were – made

⑤ Were – making

19 빈칸에 들어갈 play의 형태가 나머지와 <u>다른</u> 하나는?

① I didn't _____ tennis yesterday.

② Will you _____ outside this weekend?

③ My sister is _____ the piano now.

④ Are they going to _____ baseball this afternoon?

⑤ He won't _____ computer games tonight.

20 우리말을 영어로 <u>잘못</u> 옮긴 것은?

① 내일은 비가 내릴 것이다.

  → It will rain tomorrow.

② 너는 지금 라디오를 듣고 있니?

  → Are you listening to the radio now?

③ 그녀는 내일 도서관에 가지 않을 것이다.

  → She is not going to go to the library tomorrow.

④ 너는 새 컴퓨터를 살 거니?

  → Did you buy a new computer?

⑤ Sam은 오늘 아침에 숙제를 했다.

  → Sam did his homework this morning.

21 그림을 보고, 보기 에서 알맞은 말을 골라 글을 완성하시오. (현재진행형으로 쓸 것)

| 보기 | sleep | play | build |

Lucy _____ a sandcastle.
Gisu _____ under a beach umbrella. Aron and Mina _____ with a ball.

22 주어진 문장을 괄호 안의 지시대로 바꿔 쓰시오.

(1) Amy and Tom are running in the park.
(부정문으로)

→ _____

(2) He will buy a new smartphone. (의문문으로)

→ _____

(3) She was watering the plants at that time.
(의문문으로)

→ _____

(4) Kate visited her grandmother. (과거진행형으로)

→ _____

23 수미의 일정표와 내용이 일치하도록 조건 에 맞게 문장을 완성하시오.

Friday	make a cake
Saturday (Today)	play basketball
Sunday	go shopping

조건   1. (1), (2)는 과거시제로 쓸 것
      2. (3)은 be going to를 이용할 것

(1) Sumi _____
yesterday.

(2) Sumi _____
today.

(3) Sumi _____
tomorrow.

24 빈칸에 알맞은 말을 넣어 대화를 완성하시오.

(1) A: Will you have a hamburger for lunch?

B: _____, _____ _____.
I will have a sandwich.

(2) A: _____ _____ _____
_____ climb a mountain this
weekend?

B: No, I'm not. I'm going to stay home.

고난도
25 우리말과 일치하도록 괄호 안의 말을 이용하여 영작하시오.

(1) 나는 매일 요가를 연습한다. (practice, yoga)

→ _____

(2) 그녀는 지난주에 영화를 보았다. (watch, a movie)

→ _____

(3) 그들은 지금 저녁을 요리하고 있니? (cook, dinner)

→ _____

6 조동사

조동사는 동사의 앞에 위치하여 동사를 도와 능력, 추측, 의무 등의 의미를 더해 준다.

조동사의 개념

정답 및 해설 p.17

조동사는 동사 앞에 쓰여서 능력, 추측, 의무 등의 의미를 더해 주는 말이다. 조동사는 주어의 인칭이나 수에 따라 형태가 변하지 않으며, 뒤에는 항상 동사원형이 온다.☆

	조동사	동사원형		
I	can	play	the piano.	나는 피아노를 **연주할 수 있다**.
It	may	rain	tomorrow.	내일 **비가 올지도 모른다**.
She	will	join	the club.	그녀는 동아리에 **가입할 것이다**.
We	should	take	the train.	우리는 기차를 **타야 한다**.
You	must	wear	sunglasses.	너는 선글라스를 **써야 한다**.

주의 조동사 뒤에 be동사가 올 때는 동사원형인 be를 쓴다.
She **may be** at the beach. 그녀는 해변에 있을지도 모른다.

개념확인 **조동사 찾기**

1 Anne will arrive soon. **2** You must wash your hands. **3** He can ride a bicycle.

기본연습 **A** 괄호 안에서 알맞은 것을 고르시오.

1 I will (am / be) very busy tomorrow.

2 We (meet will / will meet) again soon.

3 My dad (should / shoulds) take a rest.

4 Jenny (may / mays) be late for school today.

5 You (keep must / must keep) the traffic rules.

B 우리말과 일치하도록 괄호 안의 말을 바르게 배열하여 문장을 완성하시오.

1 나는 바이올린을 연주할 수 있다. (can, play, I)

→ _____ the violin.

2 민호는 도서관에 갈 것이다. (will, Minho, go)

→ _____ to the library.

3 너는 플라스틱을 재활용해야 한다. (must, recycle, you)

→ _____ plastics.

4 Brown 씨는 Andy의 주소를 알지도 모른다. (Mr. Brown, know, may)

→ _____ Andy's address.

POINT 2 조동사의 부정문

조동사의 부정문은 조동사 바로 뒤에 **not**을 붙여 만든다. 「조동사+not」은 줄여 쓸 수 있다.

조동사	not	동사원형			줄임말
I	**cannot**		**play**	the piano.	나는 피아노를 연주할 수 없다.	can't
It	**may**	not	**rain**	tomorrow.	내일 비가 오지 않을지도 모른다.	mayn't
She	**will**	not	**join**	the club.	그녀는 동아리에 가입하지 않을 것이다. →	won't
We	**should**	not	**take**	the train.	우리는 기차를 타지 말아야 한다.	shouldn't
You	**must**	not	**wear**	sunglasses.	너는 선글라스를 쓰면 안 된다.	mustn't

주의 can의 부정은 띄어 쓰지 않고 cannot으로 쓴다. may not은 주로 줄여 쓰지 않는다.

개념확인 줄여 쓸 수 있는 말 찾기

1 Penguins cannot fly.　　　**2** You must not swim here.　　　**3** Liz will not go out tonight.

기본연습 다음 문장을 부정문으로 바꿔 쓰시오.

1 My father can drive a car.

→ _____ a car.

2 Kevin may be sick.

→ _____ sick.

3 You must park here.

→ _____ here.

4 Sam should take a taxi to the airport.

→ _____ a taxi to the airport.

5 My family will visit Busan this weekend.

→ _____ Busan this weekend.

틀리기 쉬운 내/신/포/인/트

조동사의 부정문은 「주어+조동사 +not+동사원형 ~」으로 써요.

밑줄 친 부분이 어법상 틀린 것은?

① He <u>cannot speak</u> French.
② It <u>will not be</u> sunny tomorrow.
③ She <u>may don't take</u> the subway.
④ You <u>shouldn't play</u> computer games for too long.

POINT 3 조동사의 의문문

조동사의 의문문은 「조동사＋주어＋동사원형 ～?」의 형태로 쓴다.

조동사	주어	동사원형		
Can	you	**play**	the piano?	너는 피아노를 연주할 수 있니?

조동사가 있는 의문문에 대한 대답은 조동사를 사용하여 한다.

의문문	긍정의 대답	부정의 대답
Should I take the train? ➡	Yes, you **should**.	No, you **shouldn't**.

개념확인 조동사와 동사원형 찾기

1 Can your brother drive?　　**2** Will you buy this red scarf?　　**3** Should I wear a suit?

기본연습 **A** 다음 문장을 의문문으로 바꿔 쓰시오.

1 He can speak Korean.

→ ＿＿＿＿＿＿＿＿＿＿＿＿＿＿＿＿＿ Korean?

2 We should cancel the picnic.

→ ＿＿＿＿＿＿＿＿＿＿＿＿＿＿＿＿＿ the picnic?

3 I must call the police right now.

→ ＿＿＿＿＿＿＿＿＿＿＿＿＿＿＿＿＿ the police right now?

4 Mina will go to the concert tomorrow.

→ ＿＿＿＿＿＿＿＿＿＿＿＿＿＿＿＿＿ to the concert tomorrow?

B 빈칸에 알맞은 말을 넣어 의문문에 대한 답을 완성하시오.

1 A: Should I bring some food?

B: Yes, ＿＿＿＿＿ ＿＿＿＿＿.

2 A: Will she move to Seoul?

B: No, ＿＿＿＿＿ ＿＿＿＿＿.

3 A: Can your brother ride a horse?

B: No, ＿＿＿＿＿ ＿＿＿＿＿.

4 A: Will Mary travel to Jeju-do?

B: Yes, ＿＿＿＿＿ ＿＿＿＿＿.

5 A: Can your sister cook spaghetti?

B: Yes, ＿＿＿＿＿ ＿＿＿＿＿.

6 A: Must I wear a safety jacket?

B: Yes, ＿＿＿＿＿ ＿＿＿＿＿.

7 A: Should I leave my key here?

B: No, ＿＿＿＿＿ ＿＿＿＿＿.

8 A: May I borrow your book for a day?

B: Yes, ＿＿＿＿＿ ＿＿＿＿＿.

POINT 4 can

can은 능력, 허가, 요청의 의미를 나타낸다.

~할 수 있다 〈능력〉	Minsu **can** speak Japanese.	민수는 일본어를 할 수 있다.
	Jack **cannot(can't)** drive a car.	Jack은 차를 운전할 수 없다. (~할 수 없다)
	Brian **could** dance very well.	Brian은 춤을 아주 잘 출 수 있었다. ↝ 능력을 나타내는 can의 과거형은 could로 써요.
~해도 좋다 〈허가〉	You **can** touch the painting.	너는 그 그림을 만져도 좋다.
	You **cannot(can't)** go now.	너는 지금 가면 안 된다. (~하면 안 된다)
	Can I use this fax machine?	이 팩스기를 사용해도 될까?
~해 줄래? 〈요청〉	**Can** you close the window?	창문을 닫아 줄래?
	Could you turn the music down?	음악 소리 좀 줄여 주시겠어요?

↝ 요청의 의미로 could를 써서 질문하면 더 정중한 표현이 돼요.

주의 '~할 수 있다'는 의미의 can은 be able to로 바꿔 쓸 수 있다. 과거의 능력을 나타낼 때는 was/were able to로 쓰고, 미래의 능력을 나타낼 때는 will be able to를 쓴다.
He **was able to** jump rope really well. 〈과거〉 그는 줄넘기를 정말 잘 할 수 있었다.
He **will be able to** jump rope well soon. 〈미래〉 그는 곧 줄넘기를 잘할 수 있을 것이다.
↝ 조동사는 두 개를 나란히 쓸 수 없어서 will can으로는 쓸 수 없어요.

주의 be able to의 부정형은 be not able to로 쓰고, 의문문은 「Be동사＋주어＋able to＋동사원형 ~?」으로 쓴다.
I **was not able to** buy the ticket. 나는 그 표를 살 수 없었다.
Were you **able to** buy the ticket? 너는 그 표를 살 수 있었니?

개념확인 옳은 해석 고르기

1 I can bake potato chips.
☐ ~해도 좋다 ☐ ~할 수 있다

2 Can you help me?
☐ ~해 줄래? ☐ ~해도 될까?

3 You cannot swim here.
☐ ~할 수 없다 ☐ ~하면 안 된다

기본연습 **A** 밑줄 친 can과 could의 의미로 알맞은 것을 고르시오.

1	He can ski very well.	☐ 능력	☐ 허가	☐ 요청
2	Could you close the door?	☐ 능력	☐ 허가	☐ 요청
3	You can ride my bike.	☐ 능력	☐ 허가	☐ 요청
4	Can you move this table for me?	☐ 능력	☐ 허가	☐ 요청
5	Can I play a computer game now?	☐ 능력	☐ 허가	☐ 요청
6	Could you check the email from Mr. Kim?	☐ 능력	☐ 허가	☐ 요청
7	My mom can cook French food.	☐ 능력	☐ 허가	☐ 요청
8	Can I try on this skirt?	☐ 능력	☐ 허가	☐ 요청
9	I can say "hello" in five languages.	☐ 능력	☐ 허가	☐ 요청

B 우리말과 일치하도록 괄호 안의 말을 이용하여 문장을 완성하시오.

1 Kate는 젓가락을 사용할 수 있다. (can, use)

→ _____ chopsticks.

2 너는 이번 주 일요일에 우리 집을 방문해도 된다. (can, visit)

→ _____ my house this Sunday.

3 제가 제 음식을 여기서 먹어도 될까요? (can, eat)

→ _____ my own food here?

4 당신이 이 편지 좀 부쳐 줄래요? (can, post)

→ _____ this letter, please?

5 당신이 제 숙제 좀 도와 주시겠어요? (could, help)

→ _____ me with my homework?

6 네가 불을 좀 켜 줄래? (can, turn on)

→ _____ the light?

7 Billy는 그 문제를 이해할 수 없었다. (could, understand)

→ _____ the question.

8 너는 도서관에서 떠들면 안 된다. (can, make)

→ _____ any noise in the library.

9 그녀는 그 주문을 취소할 수 있었다. (be able to, cancel)

→ _____ the order.

10 나는 언젠가 우주를 여행할 수 있을 것이다. (be able to, travel)

→ _____ in space someday.

11 그는 어제 경주를 끝낼 수 없었다. (be able to, finish)

→ _____ the race yesterday.

틀 리 기 쉬 운
내/신/포/인/트

can은 '~할 수 있다',
'~해도 좋다', '~해 줄래?'
라는 뜻으로 쓰여요.

밑줄 친 부분의 쓰임이 나머지와 다른 하나는?

① Can I go to the concert?
② You can take photos here.
③ Can you open the door?
④ Can I use your cell phone?

POINT 5 may

may는 약한 추측과 허가의 의미를 나타낸다.

~일지도 모른다 〈약한 추측〉	The key **may** be in my bag.	그 열쇠는 내 가방에 있**을지도 모른다**.
	He **may not** come today.	그는 오늘 오지 **않을지도 모른다**. (~이 아닐지도 모른다)
~해도 좋다 〈허가〉	You **may** go home early.	너는 일찍 집에 가**도 된다**.
	You **may not** eat food here.	너는 여기에서 음식을 먹**으면 안 된다**. (~하면 안 된다)
	May I use this computer?	이 컴퓨터를 사용**해도 되나요**?

궁금해요!
'허가'의 의미로 쓰이는 can과 may에는 어떤 차이가 있나요?

may가 더 공손한 표현이에요.

개념확인 옳은 해석 고르기

1 She may be sick.
- ☐ ~해도 좋다
- ☐ ~일지도 모른다

2 May I go out?
- ☐ ~해 줄래요?
- ☐ ~해도 될까요?

3 You may leave now.
- ☐ ~해도 좋다
- ☐ ~하면 안 된다

기본연습 **A** 밑줄 친 may의 의미로 알맞은 것을 고르시오.

1 You <u>may</u> turn on the TV. ☐ 약한 추측 ☐ 허가

2 <u>May</u> I use the bathroom? ☐ 약한 추측 ☐ 허가

3 James <u>may</u> not be home. ☐ 약한 추측 ☐ 허가

4 The story <u>may</u> be true. ☐ 약한 추측 ☐ 허가

5 You <u>may</u> not use your cell phone in class. ☐ 약한 추측 ☐ 허가

6 My brother <u>may</u> become a nurse. ☐ 약한 추측 ☐ 허가

7 You <u>may</u> not wear your shoes here. ☐ 약한 추측 ☐ 허가

8 She <u>may</u> come to my birthday party. ☐ 약한 추측 ☐ 허가

B 우리말과 일치하도록 빈칸에 can과 may 중 알맞은 것을 쓰시오.

1 I _____ visit my uncle. (나는 삼촌을 방문할지도 모른다.)

2 You _____ be right. (네가 옳을지도 모른다.)

3 Mina _____ ride a bike. (미나는 자전거를 탈 수 있다.)

4 I _____ finish it by tomorrow. (나는 그것을 내일까지 끝낼 수 있다.)

5 Alice _____ be busy now. (Alice는 지금 바쁠지도 모른다.)

6 Mike _____ not go to the library this afternoon. (Mike는 오늘 오후에 도서관에 가지 않을지도 모른다.)

POINT 6 will, would

정답 및 해설 p.18

will은 미래와 요청의 의미를 나타낸다.

~할 것이다 〈미래〉	I **will** get up at six tomorrow.	나는 내일 6시에 일어날 **것이다**.
	He **will not(won't)** go out tonight.	그는 오늘 밤에 외출하지 **않을 것이다**.
	Will you meet Tom this weekend?	너는 이번 주말에 Tom을 만날 **거니**?
~해 줄래? 〈요청〉	**Will** you open the door, please?	문을 열어 **줄래요**?
	Would you speak more clearly?	더 분명하게 말씀해 **주시겠어요**?

> 요청의 의미로 would를 써서 질문하면 더 정중한 표현이 돼요.

「would like+명사(구)」는 '~을 원하다'라는 뜻이고, 「would like to+동사원형」은 '~을 하고 싶다'라는 뜻이다.

> would는 'd로 줄여 쓸 수 있어요.

| would like+명사(구) | ~을 원하다 | **I'd like** a cold drink. | 나는 차가운 마실 것을 **원한다**. |
| would like to+동사원형 | ~을 하고 싶다 | I **would like to** climb that mountain. | 나는 저 산을 올라가고 **싶다**. |

개념확인 옳은 해석 고르기

1 Will you jog today?　　□ ~할 거니?　□ ~해 줄래?

2 I would like some coffee.　　□ ~을 좋아하다　□ ~을 원하다

3 Would you close the door?　　□ ~해도 될까요?　□ ~해 줄래요?

기본연습 우리말과 일치하도록 괄호 안의 말을 이용하여 문장을 완성하시오.

1 나는 내년에 15살이 될 것이다. (will, be)

→ _____ 15 years old next year.

2 그는 올해 새 자동차를 사지 않을 것이다. (will, buy)

→ _____ a new car this year.

3 당신이 나를 도와 줄래요? (would, help)

→ _____ me?

4 당신이 이쪽으로 와 주실래요? (would, come)

→ _____ this way?

5 너는 초콜릿 쿠키를 먹고 싶니? (would, eat)

→ _____ chocolate cookies?

6 그녀는 오늘 밤에 영화를 보러 가고 싶어 한다. (would, go)

→ _____ to the movies tonight.

POINT 7 must

must는 강한 의무와 강한 추측의 의미를 나타낸다.

~해야 한다 〈강한 의무〉	We **must** follow the rules.	우리는 규칙을 따라야 한다.
	You **must** wear a seat belt.	너는 안전벨트를 매야 한다.
~임에 틀림없다 〈강한 추측〉	They **must** be very tired.	그들은 매우 피곤함에 틀림없다.
	She **must** be a singer.	그녀는 가수임에 틀림없다.

> **주의** '~일 리가 없다'라는 뜻으로 강한 부정의 추측은 cannot(can't)으로 쓴다.
> The rumor **cannot** be true. 그 소문은 사실일 리가 없다.

must not은 금지의 의미를 나타낸다.

| ~해서는 안 된다
〈금지〉 | You **must not** go out now. | 너는 지금 외출하면 안 된다. |
| | You **must not** swim here. | 너는 여기서 수영을 하면 안 된다. |

개념확인 옳은 해석 고르기

1 You must get up early.
- ☐ ~해야 한다
- ☐ ~임에 틀림없다

2 He must be smart.
- ☐ ~해도 좋다
- ☐ ~임에 틀림없다

3 You must not lie to me.
- ☐ ~일 리가 없다
- ☐ ~해서는 안 된다

기본연습 **A** 밑줄 친 부분의 의미로 알맞은 것을 고르시오.

1 We <u>must</u> go to bed early tonight. ☐ 의무 ☐ 추측 ☐ 금지

2 He <u>cannot</u> be honest. ☐ 의무 ☐ 추측 ☐ 금지

3 You <u>must not</u> tell anybody about it. ☐ 의무 ☐ 추측 ☐ 금지

4 My sister didn't have breakfast. She <u>must</u> be hungry. ☐ 의무 ☐ 추측 ☐ 금지

B 우리말과 일치하도록 빈칸에 can, may, must 중 알맞은 것을 쓰시오.

1 She _____ be rich. (그녀는 부자임에 틀림없다.)

2 She _____ do magic tricks. (그녀는 마술을 할 수 있다.)

3 You _____ clean the windows. (너는 창문을 닦아야 한다.)

4 He _____ not pass the exam. (그는 시험을 통과하지 못할지도 모른다.)

5 Large trucks _____ not use this bridge. (대형 트럭은 이 다리를 이용하면 안 된다.)

POINT 8 have to

'~해야 한다'라는 의무의 의미를 나타내는 must는 have to로 바꿔 쓸 수 있다.

| ~해야 한다 〈의무〉 | You **have to** wash your hands first. = You **must** wash your hands first. | 너는 먼저 손을 씻어야 한다. |

have to는 주어가 3인칭 단수일 때는 has to로 쓴다. 과거의 의무는 had to로 쓰고, 미래의 의무는 will have to로 쓴다.

현재		**has to**		그녀는 교실을 청소해야 한다.
과거	She	**had to**	clean the classroom.	그녀는 교실을 청소해야 했다.
미래		**will have to**		그녀는 교실을 청소해야 할 것이다.

must는 과거형으로 쓰거나 미래를 나타내기 위해 앞에 will을 쓸 수 없어요.

don't have to는 '~할 필요가 없다'라는 의미로 불필요를 나타내고, must not은 '~해서는 안 된다'라는 의미로 금지를 나타낸다.

~해야 한다 〈의무〉
have to = must

→ ~할 필요가 없다 〈불필요〉 **don't have to** | You **don't have to** hurry. 너는 서두를 필요가 없다.

→ ~해서는 안 된다 〈금지〉 **must not** | You **must not** tell a lie. 너는 거짓말을 해서는 안 된다.

개념확인 옳은 해석 고르기

1 We have to be honest.
□ ~해야 한다   □ ~할 필요가 없다

2 You don't have to wait for the bus.
□ ~해서는 안 된다   □ ~할 필요가 없다

기본연습 **A** 밑줄 친 부분의 의미로 알맞은 것을 고르시오.

1 We have a test soon. We must study hard. □의무 □금지 □불필요
2 We have to cross the street on a green light. □의무 □금지 □불필요
3 You must not run in the classroom. □의무 □금지 □불필요
4 She doesn't have to go to school today. □의무 □금지 □불필요

B 우리말과 일치하도록 must나 have to를 이용하여 문장을 완성하시오.

1 미나는 오전에 꽃에 물을 줘야 한다.
→ Mina _____ the flowers in the morning.

2 너는 그 문제에 대해 걱정할 필요가 없다.
→ You _____ about the problem.

3 그는 내일 병원에 가야 할 것이다.

→ He _____ to the hospital tomorrow.

4 우리는 어제 숙제를 먼저 해야 했다.

→ We _____ our homework first yesterday.

5 너는 여기서 담배를 피워서는 안 된다.

→ You _____ here.

6 Daniel은 어제 늦게까지 일해야 했다.

→ Daniel _____ late yesterday.

7 너는 도서관에서 조용히 해야 한다.

→ You _____ quiet in the library.

8 너는 내일 외투를 입어야 할 것이다.

→ You _____ a coat tomorrow.

9 너는 수업 중에 잠을 자서는 안 된다.

→ You _____ in class.

10 나는 창문 값을 지불할 필요가 없다.

→ I _____ for the window.

11 John은 어젯밤에 그 프로젝트를 끝내야 했다.

→ John _____ the project last night.

12 나는 지금 런던으로 가는 표를 교환해야 한다.

→ I _____ my ticket to London now.

13 그녀는 바닥을 청소할 필요가 없다.

→ She _____ the floor.

빈칸에 알맞은 말이 순서대로 짝 지어진 것은?

- Mary _____ walk home these days.
- I _____ do my homework after school yesterday.

① have to – has to   ② have to – had to
③ has to – had to   ④ has to – will have to

POINT 9 should, had better

should는 약한 의무와 충고의 의미를 나타낸다.

~해야 한다 〈약한 의무 · 충고〉	We **should** be kind to other people.	우리는 다른 사람들에게 친절**해야 한다**.
	You **shouldn't** drink too much soda.	너는 탄산음료를 너무 많이 마시지 **말아야 한다**.

> **Tips** must는 필수적으로 꼭 해야 함을 나타내고, should는 '그렇게 하는 것이 좋겠다'라는 정도의 의미를 나타낸다.
> You **must** wear a seat belt. 너는 안전벨트를 매야 한다.
> You **should** help each other. 너희는 서로 도와야 한다.

had better는 '~하는 게 좋겠다'라는 뜻으로 강한 충고의 의미를 나타낸다.

~하는 게 좋겠다 〈강한 충고〉	You **had better** take an umbrella.	너는 우산을 가지고 가는 게 좋겠다.
	You**'d better not** sit here.	너는 여기에 앉지 **않는** 게 좋겠다.

↳ had better는 보통 'd better로 줄여 써요.

개념확인 옳은 해석 고르기

1 You shouldn't throw trash on the floor.

　　☐ ~하지 말아야 한다　　☐ ~할 필요가 없다

2 You had better tell the truth.

　　☐ ~임에 틀림없다　　☐ ~하는 게 좋겠다

기본연습 A 보기 에서 알맞은 말을 골라 should를 이용하여 대화를 완성하시오.

보기	see	go back	drink	do	wear	stay up

1 A: I have a toothache.

　　B: You _____ a dentist.

2 A: I'm cold.

　　B: You _____ a coat.

3 A: I left my sunglasses at a restaurant yesterday.

　　B: You _____ to the restaurant and ask about them.

4 A: I have the hiccups.

　　B: You _____ a glass of water.

5 A: I have a lot of homework.

　　B: You _____ important homework first.

6 A: I need my sleep.

　　B: You _____ late.

B 보기 에서 알맞은 말을 골라 had better를 이용하여 문장을 완성하시오.

> 보기   sit   hurry   go   play   eat   set

1 It's too late. You _____ home now.

2 It is too dangerous. You _____ with fire.

3 The food smells bad. You _____ it.

4 The last train leaves in 5 minutes. We _____ .

5 The bench looks very dirty. You _____ on it.

6 You have to get up early tomorrow morning. You _____ your alarm.

C 우리말과 일치하도록 보기 에서 알맞은 말을 골라 문장을 완성하시오.

> 보기   cannot   may   shouldn't   had better   don't have to

1 너는 오늘 일찍 떠나도 된다.
→ You _____ leave early today.

2 나는 요즘 밤에 잠을 잘 수가 없다.
→ I _____ sleep at night these days.

3 너는 속도를 줄이는 게 좋겠다.
→ You _____ slow down.

4 우리는 실수를 두려워할 필요가 없다.
→ We _____ be afraid of our mistakes.

5 너는 너무 오랫동안 컴퓨터 게임을 하지 말아야 한다.
→ You _____ play computer games for too long.

틀 리 기   쉬 운
내/신/포/인/트

should는 '~해야 한다'라는
뜻으로 약한 의무나 충고의
의미를 나타내요.

대화의 빈칸에 들어갈 말로 알맞은 것은?

A: Someone stole my bike yesterday.
B: Oh, you _____ tell the police about it.
A: Okay, I'll do that.

① should
② had to
③ had better not
④ don't have to

STEP 1 Map으로 개념 정리하기

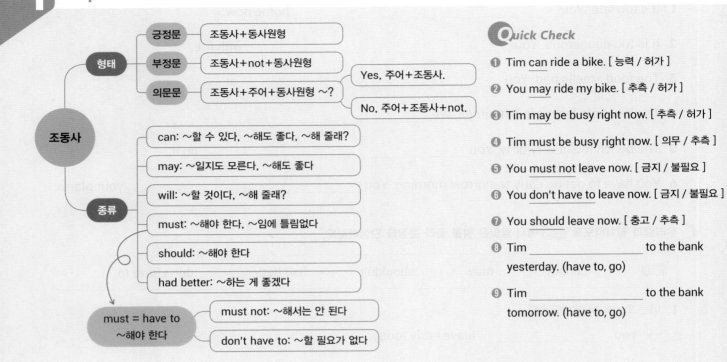

Quick Check

❶ Tim can ride a bike. [능력 / 허가]

❷ You may ride my bike. [추측 / 허가]

❸ Tim may be busy right now. [추측 / 허가]

❹ Tim must be busy right now. [의무 / 추측]

❺ You must not leave now. [금지 / 불필요]

❻ You don't have to leave now. [금지 / 불필요]

❼ You should leave now. [충고 / 추측]

❽ Tim _____ to the bank yesterday. (have to, go)

❾ Tim _____ to the bank tomorrow. (have to, go)

STEP 2 기본 다지기

빈칸완성

A 우리말과 일치하도록 빈칸에 알맞은 말을 넣어 문장을 완성하시오.

1 그녀는 말을 탈 수 있다. → She _____ ride a horse.

2 너는 여기에 앉아도 된다. → You _____ sit here.

3 그들은 내일 떠나지 않을 것이다. → They _____ leave tomorrow.

4 나는 다음 달에 돌아올지도 모른다. → I _____ be back next month.

5 너는 수업 중에 선생님께 귀를 기울여야 한다. → You _____ listen to the teacher in class.

6 제가 지금 지불해야 하나요? → Do I _____ _____ pay now?

7 Tom은 내년에 중학생이 될 것이다. → Tom _____ be a middle school student next year.

8 막차가 곧 떠난다. 우리는 뛰는 게 좋겠다. → The last bus leaves soon. We _____ _____ run.

9 너는 버스에서 너무 큰 소리로 말하면 안 된다. → You _____ _____ talk too loudly on the bus.

B 밑줄 친 부분을 어법상 바르게 고쳐 쓰시오.

1 Kate <u>cans make</u> a kite.　　　　　→ _____

2 You <u>had take better</u> a rest.　　　　→ _____

3 She <u>don't have to</u> buy the book.　　→ _____

4 We <u>musted walk</u> home yesterday.　→ _____

5 You <u>must wore</u> a school uniform.　　→ _____

6 You <u>should to have</u> breakfast every day.　→ _____

7 <u>Do you will play</u> tennis with me tomorrow?　→ _____

C 다음 문장을 괄호 안의 지시대로 바꿔 쓰시오.

1 James could play the cello. (be able to를 이용하여)

　→ _____

2 Students must study hard. (have to를 이용하여)

　→ _____

3 He may come to our party. (부정문으로)

　→ _____

4 You have to use paper cups. (must를 이용하여 부정문으로)

　→ _____

5 He must be tired. (can을 이용하여 부정문으로)

　→ _____

6 I must take the first train. (과거시제로)

　→ _____

7 Julie must get up early tomorrow. (미래시제로)

　→ _____

8 I can't believe the news. (과거시제로)

　→ _____

9 You can get a taxi outside the station. (미래시제로)

　→ _____

서술형 따라잡기

그림이해

A Andy가 할 수 있는 것과 할 수 없는 것을 나타내는 그림을 보고, 보기 에서 알맞은 단어를 골라 문장을 완성하시오.

보기	ride	read	answer	stand

1 Andy _____ _____ Chinese.

2 Andy _____ _____ a skateboard.

3 Andy _____ _____ on his hands.

4 Andy _____ _____ the phone right now.

영작완성

B 우리말과 일치하도록 괄호 안의 말을 바르게 배열하여 문장을 쓰시오.

1 나는 오늘 오후에 우체국에 가야 한다. (go, I, to the post office, must, this afternoon)

→ _____

2 너는 그 박물관에서 사진을 찍으면 안 된다. (must, you, in the museum, take, photos, not)

→ _____

3 우리는 빨간불에 길을 건너면 안 된다. (we, on a red light, not, should, cross, the street)

→ _____

4 내 여동생은 이 치마를 좋아하지 않을지도 모른다. (not, this skirt, like, my sister, may)

→ _____

문장영작

C 우리말과 일치하도록 괄호 안의 말을 이용하여 영작하시오.

1 당신은 점심을 가져올 필요가 없다. (have to, bring, your lunch)

→ _____

2 너는 배드민턴을 치고 싶니? (would, like to, play)

→ _____

3 Kate는 그녀의 방을 청소해야 한다. (have to, clean)

→ _____

4 제가 지금 들어가도 될까요? (may, come in)

→ _____

1 빈칸에 들어갈 말로 알맞지 <u>않은</u> 것은?

> Sumi _____ feed her dog.

① must
② may
③ should
④ have to
⑤ is going to

[2-3] 대화의 빈칸에 들어갈 말로 알맞은 것을 고르시오.

2
> A: Can Henry speak Korean?
> B: No, _____.

① he does
② he doesn't
③ he can
④ he can't
⑤ he could

3
> A: Are you able to come on Saturday?
> B: Yes, _____.

① I am
② I'm not
③ I was
④ I wasn't
⑤ I do

4 밑줄 친 부분과 바꿔 쓸 수 있는 것은?

> You <u>have to</u> take the test.

① can
② must
③ would
④ may
⑤ could

5 밑줄 친 **may**의 의미가 나머지와 <u>다른</u> 하나는?

① It <u>may</u> rain tomorrow.
② He <u>may</u> know the truth.
③ You <u>may</u> use my computer.
④ The cap <u>may</u> be Suji's.
⑤ The cat <u>may</u> be hungry.

6 밑줄 친 ①~⑤ 중 어법상 <u>틀린</u> 것은?

> In the Future
> ①<u>Cars will fly.</u> ②<u>People won't drive cars.</u>
> ③<u>People will work with robots.</u> ④<u>People won't cook.</u> ⑤<u>Animals will talking with people.</u>

[7-8] 우리말을 영어로 옮길 때 빈칸에 알맞은 것을 고르시오.

7
> 우리는 나이 든 사람들을 도와야 한다.
> → We _____ help elderly people.

① should
② may
③ can
④ will
⑤ could

8
> 너는 지금 음악을 들어도 된다.
> → You _____ listen to music now.

① must
② may
③ will
④ have to
⑤ are able to

9 두 문장의 뜻이 같도록 빈칸에 들어갈 말로 알맞은 것은?

> Jake could solve the problem.
> = Jake _____ solve the problem.

① should
② must
③ was able to
④ will be able to
⑤ would like to

10 밑줄 친 부분이 어법상 올바른 것은?

① He not can climb a tree.
② Can use I your bathroom?
③ I can't sleep well these days.
④ She can plays ice hockey.
⑤ My sister cans name all the flowers in the garden.

11 짝 지어진 두 문장의 의미가 <u>다른</u> 것은?

① Minsu can lift 50 kg.
   = Minsu is able to lift 50 kg.
② She will leave Seoul next week.
   = She is going to leave Seoul next week.
③ You must do your best.
   = You have to do your best.
④ Can I try on this hat?
   = May I try on this hat?
⑤ You must not run here.
   = You don't have to run here.

12 밑줄 친 must의 의미가 보기 와 같은 것은?

> 보기 He <u>must</u> be tired.

① I <u>must</u> get up early tomorrow.
② She <u>must</u> finish her homework.
③ We <u>must</u> be quiet in the library.
④ He <u>must</u> be a police officer.
⑤ Students <u>must</u> wear school uniforms.

13 우리말을 영어로 바르게 옮긴 것은?

> 그는 회의에 참석할 필요가 없다.

① He will not attend the meeting.
② He may not attend the meeting.
③ He must not attend the meeting.
④ He should not attend the meeting.
⑤ He doesn't have to attend the meeting.

14 어법상 <u>틀린</u> 문장은?

① He may be a doctor.
② My uncle can play chess.
③ Would you say that again?
④ I'd like to buying some books.
⑤ You'd better take a shower first.

15 대화가 자연스럽지 <u>않은</u> 것은?

① A: May I see your photo?
　B: Sure. Here it is.

② A: Can I take pictures here?
　B: Yes, you can. You must not take pictures here.

③ A: Can you help me?
　B: Of course.

④ A: Should I say sorry to her?
　B: Yes, you should. It's your fault.

⑤ A: Will you play baseball?
　B: No, I won't. I have to do my homework.

16 어법상 <u>틀린</u> 부분을 바르게 고친 것은?

> Cindy don't have to call me.

① don't → doesn't
② don't have → do have not
③ have → has
④ to call → calling
⑤ me → mine

17 빈칸에 May(may)가 들어갈 수 <u>없는</u> 것은?

① _____ I use this ruler?
② He _____ be at home now.
③ _____ you turn off the light for me?
④ She _____ be very thirsty.
⑤ _____ I borrow your pen?

18 주어진 문장과 의미가 같은 것은?

> He must read this book.

① He can read this book.
② He may read this book.
③ He has to read this book.
④ He will read this book.
⑤ He is able to read this book.

고난도

19 다음 표지판이 나타내는 내용으로 알맞지 <u>않은</u> 것은?

① Do not fish here.
② You cannot fish here.
③ You may not fish here.
④ You must not fish here.
⑤ You don't have to fish here.

고난도

20 어법상 올바른 문장의 개수는?

> ⓐ He cannot be a great writer.
> ⓑ Do you will have some bread?
> ⓒ Students has to follow the school rules.
> ⓓ They will can play soccer after school.
> ⓔ You had better not stay up late.

① 1개　　② 2개　　③ 3개
④ 4개　　⑤ 5개

21 두 문장의 의미가 같도록 빈칸에 알맞은 말을 쓰시오.

(1) You must keep your promises.

= You _____ your promises.

(2) My dog can swim in the sea.

= My dog _____ in the sea.

22 주어진 질문에 알맞은 답을 써서 대화를 완성하시오.

(1) **A**: Will you meet Amy this Saturday?

B: _____, _____ _____.
I will go on a picnic with my family.

(2) **A**: Can you solve this problem?

B: _____, _____ _____.
The answer is five.

23 우리말과 일치하도록 괄호 안의 말을 이용하여 영작하시오.

(1) 이 책들 좀 옮겨 주실 수 있나요? (move, book)

→ _____

(2) 너는 내 공책을 빌려도 좋아. (borrow, notebook)

→ _____

(3) 우리는 역에 6시에 도착해야 한다.
(arrive, at the station)

→ _____

(4) 너는 이 상자를 열지 말아야 한다. (open, box)

→ _____

24 어법상 틀린 부분을 바르게 고쳐 문장을 다시 쓰시오.

(1) I'd like to eating Chinese food.

→ _____

(2) You should be not rude to people.

→ _____

(3) Minji have to study for the exam.

→ _____

고난도
25 각 사람에게 해 줄 적절한 충고의 말을 조건 에 맞게 쓰시오.

조건 1. 보기 에서 알맞은 말을 고를 것
2. had better를 이용할 것

보기 write a letter to her
eat healthy food
see an eye doctor

(1) **Mike**: I really like fast food.

→ _____

(2) **Susan**: My eyes feel strange.

→ _____

(3) **Ann**: Bora is angry with me. She doesn't talk to me.

→ _____

7 의문사

의문사는 누가, 언제, 어디서, 무엇을 등에 대해 궁금한 것을 물을 때 쓰는 말이다.

POINT 1 의문사 의문문

의문사는 who, what, which, where, when, why, how와 같은 말로, 구체적인 정보를 물을 때 쓴다.

• be동사가 있는 경우: 의문사+be동사+주어 ~?

의문사	be동사	주어	
Who	is	the boy	in the picture?

사진에 있는 남자아이는 **누구**니?

• 일반동사나 조동사가 있는 경우: 의문사+do/does/did/조동사+주어+동사원형 ~?

의문사	do/조동사	주어	동사원형
When	did	you	have	lunch?
Where	will	you	have	dinner?

너는 **언제** 점심을 먹었니?
너는 **어디에서** 저녁을 먹을 거니?

• 의문사가 주어인 경우: 의문사+동사 ~?

의문사	동사	
Who	likes	chocolate?

누가 초콜릿을 좋아하니?

↳ 주어로 쓰인 의문사는 3인칭 단수로 취급해요.

주의 의문사가 있는 의문문에 답할 때는 Yes나 No로 답하지 않고, 의문사의 의미에 따라 구체적으로 답한다.

A: **What** is your name? 너의 이름은 무엇이니?
B: My name is **Tom Smith**. 내 이름은 Tom Smith야.

궁금해요!
의문사가 없는 의문문은 어떤 형태였죠?

의문사만 빼 봐요. be동사 의문문은 Are you hungry?, 일반동사 의문문은 Did you have lunch?와 같이 써요.

개념확인 의문사 찾기

1 Who is that boy?　　　**2** What does Ann have?　　　**3** When can Rosa come?

기본연습 A 괄호 안에서 알맞은 것을 고르시오.

1 Who (is / does) your favorite singer?

2 Which (are / do) you like, milk or juice?

3 Where (is / will) Roy go for dinner?

4 Who (likes / like) strawberry ice cream?

5 How (can I / I can) go to the market?

6 Why (was / did) Jihun go to the library?

7 What (did happen / happened) here last night?

8 Why (is Emma / Emma is) absent from school?

9 When did (come Mary / Mary come) back?

B 질문에 알맞은 대답을 골라 연결하시오.

1 When is your birthday?　　·　　　　　　　　· ⓐ She studies science.

2 What does Jenny study?　·　　　　　　　　· ⓑ It's September 5th.

3 Where should we meet?　·　　　　　　　　· ⓒ Mr. Thomas teaches it.

4 Who teaches history?　　·　　　　　　　　· ⓓ Let's meet at the station.

C 밑줄 친 부분을 바르게 고쳐 쓰시오.

1 What can I <u>has</u> for dinner?　　　→ _____

2 Who <u>did make</u> the cookies?　　　→ _____

3 Which <u>does</u> your textbook?　　　→ _____

4 Why <u>you were</u> so late yesterday?　→ _____

D 우리말과 일치하도록 괄호 안의 말을 바르게 배열하시오.

1 너는 왜 화가 나 있니? (you, why, are, angry)

　→ _____

2 이 단어는 무슨 의미니? (mean, this word, does, what)

　→ _____

3 누가 축구를 하고 있니? (playing, who, is, soccer)

　→ _____

4 너는 그를 어떻게 만났니? (how, him, meet, did, you)

　→ _____

5 제가 그 책을 어디에서 찾을 수 있나요? (I, where, find, can, the book)

　→ _____

틀 리 기　쉬 운
내/신/포/인/트

의문사가 있는 의문문의
어순을 기억해요.

우리말을 영어로 바르게 옮긴 것은?

너는 방과 후에 무엇을 했니?

① What did you after school?
② What you did after school?
③ You did after school what?
④ What did you do after school?

POINT 2 who, whom, whose

의문사 who, whom, whose는 사람에 대해 물을 때 쓴다.

		질문	대답
who	누구, 누가	**Who** is that man over there? 저기 있는 저 남자는 **누구**니?	He's my father. 그는 나의 아버지셔.
who(m)	누구를	**Who(m)** did you meet? 너는 **누구를** 만났니?	I met my friend. 나는 친구를 만났어.
whose	누구의 ~ (+명사)	**Whose** *computer* is this? 이건 **누구의** 컴퓨터니?	It's mine. 그것은 내 것이야.
	누구의 것	**Whose** is this backpack? 이 배낭은 **누구의 것**이니?	It's hers. 그것은 그녀의 것이야.

일상 회화에서는 whom 대신 who가 자주 쓰여요.

개념확인 옳은 해석 고르기

1 Who likes candies?
☐ 누가 ☐ 누구를

2 Whom does Tim love?
☐ 누가 ☐ 누구를

3 Whose pen is that?
☐ 누구를 ☐ 누구의

기본연습 **A** 우리말과 일치하도록 알맞은 의문사를 쓰시오.

1 이것은 누구의 스카프니?
→ _____ scarf is this?

2 누가 그 피자를 먹었니?
→ _____ ate the pizza?

3 이 집은 누구의 것이니?
→ _____ is this house?

4 너는 어제 누구를 봤니?
→ _____ did you see yesterday?

5 저기 있는 저 여자아이는 누구니?
→ _____ is that girl over there?

B 괄호 안에서 알맞은 것을 고르시오.

1 (Who / Whose) is your favorite writer?

2 (Who / Whose) will you meet there?

3 (Who / Whose) can play the violin?

4 (Whom / Whose) scissors are these on the desk?

5 (Whom / Whose) is this camera?

6 (Who / Whom) likes the painting on the wall?

7 (Who / Whose) did Tom invite for the meeting?

8 (Who / Whom) is the woman on the bench?

C 질문에 알맞은 대답을 골라 연결하시오.

1 Who has a yellow crayon? ·   · ⓐ I called Tom.

2 Whose shoes are these? ·   · ⓑ They're Kate's.

3 Who did you call yesterday? ·   · ⓒ David has one.

4 Who should I talk to? ·   · ⓓ I like Margot Robbie.

5 Who is your favorite actor? ·   · ⓔ You should talk to Mr. Lee.

D 빈칸에 who, whom, whose 중 알맞은 것을 넣어 대화를 완성하시오.

1 A: _____ is the girl in the picture?

B: She's my little sister.

2 A: _____ song do you like?

B: I like NCT's songs.

3 A: _____ cooked this chicken?

B: My father cooked it.

4 A: _____ are you going to visit?

B: I'm going to visit my uncle.

5 A: _____ socks are these?

B: They're mine.

6 A: _____ are you waiting for?

B: I'm waiting for Mina.

7 A: _____ are these books?

B: They're Peter's.

8 A: _____ does Fred like in his class?

B: He likes Jenny.

틀리기 쉬운
내/신/포/인/트

의문사의 의미에 따른
알맞은 대답을 익혀요.

질문에 대한 대답으로 알맞지 <u>않은</u> 것은?

Whose coat is this on the chair?

① It's mine.   ② It's my coat.

③ She's Emma.   ④ It's my mother's.

POINT 3 what, which

의문사 what과 which는 사물에 대해 물을 때 쓴다.

		질문	대답
what	무엇	**What** is your favorite subject? 네가 가장 좋아하는 과목은 **무엇**이니?	I like science. 나는 과학을 좋아해.
	무슨 ~ (+명사)	**What** *color* do you like? 너는 **무슨** 색을 좋아하니?	I like yellow. 나는 노란색을 좋아해.
which	어느 것	**Which** do you like, math or music? 너는 수학과 음악 중 **어느 것**을 좋아하니?	I like music. 나는 음악을 좋아해.
	어떤 ~ (+명사)	**Which** *color* do you prefer, red or blue? 너는 빨간색과 파란색 중 **어떤** 색을 더 좋아하니?	I prefer red. 나는 빨간색을 더 좋아해.

↳ which는 정해진 범위에서 선택을 물을 때 써요.

개념확인 옳은 해석 고르기

1 What is your hobby?
□ 누구   □ 무엇

2 Who did you help?
□ 누구를   □ 무엇을

3 Which number do you like, 1 or 3?
□ 누구의   □ 어떤

기본연습 **A** 괄호 안에서 알맞은 것을 고르시오.

1 (Who / What) is your dream job?

2 (Whom / What) do you do after school?

3 (Whose / Which) pen is this on the desk?

4 (Whose / What) number does Jenny like?

5 (Who / Which) do you want, a banana or an apple?

6 (Who / What) can you tell me about Mr. Smith?

7 (Who / What) are you going to invite for the party?

8 (Whose / Which) subject do you like, science or math?

B 질문에 알맞은 대답을 골라 연결하시오.

1 What is your favorite color?   ·   · ⓐ It's Jennifer's.

2 What is the name of this school?   ·   · ⓑ I like purple a lot.

3 Who broke the window?   ·   · ⓒ My sister did it.

4 Whose wallet is that on the sofa?   ·   · ⓓ I want size 8.

5 Which size do you want, 7 or 8?   ·   · ⓔ It's Hana Middle School.

6 Which do you prefer, dogs or cats?   ·   · ⓕ I prefer dogs.

C 빈칸에 who, whom, whose, what, which 중 알맞은 것을 넣어 대화를 완성하시오.

1 A: _____ are you looking for?　　　　　B: I'm looking for my ring.

2 A: _____ is this red umbrella?　　　　　B: It's my mother's.

3 A: _____ has the key to this door?　　　B: Peter has it.

4 A: _____ is in your right hand?　　　　　B: Nothing.

5 A: _____ do you prefer, red or blue?　　B: I prefer red.

6 A: _____ did you have for breakfast?　　B: I had a bowl of soup.

7 A: _____ bus do you take, No. 12 or 20?　B: I take the No. 12 bus.

8 A: _____ time did you get up this morning?　B: At seven.

9 A: _____ season do you like, spring or fall?　B: I like spring.

10 A: _____ does Ms. Baker teach?　　　　B: She teaches high school students.

D 우리말과 일치하도록 괄호 안의 말을 바르게 배열하시오.

1 너의 남동생은 무엇이 필요하니? (does, what, your brother, need)

→ _____

2 너는 무슨 영화를 봤니? (did, you, movie, what, watch)

→ _____

3 벽에 있는 저것은 무엇이니? (what, on the wall, is, that)

→ _____

4 너는 파란색과 검정색 중 어떤 색을 원하니? (do, which, color, want, you, blue or black)

→ _____

5 그는 커피와 주스 중 어느 음료를 선택할까? (he, which, drink, will, choose, coffee or juice)

→ _____

틀리기 쉬운
내/신/포/인/트

what과 which의 쓰임을
구별하여 기억해요.

대화의 빈칸에 들어갈 말로 알맞은 것은?

A: _____ sport do you prefer, soccer or baseball?
B: I prefer soccer.

① Who　　　　② Whom　　　　③ What　　　　④ Which

의문사 where, when, why, how는 다음과 같은 뜻으로 쓴다.

		질문	대답
where	어디에, 어디서	**Where** is the school library? 학교 도서관은 **어디에** 있니?	It's next to the gym. 그것은 체육관 옆에 있어.
when	언제	**When** does your class start? 네 수업은 **언제** 시작하니?	It starts at 9 a.m. 오전 9시에 시작해.
why	왜	**Why** do you study English? 너는 **왜** 영어를 공부하니?	Because I like English. 영어를 좋아하기 때문이야. → because를 생략하여 답할 수도 있어요.
how	어떻게	**How** do you go to school? 너는 학교에 **어떻게** 가니?	I go to school on foot. 걸어서 학교에 가.
		How was school today? 오늘 학교는 **어땠니**?	It was fun. 재미있었어.

↳ how는 방법이나 상태를 물을 때 써요.

Tips 정확한 시각을 물을 때 when 대신 what time을 쓸 수 있다.
A: **What time** does the movie start? 영화는 몇 시에 시작하니?
B: It starts at 7 o'clock. 7시에 시작해.

개념확인 옳은 해석 고르기

1 When is Parents' Day?
☐ 어디에 ☐ 언제

2 Where is today's newspaper?
☐ 어디에 ☐ 언제

3 Why are you so late?
☐ 왜 ☐ 어떻게

기본연습 **A** 우리말과 일치하도록 알맞은 의문사를 쓰시오.

1 너는 왜 그녀에게 전화했니? → _____ did you call her?

2 너는 언제 일어나니? → _____ do you get up?

3 너는 집에 어떻게 가니? → _____ do you go home?

4 수민이의 고향은 어디니? → _____ is Sumin's hometown?

5 어제 콘서트는 어땠니? → _____ was the concert yesterday?

B 질문에 알맞은 대답을 골라 연결하시오.

1 Why are you so angry? •
2 How was your final exam? •
3 When does your school finish? •
4 How does Mina come here? •
5 Where do you spend your weekends? •

• ⓐ It finishes at 4 o'clock.
• ⓑ I usually stay at home.
• ⓒ Because I can't find my glasses.
• ⓓ I got good grades.
• ⓔ She comes here by bus.

C 빈칸에 where, when, why, how 중 알맞은 것을 넣어 대화를 완성하시오.

1 A: _____ are you from?　　　　B: I'm from the U.K.

2 A: _____ do you spell that word?　　B: It's J-A-Z-Z.

3 A: _____ did Mary arrive here?　　B: She arrived at 11 a.m.

4 A: _____ do you need money?　　B: Because I have to buy a ticket.

5 A: _____ should I put this dictionary?　B: Put it over there.

6 A: _____ is Children's Day in Korea?　B: It's on May 5th.

7 A: _____ was your summer vacation?　B: It was great.

8 A: _____ were you upset yesterday?　B: Because my sister was very noisy.

9 A: _____ will Tom go to the gym?　　B: He'll go there at noon.

10 A: _____ can I go to City Hall?　　B: Take the No. 120 bus.

11 A: _____ did you buy those shoes?　B: I bought them at the market.

12 A: _____ is Jim going to the library?　B: Because he should borrow a book.

D 우리말과 일치하도록 괄호 안의 말을 바르게 배열하시오.

1 버스 정류장은 어디에 있니? (where, the bus stop, is)

→ _____

2 너는 언제 출발해야 하니? (you, when, should, leave)

→ _____

3 너는 그를 어떻게 알게 되었니? (you, did, how, him, know)

→ _____

4 너는 왜 영어를 배우니? (you, learn, do, why, English)

→ _____

**틀 리 기 쉬 운
내/신/포/인/트**

의문사의 의미를 구별하여
기억해요.

대화의 빈칸에 들어갈 말로 알맞은 것은?

A: _____ do you buy your clothes?
B: I buy clothes at Star Mall.

① When　　② Where　　③ Why　　④ What

POINT 5 how+형용사/부사

「how+형용사/부사」는 '얼마나 ~한(하게)'의 뜻으로 정도를 물을 때 쓴다.

		질문	대답
how old	몇 살 〈나이〉	**How old** is your brother? 네 남동생은 **몇 살**이니?	He's 10 years old. 그는 10살이야.
how tall	얼마나 큰 〈키〉, 얼마나 높은 〈높이〉	**How tall** is your sister? 네 여동생은 **키가 얼마나 크니?**	She's 150 cm tall. 150cm야.
how long	얼마나 긴 〈길이〉	**How long** is this desk? 이 책상은 **얼마나 기니?**	It's 2 meters. 2미터야.
	얼마 동안 〈기간〉	**How long** will you stay? 너는 **얼마 동안** 머물 거니?	For one month. 한 달 동안.
how far	얼마나 먼 〈거리〉	**How far** is Busan from here? 부산은 여기에서 **얼마나 머니?**	Two hours by car. 차로 2시간이야.
how often	얼마나 자주 〈빈도〉	**How often** do you swim? 너는 **얼마나 자주** 수영을 하니?	Once a week. 일주일에 한 번.
how many	얼마나 많은 ~ 〈수〉 (+셀 수 있는 명사)	**How many** pens do you want? 너는 **얼마나 많은** 펜을 원하니?	I want five pens. 다섯 개의 펜을 원해.
how much	얼마나 많은 ~ 〈양〉 (+셀 수 없는 명사)	**How much** milk do you need? 너는 우유가 **얼마나** 필요하니?	I need one cup. 한 컵이 필요해.
	얼마 〈가격〉	**How much** is this backpack? 이 배낭은 (가격이) **얼마니?**	It's 20 dollars. 20달러야.

↗ once(한 번), twice(두 번), three times(세 번) 등 빈도를 나타내는 표현으로 답해요.

주의 how many 뒤에는 셀 수 있는 명사의 복수형을 쓰고, how much 뒤에는 셀 수 없는 명사를 쓴다.

개념확인 옳은 해석 고르기

1 How far is the station?
　□ 얼마나 먼　□ 얼마나 큰

2 How long is that river?
　□ 얼마 동안　□ 얼마나 긴

3 How tall are you?
　□ 얼마나 키가 큰　□ 얼마나 많은

기본연습 A 우리말과 일치하도록 알맞은 의문사와 형용사나 부사를 쓰시오.

1 너의 개는 몇 살이니?　→ ＿＿＿＿＿ ＿＿＿＿＿ is your dog?

2 너의 방학은 얼마 동안이니?　→ ＿＿＿＿＿ ＿＿＿＿＿ is your vacation?

3 에펠탑은 얼마나 높니?　→ ＿＿＿＿＿ ＿＿＿＿＿ is the Eiffel Tower?

4 이 운동화는 얼마니?　→ ＿＿＿＿＿ ＿＿＿＿＿ are these sneakers?

5 너는 얼마나 자주 외식을 하니?　→ ＿＿＿＿＿ ＿＿＿＿＿ do you eat out?

6 얼마나 많은 사람들이 있니?　→ ＿＿＿＿＿ ＿＿＿＿＿ people are there?

7 독도는 포항에서 얼마나 머니?　→ ＿＿＿＿＿ ＿＿＿＿＿ is Dokdo from Pohang?

B 질문에 알맞은 대답을 골라 연결하시오.

1 How tall is your brother? ·   · ⓐ It's 50 meters long.
2 How long is that bridge? ·   · ⓑ She's 8 years old.
3 How old is your little sister? ·   · ⓒ He's 160 cm tall.
4 How often do you play golf? ·   · ⓓ I play golf once a month.
5 How many cars are there? ·   · ⓔ It's 20 dollars.
6 How much is this cake? ·   · ⓕ There are four cars.
7 How far is the bus stop? ·   · ⓖ I need 5 dollars.
8 How much money do you need? ·   · ⓗ It's about 20 meters from here.

C 빈칸에 알맞은 말을 넣어 대화를 완성하시오.

1 A: _____ _____ are you?   B: I'm 14 years old.
2 A: _____ _____ does he exercise?   B: Every day.
3 A: _____ _____ is your father?   B: He's about 180 cm tall.
4 A: _____ _____ is the Nile River?   B: It's 6,650 km long.
5 A: _____ _____ water does Jim want?   B: He wants two glasses of water.
6 A: _____ _____ is your lunch time?   B: One hour.
7 A: _____ _____ tomatoes did you eat?   B: I ate two tomatoes.
8 A: _____ _____ is this camera?   B: It's 50 dollars.
9 A: _____ _____ languages does he speak?   B: He speaks three languages.
10 A: _____ _____ did you walk?   B: I walked two kilometers.

틀/리/기 쉬/운
내/신/포/인/트

how many와
how much의 쓰임을
구별하여 기억해요.

어법상 틀린 부분을 바르게 고친 것은?

How much comic books do you have?

① How → What
② much → many
③ comic books → comic book
④ do → are

개 념 완 성 TEST

정답 및 해설 p.22

STEP 1 Map으로 개념 정리하기

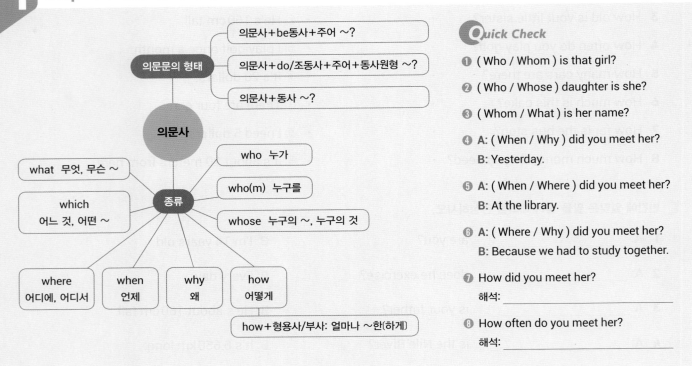

의문문의 형태
- 의문사+be동사+주어 ~?
- 의문사+do/조동사+주어+동사원형 ~?
- 의문사+동사 ~?

의문사

종류
- who 누가
- who(m) 누구를
- whose 누구의 ~, 누구의 것

- what 무엇, 무슨 ~
- which 어느 것, 어떤 ~
- where 어디에, 어디서
- when 언제
- why 왜
- how 어떻게
- how+형용사/부사: 얼마나 ~한(하게)

Quick Check

❶ (Who / Whom) is that girl?

❷ (Who / Whose) daughter is she?

❸ (Whom / What) is her name?

❹ A: (When / Why) did you meet her?
   B: Yesterday.

❺ A: (When / Where) did you meet her?
   B: At the library.

❻ A: (Where / Why) did you meet her?
   B: Because we had to study together.

❼ How did you meet her?
   해석: _____

❽ How often do you meet her?
   해석: _____

STEP 2 기본 다지기

빈칸완성

A 우리말과 일치하도록 주어진 말을 이용하여 문장을 완성하시오.

1 누가 이 음악을 좋아하니? (like) → _____ _____ this music?

2 이것은 누구의 가방이니? (bag) → _____ is this?

3 너는 그 카드를 어디에서 찾았니? (find) → _____ you _____ the card?

4 너는 언제 삼촌을 방문할 거니? (visit) → _____ you _____ your uncle?

5 너는 무엇을 잘할 수 있니? (do) → _____ you _____ well?

6 Tim은 왜 중국어를 배우고 있는 중이니? (learn) → _____ Tim _____ Chinese?

7 너는 왜 그렇게 생각하니? (think) → _____ you _____ so?

8 James는 학교에 어떻게 가니? (go) → _____ James _____ to school?

9 너는 시간이 얼마나 필요하니? (time) → _____ do you need?

10 너는 얼마나 많은 책을 가지고 있니? (book) → _____ do you have?

B 어법상 틀린 부분을 찾아 바르게 고쳐 쓰시오.

1 Whom is that tall man over there? (저기 있는 키가 큰 남자는 누구니?)

_____ → _____

2 Who know her email address? (누가 그녀의 이메일 주소를 아니?)

_____ → _____

3 What pen do you like, this or that? (너는 이것과 저것 중에서 어떤 펜이 좋니?)

_____ → _____

4 How much brothers does Joan have? (Joan은 남자 형제가 몇 명 있니?)

_____ → _____

5 How often does Mary and Alice meet each other? (Mary와 Alice는 얼마나 자주 서로 만나니?)

_____ → _____

C 밑줄 친 부분을 묻는 의문문을 완성하시오.

1 Helen doesn't drink coffee.

→ _____ doesn't drink coffee?

2 Ben lost my pen.

→ _____ _____ did Ben lose?

3 Sam is 170 cm tall now.

→ _____ _____ is Sam now?

4 Kevin will order a hamburger for lunch.

→ _____ _____ Kevin _____ for lunch?

5 Daniel bought a new car yesterday.

→ _____ _____ Daniel _____ a new car?

6 Bob and Jack went to Texas.

→ _____ _____ Bob and Jack _____?

7 The boy usually speaks very slowly.

→ _____ _____ the boy usually _____?

8 I read science books because they are interesting.

→ _____ _____ you _____ science books?

STEP 3 서술형 따라잡기

그림이해
A 그림을 보고, 빈칸에 알맞은 말을 써서 대화를 완성하시오.

1
2
3

1 A: _____ _____ is the bus?　B: It's blue.

2 A: _____ _____ is this purple scarf?　B: It's only _____ dollars.

3 A: _____ _____ people are there in the room?　B: There are _____ people.

영작완성
B 우리말과 일치하도록 괄호 안의 말을 바르게 배열하여 문장을 쓰시오.

1 너는 왜 준수를 좋아하니? (you, why, Junsu, do, like)

→ _____

2 너는 누구를 찾고 있니? (who, you, are, looking for)

→ _____

3 너는 밤에 얼마나 자니? (at night, how long, do, sleep, you)

→ _____

4 너는 펜과 연필 중 어떤 것이 필요하니? (which, a pen or a pencil, you, do, need)

→ _____

문장영작
C 우리말과 일치하도록 괄호 안의 말을 이용하여 영작하시오.

1 저 기린은 키가 얼마나 크니? (be, that giraffe)

→ _____

2 너는 언제 그 새 셔츠를 샀니? (buy, the new shirt)

→ _____

3 너의 삼촌은 어디에서 수학을 가르치시니? (teach, math)

→ _____

4 그 책상 위에 있는 저것은 누구의 스마트폰이니? (smartphone, on the desk)

→ _____

[1-3] 빈칸에 들어갈 말로 알맞은 것을 고르시오.

1

A: _____ are those people?
B: They're my parents.

① Who　　　② Whose　　　③ Whom
④ What　　　⑤ Which

2

A: _____ do you prefer, meat or fish?
B: I prefer fish.

① Who　　　② Which　　　③ How
④ When　　　⑤ Where

3

A: _____ will you go on vacation?
B: I'll go to Jeju-do.

① Why　　　② Who　　　③ Where
④ How　　　⑤ When

4 빈칸에 What이 들어갈 수 없는 것은?

① _____ subject do you like?
② _____ is your favorite sport?
③ _____ is your best friend?
④ _____ time do you get up?
⑤ _____ can I do for your birthday?

5 빈칸에 들어갈 말로 알맞지 않은 것은?

_____ does your sister exercise?

① Why　　　② Where　　　③ When
④ Whom　　　⑤ How often

[6-7] 질문에 대한 대답으로 알맞은 것을 고르시오.

6

How many days are there in March?

① It's next month.
② There are 31 days.
③ It's for one month.
④ It starts next Monday.
⑤ Yes, I'll go there in March.

7

Whose keys are these on the sofa?

① They're mine.
② No, these are keys.
③ They're from China.
④ I only have one key.
⑤ They're next to the lamp.

8 유미에 대한 정보를 보고, 대답할 수 <u>없는</u> 질문은?

Name	Lee Yumi
Age	14 years old
Date of Birth	May 10th
Email	reason@mail.com
Phone	010-1234-5678

① How old is Yumi?

② When is Yumi's birthday?

③ Where does Yumi live?

④ What is Yumi's email address?

⑤ What is Yumi's phone number?

9 빈칸에 알맞은 말이 순서대로 짝 지어진 것은?

> • How _____ does the bus come?
>
> • How _____ is your summer vacation?

① many – much   ② tall – far

③ much – long   ④ often – tall

⑤ often – long

10 주어진 대답에 대한 질문으로 알맞은 것은?

> I bought it last Sunday.

① What did you buy?

② How much was the cap?

③ When did you buy your cap?

④ Where did you buy your cap?

⑤ How many caps did you buy?

11 우리말과 일치하도록 주어진 말을 배열할 때, 네 번째로 오는 단어는?

> 너는 파티에 누구를 초대했니?
>
> (who, you, invite, for the party, did)

① you   ② invite   ③ who

④ did   ⑤ for

12 우리말을 영어로 옮길 때, 쓰이지 <u>않는</u> 단어는?

> 누가 너의 학교에서 음악을 가르치시니?

① who   ② music   ③ teaches

④ does   ⑤ your school

13 짝 지어진 대화가 어색한 것은?

① A: How tall are you?

　B: I'm 160 cm tall.

② A: How far is your school from here?

　B: It takes 10 minutes by subway.

③ A: How much is this bike?

　B: It's about one meter.

④ A: Which color do you prefer, red or blue?

　B: I prefer blue.

⑤ A: Why are you learning to swim?

　B: Because it is good for health.

14 빈칸에 Where이 들어갈 수 없는 것은?

① _____ do you live?

② _____ are my glasses?

③ _____ can I put this box?

④ _____ do you go to bed?

⑤ _____ will you go for a picnic?

18 밑줄 친 부분을 묻는 의문문으로 알맞은 것은?

Jim plays the piano every day.

① Who plays the piano?

② Why does Jim play the piano?

③ Where does Jim play the piano?

④ What does Jim do with the piano?

⑤ How often does Jim play the piano?

15 어법상 틀린 부분을 바르게 고친 것은?

A: Why you are in the hospital?

B: Because I hurt my leg.

① Why you → Why do you

② you are → are you

③ are → is

④ hurt → hurts

⑤ my → mine

고난도

19 빈칸에 들어갈 말이 같은 것끼리 짝 지어진 것은?

ⓐ _____ are you from?

ⓑ _____ is Teachers' Day?

ⓒ _____ chair is yours?

ⓓ _____ is the weather in New York?

ⓔ _____ size do you wear, 6 or 7?

① ⓐ, ⓑ   ② ⓐ, ⓓ   ③ ⓑ, ⓓ

④ ⓒ, ⓔ   ⑤ ⓓ, ⓔ

16 어법상 틀린 문장은?

① What food do you like?

② How often do you ride your bike?

③ Who is the girl in the room?

④ Who does Sue work with?

⑤ Whom opened the front door?

고난도

20 어법상 올바른 문장의 개수는?

ⓐ How long is a marathon?

ⓑ How much books do you read in a week?

ⓒ How tall is the building?

ⓓ How many money do you have in your
   pocket?

① 0개   ② 1개   ③ 2개

④ 3개   ⑤ 4개

17 빈칸에 들어갈 말이 나머지와 다른 하나는?

① _____ is wrong with you?

② _____ time is it now?

③ _____ is your full name?

④ _____ do you do after school?

⑤ _____ son is he?

21 괄호 안의 말과 알맞은 의문사를 이용하여 대답에 알맞은 질문을 쓰시오.

(1) A: _____

(Sujin, come back)

B: She came back last Sunday.

(2) A: _____

(Sam, watch, movies)

B: Once a week.

22 밑줄 친 부분을 묻는 의문문을 쓰시오.

(1) Tom entered the classroom.

→ _____

(2) This is my father's cup.

→ _____

(3) Mina can make a kite.

→ _____

23 주어진 대답에 알맞은 질문을 쓰시오.

(1) A: _____

B: My name is Lee Minho.

(2) A: _____

B: I'm fourteen years old.

(3) A: _____

B: My birthday is on April 18th.

24 학생들의 등교 현황을 묻는 다음 설문지의 질문을 완성하시오.

(1) _____ do you live?

I live in _____ .

(2) _____ do you go to school?

☐ by bus　　　　☐ by subway

☐ by car　　　　☐ on foot

(3) _____ do you go to school with?

☐ with my parents or my grandparents

☐ with my sisters or my brothers

☐ with my friends　　☐ by myself

(4) _____ _____ do you go to school?

☐ 7:00~7:30　　☐ 7:30~8:00

☐ 8:00~8:30　　☐ 8:30~9:00

고난도

25 우리말과 일치하도록 괄호 안의 말을 이용하여 조건에 맞게 영작하시오.

조건 1. 의문사를 사용할 것

　　　2. 총 여섯 단어로 쓸 것

(1) Mike는 왜 집에 일찍 갔니? (go, early)

→ _____

(2) 너의 겨울 방학은 얼마나 기니? (winter vacation)

→ _____

(3) 너는 얼마나 많은 표가 필요하니? (ticket, need)

→ _____

(4) 너는 얼마나 많은 우유를 마셨니? (milk, drink)

→ _____

8 to부정사

to부정사는 to와 함께 쓰는 품사가 정해져 있지 않은 말이라는 뜻이다.
이름처럼 to부정사는 문장 안에서 명사, 형용사, 부사처럼 쓰인다.

to부정사의 형태와 쓰임

정답 및 해설 p.24

to부정사는 「to+동사원형」의 형태로, 문장에서 명사, 형용사, 부사 역할을 한다.

명사적 용법	I like **to read** books.	나는 책을 읽는 것을 좋아한다.
형용사적 용법	I want a book **to read**.	나는 읽을 책을 원한다.
부사적 용법	I sat down **to read** a book.	나는 책을 읽기 위해 앉았다.

주의 「to+동사원형」 뒤에 여러 단어가 함께 올 수 있다.
Cathy wants **to be *a doctor***. Cathy는 의사가 되길 원한다.

궁금해요!
I go to the library to read books.에서는 to부정사가 두 개인 건가요?

아니요. to부정사는 to 뒤에 동사원형이 와요. to 뒤에 명사가 오면 전치사 to예요. the library 앞의 to는 전치사예요.

개념확인 to부정사 찾기

1 She wants to play tennis. **2** I have a magazine to read. **3** I go to the library to study.

기본연습 **A** 괄호 안에서 알맞은 것을 고르시오.

1 I plan (learn / to learn) Chinese.

2 I need someone (help / to help) me now.

3 His dream is (be / to be) a fashion model.

4 My father loves (to take / to takes) pictures.

5 Mike went to Paris (to study / to studied) music.

B 괄호 안의 말을 to부정사로 바꿔 문장을 완성하시오.

1 Robert needs a book _____ _____. (read)

2 I like _____ _____ movies. (watch)

3 He studied hard _____ _____ a doctor. (become)

4 Wendy wants _____ _____ in a big city. (live)

5 Kevin went to the mall _____ _____ a chair. (buy)

틀 리 기 쉬 운
내/신/포/인/트

to부정사는 「to+동사원형」의 형태로 써요.

우리말과 일치하도록 빈칸에 들어갈 말로 알맞은 것은?

Mark는 아이스크림 먹기를 원한다.
→ Mark wants _____ an ice cream.

① have   ② has   ③ to have   ④ to has

POINT 2 명사적 용법: 주어, 보어 역할

• **주어 역할**: to부정사가 문장에서 동사 앞에 오고, '~하는 것은'으로 해석한다. to부정사(구)가 주어로 쓰일 때는 주로 주어 자리에 가주어 It을 쓰고, 진주어인 to부정사(구)를 문장의 끝으로 보낸다.

> to부정사(구) 주어는 단수 취급한다.

| **To learn** French | is | not easy. | 프랑스어를 배우는 것은 쉽지 않다. |

→ | It | is | not easy | **to learn** French. |

> 궁금해요!
> 가주어 It은 어떻게 해석해요?
>
> 가주어 It은 해석하지 않아요. 진주어인 to부정사(구)를 주어로 해석하세요.

• **보어 역할**: to부정사가 문장에서 동사 뒤에 오고, '~하는 것(이다)'라는 뜻으로 주어를 보충 설명한다.

| My plan | is | **to learn** French. | 나의 계획은 프랑스어를 배우는 것이다. |

개념확인 to부정사의 역할 구분하기

1 It is exciting to travel by ship.
  ☐ 주어 ☐ 보어

2 My plan is to travel alone.
  ☐ 주어 ☐ 보어

기본연습 우리말과 일치하도록 괄호 안의 말을 이용하여 문장을 완성하시오.

1 그의 목표는 수학 선생님이 되는 것이다. (be)
  → His goal is _____ _____ a math teacher.

2 야구 경기를 보는 것은 재미있다. (watch)
  → It is exciting _____ _____ baseball games.

3 혼자 여행하는 것은 위험하다. (travel)
  → It is dangerous _____ _____ alone.

4 약속을 지키는 것은 중요하다. (keep)
  → It is important _____ _____ a promise.

5 나의 계획은 매일 아침 조깅을 하는 것이다. (jog)
  → My plan is _____ _____ every morning.

6 영어로 쓰는 것은 매우 어렵다. (write)
  → It is very difficult _____ _____ in English.

7 그녀의 꿈은 유명한 가수가 되는 것이다. (become)
  → Her dream is _____ _____ a famous singer.

POINT 3 명사적 용법: 목적어 역할

- 목적어 역할: to부정사가 문장에서 동사 뒤에 와서 동사의 목적어로 쓰이며, '~하는 것을'로 해석한다.

| She | wants | **to learn** French. | 그녀는 프랑스어를 **배우기를** 원한다. |

- 다음 동사들은 to부정사를 목적어로 쓴다.

| want 원하다 | hope 바라다 | expect 기대하다 | need 필요로 하다 |
| decide 결정하다 | plan 계획하다 | agree 동의하다 | promise 약속하다 |

주의 to부정사의 부정은 「not+to부정사」의 형태로 나타낸다.
He decided **not to play** soccer. 그는 축구를 하지 않기로 결정했다.

개념확인 to부정사의 역할 구분하기

1 He plans to buy a new bike.

☐ 주어 ☐ 보어 ☐ 목적어

2 His plan is to buy a new bike.

☐ 주어 ☐ 보어 ☐ 목적어

기본연습 우리말과 일치하도록 괄호 안의 말을 이용하여 문장을 완성하시오.

1 나는 시험에 합격하기를 기대했다. (expect, pass)

→ I ＿＿＿＿＿ ＿＿＿＿＿ ＿＿＿＿＿ the exam.

2 그 아이들은 책을 읽는 것을 필요로 한다. (need, read)

→ The children ＿＿＿＿＿ ＿＿＿＿＿ ＿＿＿＿＿ books.

3 나의 여동생은 뉴욕에서 살기를 바란다. (hope, live)

→ My sister ＿＿＿＿＿ ＿＿＿＿＿ ＿＿＿＿＿ in New York.

4 우리 아버지는 그 가방을 사는 것을 동의하셨다. (agree, buy)

→ My father ＿＿＿＿＿ ＿＿＿＿＿ ＿＿＿＿＿ the bag.

5 하나는 그 상자를 열지 않기로 약속했다. (promise, not, open)

→ Hana ＿＿＿＿＿ ＿＿＿＿＿ ＿＿＿＿＿ ＿＿＿＿＿ the box.

틀리기 쉬운 내/신/포/인/트

to부정사를 목적어로 쓰는 동사를 기억해요.

빈칸에 들어갈 말로 알맞은 것은?

Tom and I want ＿＿＿＿＿ table tennis.

① play   ② plays   ③ to play   ④ to plays

POINT 4 형용사적 용법

to부정사가 명사나 대명사를 꾸며 주는 형용사처럼 쓰일 때는 '~할, ~하는'으로 해석한다. 이때 to부정사는 명사를 뒤에서 수식한다.

He needs	a book	**to read**.	그는 읽을 책이 필요하다.

She has	a letter	**to write**.	그녀는 쓸 편지가 있다.

개념확인 to부정사가 꾸며 주는 말 찾기

1 I need a hat to wear.   **2** It's time to go to bed.   **3** He has no homework to do.

기본연습 A 밑줄 친 부분을 어법상 바르게 고쳐 쓰시오.

1 Ann has an essay write today.   → _____

2 They need time exercise these days.   → _____

3 My mother has a lot of to do work.   → _____

4 Steve brought some to eat snacks.   → _____

5 Nick is looking for something drink.   → _____

B 우리말과 일치하도록 괄호 안의 말을 바르게 배열하여 문장을 완성하시오.

1 우리 엄마는 읽을 신문을 샀다. (to, a newspaper, read)
→ My mom bought _____.

2 나의 남동생은 입을 재킷을 하나 원했다. (to, wear, a jacket)
→ My brother wanted _____.

3 그들은 가방을 살 약간의 돈이 필요하다. (a bag, some money, buy, to)
→ They need _____.

4 Jane은 춤을 연습할 시간이 없다. (time, the dance, practice, to)
→ Jane doesn't have _____.

5 Kate는 그녀의 차를 고쳐 줄 누군가를 찾고 있다. (fix, to, someone, her car)
→ Kate is looking for _____.

6 William은 지금 사용할 우산이 하나 필요하다. (to, an umbrella, use)
→ William needs _____ now.

POINT 5 부사적 용법

to부정사가 부사처럼 쓰일 때는 행동의 목적, 감정의 원인, 결과 등의 의미를 나타낸다.

	행동	행동의 목적(~하기 위해)	
목적	She exercises	**to stay** healthy.	그녀는 건강을 유지하기 위해 운동한다.
	I studied hard	**to pass** the exam.	나는 시험에 합격하기 위해 열심히 공부했다.
	감정	감정의 원인(~해서)	
원인	I'm so happy	**to see** you again.	나는 너를 다시 만나서 정말 기쁘다.
	I was surprised	**to hear** the news.	나는 그 소식을 듣고 놀랐다.
	일어난 일(~해서)	일의 결과(…하다)	
결과	She grew up	**to be** a scientist.	그녀는 자라서 과학자가 되었다.
	My father lived	**to be** 80 years old.	우리 아버지는 80세까지 사셨다.

> 목적을 나타낼 때는 to 대신 in order to를 쓸 수 있어요.

> 주로 grow up, live 등과 함께 쓰여요.

개념확인 옳은 해석 고르기

1 I'm happy to talk with you.

☐ 너와 이야기를 나눠서 ☐ 너와 이야기를 나누기 위해

2 I saved money to buy some clothes.

☐ 옷을 사서 ☐ 옷을 사기 위해

기본연습 **A** 밑줄 친 to부정사의 의미로 알맞은 것을 고르시오.

1 I was glad to meet you again.   ☐ 목적   ☐ 감정의 원인   ☐ 결과

2 James grew up to be a pilot.   ☐ 목적   ☐ 감정의 원인   ☐ 결과

3 Susan woke up early to exercise.   ☐ 목적   ☐ 감정의 원인   ☐ 결과

4 I'm sorry to hear the news.   ☐ 목적   ☐ 감정의 원인   ☐ 결과

5 I went to the store to buy milk.   ☐ 목적   ☐ 감정의 원인   ☐ 결과

B 우리말과 일치하도록 괄호 안의 말을 이용하여 문장을 완성하시오.

1 소민이는 나를 보기 위해 이곳에 왔다. (see, me)

→ Somin came here ＿＿＿＿＿ ＿＿＿＿＿ ＿＿＿＿＿.

2 유진이는 버스를 잡기 위해 달렸다. (run, catch)

→ Yujin ＿＿＿＿＿ ＿＿＿＿＿ ＿＿＿＿＿ the bus.

3 나는 그 소식을 듣고 정말 슬펐다. (sad, hear)

→ I was so ＿＿＿＿＿ ＿＿＿＿＿ ＿＿＿＿＿ the news.

4 그는 경기에 져서 실망했다. (disappointed, lose)

→ He was ＿＿＿＿＿ ＿＿＿＿＿ ＿＿＿＿＿ the game.

5 보미는 건강을 유지하기 위해 매일 수영을 한다. (stay, healthy)

→ Bomi swims every day _____ _____ _____.

6 지민이는 음악을 공부하기 위해 오스트리아로 갔다. (study, music)

→ Jimin went to Austria _____ _____ _____.

7 Eric은 자라서 치과의사가 되었다. (grow up, be)

→ Eric _____ _____ _____ _____ a dentist.

8 Mary는 질문을 하기 위해 손을 들었다. (ask, a question)

→ Mary raised her hand _____ _____ _____ _____.

9 나의 남동생은 시험에 합격하기 위해 열심히 공부했다. (pass, the exam)

→ My brother studied hard _____ _____ _____ _____.

10 우리 할머니는 100세까지 사셨다. (be, 100 years old)

→ My grandmother lived _____ _____ _____ _____.

C 밑줄 친 to부정사의 쓰임으로 알맞은 것을 고르시오.

		명사	형용사	부사
1	I want to run in the marathon.	☐	☐	☐
2	It is important to save energy.	☐	☐	☐
3	Steve was surprised to see her there.	☐	☐	☐
4	Robin needed some time to think.	☐	☐	☐
5	Linda listens to music to feel good.	☐	☐	☐
6	Carol bought some books to read.	☐	☐	☐
7	My dream is to become a farmer.	☐	☐	☐
8	His son grew up to be a pianist.	☐	☐	☐
9	I use my cell phone to take pictures.	☐	☐	☐
10	I'm planning to cook dinner for my mom.	☐	☐	☐

틀리기 쉬운 내/신/포/인/트

문장에서 to부정사가 어떤 역할로 쓰이는지 구별하여 기억해요.

밑줄 친 부분의 쓰임이 보기와 같은 것은?

보기 I went to the park to exercise.

① It is not easy to learn Spanish.
② He wants to meet you again.
③ We went out to see the stars in the sky.
④ Her plan is to do yoga every morning.

개 념 완 성 TEST

정답 및 해설 p.24

STEP 1 Map으로 개념 정리하기

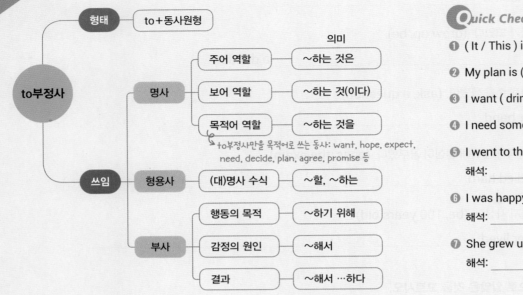

Quick Check

❶ (It / This) is not good to eat fast food.

❷ My plan is (cook / to cook) for my mom.

❸ I want (drink / to drink) some water.

❹ I need something (eat / to eat).

❺ I went to the bakery to buy some bread.
해석: _____

❻ I was happy to become a cook.
해석: _____

❼ She grew up to become a cook.
해석: _____

STEP 2 기본 다지기

빈칸완성

A 우리말과 일치하도록 빈칸에 알맞은 말을 넣어 문장을 완성하시오.

1 Jim은 그의 셔츠를 세탁할 필요가 있다. → Jim needs _____ _____ his shirt.

2 나는 요가를 배우기 위해 수업을 들었다. → I took the class _____ _____ yoga.

3 미나는 읽을 책이 많이 있다. → Mina has many books _____ _____.

4 숙제를 할 시간이야. → It's time _____ _____ your homework.

5 나는 친구들을 만나서 기뻤다. → I was happy _____ _____ my friends.

6 나는 그에게 인형을 사 주기로 약속했다. → I promised _____ _____ a doll for him.

7 나는 에너지를 절약하기 위해 불을 껐다. → I turned off the light _____ _____ energy.

8 그녀는 나쁜 소식을 듣고 너무 슬펐다. → She was so sad _____ _____ the bad news.

9 그는 자라서 유명한 무용수가 되었다. → He grew up _____ _____ a famous dancer.

10 영어를 말하는 것은 재미있다. → _____ is fun _____ _____ English.

11 올림픽을 보는 것은 흥미진진하다. → It is exciting _____ _____ the Olympics.

B 밑줄 친 부분이 어법상 바르면 ◯라고 쓰고, 틀리면 바르게 고쳐 쓰시오.

1 Sally decided <u>to not go</u> to Europe. → _____

2 It is very difficult <u>write</u> in Chinese. → _____

3 We went to the park <u>to took</u> a walk. → _____

4 <u>This</u> is not difficult to make friends. → _____

5 His hope is <u>to studies</u> in Germany. → _____

6 I'm glad <u>to meets</u> you again. → _____

7 I'm looking for someone <u>teach</u> me. → _____

8 His grandfather lived <u>to was</u> eighty. → _____

9 I want <u>to help</u> Eric with his work. → _____

C 다음 문장을 괄호 안의 지시대로 바꿔 쓰시오.

1 Henry decided to take a taxi. (to부정사를 부정하여)
→ Henry _____ .

2 Mr. Song chose to go to Tokyo. (to부정사를 부정하여)
→ Mr. Song _____ .

3 They agreed to watch a horror movie. (to부정사를 부정하여)
→ They agreed _____ .

4 To talk loudly in a library is rude. (It으로 시작하는 문장으로)
→ It is _____ .

5 Tim will climb the mountain. It is his plan. (to부정사를 이용하여 한 문장으로)
→ Tim's plan is _____ .

6 She sells concert tickets. It is her job. (to부정사를 이용하여 한 문장으로)
→ Her job is _____ .

7 Daniel will visit his grandparents. He promises. (to부정사를 이용하여 한 문장으로)
→ Daniel promises _____ .

8 Kate will stay in Singapore for two months. That is her plan. (to부정사를 이용하여 한 문장으로)
→ Kate plans _____ .

도표이해

A Julie의 계획을 보고, 문장을 완성하시오.

Thur.	go camping
Fri.	practice soccer
Sat.	watch a movie
Sun.	meet Mike at the library

1 Julie plans _____ on Thursday.

2 Julie wants _____ on Friday.

3 Julie wants _____ on Saturday.

4 Julie plans _____ on Sunday.

영작완성

B 우리말과 일치하도록 괄호 안의 말을 바르게 배열하여 문장을 쓰시오.

1 나는 이번 겨울에 프랑스어를 배우고 싶다. (I, to, want, French, learn, this winter)

→ _____

2 제가 마실 것 좀 얻을 수 있을까요? (I, can, to, have, drink, something)

→ _____

3 그는 개를 산책시키기 위해 공원에 갔다. (he, his dog, to, went, walk, to the park)

→ _____

4 마라톤을 뛰는 것은 정말 힘들다. (to, is, it, in the marathon, run, hard, very)

→ _____

문장영작

C 우리말과 일치하도록 괄호 안의 말을 이용하여 영작하시오.

1 나는 의사가 되기를 바란다. (hope, become)

→ _____

2 Ann은 내 생일 파티에 오기로 약속했다. (promise, come, to my birthday party)

→ _____

3 Mike는 그의 스마트폰을 게임하기 위해 사용한다. (use, play, games)

→ _____

4 Tony는 기차에서 읽을 책 한 권이 필요하다. (need, read, on the train)

→ _____

5 깊은 강에서 수영하는 것은 위험하다. (it, swim, in a deep river)

→ _____

[1-3] 빈칸에 들어갈 말로 알맞은 것을 고르시오.

1

Mina wants _____ home.

① go   ② goes   ③ went
④ to go   ⑤ to goes

2

_____ is exciting to watch football games.

① It   ② This   ③ That
④ What   ⑤ They

3

Kate chose her clothes _____ for the party.

① wear   ② wears   ③ wore
④ to wear   ⑤ to wore

4 ①~⑤ 중 not이 들어갈 위치로 알맞은 곳은?

Jimmy (①) promised (②) to (③) fight
(④) again (⑤).

5 빈칸에 알맞은 말이 순서대로 짝 지어진 것은?

• I'm glad _____ you again.
• He lived _____ 80 years old.

① met – was   ② met – to be
③ meet – be   ④ to meet – be
⑤ to meet – to be

[6-7] 밑줄 친 부분의 쓰임이 보기와 같은 것을 고르시오.

6

보기 My plan is to travel to Jeju-do.

① I'm sorry to hear that.
② I don't have any food to eat.
③ Do you have anything to read?
④ Tommy got up early to watch TV.
⑤ My dream is to be a movie star.

7

보기 My sister went to America to study.

① Mina has nothing to do tonight.
② My brother likes to read books.
③ Tony wants to eat chocolate cookies.
④ I drink a lot of water to stay healthy.
⑤ They need some money to buy food.

8 우리말과 일치하도록 할 때 빈칸에 들어갈 말로 알맞은 것은?

> 자전거를 고치는 것은 힘들다.
> → It is hard _____ a bike.

① fix   ② fixes   ③ fixed
④ to fix   ⑤ to fixes

9 우리말을 영어로 바르게 옮긴 것은?

> 나는 택시를 탈 돈이 없다.

① I have money not to take a taxi.
② I have money to not take a taxi.
③ I don't have to take a taxi money.
④ I don't have a taxi to take money.
⑤ I don't have money to take a taxi.

10 우리말과 일치하도록 빈칸에 들어갈 말로 알맞은 것은?

> 나는 Steve의 편지를 받고 기뻤다.
> = I was _____ Steve's letter.

① happy get to   ② happy to get
③ happy to got   ④ to get happy
⑤ getting happy

11 우리말과 일치하도록 주어진 말을 배열할 때, 네 번째로 오는 단어는?

> 친구를 사귀는 것은 재미있다.
> (to, it, is, make, fun, friends)

① it   ② is   ③ to
④ fun   ⑤ make

12 우리말을 영어로 잘못 옮긴 것은?

① 그는 그녀를 다시 만나기를 원한다.
   → He wants to meet her again.
② 그는 늦지 않기로 약속했다.
   → He promised not to be late.
③ 나는 당신과 함께 일해서 기쁘다.
   → I'm happy to work with you.
④ 비행기를 날리는 것은 쉽지 않다.
   → It is not easy to fly a plane.
⑤ 내 바람은 그 경기를 이기는 것이다.
   → My hope is win the game.

13 다음 두 문장을 to부정사를 이용하여 한 문장으로 바르게 쓴 것은?

> • Sumin will take a walk in the morning.
> • Sumin promises.

① It is promise to take a walk in the morning.
② Sumin is to promise take a walk in the morning.
③ Sumin promises to take a walk in the morning.
④ Sumin promises take to a walk in the morning.
⑤ Sumin promised to take a walk in the morning.

[14-15] 어법상 틀린 부분을 바르게 고친 것을 고르시오.

14

> To see are to believe.

① To → Too
② To see → See to
③ see → saw
④ are → is
⑤ to believe → believe

15

> This is important to save energy.

① This → It
② is → are
③ important → importance
④ to → too
⑤ save → saves

[16-17] 어법상 틀린 문장을 고르시오.

16 ① She plans to sell her old house.
　② I hope to buy a toy car for him.
　③ Robert wants study in the library.
　④ We need to work on the weekend.
　⑤ They decided not to have any fast food.

17 ① I came here to see you.
　② She ran to catches the train.
　③ He went home to have dinner.
　④ I study hard to get good grades.
　⑤ I'm saving money to buy a T-shirt.

18 밑줄 친 부분이 어법상 틀린 문장의 개수는?

> ⓐ I want to eat some nuts now.
> ⓑ Where do you want to eat?
> ⓒ I waited for an hour to eat bulgogi.
> ⓓ Her plan is to eat pizza for dinner.
> ⓔ He needs something to eat.

① 0개　　② 1개　　③ 2개
④ 3개　　⑤ 4개

19 밑줄 친 ①~⑤ 중 어법상 틀린 것은?

> I ①decided to give a birthday party for my mom. I needed someone ②to helps me. My little brother ③helped me. I ④made a cake with him. It was a surprise party. My mom was happy ⑤to see the cake.

20 어법상 올바른 문장의 개수는?

> ⓐ He got up early to exercise.
> ⓑ They went out to took a walk.
> ⓒ I use my smartphone to play chess.
> ⓓ They ran fast not to are late.

① 0개　　② 1개　　③ 2개
④ 3개　　⑤ 4개

21 주말에 수민이가 하고 싶은 일을 적은 다음 목록을 보고, 괄호 안의 동사를 활용하여 문장을 완성하시오.

> (1) watch an art movie
> (2) borrow a book from the library
> (3) play tennis with Mina

(1) Sumin _____ .
　　(want)

(2) Sumin _____ .
　　(plan)

(3) Sumin _____ .
　　(hope)

22 주어진 문장과 의미가 같도록 가주어 It을 사용하여 문장을 바꿔 쓰시오.

(1) To finish the project today is not easy.

　　→ _____

(2) To study English is very important.

　　→ _____

23 우리말과 일치하도록 to부정사를 이용하여 문장을 완성하시오.

(1) 나는 숙제를 할 시간이 필요하다.

　　→ I need _____ my homework.

(2) 나는 할 숙제가 많이 있다.

　　→ I have a lot of _____ .

24 그림을 보고, 보기 와 같이 to부정사를 사용하여 문장을 완성하시오.

> 보기 Sue went to the park to meet her friend.

(1) Tim went to the park _____

(2) Jack went to the park _____ .

고난도
25 우리말과 일치하도록 괄호 안의 말을 이용하여 조건 에 맞게 영작하시오.

> 조건 1. to부정사를 사용할 것
> 　　　 2. 현재시제로 쓸 것

(1) 내 계획은 노란색 튤립을 기르는 것이다.
　　(grow, yellow tulips)

　　→ _____

(2) Kevin은 그의 조부모님을 방문하기를 원한다.
　　(visit, his grandparents)

　　→ _____

(3) Cindy는 마실 무언가가 필요하다.
　　(something, drink)

　　→ _____

(4) 나는 그 소식을 들어서 기쁘다. (hear, the news)

　　→ _____

9 동명사

동명사는 동사원형에 -ing를 붙여 동사를 명사처럼 만든 것이다.
동명사는 문장 안에서 명사와 같은 역할을 한다.

동명사의 형태와 쓰임

동명사는 「동사원형＋-ing」의 형태로, '～하기, ～하는 것'이라는 뜻으로 쓰인다.

	동사원형			동명사	
노래하다	sing	+ -ing	➡	sing**ing**	노래하기
춤추다	dance			danc**ing**	춤추기

주의 come처럼 -e로 끝나는 동사는 e를 빼고 -ing를 붙인다. (→ coming)
lie처럼 -ie로 끝나는 동사는 ie를 y로 고치고 -ing를 붙인다. (→ lying)
shop처럼 「단모음＋단자음」으로 끝나는 동사는 자음을 한 번 더 쓰고 -ing를 붙인다. (→ shopping)

동명사는 문장에서 명사처럼 주어, 보어, 목적어로 쓰인다.

주어	**Swimming**	is always fun.	수영하는 것은 항상 재미있다.
보어	His hobby is	**cooking**.	그의 취미는 요리하는 것이다.
동사의 목적어	Mina enjoys	**watching** TV.	미나는 TV 보는 것을 즐긴다.
전치사의 목적어	He's good at	**riding** a horse.	그는 말 타기를 잘한다.

↳ 동명사는 동사의 성격을 가지고 있어서 뒤에 목적어 등이 올 수 있어요.

주의 주어로 쓰인 동명사(구)는 항상 단수 취급한다.
Drawing pictures *is* not easy. 그림을 그리는 것은 쉽지 않다.

궁금해요!
동명사의 부정은
어떻게 표현해요?

동명사의 부정은
I'm sorry for not coming to your party.와
같이 동명사 앞에 not을 써서 나타내요.

개념확인 동명사 찾기

1 Dancing is good exercise.　　**2** I enjoy riding a bike.　　**3** My hobby is singing songs.

기본연습 **A** 다음 동사를 동명사로 바꿔 쓰시오.

1 run　　→ _____　　**2** go　　→ _____

3 sit　　→ _____　　**4** lie　　→ _____

5 exercise　　→ _____　　**6** play　　→ _____

7 become　　→ _____　　**8** wait　　→ _____

B 괄호 안에서 알맞은 것을 고르시오.

1 They enjoy (go / going) to parties.

2 (Get / Getting) up early is difficult.

3 I'm thinking of (not taking / taking not) this class.

4 Drinking soda (is / are) not good for your health.

5 Playing computer games (was / were) interesting.

C 밑줄 친 동명사의 쓰임으로 알맞은 것을 고르시오.

		주어	보어	동사의 목적어	전치사의 목적어
1	Planning a trip is really fun.	☐	☐	☐	☐
2	Thank you for inviting me.	☐	☐	☐	☐
3	The little girl started crying.	☐	☐	☐	☐
4	Driving in the rain is not easy.	☐	☐	☐	☐
5	Andy's hobby is listening to music.	☐	☐	☐	☐
6	I will finish reading this book soon.	☐	☐	☐	☐
7	She's thinking about living in Canada.	☐	☐	☐	☐
8	My dream is meeting my favorite singer.	☐	☐	☐	☐

D 빈칸에 들어갈 말을 보기 에서 골라 동명사 형태로 바꿔 문장을 완성하시오.

보기	be	eat	study	sing	swim	take	worry	collect

1 _____ songs is a lot of fun.

2 Her hobby is _____ stamps.

3 I'm sorry for _____ late again.

4 Jessica enjoys _____ Korean food.

5 I'm interested in _____ science.

6 I stopped _____ about the math test.

7 _____ pictures of animals is exciting.

8 My favorite activity is _____ in the sea.

틀 리 기 쉬 운
내/신/포/인/트

동명사가 문장에서 주어,
보어, 목적어 중 어떤 역할을
하는지 구별해요.

밑줄 친 부분의 쓰임이 보기 와 같은 것은?

보기 I like meeting new people.

① His hobby is watching movies.
② Studying history is important.
③ Playing table tennis is exciting.
④ They enjoy running in the park.

POINT **2** 동명사를 목적어로 쓰는 동사

다음 동사들은 동명사를 목적어로 쓴다. ★

enjoy 즐기다	Jessica **enjoys singing** songs.	Jessica는 노래 부르는 것을 즐긴다.
finish 끝내다	Ben **finished cleaning** his room.	Ben은 그의 방을 청소하는 것을 끝냈다.
mind 꺼리다	I don't **mind being** alone.	나는 혼자 있는 것을 꺼리지 않는다.
stop 멈추다	Jiwoo **stopped drinking** water.	지우는 물을 마시는 것을 멈췄다.
keep 계속 ~하다	I **kept talking** with my friends.	나는 친구들과 계속 이야기했다.
practice 연습하다	He **practiced skiing** every day.	그는 매일 스키 타는 것을 연습했다.
give up 포기하다, 그만두다	Angela **gave up drinking** coke.	Angela는 콜라를 마시는 것을 그만뒀다.

주의 stop 뒤에 to부정사가 오면 목적을 나타내는 부사적 용법으로, '~하기 위해 멈추다'라는 뜻으로 쓰인다.
Jiwoo **stopped** *to drink* water. 지우는 물을 마시기 위해 멈췄다.

다음 동사들은 동명사와 to부정사 모두를 목적어로 쓴다. ★

| like 좋아하다 | love 사랑하다 | hate 싫어하다 |
| begin 시작하다 | start 시작하다 | continue 계속하다 |

I love **jogging** in the morning. 나는 아침에 조깅하는 것을 정말 좋아한다.
= I love **to jog** in the morning.

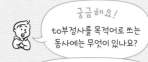

궁금해요!
to부정사를 목적어로 쓰는 동사에는 무엇이 있나요?

want, hope, need, plan, promise 등이 있어요.
Chapter 8의 Point 3을 보세요.

개념확인 동사와 목적어 찾기

1 My brother kept laughing.   **2** Ms. Smith likes swimming.   **3** Do you enjoy dancing?

기본연습 **A** 괄호 안에서 알맞은 것을 고르시오.

1 My dog wants (to play / playing) with me.

2 Do you mind (to open / opening) the window?

3 Kevin hopes (to buy / buying) a new drone.

4 Did you finish (to do / doing) your homework?

5 Junsu gave up (to wait / waiting) for the bus.

6 He practiced (to drive / driving) every day.

7 Emma kept (to play / playing) the piano for an hour.

8 Tim needs (to get up / getting up) early in the morning.

9 They're planning (to paint / painting) the wall at 2 o'clock.

10 My sister and I enjoy (to watch / watching) movies.

B 우리말과 일치하도록 괄호 안의 말을 이용하여 문장을 완성하시오.

1 너는 정원을 청소하는 것을 언제 끝냈니? (finish, clean)

→ When did you _____ the garden?

2 오후 3시에 눈이 내리는 것이 멈췄다. (stop, snow)

→ It _____ at 3 p.m.

3 너는 다른 나라로 여행하는 것을 즐기니? (enjoy, travel)

→ Do you _____ to other countries?

4 유미는 매일 노래하는 것을 연습한다. (practice, sing)

→ Yumi _____ every day.

5 그 여자는 전화로 계속 말했다. (keep, talk)

→ The woman _____ on the phone.

6 그는 오래 기다리는 것을 꺼리지 않는다. (mind, wait)

→ He doesn't _____ long.

7 나는 그 책을 읽는 것을 포기했다. (give up, read)

→ I _____ the book.

C 괄호 안의 말을 이용하여 문장을 완성하시오.

1 I hate _____ to the dentist. (go)

2 Danny will keep _____ Spanish. (learn)

3 Amy wants _____ Chinese well. (speak)

4 Mike finished _____ dinner for his parents. (cook)

5 The students continued _____ about the project. (talk)

6 My family won't stop _____ for our lost dog. (look)

7 Emily loves _____ baseball games on TV. (watch)

8 Sora enjoys _____ her diary in English. (write)

틀/리/기/쉬/운
내/신/포/인/트

목적어로 동명사를 쓰는 동사와
to부정사를 쓰는 동사를
구별해요.

빈칸에 들어갈 말로 알맞지 <u>않은</u> 것은?

My brothers _____ to play badminton.

① began   ② enjoy   ③ like   ④ love

POINT 3 동명사 vs. 진행형

보어로 쓰이는 동명사와 진행형에 쓰이는 「동사원형＋-ing」는 형태가 같으므로 주의한다.

동명사	～하기, ～하는 것	His hobby is **reading** books. 보어 <His hobby = reading books>	그의 취미는 책 읽는 것이다.
진행형	～하고 있다, ～하는 중이다	He is **reading** a book. 현재진행형 <He ≠ reading a book>	그는 책을 읽는 중이다.

개념확인 옳은 해석 고르기

1 I am writing a letter.

☐ 쓰는 것이다 ☐ 쓰는 중이다

2 My job is baking cookies.

☐ 굽는 것이다 ☐ 굽는 중이다

3 They are running away.

☐ 도망치는 것이다 ☐ 도망치는 중이다

기본연습 밑줄 친 부분의 쓰임과 같은 것을 보기 에서 골라 그 기호를 쓰시오.

> 보기 ⓐ Tony stopped eating hamburgers.
> ⓑ The children are singing together.

1 His job is driving a bus. _____

2 My dog is sleeping on the sofa. _____

3 My dream is working in Hong Kong. _____

4 Thank you for helping me with my homework. _____

5 The students are cleaning the classroom. _____

6 Eric and his brother were climbing the mountain. _____

7 My hobby is going to museums. _____

8 Jessy is listening to music in her room. _____

9 We were playing basketball at that time. _____

10 My bad habit is biting my nails. _____

틀 리 기 쉬 운 내/신/포/인/트

「동사원형＋-ing」 형태가
동명사로 쓰일 때와
진행형으로 쓰일 때를
구별해야 해요.

밑줄 친 부분의 쓰임이 나머지와 다른 하나는?

① The baby started crying.
② Her job is taking care of the pandas.
③ His bad habit is being late for school.
④ My father is washing the dishes.

POINT 4 동명사의 관용 표현

go -ing	~하러 가다	We **went fishing** last weekend. 우리는 지난 주말에 낚시하러 갔다.
be busy -ing	~하느라 바쁘다	She **is busy doing** her homework. 그녀는 숙제를 하느라 바쁘다.
feel like -ing	~하고 싶다	I **feel like having** lunch with you. 나는 너와 점심을 먹고 싶다.
be good at -ing	~하는 것을 잘하다	The boys **are good at dancing**. 그 소년들은 춤을 잘 춘다.
be interested in -ing	~하는 것에 관심이 있다	He **is interested in growing** plants. 그는 식물을 키우는 것에 관심이 있다.
spend+시간/돈+-ing	~하는 데 시간/돈을 쓰다	He **spends a lot of time cooking**. 그는 요리하는 데 많은 시간을 쓴다.
How/What about -ing?	~하는 게 어때?	**How about joining** our soccer team? 우리 축구팀에 들어오는 게 어때?

개념확인 옳은 해석 고르기

1 He goes swimming on Sundays.
- ☐ 수영하러 가다
- ☐ 수영하고 싶다

2 How about meeting at 6?
- ☐ 만나러 가다
- ☐ 만나는 게 어때

3 I am busy cleaning my room.
- ☐ 청소하고 싶다
- ☐ 청소하느라 바쁘다

기본연습 우리말과 일치하도록 괄호 안의 말을 이용하여 문장을 완성하시오.

1 하준이는 그 노래를 연습하는 데 일주일을 썼다. (practice)
→ Hajun _____ a week _____ the song.

2 우리 가족은 이번 주말에 캠핑하러 갈 것이다. (camp)
→ My family will _____ _____ this weekend.

3 지금 길을 건너는 게 어때? (cross)
→ _____ _____ _____ the street now?

4 시온이는 새 옷을 사는 데 많은 돈을 쓴다. (buy)
→ Sion _____ a lot of money _____ new clothes.

5 나의 할아버지는 스마트폰을 사용하는 것을 잘하신다. (use)
→ My grandfather _____ _____ _____ his smartphone.

6 주안이는 학교 밴드에 가입하는 것에 관심이 있다. (join)
→ Juan _____ _____ _____ _____ the school band.

개 념 완 성 TEST

정답 및 해설 p.27

STEP 1 Map으로 개념 정리하기

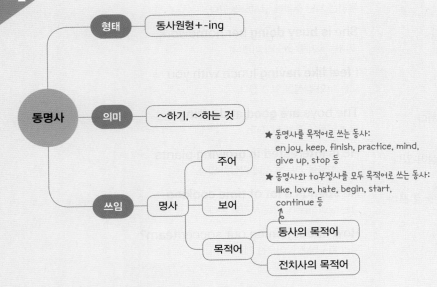

동명사

- 형태 ─ 동사원형+-ing
- 의미 ─ ~하기, ~하는 것
- 쓰임 ─ 명사 ─ 주어
  - 보어
  - 목적어 ─ 동사의 목적어
  - 전치사의 목적어

★ 동명사를 목적어로 쓰는 동사:
enjoy, keep, finish, practice, mind, give up, stop 등
★ 동명사와 to부정사를 모두 목적어로 쓰는 동사:
like, love, hate, begin, start, continue 등

Quick Check

❶ Making cookies (is / are) lots of fun.

❷ I'm thinking of (to make / making) cookies.

❸ I enjoy making cookies.
해석: _____

❹ My hobby is (make / making) cookies.

❺ I am making cookies.
해석: _____

❻ I feel like making cookies.
해석: _____

❼ I am busy making cookies.
해석: _____

STEP 2 기본 다지기

빈칸완성

A 우리말과 일치하도록 빈칸에 알맞은 말을 넣어 문장을 완성하시오.

1 그의 직업은 시를 쓰는 것이다.
→ His job is _____ poems.

2 여행을 계획하는 것은 매우 흥미진진하다.
→ _____ a trip is very exciting.

3 언제 비가 내리는 것이 멈췄나요?
→ When did it stop _____?

4 나는 내 지갑을 찾는 것을 포기했다.
→ I gave up _____ for my wallet.

5 수호는 친구들과 계속 이야기했다.
→ Suho kept _____ with his friends.

6 내 노래를 들어 줘서 고마워.
→ Thank you for _____ to my song.

7 수미는 그녀의 자전거를 수리하느라 바쁘다.
→ Sumi is busy _____ her bicycle.

8 나는 밤에 일하는 것을 꺼리지 않는다.
→ I don't mind _____ at night.

9 나는 수학을 공부하는 데 많은 시간을 쓴다.
→ I spend a lot of time _____ math.

10 준호는 차로 여행하는 것에 관심이 있다.
→ Junho is interested in _____ by car.

11 유주는 그녀의 방에서 자는 중이다.
→ Yujoo _____ in her room.

B 밑줄 친 부분이 어법상 바르면 ○라고 쓰고, 틀리면 바르게 고쳐 쓰시오.

1 I don't feel like <u>to meet</u> her today. → _____

2 Daniel hopes <u>passing</u> the exam. → _____

3 They were <u>play</u> baseball at that time. → _____

4 Climbing mountains <u>are</u> very difficult. → _____

5 How about <u>go</u> to the park after school? → _____

6 My sister enjoys <u>to take</u> the French class. → _____

7 My grandfather went <u>swimming</u> in the river. → _____

C 다음 문장을 괄호 안의 지시대로 바꿔 쓰시오.

1 Tina likes to go to the zoo in summer. (동사의 목적어를 동명사로)

→ _____

2 Harry loves to listen to K-pop music. (동사의 목적어를 동명사로)

→ _____

3 Jessy watched a sci-fi movie. She enjoyed it. (한 문장으로)

→ _____

4 Mike plays the piano. He practices every day. (한 문장으로)

→ _____

5 Jack read the book last night. He finished it. (한 문장으로)

→ _____

6 Sarah is busy. She is washing her dog. (한 문장으로)

→ _____

7 I draw flowers. I'm good at it. (한 문장으로)

→ _____

8 It is difficult to choose a gift. (주어를 동명사로)

→ _____

9 It is expensive to heat a big house. (주어를 동명사로)

→ _____

STEP 3 서술형 따라잡기

그림이해

A 그림을 보고, 괄호 안의 말을 이용하여 문장을 완성하시오.

1

2

3

1 Bob _____ with his friends. (enjoy, dance)

2 Kate should _____ her salad. (finish, eat)

3 Roy _____ the plants. (busy, water)

영작완성

B 우리말과 일치하도록 괄호 안의 말을 바르게 배열하여 문장을 쓰시오.

1 그의 직업은 택시를 운전하는 것이다. (driving, his job, a taxi, is)

→ _____

2 그들은 버스를 기다리는 것을 포기했다. (gave up, they, the bus, waiting for)

→ _____

3 바다에서 수영하는 것은 쉽지 않다. (not, swimming, is, in the sea, easy)

→ _____

4 지나와 나는 공원에서 농구를 하고 있었다. (in the park, were, basketball, Jina and I, playing)

→ _____

문장영작

C 우리말과 일치하도록 괄호 안의 말을 이용하여 영작하시오.

1 나는 피아노 치는 것에 관심이 있다. (interested, play, the piano)

→ _____

2 우리 어머니는 사진 찍는 것을 연습하신다. (practice, take, pictures)

→ _____

3 Ben은 그의 정원에서 일하는 데 시간을 보냈다. (spend, work, in his garden)

→ _____

4 너는 지난 주말에 친구들과 스키 타러 갔니? (ski, with your friends)

→ _____

[1-2] 빈칸에 들어갈 말로 알맞은 것을 고르시오.

1

_____ in snow is dangerous.

① Drive ② Drives ③ Drove
④ To driving ⑤ Driving

2

Rena's job is _____ computer games.

① invent ② invents ③ invented
④ inventing ⑤ to invented

3 빈칸에 들어갈 말로 알맞지 <u>않은</u> 것은?

Nancy _____ reading comic books.

① keeps ② enjoys ③ hates
④ likes ⑤ wants

4 빈칸에 공통으로 들어갈 말로 알맞은 것은?

· Tony finished _____ the dishes.
· Ms. Green is busy _____ her car.

① wash ② washes ③ washed
④ washing ⑤ to wash

5 밑줄 친 부분이 어법상 올바른 것은?

① It started <u>to rain</u> heavily.
② He is <u>send</u> a text message.
③ How about <u>to raise</u> a dog?
④ The baby suddenly stopped <u>to cry</u>.
⑤ Alice is thinking of <u>to eat</u> lunch.

[6-7] 밑줄 친 부분의 쓰임이 나머지와 <u>다른</u> 하나를 고르시오.

6 ① She finished <u>taking</u> a shower.
② My sister and I love <u>watching</u> TV.
③ Allen enjoys <u>swimming</u> in the pool.
④ He practices <u>speaking</u> English every day.
⑤ My favorite activity is <u>climbing</u> mountains.

7 ① <u>Baking</u> cookies is her hobby.
② She's <u>watching</u> a soccer game.
③ He's thinking of <u>buying</u> a new car.
④ Do you mind <u>opening</u> the window?
⑤ My dad is interested in <u>running</u> a marathon.

8 빈칸에 알맞은 말이 순서대로 짝 지어진 것은?

> • Jiho is good at _____ soccer.
> • Do you mind _____ for me?

① play – wait
② playing – to wait
③ play – waiting
④ playing – waiting
⑤ to play – to wait

9 밑줄 친 부분의 쓰임이 보기 와 같은 것은?

> 보기 She loves playing the guitar.

① John is reading a book.
② My sister was sleeping.
③ His job is teaching science.
④ We were running in the park.
⑤ David is not listening to the radio.

10 우리말을 영어로 바르게 옮긴 것은?

> 우리는 그 문제에 대해 계속 이야기할 것이다.

① We keep talk about the problem.
② We keep to talk about the problem.
③ We kept talking about the problem.
④ We will keep talking about the problem.
⑤ We will keep to talk about the problem.

11 밑줄 친 부분을 어법상 바르게 고친 것은?

> Tom left without say goodbye.

① says ② said ③ saying
④ to say ⑤ to saying

12 밑줄 친 부분이 어법상 틀린 문장의 개수는?

> ⓐ Cooking is always fun.
> ⓑ I feel like going out for lunch.
> ⓒ Ben began to read the letter.
> ⓓ Making friends is easy.

① 0개 ② 1개 ③ 2개
④ 3개 ⑤ 4개

13 밑줄 친 부분이 어법상 올바른 것을 모두 고르면?

① I'm sorry for be late again.
② Winning the game is my goal.
③ He doesn't mind to eat alone.
④ My sister hates to get up early.
⑤ Harry hopes meeting his old friend.

14 빈칸에 riding을 쓸 수 없는 것은?

① How about _____ a bike?
② Wendy is _____ a bike now.
③ My hobby is _____ a horse.
④ Kathy wants _____ a roller coaster.
⑤ Julie enjoys _____ a bicycle in the park.

15 우리말과 일치하도록 빈칸에 들어갈 말로 알맞은 것은?

> Owen은 그 표지판을 보기 위해 멈췄다.
> → Owen stopped _____ the sign.

① see ② sees ③ saw
④ seeing ⑤ to see

16 어법상 <u>틀린</u> 부분을 바르게 고친 것은?

> Getting good grades are her goal.

① Getting → Get
② Getting → To get
③ grades → grade
④ are → is
⑤ goal → goals

17 영어를 우리말로 <u>잘못</u> 옮긴 것은?

① Minha is good at playing soccer.
   → 민하는 축구를 잘한다.
② She felt like going to bed early.
   → 그녀는 일찍 잠자리에 드는 것을 좋아했다.
③ Jiwoo is interested in writing novels.
   → 지우는 소설을 쓰는 데 관심이 있다.
④ How about going for a walk?
   → 산책하러 가는 게 어때?
⑤ I spent two hours cooking dinner.
   → 나는 저녁을 요리하는 데 두 시간을 썼다.

18 대화의 빈칸에 알맞은 말이 순서대로 짝 지어진 것은?

> **A:** Did you finish _____ your homework last night?
> **B:** No. I was busy _____ my mom.

① do – help ② doing – help
③ doing – helping ④ to do – helping
⑤ to do – to help

19 빈칸 (A)~(C)에 들어갈 말이 바르게 짝 지어진 것은?

> • Kate gave up ___(A)___ Chinese.
> • Bill continued ___(B)___ his dog.
> • My sister practices ___(C)___ pop songs.

	(A)	(B)	(C)
①	learn	– look for	– sing
②	learn	– looking for	– singing
③	learning	– looking for	– singing
④	learning	– to look for	– to sing
⑤	to learn	– to look for	– to sing

20 어법상 올바른 문장의 개수는?

> ⓐ Thank you for come to my party.
> ⓑ Reading many books is helpful.
> ⓒ You need eating healthy food.
> ⓓ What about meeting at 6 o'clock?
> ⓔ I enjoy to meet people.

① 0개 ② 1개 ③ 2개
④ 3개 ⑤ 4개

21 어법상 틀린 부분을 찾아 바르게 고쳐 쓰시오.

(1)
> Mike didn't give up to travel by bike.

_____ → _____

(2)
> Making good friends are important.

_____ → _____

22 우리말과 일치하도록 괄호 안의 말을 이용하여 문장을 완성하시오.

(1) 지호는 뛰는 것을 멈췄고 물을 조금 마셨다.
(stop, run)

→ Jiho _____
and drank some water.

(2) Sophie는 벤치에 앉고 싶었다. (feel, sit)

→ Sophie _____
on the bench.

23 우리말과 일치하도록 괄호 안의 말을 이용하여 문장을 쓰시오.

> Jacob is from Canada. (1)그는 춤추는 것을 잘한다. (2)그는 K-pop 듣는 것을 즐긴다. (3)그는 지난주에 한국어를 배우기 시작했다.

(1) (good, dance)

→ He _____.

(2) (enjoy, listen to)

→ He _____.

(3) (begin, learn)

→ He _____
last week.

24 그림을 보고, 조건 에 맞게 대화를 완성하시오.

> 조건 mind, open, take off를 이용할 것

Bora: Do you (1) _____ _____ the window? It's very hot.

Tony: Sorry. It's raining outside. How about (2) _____ _____ your jacket?

Bora: Okay.

고난도
25 각 학생들이 지난 주말에 한 일에 관한 표를 보고, 괄호 안의 말을 이용하여 문장을 완성하시오.

Danny	played the guitar
Bomi	fished in the river
Sora	did her homework
Jessy	made model planes

(1) Danny _____
last weekend. (practice)

(2) Bomi _____
last weekend. (enjoy)

(3) Sora _____
last weekend. (busy)

(4) Jessy _____ last weekend _____
_____. (spend)

CHAPTER

10

문장의 종류

평서문과 의문문 이외에도 특정한 의도를 나타내는 명령문, 제안문, 감탄문 등 다양한 종류의 문장이 있다.

POINT 1 명령문

명령문은 상대방에게 명령이나 요청할 때 사용하며, <u>주어 없이 동사원형으로 시작한다.</u>
부정 명령문은 동사원형 앞에 **Don't**를 붙인다.

긍정	**동사원형 ~.** (~해라)	**Open** the window.	창문을 열어라.
		Be quiet.	조용히 해라.
부정	**Don't+동사원형 ~.** (~하지 마라)	**Don't open** the door.	문을 열지 마라.
		Don't be late again.	다시는 늦지 마라.

↪ am, are, is는 원형인 be로 써요.

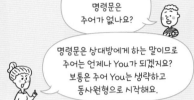

> 궁금해요!
> 명령문은 주어가 없나요?
>
> 명령문은 상대방에게 하는 말이므로 주어는 언제나 You가 되겠지요? 보통은 주어 You는 생략하고 동사원형으로 시작해요.

Tips 명령문의 앞이나 뒤에 please를 붙이면 좀 더 공손한 표현이 된다.
Please close the door. (= Close the door, **please**.) 문을 닫아 주세요.

개념확인 동사 찾기

1 Be kind to your friends.　　**2** Come here tomorrow.　　**3** Wash your hands, please.

기본연습 **A** 괄호 안에서 알맞은 것을 고르시오.

1 (Do / Be) nice to your parents.　　**2** Don't (talk / talking) during the test.

3 Please (sit / sat) in this chair.　　**4** (Open / To open) your book, please.

5 The coffee is very hot. (Be / Is) careful.　　**6** Jim is okay. (Not / Don't) be sad for him.

7 (Don't / Doesn't) use your phone too much.　　**8** I will help you. (Don't / Don't be) afraid.

B 우리말과 일치하도록 괄호 안의 말을 이용하여 문장을 완성하시오.

1 도서관에서 조용히 해라. (quiet)　　→ _____ _____ in the library.

2 이 호수에서 수영하지 마라. (swim)　　→ _____ _____ in this lake.

3 빨간불일 때 길을 건너지 마라. (cross)　　→ _____ _____ the road at a red light.

4 학교에 늦지 마라. (late)　　→ _____ _____ _____ for school.

틀 리 기 쉬 운
내/신/포/인/트

긍정 명령문과 부정 명령문의 형태를 기억해요.

우리말과 일치하도록 빈칸에 들어갈 말로 알맞은 것은?

눈을 감지 마라.
→ _____ close your eyes.

① Be　　② Not　　③ Don't　　④ Doesn't

POINT **2** 제안문

Let's ~.는 상대방에게 제안할 때 사용하며, 뒤에 동사원형이 온다. 부정 제안문은 Let's 뒤에 not을 쓴다.

긍정	Let's+동사원형 ~. (~하자)	**Let's watch** a movie.	영화를 보자.
		Let's play badminton.	배드민턴을 치자.
부정	Let's not+동사원형 ~. (~하지 말자)	**Let's not eat** lunch.	점심을 먹지 말자.
		Let's not waste time.	시간을 낭비하지 말자.

주의 Let's ~.에 대한 긍정의 대답은 Yes, let's./Okay./All right./Sure. 등으로 하고, 부정의 대답은 No, let's not./I'm sorry, but I can't. 등으로 한다.
A: **Let's eat** dinner. 저녁을 먹자.
B: **Yes, let's. / No, let's not.** 그래, 그러자. / 아니, 그러지 말자.

개념확인 옳은 해석 고르기

1 Let's go outside.
☐ 가라 ☐ 가자

2 Let's eat some apples.
☐ 먹어라 ☐ 먹자

3 Let's not order hamburgers.
☐ 주문하지 마라 ☐ 주문하지 말자

기본연습 A 괄호 안에서 알맞은 것을 고르시오.

1 Don't give up. (Let / Let's) try again.

2 Let's (do / be) quiet in the movie theater.

3 It's too hot. Let's (drink / drinks) some water.

4 It's very cold outside. Let's (not / don't) go out.

5 It smells bad. Let's (not eat / eat not) this food.

6 It's beginning to rain. Let's (walk / walking) fast.

7 A: Let's visit the art museum this Saturday.　　B: No, (let's / let's not). I have other plans.

8 A: Let's watch the soccer game on TV.　　B: Yes, (let's / let's not) watch it.

B 우리말과 일치하도록 괄호 안의 말을 이용하여 문장을 완성하시오.

1 정직해지자. (be)　　→ _____ _____ honest.

2 오늘 밤에 파티를 하자. (have)　　→ _____ _____ a party tonight.

3 그 TV를 사지 말자. (buy)　　→ _____ _____ _____ the TV.

4 오늘 동물원에 가지 말자. (go)　　→ _____ _____ _____ to the zoo today.

POINT 3 감탄문

감탄문은 '정말 ~하구나!'라는 의미로 기쁨, 놀람, 슬픔 등의 감정을 표현하는 문장으로, What 또는 How로 시작한다.

| What 감탄문 | **What** | (a/an) | 형용사 | 명사 | (주어+동사)! | 명사를 강조해요. |
| How 감탄문 | **How** | | | 형용사/부사 | | (주어+동사)! | 형용사나 부사를 강조해요. |

What a beautiful flower (it is)! (그것은) 정말 예쁜 꽃이구나!
(← It is a very beautiful flower.)
How exciting (the game is)! (그 경기는) 정말 흥미진진하구나!
(← The game is very exciting.)

Tips 감탄문의 주어와 동사는 생략하여 쓰는 경우가 많다.
What a nice car! 정말 멋진 차구나!
How cute! 정말 귀엽구나!

주의 What 감탄문에서 명사가 복수형이거나 셀 수 없는 명사이면 a/an을 쓰지 않는다.
What smart **students** they are! 그들은 정말 똑똑한 학생들이구나!

주의 의문문의 어순과 헷갈리지 않도록 주의한다.
How long the bridge is! 〈감탄문〉 그 다리는 정말 길구나!
How long is the bridge? 〈의문문〉 그 다리는 얼마나 기니?

개념확인 강조하는 말 찾기

1 What a beautiful day!   **2** What cute birds!   **3** How terrible!

기본연습 **A** 빈칸에 What 또는 How를 써서 감탄문을 완성하시오.

1 _____ pretty bugs they are!

2 _____ slow the snail moves!

3 _____ cute this doll is!

4 _____ a great actor he is!

5 _____ sweet this chocolate cake is!

6 _____ expensive the smartphone was!

7 _____ sharp teeth the snake has!

8 _____ sad the movie was!

9 _____ an interesting book!

B 다음 문장을 감탄문으로 바꿀 때 빈칸에 알맞은 말을 쓰시오.

1 The light is so bright.　→　_____ _____ the light is!

2 The horse is running very fast.　→　_____ _____ the horse is running!

3 She finished her meal very quickly.　→　_____ _____ she finished her meal!

4 The old man has really big feet.　→　_____ _____ _____ the old man has!

5 That is a really huge whale.　→　_____ _____ _____ _____ that is!

6 That idea is great.　→　_____ _____ _____ idea!

C 우리말과 일치하도록 괄호 안의 말을 이용하여 문장을 완성하시오.

1 그는 정말 똑똑하구나! (clever)

→ _____ _____ he is!

2 이 스웨터는 정말 따뜻하구나! (warm)

→ _____ _____ this sweater is!

3 그 학생들은 정말 열심히 공부하고 있구나! (hard)

→ _____ _____ the students are studying!

4 그녀는 정말 그림을 잘 그리는구나! (well)

→ _____ _____ she paints!

5 이것은 정말 재미있는 소설이구나! (interesting, novel)

→ _____ _____ _____ _____ this is!

6 그것은 정말 흥미진진한 쇼이구나! (exciting, show)

→ _____ _____ _____ _____ it is!

7 정말 예쁜 꽃들이구나! (lovely, flowers)

→ _____ _____ _____ !

틀리기 쉬운
내/신/포/인/트

명사를 강조하려면
What 감탄문을 쓰고,
형용사나 부사를 강조하려면
How 감탄문을 써요.

다음 문장을 감탄문으로 바꿀 때 빈칸에 알맞은 것은?

These are very pretty dolls.
→ _____ pretty dolls these are!

① Which　　② Why　　③ How　　④ What

POINT 4 부가의문문

부가의문문은 평서문 뒤에 덧붙이는 의문문으로, '그렇지?' 또는 '그렇지 않니?'라는 의미로 상대방에게 확인이나 동의를 구할 때 쓴다.

부정의 부가의문문은 줄임말로 써요.

| This book | is | fun, | **isn't** | **it?** | 이 책은 재미있어, 그렇지 않니? |

— ①, ② —
— ③ —

① 긍정문 뒤에는 부정의 부가의문문, 부정문 뒤에는 긍정의 부가의문문을 쓴다.
② 앞에 나온 동사가 be동사와 조동사이면 그대로 사용하고, 일반동사이면 do/does/did를 사용한다. 시제는 앞 문장과 일치시킨다.
③ 앞 문장의 주어는 대명사로 바꿔 쓴다.

Jenny **can't** swim, **can she**? Jenny는 수영을 못 해, 그렇지?
Alex and Tom **cleaned** the room, **didn't they**? Alex와 Tom은 그 방을 청소했어, 그렇지 않니?

부가의문문에 대한 대답은 대답하는 내용이 긍정이면 Yes로, 부정이면 No로 답한다.

A: You didn't do your homework, **did you**? 너는 네 숙제를 하지 않았어, 그렇지?

B: **Yes, I did.** (숙제를 했음) / **No, I didn't.** (숙제를 하지 않았음)

Tips 앞 문장이 긍정이든 부정이든 상관없이 명령문의 부가의문문은 will you?로 쓰고, 제안문의 부가의문문은 shall we?로 쓴다.
Close the window, **will you**? 〈명령문〉 창문을 닫아라, 그래 줄래?
Let's turn on the TV, **shall we**? 〈제안문〉 TV를 켜자, 그럴래?

개념확인 부가의문문 찾기

1 He is a singer, isn't he?   **2** You can't come, can you?   **3** Amy cried, didn't she?

기본연습 **A** 괄호 안에서 알맞은 것을 고르시오.

1 The weather is nice, (is / isn't) it?

2 Hold this rope tight, (do / will) you?

3 Martin has two dogs, (does / doesn't) he?

4 Let's go to the beach tomorrow, (shall / let's) we?

5 Martha couldn't go to school, (could / couldn't) she?

6 The boys were not playing soccer, (are / were) they?

B 빈칸에 알맞은 부가의문문을 쓰시오.

1 Your aunt lives in London, _____ _____?

2 She will go with you, _____ _____?

3 You couldn't help me, _____ _____?

4 Mr. White is your English teacher, _____ _____?

5 You won't be late for school, _____ _____?

6 You didn't forget his birthday, _____ _____?

7 Jessie and Tom are riding their bikes, _____ _____?

8 James doesn't have class today, _____ _____?

9 This smartphone is too expensive, _____ _____?

10 Let's have lunch at the restaurant, _____ _____?

11 He washed his car this morning, _____ _____?

C 보기 와 같이 질문에 대한 대답이 괄호 안의 내용과 일치하도록 빈칸에 쓰시오.

> 보기 A: It's raining, isn't it?
> B: <u>No, it isn't</u>. (It isn't raining.)

1 A: Penguins can't fly, can they?

  B: _____, _____ _____. (They can't fly.)

2 A: You know my name, don't you?

  B: _____, _____ _____. (I know your name.)

3 A: This umbrella is yours, isn't it?

  B: _____, _____ _____. (It isn't my umbrella.)

4 A: Your sister doesn't like pizza, does she?

  B: _____, _____ _____. (She likes pizza.)

5 A: The math exam wasn't easy, was it?

  B: _____, _____ _____. (It wasn't easy.)

6 A: He fixed the machine, didn't he?

  B: _____, _____ _____. (He fixed the machine.)

틀리기 쉬운 내/신/포/인/트

앞 문장의 동사의 종류와 시제에 따라 부가의문문의 동사가 달라짐에 주의해요.

빈칸에 공통으로 들어갈 말로 알맞은 것은?

• She didn't cut my hair, _____ she?
• He didn't watch the movie, _____ he?

① does   ② doesn't   ③ did   ④ didn't

POINT **5** There is/are ~

There is/are ~.는 '~이 있다'라는 뜻으로, 뒤에 오는 명사가 주어이다. There is 뒤에는 단수 명사나 셀 수 없는 명사가 오고, There are 뒤에는 복수 명사가 온다.

There is	+단수 명사	~이 있다	There	is	an orange	on the plate.	접시 위에 오렌지가 하나 **있다.**
	+셀 수 없는 명사		There	is	some milk	in the cup.	컵 안에 우유가 조금 **있다.**
There are	+복수 명사		There	are	two apples	on the table.	식탁 위에 사과가 두 개 **있다.**

부정문은 There is/are not ~.으로 쓰고, '~이 없다'라는 뜻이다.

| There | is | not | much tea in the pot. | 주전자에 차가 많이 **없다.** |
| There | are | not | many stars in the sky. | 하늘에 별이 많이 **없다.** |

의문문은 Is/Are there ~?로 쓰고, '~이 있니?'라는 뜻이다.

A: **Is there** any water in the glass? 컵 안에 물이 있니?
B: Yes, there is. / No, there isn't. 응, 있어. / 아니, 없어.

주의 there는 장소나 방향을 나타내어 '거기에, 저기에'라는 뜻으로도 쓰인다.
They stayed **there** for seven days. 그들은 거기에 7일 동안 머물렀다.

Tips There is는 There's로, There are는 There're로 줄여 쓸 수 있다.

궁금해요!
'~이 있었다'는 어떻게 써요?

There was/were ~.와 같이 be동사를 과거형으로 쓰세요.

 주어 찾기

1 There is a cat on the bed.　　2 There are two ducks on the river.　　3 There is dust everywhere.

기본연습 A 괄호 안에서 알맞은 것을 고르시오.

1 (There is / There are / Is there) a fly in my soup.

2 (There isn't / There aren't / Are there) any water in this bottle.

3 (There was / There were / Was there) three cats on the roof.

4 (There is / There are / Are there) two birds in the tree.

5 (There are / Is there / Are there) a bus stop near here?

6 (There is / There are / Were there) many books in the library.

7 (There wasn't / There weren't / Was there) any candles on the cake.

8 (Is there / Are there / Was there) any apples in the fridge?

9 (Is there / Are there / Were there) a meeting today?

10 (There is / There was / There were) lots of flowers in the garden.

B 우리말과 일치하도록 괄호 안의 말을 바르게 배열하시오.

1 교실에는 학생들이 없다. (aren't, there, any, students)

→ _____ in the classroom.

2 접시 위에 치즈가 조금 있다. (cheese, is, there, some)

→ _____ on the plate.

3 일 년에는 열두 달이 있다. (months, are, there, twelve)

→ _____ in a year.

4 이 동물원에 기린이 있나요? (a, giraffe, is, there)

→ _____ in this zoo?

5 벽에 아름다운 그림 하나가 있었다. (was, beautiful, a, picture, there)

→ _____ on the wall.

6 전에는 공원에 나무가 많지 않았다. (trees, many, there, weren't)

→ _____ in the park before.

C 우리말과 일치하도록 there와 괄호 안의 말을 이용하여 문장을 완성하시오.

1 무지개에는 일곱 가지 색이 있다. (color)

→ _____ in a rainbow.

2 거실에는 큰 텔레비전이 있었다. (a big television)

→ _____ in the living room.

3 내 지갑에는 돈이 없었다. (any money)

→ _____ in my wallet.

4 이 근처에 도서관이 있나요? (a library)

→ _____ near here?

5 선반에 설탕이 있었니? (any sugar)

→ _____ on the shelf?

틀리기 쉬운 내/신/포/인/트

There is/are ~. 문장에서 be동사는 뒤에 오는 명사의 수에 일치시켜야 해요.

빈칸에 알맞은 말이 순서대로 짝 지어진 것은?

- There _____ a lot of food here.
- There _____ 31 days in January.

① is – is   ② is – are   ③ are – is   ④ are – are

개 · 념 · 완 · 성 T E S T

정답 및 해설 p.30

STEP 1 Map으로 개념 정리하기

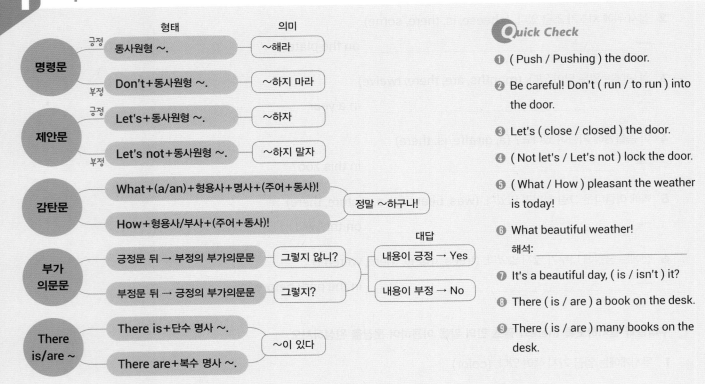

Quick Check

1 (Push / Pushing) the door.

2 Be careful! Don't (run / to run) into the door.

3 Let's (close / closed) the door.

4 (Not let's / Let's not) lock the door.

5 (What / How) pleasant the weather is today!

6 What beautiful weather!
해석: _____

7 It's a beautiful day, (is / isn't) it?

8 There (is / are) a book on the desk.

9 There (is / are) many books on the desk.

STEP 2 기본 다지기

빈칸완성

A 우리말과 일치하도록 빈칸에 알맞은 말을 넣어 문장을 완성하시오.

1 칼 조심해라. → _____ careful with the knife.

2 그녀는 정말 아름답게 노래하는구나! → _____ beautifully she sings!

3 이것은 정말 멋있는 선글라스구나! → _____ nice sunglasses these are!

4 시험은 내일이야, 그렇지 않니? → The test is tomorrow, _____ _____?

5 선반에 버터가 없다. → _____ _____ any butter on the shelf.

6 그녀는 James를 몰랐어, 그렇지? → She didn't know James, _____ _____?

7 할머니께 편지를 쓰자. → _____ _____ a letter to our grandmother.

8 컴퓨터 게임을 너무 많이 하지 마라. → _____ _____ computer games too much.

9 경기장에 많은 사람들이 있었다. → _____ _____ many people in the stadium.

B 밑줄 친 부분이 어법상 바르면 ○라고 쓰고, 틀리면 바르게 고쳐 쓰시오.

1 How an exciting movie! → _____

2 Let's not think about it too much. → _____

3 There is seven days in a week. → _____

4 Turn off your computer, please. → _____

5 What huge the elephants are! → _____

6 The boy can ride a horse, can't it? → _____

7 Don't fighting with your little brother. → _____

8 Are there a good restaurant near here? → _____

9 Let's have sandwiches for lunch, will we? → _____

C 다음 문장을 괄호 안의 지시대로 바꿔 쓰시오.

1 This building is very tall. (how를 사용한 감탄문으로)

→ _____

2 Your sister has a really beautiful smile. (what을 사용한 감탄문으로)

→ _____

3 You should order a book on the Internet. (명령문으로)

→ _____

4 You can't park your car here. (부정 명령문으로)

→ _____

5 Steve and Lucy are from Canada. (부가의문문이 있는 문장으로)

→ _____

6 It isn't hot in Seoul now. (부가의문문이 있는 문장으로)

→ _____

7 They played basketball last Saturday. (부가의문문이 있는 문장으로)

→ _____

8 A new bookstore is on the first floor. (There is/are ~ 문장으로)

→ _____

STEP 3 서술형 따라잡기

그림이해

A 그림을 보고, 동물의 수와 위치를 설명하는 문장을 완성하시오. (현재시제로 쓸 것)

1

There ＿＿＿＿＿ ＿＿＿＿＿＿ ＿＿＿＿＿ on the sofa.

2

There ＿＿＿＿＿ ＿＿＿＿＿ ＿＿＿＿＿ in the box.

영작완성

B 우리말과 일치하도록 괄호 안의 말을 바르게 배열하여 문장을 쓰시오.

1 너의 코를 만지지 마라. (nose, touch, don't, your)

→ ＿＿＿＿＿＿＿＿＿＿＿＿＿＿＿＿＿＿＿＿＿＿＿＿＿＿＿＿＿

2 길거리 음식에 대해 알아보자. (find out, street food, let's, about)

→ ＿＿＿＿＿＿＿＿＿＿＿＿＿＿＿＿＿＿＿＿＿＿＿＿＿＿＿＿＿

3 정말 좋은 선생님이구나! (teacher, what, nice, a)

→ ＿＿＿＿＿＿＿＿＿＿＿＿＿＿＿＿＿＿＿＿＿＿＿＿＿＿＿＿＿

4 너는 그 박물관을 방문할 거야, 그렇지 않니? (will, you, visit, you, won't, the museum)

→ ＿＿＿＿＿＿＿＿＿＿＿＿＿＿＿＿＿＿＿＿＿＿＿＿＿＿＿＿＿

문장영작

C 우리말과 일치하도록 괄호 안의 말을 이용하여 영작하시오.

1 그 강은 정말 넓구나! (wide, the river)

→ ＿＿＿＿＿＿＿＿＿＿＿＿＿＿＿＿＿＿＿＿＿＿＿＿＿＿＿＿＿

2 이 호수에서 수영하지 말자. (swim, in this lake)

→ ＿＿＿＿＿＿＿＿＿＿＿＿＿＿＿＿＿＿＿＿＿＿＿＿＿＿＿＿＿

3 James는 너를 초대하지 않았어, 그렇지? (invite)

→ ＿＿＿＿＿＿＿＿＿＿＿＿＿＿＿＿＿＿＿＿＿＿＿＿＿＿＿＿＿

4 너의 친구들에게 친절하게 대해라. (nice, to)

→ ＿＿＿＿＿＿＿＿＿＿＿＿＿＿＿＿＿＿＿＿＿＿＿＿＿＿＿＿＿

[1-2] 빈칸에 들어갈 말로 알맞은 것을 고르시오.

1

> Please _____ quiet in the library.

① do ② be ③ is

④ don't ⑤ let's

2

> Sally can speak French, _____ she?

① is ② isn't ③ does

④ can ⑤ can't

3 빈칸에 들어갈 말로 알맞지 않은 것은?

> Is there _____ in the kitchen?

① a potato ② a knife

③ children ④ any bread

⑤ any sugar

4 빈칸에 Let's를 쓸 수 없는 문장은?

① _____ watch a movie.

② _____ swim together.

③ _____ take the subway.

④ _____ turn on the radio.

⑤ _____ careful on the stairs.

5 빈칸에 알맞은 말이 순서대로 짝 지어진 것은?

> • _____ strong the wind is!
>
> • _____ a nice coat this is!

① How – Don't ② What – How

③ How – What ④ What – Let's

⑤ How – Let's

6 대화의 밑줄 친 문장과 전달하는 의미가 같은 것은?

> **A:** You didn't call me, did you?
>
> **B:** No, I didn't.

① I called you.

② I didn't call you.

③ I cannot call you.

④ You called me.

⑤ You didn't call me.

7 짝 지어진 대화가 어색한 것은?

① **A:** Please close the door.

　B: Sure.

② **A:** Let's listen to music.

　B: No, let's not.

③ **A:** Let's go on a picnic.

　B: Yes, let's stay home today.

④ **A:** Is there a piano on the stage?

　B: Yes, there is.

⑤ **A:** He'll come to the party, won't he?

　B: Yes, he will.

8 밑줄 친 there 중 보기 와 쓰임이 같은 것은?

> 보기 There is some milk in the glass.

① Is it cold out there?
② Look at that girl over there.
③ Are there many sheep on the farm?
④ They will get there tomorrow.
⑤ He lived there for thirty years.

9 다음 문장을 감탄문으로 바꿀 때 쓰이지 않는 것은?

> This house has a very beautiful garden.

① has   ② how   ③ a
④ garden   ⑤ beautiful

10 어법상 틀린 부분을 찾아 바르게 고친 것은?

> Let's don't waste our time, shall we?

① Let's → Let   ② don't → not
③ waste → wastes   ④ shall → will
⑤ we → you

11 빈칸에 들어갈 말이 나머지와 다른 하나는?

① _____ cute dolls she has!
② _____ fast the train is going!
③ _____ tall buildings they are!
④ _____ an amazing story it is!
⑤ _____ difficult questions these are!

12 다음 그림을 설명하는 문장으로 틀린 것은?

① There is a balloon in the sky.
② There are two birds on the bench.
③ There are two dogs with a boy.
④ There is not much water in the lake.
⑤ There are two children on the grass.

13 어법상 올바른 문장은?

① Please turns off the light.
② What big the elephant is!
③ Let's have a birthday party.
④ They watched the movie, didn't?
⑤ There is five students in the classroom.

14 빈칸에 들어갈 말이 보기 와 같은 것은?

> 보기 There _____ four members in my
> family.

① Please _____ nice to my guests.
② You were sleeping, _____ you?
③ There _____ a bookstore near here.
④ There _____ some juice in the bottle.
⑤ Jane and Linda aren't sisters, _____ they?

[15-16] 우리말을 영어로 바르게 옮긴 것을 고르시오.

15

그는 파란색 티셔츠를 입고 있어, 그렇지 않니?

① Is he wearing a blue T-shirt?

② He wore a blue T-shirt, didn't he?

③ He didn't wear a blue T-shirt, did he?

④ He isn't wearing a blue T-shirt, is he?

⑤ He is wearing a blue T-shirt, isn't he?

16

정말 재미있는 게임이구나!

① How interesting game!

② How interesting is game!

③ What interesting game!

④ What an interesting game!

⑤ What an interesting game is!

고난도

17 밑줄 친 부분이 어법상 **틀린** 문장의 개수는?

ⓐ What big her eyes are!

ⓑ It's time to sleep, isn't it?

ⓒ Let watch a baseball game.

ⓓ There is some good news for you.

ⓔ Checks the weather first.

① 1개   ② 2개   ③ 3개

④ 4개   ⑤ 5개

18 밑줄 친 부분이 어법상 **틀린** 것은?

① It is very cold, isn't it?

② Don't be angry with me.

③ Let's plays games together.

④ There is a camera in the bag.

⑤ You didn't wash your hands, did you?

고난도

19 어법상 올바른 것끼리 짝 지어진 것은?

ⓐ Don't be afraid now.

ⓑ How a funny photo this is!

ⓒ Close your eyes for a moment.

ⓓ Sarah and Sam remembered her, don't they?

ⓔ Are there any pencils on the desk?

① ⓐ, ⓑ, ⓓ   ② ⓐ, ⓒ, ⓓ

③ ⓐ, ⓒ, ⓔ   ④ ⓑ, ⓒ, ⓔ

⑤ ⓑ, ⓓ, ⓔ

고난도

20 빈칸 (A)~(C)에 들어갈 말이 바르게 짝 지어진 것은?

· Dogs can't see red, ___(A)___ they?

· ___(B)___ nice sunglasses she is wearing!

· There ___(C)___ three eggs on the table.

	(A)	(B)	(C)
①	can	What	are
②	can	How	is
③	can	How	are
④	can't	What	are
⑤	can't	How	is

21 다음 문장을 감탄문으로 바꿔 쓸 때, 빈칸에 알맞은 말을 쓰시오.

(1) Mr. Son is a great player.

→ _____ _____ _____

_____ Mr. Son is!

(2) My mom's cookies are really delicious.

→ _____ _____ my mom's

cookies are!

22 우리말과 일치하도록 괄호 안의 말을 이용하여 문장을 완성하시오.

(1) 냉장고에 사과 다섯 개와 우유 한 병이 있다.

(there, apple, milk)

→ _____

in the refrigerator.

(2) 가게에서 계란 두 개와 오렌지 세 개를 사자.

(buy, egg, orange)

→ _____

in the store.

23 밑줄 친 ①~⑤ 중 어법상 틀린 것을 찾아 바르게 고친 후, 틀린 이유를 쓰시오.

A: ① Look at this little boy.
B: ② How cute he is! He is sleeping, ③ doesn't he?
A: Yes, he is. ④ Please keep your voice down.
B: Sure. ⑤ Let's not wake him up.

→ _____

틀린 이유: _____

24 다음 그림을 보고, 보기 에서 알맞은 말을 골라 동물원 이용 수칙을 설명하는 글을 완성하시오.

보기   shout   throw   bring

Welcome to the zoo!
Please keep the rules in the zoo.
(1) _____ any pets.
(2) _____ trash in the trash can.
(3) _____ at the animals.
Enjoy your visit!

고난도
25 다음 영화 상영 시간표를 보고, 조건 에 맞게 대화를 완성하시오.

Time	Saturday	Sunday
10 a.m.	Snow White	–
12 p.m.	Super Panda	Snow White
2 p.m.	–	Super Panda

조건 제안문, 부가의문문, 감탄문을 포함할 것

A: I'd like to watch the movie, *Super Panda*.
B: OK. (1) _____ _____ it on Sunday.
A: Great. It starts at 2 p.m., (2) _____ _____?
B: Yes, (3) _____.
I'll book the tickets.
A: (4) _____ kind you are! Thanks.
B: You're welcome.

CHAPTER

11 문장의 구조

문장을 이루는 가장 작은 단위는 주어와 동사이며, 동사 뒤에 어떤 문장 요소가
오는지에 따라서 다섯 가지의 문장 형식으로 구분한다.

1형식 문장은 「주어＋동사」만으로 성립되는 문장이다.

주어 ＋	동사	수식어(구)
Time	**flies.**	
Christine	**walks**	to school every day.

➜ 수식어구는 문장의 필수 요소가 아니며, 문장 형식에 영향을 주지 않아요.

시간이 아주 빨리 흐른다.

Christine은 매일 걸어서 학교에 간다.

주의 1형식 문장에 쓰이는 동사에는 be(~에 있다), go(~에 가다), come, arrive, run, live, sing, sleep 등이 있다.

2형식 문장은 「주어＋동사＋주격 보어」로 이루어진 문장이다. 주격 보어란 주어의 상태나 동작을 설명하는 말이며, 명사나 형용사가 온다.

주어 ＋	동사 ＋	주격 보어	수식어(구)
This	**is**	my pen.	
The leaves	**turn**	yellow	in fall.

이것은 내 펜이다.

나뭇잎은 가을에 노랗게 변한다.

주의 주격 보어가 필요한 동사에는 be(~이다), go(~되다), become(~이 되다), get(~해지다), turn(~하게 변하다), keep(~한 상태를 유지하다) 등이 있다.

개념확인 동사 찾기

1 Jimin became rich.　　2 Richard is smart.　　3 The baby cried loudly.

기본연습 다음 문장이 1형식인지 2형식인지 고르시오.

1 Kevin lives in San Francisco.　　□1형식　□2형식

2 She works for a design company.　　□1형식　□2형식

3 James and his brothers are always kind.　　□1형식　□2형식

4 The boys sat on the grass.　　□1형식　□2형식

5 The dog jumped through the window.　　□1형식　□2형식

6 My mother got angry this morning.　　□1형식　□2형식

7 Her hair is going gray.　　□1형식　□2형식

8 The birds in the tree sang beautifully.　　□1형식　□2형식

9 He played with his dog.　　□1형식　□2형식

10 The song became popular all over the world.　　□1형식　□2형식

11 His face turned red with anger.　　□1형식　□2형식

12 The students kept quiet.　　□1형식　□2형식

POINT 2 2형식: 감각동사

감각동사는 감각을 나타내는 2형식 동사로, 「주어＋감각동사＋주격 보어」의 형태로 쓴다. 주격 보어는 부사처럼 '～하게'로 해석되지만 형용사가 쓰인다. ☆

주어	+	감각동사	+ 주격 보어(형용사)	
You		**look** ～하게 보이다	tired.	너는 피곤해 보인다.
Her voice		**sounds** ～하게 들리다	strange.	그녀의 목소리가 이상하게 들린다.
This fish		**smells** ～한 냄새가 나다	bad.	이 생선은 상한 냄새가 난다.
This soup		**tastes** ～한 맛이 나다	salty.	이 수프는 짠맛이 난다.
I		**feel** ～하게 느끼다	dizzy.	나는 어지러움을 느낀다.

주의 감각동사 뒤에 명사가 오는 경우에는 「감각동사＋like＋명사」의 형태로 쓴다.
My room **smells like** a hospital. 내 방은 병원 같은 냄새가 난다.

개념확인 주격 보어 찾기

1 This blanket feels soft.　　**2** This tea smells sweet.　　**3** She looks very sad.

기본연습 A 괄호 안에서 알맞은 것을 고르시오.

1 He felt (sad / sadly) yesterday.

2 This pie tastes (wonderful / wonderfully).

3 That pancake smells (delicious / deliciously).

4 This music sounds (romantic / romantically).

5 Everything looks (fresh / freshly) in spring.

6 This rock (looks / looks like) a lion.

B 보기 에서 알맞은 말을 골라 문장을 완성하시오. (한 번씩만 사용할 것)

보기	looks	sounds	smells	tastes	feels

1 The song ＿＿＿＿＿＿ beautiful.

2 The wind ＿＿＿＿＿＿ very cold.

3 This lemon juice ＿＿＿＿＿＿ sour.

4 This shampoo ＿＿＿＿＿＿ nice.

5 She ＿＿＿＿＿＿ pretty in her new dress.

밑줄 친 부분이 어법상 바르면 ○라고 쓰고, 틀리면 바르게 고쳐 쓰시오.

1 Your house looks so <u>beautifully</u>.   → _____

2 The snow <u>looks</u> sugar.   → _____

3 I <u>felt</u> a movie star at the moment.   → _____

4 These cookies <u>taste like</u> too sweet.   → _____

5 Our kitchen <u>smells like</u> a Chinese restaurant.   → _____

D 우리말과 일치하도록 괄호 안의 말을 배열하여 문장을 완성하시오.

1 이 음료는 딸기 맛이 난다. (tastes, this drink, strawberries, like)
→ _____

2 그 아기의 피부는 정말 부드럽다. (the baby's skin, so soft, feels)
→ _____

3 너는 신사처럼 보인다. (a gentleman, like, you, look)
→ _____

4 이 꽃은 달콤한 냄새가 난다. (sweet, this flower, smells)
→ _____

5 그녀는 이 사진에서 아름답게 보인다. (she, beautiful, in this photo, looks)
→ _____

6 그의 목소리는 즐겁게 들린다. (sounds, his voice, pleasant)
→ _____

7 왜 이 수프는 이상한 맛이 나지? (why, this soup, taste, does, strange)
→ _____

틀/리/기 쉬/운
내/신/포/인/트

look, sound, smell, taste, feel 같은 감각동사의 보어로는 형용사가 쓰여요.

빈칸에 들어갈 말로 알맞지 <u>않은</u> 것은?

This ice cream looks _____.

① good   ② delicious
③ soft   ④ sweetly

POINT 3 3형식, 4형식

3형식 문장은 「주어＋동사＋목적어」로 이루어진 문장이다. 목적어는 동사의 대상이 되는 말로, 목적어 자리에는 다양한 명사 어구가 온다.

주어	+	동사	+	목적어	수식어(구)	
We		**played**		soccer	yesterday.	우리는 어제 축구를 했다.
My sister		**likes**		to swim. ↗ to부정사 목적어예요.		내 여동생은 수영하는 것을 좋아한다.
Andy		**enjoyed**		shopping	with his mother.	Andy는 그의 어머니와 쇼핑하는 것을 즐겼다.

↳ 동명사 목적어예요.

Tips 목적어가 필요한 동사에는 eat, want, know, buy, need, find, meet, see, use 등이 있다.

4형식 문장은 「주어＋동사＋간접목적어(～에게)＋직접목적어(～을)」로 이루어진 문장이다. 주로 간접목적어에는 사람이 오고, 직접목적어에는 사물이 온다.

주어	+	동사	+	간접목적어(사람)	+	직접목적어(사물)	
My dad		**gave**		me		a bike.	우리 아빠는 나에게 자전거를 주셨다.
She		**bought**		her son		a new bag.	그녀는 아들에게 새 가방을 사 주었다.
Sarah		**asked**		Jina		a question.	Sarah는 지나에게 질문을 했다.

Tips 목적어가 두 개 필요한 동사를 수여동사라고 부른다. 수여동사에는 give, send, make, buy, write, teach, show, ask, tell, bring 등이 있다.

개념확인 동사 찾기

1 He opened the window. **2** He taught me Spanish. **3** I sent you a postcard.

기본연습 **A** **보기**와 같이 주어, 동사, 목적어나 주어, 동사, 간접목적어, 직접목적어를 구분하여 쓰시오.

보기	I / love / apple juice.		He / lent / his sister / a bag.
	주어 동사 목적어		주어 동사 간접목적어 직접목적어

1 They have a piano.

2 He showed me his photos.

3 She sent her cousin a text.

4 Adam writes children's books.

5 My brother broke his arm.

6 She didn't leave him any messages.

B 보기에서 알맞은 말을 골라 문장을 완성하시오. (한 번씩만 사용할 것)

보기	bought	met	entered	wrote	gave

1 He _____ me a bottle of water.

2 Someone _____ the room behind me.

3 I _____ my friends at the café yesterday.

4 Jina _____ her mom a thank-you note.

5 The teacher _____ us lots of homework.

C 우리말과 일치하도록 괄호 안의 말을 배열하여 문장을 완성하시오.

1 그들은 상점에서 옷을 좀 샀다. (bought, some clothes, at the store, they)

→ _____

2 그는 나에게 크리스마스 카드를 보냈다. (he, me, sent, a Christmas card)

→ _____

3 그녀는 우리에게 맛있는 과자를 줬다. (gave, she, some delicious snacks, us)

→ _____

4 Jake는 내게 질문을 하나 했다. (Jake, me, a question, asked)

→ _____

5 엄마가 우리에게 재미있는 이야기를 읽어주셨다. (us, an interesting story, read, my mom)

→ _____

6 너는 도움이 필요하니? (you, need, do, any help)

→ _____

7 오늘 저녁에 네 차를 빌려 줄 수 있니? (you, me, can, this evening, your car, lend)

→ _____

틀리기 쉬운
내/신/포/인/트

4형식 문장은
「주어＋동사＋간접목적어＋
직접목적어」의 어순으로 써요.

빈칸에 들어갈 말로 알맞은 것은?

He gave _____.

① his brother a book ② a book his brother
③ to his brother a book ④ a book for his brother

4형식 문장은 「직접목적어 + 전치사 + 간접목적어」 형태의 3형식 문장으로 바꿀 수 있다.

	주어	동사	간접목적어	직접목적어	
4형식	She	gave	Andy	a rose.	그녀는 Andy에게 장미 한 송이를 줬다.

	주어	동사	직접목적어		간접목적어
3형식	She	gave	a rose	to	Andy.

4형식 문장을 3형식으로 바꿀 때 쓰는 전치사는 동사에 따라 to, for, of를 쓴다.

to를 쓰는 동사	bring, give, lend, send, show, teach, tell, write 등	Brian **sent** his mother a necklace. → Brian **sent** a necklace **to** his mother. Brian은 그의 어머니에게 목걸이를 보냈다.
for를 쓰는 동사	buy, build, cook, find, get, make 등	My dad **bought** me a book. → My dad **bought** a book **for** me. 아빠는 나에게 책을 한 권 사 주셨다.
of를 쓰는 동사	ask 등	Anna **asked** me a favor. → Anna **asked** a favor **of** me. Anna는 나에게 부탁을 했다.

개념확인 목적어 찾기

1 Kate lent me her camera.   **2** He bought his son a watch.   **3** I asked him a question.

기본연습 **A** 괄호 안에서 알맞은 것을 고르시오.

1 My mom cooked some noodles (to / for / of) me.

2 Please lend your car (to / for / of) me.

3 My teacher told the class rules (to / for / of) us.

4 Jenny showed her new sneakers (to / for / of) Jake.

5 Can you get a glass of water (to / for / of) her?

6 Could you buy some apples (to / for / of) me?

7 He built a house (to / for / of) his parents 3 years ago.

8 I gave a movie ticket (to / for / of) my friend.

9 Alice sent a text message (to / for / of) her sister.

10 My father made a model car (to / for / of) me.

11 I asked a favor (to / for / of) him.

B 다음 4형식 문장을 3형식 문장으로 바꿔 쓰시오.

1 The pen brings him good luck.   → The pen _____.

2 Brian cooked his friends some dishes.   → Brian _____.

3 Jake gave Susan a gold ring.   → Jake _____.

4 She bought him a cap on his birthday.   → She _____.

5 My mom made me a warm sweater.   → My mom _____.

6 He showed the visitors the painting.   → He _____.

C 우리말과 일치하도록 빈칸에 알맞은 말을 쓰시오.

1 Susan은 나에게 영어를 가르칠 것이다.
　→ Susan will teach _____ _____.

2 나는 그에게 영어로 이메일을 보낼 것이다.
　→ I will send _____ _____ _____ in English.

3 나는 그녀에게 내 주소를 말했다.
　→ I told _____ _____ _____.

4 Susan은 그에게 꽃 한 송이를 사 주었다.
　→ Susan bought _____ _____ _____ _____.

5 당신의 책을 나에게 주세요.
　→ Please give _____ _____ _____ _____.

6 내 남동생은 나에게 어려운 질문을 하나 했다.
　→ My brother asked _____ _____ _____ _____.

7 내게 내 코트 좀 가져다 줄래요?
　→ Could you bring _____ _____ _____?

빈칸에 들어갈 말로 알맞지 <u>않은</u> 것은?

Mary _____ some flowers to her mother.

① sent   ② brought
③ bought   ④ gave

POINT 5 5형식

5형식 문장은 「주어＋동사＋목적어＋목적격 보어」로 이루어진 문장이다. 목적격 보어는 목적어의 상태나 동작을 설명하는 말로 목적격 보어 자리에는 명사와 형용사 등이 온다.

주어	+	동사	+	목적어	+	목적격 보어(명사)	
We		**call**		our dog		Stubby.	우리는 우리 개를 Stubby라고 부른다.
The song		**made**		her		a superstar.	그 노래가 그녀를 슈퍼스타로 만들었다.

call: (~을 …라고) 부르다
make: (~을 …로) 만들다

주어	+	동사	+	목적어	+	목적격 보어(형용사)	
She		**found**		the book		interesting.	그녀는 그 책이 재미있다는 것을 알게 되었다.
This coat		**keeps**		me		warm.	이 코트는 나를 따뜻하게 해 준다.
Jake		**made**		her		angry.	Jake는 그녀를 화나게 했다.

→ 목적격 보어 자리에 부사를 쓰지 않도록 주의해요.

find: (~이 …하다는 것을) 알게 되다
keep: (~을 …하게) 유지하다
make: (~을 …하게) 만들다[하다]

개념확인 동사 찾기

1 She always makes me happy.　　**2** People call him Big Mouth.　　**3** I found the book strange.

기본연습 보기와 같이 주어, 동사, 목적어, 목적격 보어를 구분하여 쓰시오.

> 보기 My father / calls / me / a princess.
> 　　　주어　　　동사　목적어　목적격 보어

1 My family calls Judy a tomboy.

2 This blanket will keep you warm.

3 The news made people angry.

4 She found the science exam difficult.

5 The movie made him famous.

6 Ms. Wilson keeps her room clean.

틀리기 쉬운
내/신/포/인/트

목적격 보어 자리에 부사를
쓸 수 없어요.

빈칸에 들어갈 말로 알맞은 것은?

The speech made me _____.

① sadly　　　　　　② angrily
③ sleepy　　　　　　④ happily

개 념 완 성 **TEST**

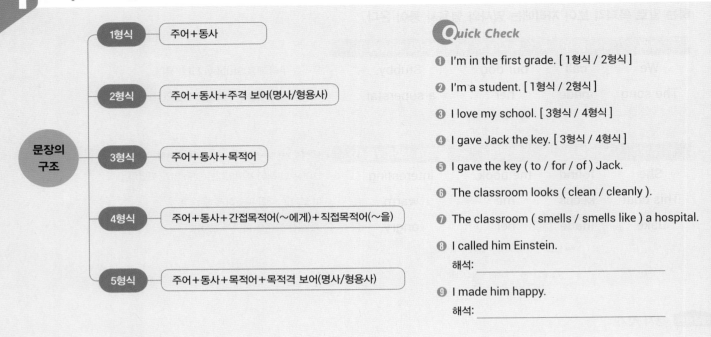

Quick Check

❶ I'm in the first grade. [1형식 / 2형식]

❷ I'm a student. [1형식 / 2형식]

❸ I love my school. [3형식 / 4형식]

❹ I gave Jack the key. [3형식 / 4형식]

❺ I gave the key (to / for / of) Jack.

❻ The classroom looks (clean / cleanly).

❼ The classroom (smells / smells like) a hospital.

❽ I called him Einstein.
해석: _____

❾ I made him happy.
해석: _____

STEP 2 기본 다지기

빈칸완성

A 우리말과 일치하도록 빈칸에 알맞은 말을 넣어 문장을 완성하시오.

1 나는 어젯밤에 잘 자지 못했다. → I didn't _____ well last night.

2 내 양말은 고약한 냄새가 났다. → My socks _____ terrible.

3 Lucy는 아이들에게 종이비행기를 만들어 주었다. → Lucy _____ her children paper planes.

4 Alice는 내게 새 컴퓨터를 사 주었다. → Alice _____ me a new computer.

5 그녀는 그녀의 가족에게 엽서를 보냈다. → She sent a postcard _____ her family.

6 나는 어제 내 방을 청소했다. → I _____ my room yesterday.

7 Erick은 나를 '천사'라고 불렀다. → Erick _____ me "Angel."

8 당신의 책을 나에게 보여 주세요. → Please _____ me your book.

9 나에게 빵 좀 가져다 주세요. → Please get some bread _____ me.

10 그녀의 이야기는 나를 슬프게 만들었다. → Her story _____ me sad.

11 그는 부모님을 위해 케이크를 만들었다. → He made a cake _____ his parents.

B 밑줄 친 부분을 어법상 바르게 고쳐 쓰시오.

1 It usually rains <u>heavy</u> in summer. → _____

2 This book looks very <u>difficulty</u>. → _____

3 This sand feels very <u>softly</u>. → _____

4 Chris taught <u>a new song me</u>. → _____

5 Jim bought Julia <u>to a bag</u>. → _____

6 He told <u>to the kid</u> a funny story. → _____

7 This coat kept him <u>warmth</u> during the winter. → _____

C 다음 문장을 괄호 안의 지시대로 바꿔 쓰시오.

1 The young girl looks cute. (cute을 an angel로 바꿔서)

→ _____

2 He cooked me dinner. (3형식으로)

→ _____

3 May I ask you a favor? (3형식으로)

→ _____

4 I made my cat a new cat tower. (3형식으로)

→ _____

5 I gave my horse some carrots. (3형식으로)

→ _____

6 Mr. Kim sends his wife some flowers every day. (3형식으로)

→ _____

7 She teaches Spanish to us. (4형식으로)

→ _____

8 Tom bought comic books for his brother. (4형식으로)

→ _____

9 Can you get a hotcake for me? (4형식으로)

→ _____

STEP 3 서술형 따라잡기

그림이해

A 그림을 보고, 내가 받은 생일 선물들에 대한 문장을 괄호 안의 지시대로 완성하시오.

1 My mom made _____. (4형식으로)

2 My dad bought _____. (3형식으로)

3 My sister, Mina, wrote _____. (4형식으로)

4 My friend, Tony, gave _____. (3형식으로)

영작완성

B 우리말과 일치하도록 괄호 안의 말을 바르게 배열하여 문장을 쓰시오.

1 그 소파는 편안해 보인다. (looks, comfortable, the sofa)

→ _____

2 너는 사진 찍는 것을 즐기니? (you, taking, pictures, enjoy, do)

→ _____

3 우리는 그를 피터팬이라고 부를 것이다. (call, we, are going to, him, Peter Pan)

→ _____

4 그는 내게 탐정 이야기를 말해 주었다. (told, he, me, a detective story)

→ _____

문장영작

C 우리말과 일치하도록 괄호 안의 말을 이용하여 영작하시오.

1 나는 지금 춥게 느껴진다. (feel)

→ _____

2 그 비누는 장미향이 난다. (smell, roses)

→ _____

3 나는 Danny에게 내 그림들을 보여 줬다. (show, my drawings)

→ _____

4 나는 창문이 열려 있는 것을 알게 되었다. (find, the window)

→ _____

1 문장의 형식이 잘못 연결된 것은?

① He often gets up early. – 1형식

② She is a clever student. – 2형식

③ I have a lot of friends. – 3형식

④ I will send my photos to my parents. – 4형식

⑤ People call New York the Big Apple. – 5형식

[2-3] 빈칸에 들어갈 말로 알맞은 것을 고르시오.

2

That cloud _____ a rabbit.

① looks ② looks like ③ feels

④ feels like ⑤ sounds like

3

The movie _____ James angry.

① gave ② sent ③ found

④ made ⑤ became

[4-5] 빈칸에 들어갈 말로 알맞지 않은 것을 고르시오.

4

This food smells _____ .

① good ② bad ③ sweetly

④ delicious ⑤ nice

5

She _____ the sunglasses to me.

① sent ② gave ③ showed

④ got ⑤ brought

6 대화의 빈칸에 들어갈 말로 알맞은 것은?

A: Can I _____ a favor of you?

B: Sure. What is it?

A: Can you watch my bags for a moment?

B: No problem.

① make ② give ③ send

④ show ⑤ ask

[7-8] 문장의 형식이 주어진 문장과 같은 것을 고르시오.

7

Kate lent me her camera.

① I will make my family happy.

② We want to eat pizza.

③ You gave a lot of things to me.

④ Mr. Kim teaches us science.

⑤ She cannot answer the phone right now.

8

The sunny weather made me happy.

① She gave Jack a white tulip.

② We call Mars the Red Planet.

③ Tom made me a cup of coffee.

④ Julia looked sick yesterday.

⑤ My father plays badminton every Sunday.

9 빈칸에 들어갈 말이 나머지와 <u>다른</u> 하나는?

① She gave her phone number _____ Mike.

② I made a beautiful scarf _____ my mother.

③ My mom teaches yoga _____ kids.

④ Did you send your book _____ John?

⑤ He showed the garden _____ me.

10 밑줄 친 부분의 쓰임이 나머지와 <u>다른</u> 하나는?

① The book was so <u>boring</u>.

② His father is an <u>inventor</u>.

③ The sky turned <u>dark</u>.

④ Time flies <u>very fast</u>.

⑤ The man became <u>hungry</u>.

11 우리말을 영어로 바르게 옮긴 것은?

> 그 새 스카프는 하루 종일 그를 따뜻하게 유지해 줬다.

① The new scarf kept him warm all day.

② The new scarf kept him warmly all day.

③ The new scarf kept warm him all day.

④ The new scarf kept warmly him all day.

⑤ The new scarf kept warm to him all day.

12 어법상 <u>틀린</u> 문장은?

① They call their dog Hairy.

② My mom looks worried today.

③ Can I ask you a favor?

④ The teacher entered the classroom.

⑤ They are acting wonderful on the stage.

[13-14] 빈칸에 공통으로 들어갈 말로 알맞은 것을 고르시오.

13

> • Julia bought a watch _____ me.
> • Mom made egg sandwiches _____ us.

① to   ② for   ③ of

④ in   ⑤ with

14

> • This candy tastes _____ oranges.
> • The rock looks _____ an elephant.

① of   ② with   ③ like

④ to   ⑤ for

15 빈칸에 알맞은 말이 순서대로 짝 지어진 것은?

> · The pasta _____ salty.
> · The blanket _____ very soft.

① sounds – tastes
② sounds – feels
③ tastes – smells
④ tastes – feels
⑤ tastes – touches

16 어법상 올바른 문장은?

① He drives very careful.
② Her heart is beating normal.
③ His new novel is amazing.
④ My brother is quietly.
⑤ This hamburger tastes badly.

17 주어진 문장을 3형식으로 바르게 바꾼 것은?

> Mr. Jackson bought his son bibimbab.

① Mr. Jackson bought his son for bibimbab.
② Mr. Jackson bought his son to bibimbab.
③ Mr. Jackson bought bibimbab for his son.
④ Mr. Jackson bought bibimbab to his son.
⑤ Mr. Jackson bought bibimbab of his son.

18 문장의 형식이 나머지와 다른 하나는?

① The baby makes me happy.
② Kelly made me very upset.
③ Working in the garden makes me very tired.
④ My dad made me a glass of orange juice.
⑤ The color green makes my eyes comfortable.

19 밑줄 친 ①~⑤ 중 어법상 틀린 것은?

> I want to introduce my friend, Susan. ① She is good at singing. ② She has a beautiful voice. ③ She likes baking a lot. ④ She often makes sweet cookies to me. ⑤ So I call her Sweet Hands.

20 어법상 올바른 문장의 개수는?

> ⓐ Emily became a pianist.
> ⓑ Jina sang cheerfully.
> ⓒ He looks like young.
> ⓓ I found very interesting this book.
> ⓔ Can I call you Uncle John?

① 1개 　　 ② 2개 　　 ③ 3개
④ 4개 　　 ⑤ 5개

21 그림을 보고, 보기 에 주어진 말을 이용하여 지시에 맞게 문장을 완성하시오. (과거시제로 쓸 것)

| 보기 | buy | a teddy bear | Jane |

(1) (4형식 문장으로)

Steve _____ .

(2) (3형식 문장으로)

Steve _____ .

22 우리말과 일치하도록 괄호 안의 말을 이용하여 문장을 쓰시오.

(1) 너는 오늘 모델처럼 보인다. (look, a model)

→ _____

(2) 너의 새 장갑은 따뜻해 보인다. (gloves, look, warm)

→ _____

23 괄호 안의 말을 바르게 배열하여 문장을 완성하시오.

(1) (plan, to learn, we, French, this year)

→ _____

(2) (show, I'll, my new shoes, you)

→ _____

(3) (call, people, Bach, the father of music)

→ _____

24 어법상 틀린 문장을 찾아 바르게 고친 후, 틀린 이유를 쓰시오.

ⓐ He looks so friendly.
ⓑ I read the letter careful.
ⓒ She bought the boy a cell phone.
ⓓ I will make a sandwich for you.

_____ → _____

틀린 이유: _____

_____

🔺고난도

25 그림을 보고, 괄호 안의 말을 이용하여 문장을 쓰시오.
(과거시제로 쓸 것)

(1)   (2)

(3)

(1) (the machine, keep, the water)

→ _____

(2) (the fan, make, the boy)

→ _____

(3) (the boy, call, his dad)

→ _____

12

형용사와 부사

형용사는 명사의 색깔, 모양, 크기, 성질 등을 나타내는 말이고,
부사는 방법, 정도, 빈도 등을 설명하는 말이다.

A **black** cat is sleeping **happily**.

POINT 1 형용사의 쓰임

형용사는 사람이나 사물의 색깔, 모양, 성질, 상태 등을 나타내는 말이다.

색깔	yellow 노란색의	red 빨간색의	white 흰색의	black 검은색의	green 초록색의	blue 파란색의 ...
외모, 모양	long 긴	short 짧은	tall 키가 큰, 높은	big 큰	small 작은	thin 마른 ...
감정, 성질	kind 친절한	nice 다정한	funny 웃기는	angry 화난	happy 행복한	sad 슬픈 ...
상태	hungry 배고픈	clean 깨끗한	old 오래된, 나이 든	young 어린	slow 느린	fast 빠른 ...

형용사는 명사를 꾸며 주거나, 주어나 목적어를 보충 설명하는 보어로 쓰인다.

명사 수식	형용사+명사	She is a **tall girl**.	그녀는 키가 큰 소녀이다.
보어	주어 보충 설명	**She** is **happy**.	그녀는 행복하다. 〈She = happy〉
	목적어 보충 설명	She made **me happy**.	그녀는 나를 행복하게 만들었다. 〈me = happy〉

Tips 형용사는 두 개 이상 함께 쓸 수 있다.
She has **long red** hair. 그녀는 **긴 빨간색** 머리를 가지고 있다.

주의 관사(a/an, the), 수를 나타내는 말(one, two 등), 지시형용사(this, that 등), 소유격 인칭대명사(my, your 등)는 형용사 앞에 쓴다.
The house has **two big** windows. 그 집에는 **두 개의 큰** 창문이 있다.
Look at **this beautiful** flower. **이 아름다운** 꽃을 봐.

개념확인 형용사 찾기

1 Mike has short hair.   **2** I bought a green T-shirt.   **3** The dress is beautiful.

기본연습 **A** 우리말과 일치하도록 빈칸에 알맞은 형용사를 쓰시오.

1 오래된 집 → an _____ house
2 배고픈 고양이들 → _____ cats
3 깨끗한 창문 → a _____ window
4 나의 작은 가방 → my _____ bag
5 검은 양말 → _____ socks
6 저 빠른 자동차 → that _____ car
7 어린 화가 → a _____ artist
8 웃기는 이야기 → a _____ story
9 긴 갈색 머리 → _____ brown hair
10 세 마리 하얀 개 → three _____ dogs
11 슬픈 소식 → _____ news
12 친절한 선생님 → a _____ teacher
13 파란 하늘 → the _____ sky
14 높은 건물들 → _____ buildings
15 노란색 드레스 → a _____ dress
16 아름다운 꽃들 → _____ flowers
17 이 빨간 사과 → this _____ apple
18 짧은 꼬리 → a _____ tail

B 밑줄 친 형용사의 쓰임으로 알맞은 것을 고르시오.

1 The puppy is cute. □ 명사 수식 □ 보어

2 Henry is a smart student. □ 명사 수식 □ 보어

3 The song made me sad. □ 명사 수식 □ 보어

4 I made these sweet cookies. □ 명사 수식 □ 보어

5 Mike has an old computer. □ 명사 수식 □ 보어

6 Those bananas look fresh. □ 명사 수식 □ 보어

7 The elephant has a long nose. □ 명사 수식 □ 보어

8 This jacket keeps me warm. □ 명사 수식 □ 보어

9 They were in a large room. □ 명사 수식 □ 보어

10 This question is really easy. □ 명사 수식 □ 보어

C 밑줄 친 부분이 어법상 바르면 ○라고 쓰고, 틀리면 바르게 고쳐 쓰시오.

1 Brian is close my friend. → _____

2 I love their new songs. → _____

3 Yellow her bag is pretty. → _____

4 Can you solve difficult these questions? → _____

5 Sue is wearing long a skirt. → _____

6 Let's climb high that mountain. → _____

7 We need clean two glasses. → _____

8 My sister wants fresh ten oranges. → _____

9 Look at that red car over there. → _____

10 Ms. Brown knows old that man. → _____

틀리기 쉬운
내/신/포/인/트

'~하게'라고 해석되더라도
보어 자리에는 형용사가
온다는 것을 기억해요.

빈칸에 알맞은 말이 순서대로 짝 지어진 것은?

• She was a _____ person.
• The movie made me _____.

① happy – sad   ② happily – sad
③ happy – sadly   ④ happily – sadly

수량형용사: many, much, a lot of 정답 및 해설 p.34

many, much, a lot of는 모두 '많은'이라는 뜻을 나타낸다. many는 셀 수 있는 명사와 함께 쓰고,
much는 셀 수 없는 명사와 함께 쓴다.

many (수가) 많은	+ 셀 수 있는 명사의 복수형	I have **many friends**.	나는 친구들이 많다.
much (양이) 많은	+ 셀 수 없는 명사	I don't have **much time**.	나는 시간이 많이 없다.
a lot of (= lots of) (수 · 양이) 많은	+ 셀 수 있는 명사의 복수형	I have **a lot of pencils**.	나는 연필이 많다.
	+ 셀 수 없는 명사	I have **lots of homework**.	나는 숙제가 많다.

개념확인 형용사와 형용사가 꾸며 주는 명사 찾기

1 Jane reads many books.   **2** I don't have much money.   **3** There are many bottles.

기본연습 **A** 괄호 안에서 알맞은 것을 고르시오.

1 She doesn't have (many / much) time.

2 My father drinks too (many / much) coffee.

3 I saw (many / much) people at the party.

4 Sam grows (many / much) roses in his garden.

5 There is (many / a lot of) sand in his shoes.

6 You should eat (much / lots of) vegetables.

B 밑줄 친 부분을 어법상 바르게 고쳐 쓰시오.

1 Amy doesn't save <u>many</u> money every month.   → _____

2 You can see <u>much</u> stars in the sky at night.   → _____

3 Did you borrow <u>much</u> books from the library?   → _____

4 There are <u>lot of desk</u> in this classroom.   → _____

틀 리 기 쉬 운
내/신/포/인/트

명사가 셀 수 있는지 없는지에
따라 many와 much를
구별하여 써야 해요.

빈칸에 들어갈 말로 알맞지 <u>않은</u> 것은?

There are _____ flowers on the table.

① many   ② much   ③ a lot of   ④ lots of

POINT 3 수량형용사: (a) few, (a) little

a few, a little은 '약간의, 조금 있는'이라는 뜻이고, few, little은 '거의 없는'이라는 뜻이다.
a few, few는 셀 수 있는 명사와 함께 쓰고, a little, little은 셀 수 없는 명사와 함께 쓴다.

a few 약간의, 조금 있는	+ 셀 수 있는 명사의 복수형	I have **a few** questions.	나는 질문이 조금 있다.
few 거의 없는		I have **few** questions.	나는 질문이 거의 없다.
a little 약간의, 조금 있는	+ 셀 수 없는 명사	We have **a little** time.	우리는 시간이 조금 있다.
little 거의 없는		We have **little** time.	우리는 시간이 거의 없다.

주의 few와 little은 부정적인 의미가 있으므로 부정어와 함께 쓰지 않는다.

개념확인 옳은 해석 고르기

1 I borrowed a few books.
□ 약간의 □ 거의 없는

2 He has little money now.
□ 약간의 □ 거의 없는

3 There are few stars in the sky.
□ 약간의 □ 거의 없는

기본연습 A 괄호 안에서 알맞은 것을 고르시오.

1 There are (few / little) flowers in winter.

2 I put (a few / a little) salt in my soup.

3 There is (a few / a little) juice in the glass.

4 Amy knows (a few / a little) Chinese words.

5 My team had (few / little) luck in the game.

6 She left (a few / a little) days ago.

B 우리말과 일치하도록 빈칸에 알맞은 수량형용사를 쓰시오.

1 나는 방 안의 사람들을 거의 모른다.
→ I know _____ people in the room.

2 이번 겨울에는 눈이 거의 안 왔다.
→ We had _____ snow this winter.

3 그는 약간의 시간을 아들과 함께 보냈다.
→ He spent _____ time with his son.

4 우진이와 미나는 약간의 책을 샀다.
→ Woojin and Mina bought _____ books.

5 Smith 씨는 지갑에 돈이 거의 없다.
→ Mr. Smith has _____ money in his wallet.

틀리기 쉬운 내/신/포/인트

(a) few, (a) little의 뜻과 쓰임을 구별하여 기억해요.

빈칸에 들어갈 말로 알맞은 것은?

Luke has _____ friends. He is very lonely.

① many ② a little ③ few ④ little

수량형용사: some, any

정답 및 해설 p.35

some과 any는 '약간의, 조금의'라는 뜻으로, 셀 수 있는 명사와 셀 수 없는 명사 모두와 함께 쓸 수 있다.
some은 주로 긍정문과 권유문에 쓰고, any는 주로 부정문과 의문문에 쓴다.

some	긍정문	I have **some** books in my bag.	나는 가방에 책이 조금 있다.
	권유문	Would you like **some** juice?	주스 좀 드시겠어요?
any	부정문	I don't have **any** classes today.	나는 오늘 수업이 없다.
	의문문	Do you have **any** questions?	질문이 있나요?

개념확인 some이나 any가 들어갈 곳 찾기

1 I have sugar.

2 I can't find stamps.

3 He didn't buy clothes.

기본연습 **A** 괄호 안에서 알맞은 것을 고르시오.

1 Would you like (some / any) water?

2 I don't have (some / any) time right now.

3 He needs (some / any) boxes and tape.

4 Here are (some / any) sandwiches for you.

5 Do you have (some / any) plans for the weekend?

B 우리말과 일치하도록 빈칸에 some과 any 중 알맞은 것을 쓰시오.

1 그들은 몸무게를 좀 줄일 필요가 있다. → They need to lose _____ weight.

2 지민이는 약간의 채소를 샀다. → Jimin bought _____ vegetables.

3 내 여동생은 사진을 조금도 찍지 않았다. → My sister didn't take _____ pictures.

4 동수는 약간의 동전을 지갑에 넣었다. → Dongsu put _____ coins into his wallet.

5 너는 작년에 책을 좀 읽었니? → Did you read _____ books last year?

틀리기 쉬운 내/신/포/인/트

주로 some은 긍정문과 권유문에, any는 부정문과 의문문에 써요.

빈칸에 알맞은 말이 순서대로 짝 지어진 것은?

- There are _____ girls in the park.
- I don't want _____ salt in my soup.

① some – any
② some – some
③ any – some
④ any – any

감정 형용사

정답 및 해설 p.35

-ing로 끝나는 형용사는 감정을 느끼게 하는 대상에 쓰고, -ed로 끝나는 형용사는 감정을 느끼는 주체(사람)에 쓴다.

이야기가 흥미로운 감정을 느끼게 하는 대상이에요.

-ing 형용사: ~한 감정을 느끼게 하는	interesting 흥미로운	The story was **interesting**.	그 이야기는 흥미로웠다.
	surprising 놀라게 하는	The news was **surprising**.	그 뉴스는 놀라웠다.
	boring 지루한	The movie was **boring**.	그 영화는 지루했다.
	exciting 신나게 하는	The trip to L.A. was **exciting**.	L.A.로의 여행은 신이 났다.
-ed 형용사: ~한 감정을 느끼는	interested 흥미로워하는	I was **interested** in the story.	나는 그 이야기에 흥미로워했다.
	surprised 놀란	I was **surprised** at the news.	나는 그 뉴스에 놀랐다.
	bored 지루해하는	I was **bored** with the movie.	나는 그 영화에 지루해했다.
	excited 신이 난	I'm **excited** about the trip.	나는 여행에 신이 났다.

여행 때문에 'I'가 신이 난 감정을 느껴요.

개념확인 옳은 해석 고르기

1 The book is <u>interesting</u>.
　□ 흥미로운　□ 흥미로워하는

2 The girl looks <u>bored</u>.
　□ 지루한　□ 지루해하는

3 The game was very <u>exciting</u>.
　□ 신나게 하는　□ 신이 난

기본연습 A 괄호 안에서 알맞은 것을 고르시오.

1 Tom is (interesting / interested) in arts.

2 This is an (interesting / interested) movie.

3 I felt very (boring / bored) at the party.

4 The history class was very (boring / bored).

5 Their story was very (surprising / surprised).

6 My mother looked very (surprising / surprised).

7 I'm so (exciting / excited) by the news.

8 We learned some (exciting / excited) news from her.

B 우리말과 일치하도록 빈칸에 알맞은 말을 쓰시오.

1 준호는 그때 신이 나 보였다.
　→ Junho looked ＿＿＿＿＿＿ then.

2 미나는 흥미로운 이야기를 읽었다.
　→ Mina read an ＿＿＿＿＿＿ story.

3 그의 대답은 정말 놀라웠다.
　→ His answer was really ＿＿＿＿＿＿.

4 내 남동생은 오늘 너무 지루해했다.
　→ My brother was very ＿＿＿＿＿＿ today.

POINT 6 부사의 쓰임

정답 및 해설 p.35

부사는 동사, 형용사, 다른 부사 또는 문장 전체를 꾸며 준다.

동사 수식	The bus **moved slowly**.	그 버스는 느리게 움직였다.
형용사 수식	The bus was **really slow**.	그 버스는 정말 느렸다.
다른 부사 수식	The bus moved **very slowly**.	그 버스는 정말 느리게 움직였다.
문장 전체 수식	**Luckily, the bus moved**.	다행히, 그 버스가 움직였다.

> 궁금해요!
> 동사를 꾸미는 부사는 동사 뒤에 써야 하나요?
>
> 동사를 꾸미는 부사는 동사의 앞이나 뒤에 모두 올 수 있어요. 하지만 주로 동사 뒤에 써요.

개념확인 부사 찾기

1 Hojin eats quickly. **2** You are really smart. **3** They welcomed him joyfully.

기본연습  밑줄 친 부사가 꾸며 주는 부분에 ○로 표시하시오.

1 The airplane flies <u>very</u> fast.

2 They lived <u>happily</u> in the town.

3 Mina speaks English <u>well</u>.

4 Suji and I worked <u>very</u> hard.

5 My sister opened the door <u>slowly</u>.

6 The cheetah runs <u>quickly</u>.

7 The math exam was <u>very</u> difficult.

8 Somi and I talked <u>quietly</u> in the library.

9 Ms. Smith is a <u>really</u> kind person.

10 You have to listen <u>carefully</u>.

11 Mr. Han is a <u>very</u> good teacher.

12 Judy and Mary ate <u>too</u> much dinner.

13 <u>Surprisingly</u>, he agreed right away.

14 The cat <u>really</u> likes fish.

15 Jinho and Andy were <u>very</u> happy yesterday.

16 I think <u>differently</u> from my parents.

17 That actor is <u>very</u> famous in Korea.

부사는 대부분 형용사에 -ly를 붙인 형태이다.

대부분의 형용사+-ly	sad 슬픈 → sadly 슬프게 quick 빠른 → quickly 빨리	slow 느린 → slowly 느리게 careful 주의 깊은 → carefully 주의 깊게
-y로 끝나는 형용사는 y를 i로 바꾸고+-ly	easy 쉬운 → easily 쉽게 busy 바쁜 → busily 바쁘게	happy 행복한 → happily 행복하게 lucky 운이 좋은 → luckily 운 좋게
-le로 끝나는 형용사는 e를 없애고+-y	terrible 심한 → terribly 몹시 simple 간단한 → simply 간단히	gentle 온화한 → gently 다정하게 possible 가능한 → possibly 아마
불규칙 변화	good 좋은 → well 잘, 좋게	

Tips very(매우), almost(거의), too(너무)처럼 「형용사+-ly」의 형태가 아닌 부사도 있다.
The box was **too** heavy. 그 상자는 너무 무거웠다.

주의 lovely(사랑스러운), friendly(친절한), ugly(못생긴)는 -ly로 끝나는 형용사이다.
The doll looked **lovely**. 그 인형은 사랑스러워 보였다.

개념확인 옳은 해석 고르기

1 Tom walks <u>quickly</u>.
  ☐ 빠른 ☐ 빨리

2 Jane drives <u>slowly</u>.
  ☐ 느린 ☐ 느리게

3 They sing <u>beautifully</u>.
  ☐ 아름다운 ☐ 아름답게

기본연습 **A** 다음 형용사의 부사형을 쓰시오.

1 real – _____

2 happy – _____

3 quiet – _____

4 clear – _____

5 good – _____

6 nice – _____

7 bad – _____

8 angry – _____

9 sad – _____

10 possible – _____

11 useful – _____

12 deep – _____

13 comfortable – _____

14 serious – _____

15 strange – _____

16 sweet – _____

17 simple – _____

18 safe – _____

19 kind – _____

20 perfect – _____

21 light – _____

22 similar – _____

B 우리말과 일치하도록 괄호 안에서 알맞은 것을 고르시오.

1 우리 어머니는 밝게 웃으셨다. → My mother smiled (bright / **brightly**).

2 그 아이들은 춤을 매우 잘 춘다. → The kids dance very (good / **well**).

3 그 버스는 갑자기 멈췄다. → The bus stopped (sudden / **suddenly**).

4 사람들은 현명한 지도자를 원한다. → People want a (**wise** / wisely) leader.

5 어제 눈이 심하게 내렸다. → It snowed (heavy / **heavily**) yesterday.

6 그는 아름다운 목소리를 가지고 있다. → He has a (**beautiful** / beautifully) voice.

C 괄호 안에 주어진 말을 이용하여 문장을 완성하시오.

1 _____, I passed the test. (lucky)

2 Ryan fixed my bike _____. (easy)

3 I was _____ sick yesterday. (terrible)

4 Wendy looks so _____ today. (different)

5 Daniel _____ listened to my story. (careful)

6 My older sister is _____ to everyone. (kind)

7 The woman _____ hugged her baby. (gentle)

8 Swimming in the sea can be _____. (dangerous)

D 두 문장의 뜻이 같도록 빈칸에 알맞은 말을 쓰시오.

1 Tony is a good soccer player.

= Tony plays soccer very _____.

2 My grandmother is a careful driver.

= My grandmother drives _____.

틀/리/기 쉬운
내/신/포/인/트

-ly로 끝나지만 부사가
아니라 형용사인 단어들을
구별하여 기억해요.

짝 지어진 두 단어의 관계가 보기 와 다른 것은?

보기	happy – happily

① easy – easily   ② good – well

③ love – lovely   ④ possible – possibly

다음 단어는 형용사와 부사의 형태가 같다.

fast	형 빠른	Juwon is a **fast** runner.	주원이는 **빠른** 주자이다.
	부 빨리	Children grow up **fast**.	아이들은 **빨리** 자란다.
early	형 이른	They had **early** dinner.	그들은 **이른** 저녁을 먹었다.
	부 일찍	The train arrived **early**.	기차가 **일찍** 도착했다.
late	형 늦은	Ann was **late** for school.	Ann은 학교에 **늦었다**.
	부 늦게	Mom goes to bed **late**.	엄마는 **늦게** 주무신다.
high	형 높은	Sujin has a **high** fever.	수진이는 열이 **높다**.
	부 높이	She kicked the ball **high**.	그녀는 공을 **높이** 찼다.
long	형 (길이 · 거리가) 긴	Mr. Smith has **long** hair.	Smith 씨는 머리가 **길다**.
	부 오래, 오랫동안	We worked very **long**.	우리는 매우 **오래** 일했다.
hard	형 어려운, 단단한	This exam was very **hard**.	이번 시험은 매우 **어려웠다**.
	부 열심히	My brother studies **hard**.	내 남동생은 **열심히** 공부한다.

개념확인 옳은 해석 고르기

1 I can jump high.
　□ 높은　□ 높이

2 The toy car is very fast.
　□ 빠른　□ 빨리

3 I get up early every morning.
　□ 이른　□ 일찍

기본연습 밑줄 친 부분의 품사로 알맞은 것을 고르시오.

1 How high is the mountain?　　□ 형용사　□ 부사

2 This is a really hard question.　　□ 형용사　□ 부사

3 He was late for the class again.　　□ 형용사　□ 부사

4 Spring came late this year.　　□ 형용사　□ 부사

5 The eagle can fly very high.　　□ 형용사　□ 부사

6 My little sister is a fast learner.　　□ 형용사　□ 부사

7 You don't have to wait too long.　　□ 형용사　□ 부사

8 The bus arrived 10 minutes early.　　□ 형용사　□ 부사

9 I went jogging in the early morning.　　□ 형용사　□ 부사

10 Please do not eat too fast.　　□ 형용사　□ 부사

11 The young farmer worked very hard.　　□ 형용사　□ 부사

12 The woman is wearing a long jacket.　　□ 형용사　□ 부사

POINT 9 빈도부사

정답 및 해설 p.36

빈도부사는 어떤 일이 얼마나 자주 일어나는지 나타내는 말이다. ☆

	100%		
always 항상, 늘		My mom **always** wakes up early.	우리 엄마는 **항상** 일찍 일어난다.
usually 보통, 대개		Robert **usually** comes home late.	Robert는 **대개** 집에 늦게 온다.
often 자주		Sam **often** plays computer games.	Sam은 **자주** 컴퓨터 게임을 한다.
sometimes 가끔, 때때로		Mina is **sometimes** late for school.	미나는 **때때로** 학교에 지각한다.
never 전혀 ~ 않다	0%	My brother **never** skips breakfast.	내 남동생은 **절대** 아침을 거르지 **않는다.**

주의 빈도부사는 주로 be동사와 조동사의 뒤, 일반동사의 앞에 쓴다.
She is **always** busy. 그녀는 항상 바쁘다.
You will **never** forget him. 너는 그를 절대 잊지 않을 것이다.
I **usually** eat breakfast. 나는 보통 아침을 먹는다.

개념확인 **빈도부사 찾기**

1 I sometimes eat fast food.　　**2** We always have breakfast.　　**3** Jim never drinks coffee.

기본연습 **A 우리말과 일치하도록 빈칸에 알맞은 빈도부사를 쓰시오.**

1 하나는 우리에게 항상 친절하다.　→　Hana is _____ kind to us.

2 한국에 4월에 가끔 눈이 온다.　→　It _____ snows in April in Korea.

3 유미는 체육관에서 자주 운동을 한다.　→　Yumi _____ exercises in the gym.

4 그녀는 절대 돌아오지 않을 것이다.　→　She will _____ come back.

5 버스는 항상 제시간에 도착한다.　→　The bus _____ arrives on time.

6 우리 아빠는 때때로 아침을 거른다.　→　My dad _____ skips breakfast.

7 나는 절대 일요일에 일하지 않는다.　→　I _____ work on Sundays.

8 나는 자주 자전거를 타고 학교에 간다.　→　I _____ go to school by bicycle.

9 Susan은 보통 하루에 8시간을 잔다.　→　Susan _____ sleeps 8 hours a day.

10 그들은 대개 12시에 점심을 먹는다.　→　They _____ have lunch at twelve.

11 그는 가끔 수업에 늦는다.　→　He is _____ late for class.

12 나는 자주 공원에서 산책한다.　→　I _____ take a walk in the park.

13 너는 토요일에 보통 무엇을 하니?　→　What do you _____ do on Saturday?

B 괄호 안의 빈도부사가 들어갈 곳을 고르시오.

1 (always)   I ① drink ② milk ③ in the morning.

2 (always)   Mr. Smith ① is ② late ③ for the meeting.

3 (usually)   My dad ① is ② at home ③ on weekends.

4 (usually)   My brother's room ① is ② clean ③ and warm.

5 (often)   The weather ① is ② very cold ③ here.

6 (often)   Eric ① exercises ② in the evening ③ with his friend.

7 (sometimes)   I ① work ② nine hours ③ in a day.

8 (sometimes)   She ① visits ② her grandparents ③ after school.

9 (never)   I ① will ② shop ③ at that store again.

10 (never)   Anna ① wakes up ② before ③ seven.

C 미라의 활동을 나타낸 표를 보고, 빈칸에 알맞은 빈도부사를 보기에서 골라 쓰시오.

	Mon.	Tue.	Wed.	Thur.	Fri.	Sat.	Sun.
go jogging	×	×	×	×	×	×	×
have breakfast	○	○	○	○	○	○	○
walk her dog	○	×	○	×	○	○	○
watch movies	×	○	×	○	×	×	×

보기	sometimes	always	never	often

1 Mira _____ goes jogging.

2 She _____ has breakfast.

3 She _____ walks her dog.

4 She _____ watches movies.

틀리기 쉬운
내/신/포/인/트

빈도부사는 주로 be동사와
조동사의 뒤, 일반동사의
앞에 와요.

밑줄 친 빈도부사의 위치가 어색한 것은?

① I usually wake up at 7.
② She will never forget him.
③ Kate is often late for school.
④ Sam always is kind to his friends.

개 | 념 | 완 | 성 TEST

정답 및 해설 p.36

STEP 1 Map으로 개념 정리하기

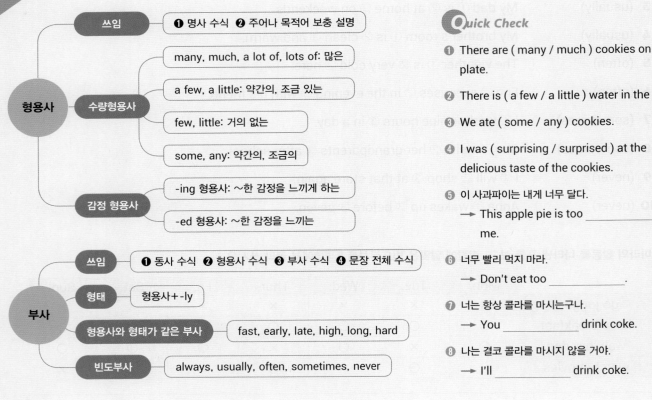

쓰임 ❶ 명사 수식 ❷ 주어나 목적어 보충 설명

형용사

수량형용사
- many, much, a lot of, lots of: 많은
- a few, a little: 약간의, 조금 있는
- few, little: 거의 없는
- some, any: 약간의, 조금의

감정 형용사
- -ing 형용사: ~한 감정을 느끼게 하는
- -ed 형용사: ~한 감정을 느끼는

부사

쓰임 ❶ 동사 수식 ❷ 형용사 수식 ❸ 부사 수식 ❹ 문장 전체 수식

형태 형용사+-ly

형용사와 형태가 같은 부사 fast, early, late, high, long, hard

빈도부사 always, usually, often, sometimes, never

Quick Check

❶ There are (many / much) cookies on the plate.

❷ There is (a few / a little) water in the glass.

❸ We ate (some / any) cookies.

❹ I was (surprising / surprised) at the delicious taste of the cookies.

❺ 이 사과파이는 내게 너무 달다.
→ This apple pie is too _____ for me.

❻ 너무 빨리 먹지 마라.
→ Don't eat too _____.

❼ 너는 항상 콜라를 마시는구나.
→ You _____ drink coke.

❽ 나는 결코 콜라를 마시지 않을 거야.
→ I'll _____ drink coke.

STEP 2 기본 다지기

빈칸완성

A 우리말과 일치하도록 빈칸에 알맞은 말을 넣어 문장을 완성하시오.

1 수진이는 귀여운 고양이를 봤다.
→ Sujin saw a _____ cat.

2 보미는 흥미로운 TV 쇼를 봤다.
→ Bomi watched an _____ TV show.

3 너는 어젯밤에 일찍 자러 갔니?
→ Did you go to sleep _____ last night?

4 나는 보통 7시에 아침을 먹는다.
→ I _____ have breakfast at 7 a.m.

5 미주는 자매가 있니?
→ Does Miju have _____ sisters?

6 지훈이는 중국어 단어를 거의 모른다.
→ Jihun knows _____ Chinese words.

7 거리에 약간의 얼음이 있다.
→ There is _____ _____ ice on the street.

8 민수는 많은 친구를 사귀었다.
→ Minsu made _____ _____ _____ friends.

오류수정

B 밑줄 친 부분을 어법상 바르게 고쳐 쓰시오.

1 My brother drinks too <u>many</u> soda. → _____

2 I can finish the science project <u>easy</u>. → _____

3 There was <u>few</u> water in the bowl. → _____

4 <u>A little</u> birds are sitting in the trees. → _____

5 My little sister walked <u>slowly too</u>. → _____

6 My English teacher usually speaks too <u>fastly</u>. → _____

7 They picked up <u>any</u> trash in the park. → _____

8 There are <u>yellow three</u> chairs in the room. → _____

9 It <u>normal</u> takes 20 minutes to get there. → _____

문장해석

C 밑줄 친 부분에 유의하여 우리말로 해석하시오.

1 He fixed the old car <u>easily</u>.

→ _____

2 Lisa <u>usually</u> walks to school.

→ _____

3 John <u>sometimes</u> play baseball with his friends.

→ _____

4 They studied <u>hard</u> for the test.

→ _____

5 She has <u>long black</u> hair.

→ _____

6 I found <u>a few</u> coins in my pocket.

→ _____

7 <u>Many</u> students have smartphones.

→ _____

8 They don't want <u>any</u> milk.

→ _____

STEP 3 서술형 따라잡기

그림이해
A 그림을 보고, 빈칸에 알맞은 말을 보기 에서 골라 쓰시오. (한 번씩만 쓸 것)

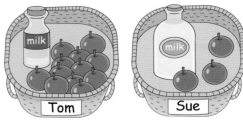

보기	many	lots of	a few	a little

1 Sue has _____ milk, but Tom has _____ milk.

2 Tom has _____ apples, but Sue has _____ apples.

영작완성
B 우리말과 일치하도록 괄호 안의 말을 바르게 배열하여 문장을 쓰시오.

1 우리는 항상 너를 기억할 것이다. (you, always, we, will, remember)

→ _____

2 하준이는 약간의 양파와 당근이 필요하다. (some, Hajun, and, onions, needs, carrots)

→ _____

3 지호는 체중을 줄이기 위해 열심히 운동했다. (lose, exercised, to, hard, Jiho, weight)

→ _____

4 도서관에 사람이 거의 없었다. (in the library, few, there, people, were)

→ _____

문장영작
C 우리말과 일치하도록 괄호 안의 말을 이용하여 영작하시오.

1 우리는 복도에서 조용히 걸었다. (quiet, in the hall)

→ _____

2 Alice는 거실에 너무 많은 가구를 샀다. (buy, furniture, for the living room)

→ _____

3 Ron은 그의 방을 결코 청소하지 않는다. (clean)

→ _____

4 Amy는 그녀의 차에 약간의 꿀을 넣었다. (put, honey, in her tea)

→ _____

1 짝 지어진 단어의 관계가 나머지와 <u>다른</u> 하나는?

① sad – sadly   ② love – lovely

③ busy – busily   ④ normal – normally

⑤ happy – happily

5 빈칸에 알맞은 말이 순서대로 짝 지어진 것은?

> • I don't have _____ questions.
>
> • Mike eats _____ cheese every day.

① any – any   ② any – many

③ any – some   ④ some – any

⑤ some – much

[2-3] 빈칸에 들어갈 말로 알맞지 <u>않은</u> 것을 고르시오.

2
> The cookies smell _____.

① sweet   ② good   ③ nice

④ delicious   ⑤ well

[6-8] 빈칸에 공통으로 들어갈 말로 알맞은 것을 고르시오.

6
> • Mr. Kim gave us _____ homework.
>
> • Luna invited _____ friends to her birthday party.

① many   ② much   ③ a lot of

④ a few   ⑤ a little

3
> My little sister and I usually eat dinner _____.

① early   ② late   ③ slowly

④ friendly   ⑤ quietly

7
> • John studied very _____.
>
> • It is _____ to believe her.

① hard   ② well   ③ easy

④ difficult   ⑤ good

8
> • My brother always eats too _____.
>
> • I'd like to buy a _____ car.

4 단어의 성격이 나머지와 <u>다른</u> 하나는?

① sadly   ② ugly   ③ terribly

④ luckily   ⑤ gently

① slowly   ② high   ③ heavily

④ fast   ⑤ late

9 밑줄 친 부분이 어법상 올바른 것은?

① I saved <u>a few</u> money in the bank.

② Let's add <u>any</u> sugar to the soup.

③ There isn't <u>many</u> information in the book.

④ Were there <u>much</u> food at the party?

⑤ They asked Mr. Jones <u>much</u> questions.

12 밑줄 친 단어와 바꿔 쓸 수 있는 것은?

> There are <u>a lot of</u> cafés near my house.

① little   ② any   ③ much

④ a little   ⑤ many

10 대화의 빈칸에 알맞은 말이 순서대로 짝 지어진 것은?

> A: How _____ do you skip breakfast?
>
> B: I _____ skip breakfast. I have breakfast every day.

① often − always   ② often − usually

③ often − never   ④ many − often

⑤ many − never

13 밑줄 친 단어의 쓰임이 나머지와 다른 하나는?

① Did you sleep <u>late</u> last night?

② The bus arrived two hours <u>late</u>.

③ You will be <u>late</u> for the meeting.

④ Dad came home <u>late</u> yesterday.

⑤ The store is open <u>late</u> on Sundays.

11 어법상 틀린 문장은?

① Tony is a famous actor.

② This is my new computer.

③ Sujin has cute two puppies.

④ The cake is very delicious.

⑤ I want these beautiful flowers.

고난도
14 어법상 틀린 것끼리 짝 지어진 것은?

> ⓐ Let's take a little pictures.
>
> ⓑ Do you have any paper bags?
>
> ⓒ I don't have some homework today.
>
> ⓓ How much money did you spend?
>
> ⓔ I put lots of coins in my piggy bank.

① ⓐ, ⓑ   ② ⓐ, ⓒ   ③ ⓑ, ⓒ

④ ⓒ, ⓓ   ⑤ ⓒ, ⓔ

[15-16] 밑줄 친 부분이 어법상 틀린 것을 고르시오.

15 ① I couldn't hear clearly.

② Fred can dance very well.

③ His story is almost true.

④ Oliver kind helped us.

⑤ They talked loudly in the bus.

16 ① I felt bored yesterday.

② William is an interesting boy.

③ They are interested in music.

④ It is surprised to see her there.

⑤ We were excited to hear the news.

17 빈칸 (A)~(C)에 들어갈 말이 바르게 짝 지어진 것은?

| • We had ___(A)___ snow last winter. |
| • Don't drink too ___(B)___ coffee. |
| • There are ___(C)___ clouds in the sky. |

    (A)   (B)   (C)

① few   – much – any

② few   – many – some

③ little – much – any

④ little – many – some

⑤ little – much – some

18 표의 내용을 잘못 이해한 사람은?

How often do you read books?

	Mon.	Tue.	Wed.	Thur.	Fri.	Sat.	Sun.
Lia	×	×	×	×	×	×	×
Ron	×	×	×	×	×	○	○
Mira	×	○	×	×	○	×	×
Jun	○	○	×	○	○	×	×
Eric	○	○	○	○	○	○	○

① 소민: Lia never reads books.

② 호진: Ron sometimes reads books.

③ 지나: Mira always reads books.

④ 민호: Jun often reads books.

⑤ 영지: Eric always reads books.

19 밑줄 친 부분을 잘못 고친 것은?

① I couldn't sleep good yesterday.

           → well

② Mr. Davis drives too fast.

           → fastly

③ The rainy season came earlily.

           → early

④ Do I have to wait longly?

           → long

⑤ The children were sitting quiet.

           → quietly

고난도

20 어법상 올바른 문장의 개수는?

| ⓐ This is a difficult question. |
| ⓑ Ms. Han often bakes some cookies. |
| ⓒ You should think carefully about it. |
| ⓓ I feel like having a little rest now. |

① 0개   ② 1개   ③ 2개

④ 3개   ⑤ 4개

21 두 문장의 의미가 같도록 문장을 완성하시오.

(1) There was a sudden change in the weather.

= The weather changed _____.

(2) This shirt is expensive.

= This is a(n) _____ _____.

22 괄호 안의 단어를 알맞은 형태로 바꿔 문장을 완성하시오.

(1) The airplane arrived _____. (safe)

(2) Jinho doesn't scare _____. (easy)

(3) Minsu came _____ this morning. (late)

23 그림을 보고, 빈칸에 알맞은 말을 보기 에서 골라 쓰시오.

| 보기 | lots of   much   any   a few   a little |

(1) There are _____ books on the desk.

(2) There is _____ orange juice in the glass.

(3) There aren't _____ pencils on the desk.

24 어법상 틀린 부분을 찾아 바르게 고쳐 쓰시오.

(1) I love beautiful your dress.

_____ → _____

(2) Would you like any hot water?

_____ → _____

(3) I saw an excited game on TV.

_____ → _____

(4) An eagle flies highly in the sky.

_____ → _____

고난도
25 인터뷰 내용과 일치하도록 알맞은 빈도부사를 사용하여 문장을 완성하시오.

A: Suji, do you get up early?
B: Yes, I get up early every morning.
A: Do you go jogging?
B: Yes, I go jogging on Mondays and Fridays near my house.
A: Do you walk to school?
B: No, I don't. My school is not close.

(1) Suji _____ _____ _____ early.

(2) Suji _____ _____ near her house.

(3) Suji _____ _____ to school.

13

비교 구문

비교 구문은 형용사나 부사의 표현을 활용하여 둘 이상의 대상을 비교할 때 사용한다.

원급은 형용사나 부사의 원래 형태이며, 비교급은 대개 원급에 -er을 붙이고, 최상급은 -est를 붙여서 만든다. 비교급은 '더 ~한/하게'라는 뜻이고, 최상급은 '가장 ~한/하게'라는 뜻이다.★

		원급	비교급	최상급
대부분의 경우	+-er/-est	tall	taller	tallest
-e로 끝나는 경우	+-r/-st	large	larger	largest
-y로 끝나는 경우	y를 i로 바꾸고 +-er/-est	easy pretty	easier prettier	easiest prettiest
「단모음+단자음」으로 끝나는 경우	자음을 한 번 더 쓰고 +-er/-est	hot big	hotter bigger	hottest biggest
3음절 이상, -ful, -ous, -ing, -ive 등으로 끝나는 2음절인 경우	more/most + 원급	useful famous important	more useful more famous more important	most useful most famous most important

↳ '음절'은 한 번에 발음되는 모음을 포함한 소리 단위를 말해요.

개념확인 옳은 표현 고르기

1 가장 긴
☐ longer ☐ longest

2 더 추운
☐ colder ☐ coldest

3 더 유용한
☐ more useful ☐ most useful

기본연습 다음 단어의 비교급과 최상급을 쓰시오.

1 fast – _____ – _____

2 big – _____ – _____

3 loud – _____ – _____

4 tall – _____ – _____

5 high – _____ – _____

6 happy – _____ – _____

7 large – _____ – _____

8 thin – _____ – _____

9 cute – _____ – _____

10 strong – _____ – _____

11 difficult – _____ – _____

12 easy – _____ – _____

13 nice – _____ – _____

14 busy – _____ – _____

15 hard – _____ – _____

16 exciting – _____ – _____

17 short – _____ – _____

18 small – _____ – _____

19 hot – _____ – _____

20 cheap – _____ – _____

21 young – _____ – _____

22 delicious – _____ – _____

23 beautiful – _____ – _____

24 heavy – _____ – _____

비교급과 최상급: 불규칙 변화

정답 및 해설 p.38

일부 형용사와 부사의 비교급과 최상급은 일정한 규칙 없이 변화한다.

원급		비교급	최상급
good	좋은	better	best
well	건강한, 잘		
bad	나쁜	worse	worst

원급		비교급	최상급
many	(수가) 많은	more	most
much	(양이) 많은, 많이		
little	(양이) 적은	less	least

개념확인 옳은 표현 고르기

1 더 잘
☐ well ☐ better

2 가장 (양이) 적은
☐ less ☐ least

3 더 나쁜
☐ worse ☐ worst

기본연습 다음 단어의 비교급과 최상급을 쓰시오.

1 little – _____ – _____   **2** bright – _____ – _____

3 thick – _____ – _____   **4** well – _____ – _____

5 slow – _____ – _____   **6** pretty – _____ – _____

7 bad – _____ – _____   **8** much – _____ – _____

9 active – _____ – _____   **10** tasty – _____ – _____

11 cold – _____ – _____   **12** famous – _____ – _____

13 long – _____ – _____   **14** dark – _____ – _____

15 many – _____ – _____   **16** dirty – _____ – _____

17 good – _____ – _____   **18** early – _____ – _____

19 sweet – _____ – _____   **20** weak – _____ – _____

21 expensive – _____ – _____   **22** interesting – _____ – _____

틀리기 쉬운 내/신/포/인/트

형용사나 부사의 비교급과 최상급의 변화형을 기억해요.

형용사의 비교급과 최상급이 <u>잘못</u> 짝 지어진 것은?

① bad – worse – worst
② good – gooder – goodest
③ happy – happier – happiest
④ useful – more useful – most useful

비교급을 이용한 비교

정답 및 해설 p.38

비교급 문장은 「비교급+than」의 형태로 쓰며, 두 개의 대상을 비교하여 '~보다 더 …한/하게'라는 의미를 나타낸다.

A	동사	비교급+than	B.	A가 B보다 더 ~하다.
Sujin	is	older than	Miyeong.	수진이는 미영이보다 나이가 더 많다.
Henry	ran	slower than	his sister.	Henry는 그의 여동생보다 더 느리게 달렸다.

↪ '그때'라는 뜻의 then을 쓰지 않도록 주의해요.

주의 비교하는 두 대상은 동등한 성질이거나 형태여야 한다.
The movie is more interesting than **the book**. 영화가 책보다 더 재미있다.
↪ 영화와 책은 재미를 비교할 수 있다는 점에서 같은 성질이에요.

개념확인 비교급 찾기

1 I am younger than Jenny.　**2** Suho swam faster than me.　**3** Liz danced better than Tom.

기본연습 **A** 괄호 안에서 알맞은 것을 고르시오.

1 The Earth is (small / smaller) than the sun.

2 Mike worked (harder / more hard) than Tim.

3 Oranges are (sweet / sweeter) than lemons.

4 My kite flew higher than (you / yours).

5 This show is more interesting (than / then) that one.

B 우리말과 일치하도록 괄호 안의 말을 이용하여 문장을 완성하시오.

1 너의 방은 나의 것보다 더 커 보인다. (big)

→ Your room looks _____ _____ mine.

2 유진이는 민수보다 더 나이가 많다. (old)

→ Yujin is _____ _____ Minsu.

3 이 자동차는 저 트럭보다 더 가볍다. (light)

→ This car is _____ _____ that truck.

4 우리 엄마는 항상 나보다 더 일찍 일어난다. (early)

→ My mom always gets up _____ _____ me.

5 개는 인간보다 더 잘 들을 수 있다. (well)

→ Dogs can hear _____ _____ humans.

6 그 탑은 그 건물보다 더 높다. (tall)

→ The tower is _____ _____ the building.

7 시간은 돈보다 더 중요하다. (important)

→ Time is _____ _____ _____ money.

8 Sam은 대개 Eric보다 더 조심스럽게 운전한다. (carefully)

→ Sam usually drives _____ _____ _____ Eric.

9 준하는 민수보다 더 인기가 많다. (popular)

→ Junha is _____ _____ _____ Minsu.

C 그림을 보고, 괄호 안에서 알맞은 말을 골라 비교하는 문장을 완성하시오.

1

2

3

4

5

5
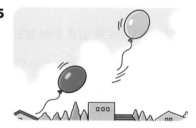

1 Tony is _____ _____ Emma. (short / tall)

2 Brian is running _____ _____ Kevin. (slow / fast)

3 The elephant is _____ _____ the hippo. (light / heavy)

4 The red book is _____ _____ the blue one. (thin / thick)

5 The pink hat is _____ _____ the purple cap. (cheap / expensive)

6 The yellow balloon is flying _____ _____ the green one. (low / high)

틀리기 쉬운 내/신/포/인/트

비교급은 than과 함께 쓰여 '~보다 더 …한/하게'라는 뜻을 나타내요.

대화의 빈칸에 들어갈 말로 알맞은 것은?

A: How's the weather today?

B: Today is _____ than yesterday.

① hot　　② windy　　③ sunny　　④ colder

비교급을 강조할 때는 비교급 앞에 **much, still, even, far, a lot** 등의 부사를 쓰며, '훨씬'이라는 의미를 나타낸다.

부사		비교급
much, still, even, far, a lot	+	형용사/부사의 비교급

The sun is **much bigger** than the Earth. 태양은 지구보다 훨씬 더 크다.

Health is **a lot more important** than money. 건강이 돈보다 훨씬 더 중요하다.

주의 부사 very(매우)는 비교급이 아닌 원급을 강조한다.
Jane is **very** quiet. Jane은 매우 조용하다.

개념확인 비교급을 강조하는 부사 찾기

1 Andy is much taller than Homin.   **2** The ant is even smaller than the spider.

기본연습 우리말과 일치하도록 괄호 안의 말을 이용하여 문장을 완성하시오.

1 빛은 소리보다 훨씬 더 빨리 이동한다. (much, fast)

→ Light travels ＿＿＿＿＿ ＿＿＿＿＿ ＿＿＿＿＿ sound.

2 거북이는 코끼리보다 훨씬 더 오래 산다. (even, long)

→ A turtle lives ＿＿＿＿＿ ＿＿＿＿＿ ＿＿＿＿＿ an elephant.

3 오늘의 날씨는 어제의 날씨보다 훨씬 더 나쁘다. (still, bad)

→ Today's weather is ＿＿＿＿＿ ＿＿＿＿＿ ＿＿＿＿＿ yesterday's.

4 민호는 대개 나보다 훨씬 더 노래를 잘한다. (a lot, well)

→ Minho usually sings ＿＿＿＿＿ ＿＿＿＿＿ ＿＿＿＿＿ ＿＿＿＿＿ me.

5 이 피자가 저 피자보다 훨씬 더 맛있다. (far, delicious)

→ This pizza is ＿＿＿＿＿ ＿＿＿＿＿ ＿＿＿＿＿ ＿＿＿＿＿ that one.

6 그의 컴퓨터는 내 것보다 훨씬 더 비싸다. (much, expensive)

→ His computer is ＿＿＿＿＿ ＿＿＿＿＿ ＿＿＿＿＿ ＿＿＿＿＿ mine.

**틀리기 쉬운
내/신/포/인/트**

비교급을 강조할 때 쓰는
부사를 기억해요.

빈칸에 들어갈 말로 알맞지 <u>않은</u> 것은?

My car is ＿＿＿＿＿ older than yours.

① much   ② even   ③ far   ④ very

POINT 5 최상급을 이용한 비교

최상급 문장은 「the+최상급」의 형태로 쓰며, 셋 이상의 대상을 비교하여 '가장 …한/하게'라는 의미를 나타낸다.
뒤에 in이나 of를 사용하여 비교 범위를 나타낼 수 있다.

the+최상급	+in+장소/집단 ~에서 가장 …한/하게	Tom is **the tallest** boy **in** his class.	Tom은 반에서 가장 키가 큰 남자아이이다.
	+of+기간/복수 명사 ~ 중에서 가장 …한/하게	Today is **the happiest** day **of** my life.	오늘은 내 인생에서 가장 행복한 날이다.

주의 「the+최상급+명사」로 최상급을 나타낼 때, 문맥상 짐작이 가능하면 명사를 생략하기도 한다.
Mina is **the youngest** (girl) **of** the three sisters. 미나는 세 자매들 중에서 가장 어리다.

개념확인 최상급 찾기

1 Ann is the smartest of the four students.　　**2** Kevin is the strongest in his team.

기본연습 A 괄호 안에서 알맞은 것을 고르시오.

1 I am the (shortest / most short) person in my family.

2 This problem is the (difficultest / most difficult) of them all.

3 We stayed in the (nicest / most nice) room in the hotel.

4 Science is (interestingest / the most interesting) subject to me.

5 That is (worse / the worst) movie of the five.

6 This is (older / the oldest) house in the town.

7 Jack is (taller / the tallest) of the four boys.

8 Canada is (bigger / the biggest) than China.

9 Mt. Everest is (higher / the highest) mountain in the world.

10 This T-shirt is (more expensive / the most expensive) than that dress.

B 괄호 안의 말을 이용하여 최상급 문장을 완성하시오.

1 It was _____ _____ day of his life. (sad)

2 Alaska is _____ _____ state in the U.S. (big)

3 The Nile is _____ _____ river in Africa. (long)

4 Bulgogi is _____ _____ _____ dish in this restaurant. (delicious)

5 Andy is _____ _____ student in my science class. (bright)

6 January is usually _____ _____ month of the year. (cold)

7 Where is _____ _____ desert in the world? (hot)

8 Amy has _____ _____ voice in her class. (loud)

9 Math is _____ _____ _____ subject for me. (difficult)

10 Health is _____ _____ _____ thing of all. (important)

11 I'm _____ _____ member in the book club. (young)

12 The Louvre is _____ _____ _____ museum in France. (famous)

C 표를 보고, 보기 에서 알맞은 말을 골라 최상급 문장을 완성하시오.

	나이	키	몸무게	최고 속도
Cheetah	5 years old	0.9 m	70 kg	93 km/h
Giraffe	12 years old	6 m	800 kg	60 km/h
Hippo	25 years old	1.5 m	1,500 kg	48 km/h
Turtle	55 years old	0.9 m	120 kg	0.4 km/h

보기	tall	fast	old	heavy

1 The cheetah is _____ _____ animal of the four.

2 The turtle is _____ _____ animal of the four.

3 The hippo is _____ _____ animal of the four.

4 The giraffe is _____ _____ animal of the four.

틀리기 쉬운
내/신/포/인/트

최상급은 「the + 최상급 +
in/of ~」의 형태로
'~(중)에서 가장 …한/하게'
라는 뜻을 나타내요.

빈칸에 들어갈 말로 알맞은 것은?

Soccer is the _____ sport in Brazil.

① popularer　　　　　② more popular
③ popularest　　　　④ most popular

POINT 6 원급을 이용한 비교

두 대상의 정도가 같음을 표현할 때 「as＋원급＋as」의 형태로 쓰며, '～만큼 …한/하게'라는 의미를 나타낸다.

A	동사	as＋원급＋as	B.	
Jinsu	is	**as tall as**	his father.	A는 B만큼 ～하다. 진수는 그의 아버지**만큼** 키가 크다.
Mike	runs	**as fast as**	Matthew.	Mike는 Matthew**만큼** 빠르게 달린다.

Tips 원급 비교의 부정은 「not as(so)＋원급＋as」의 형태로 쓰며, '～만큼 …하지 않은/않게'라는 의미를 나타낸다.
Today is **not as(so) hot as** yesterday. 오늘은 어제만큼 덥지 않다.

주의 비교하는 두 대상은 동등한 성질이거나 형태여야 한다.
My bag is **as heavy as** yours. 내 가방은 네 것만큼 무겁다. 〈yours = your bag〉

개념확인 원급 찾기

1 John is as old as me.

2 She sleeps as much as her son.

기본연습 우리말과 일치하도록 괄호 안의 말을 이용하여 문장을 완성하시오.

1 하나는 지호만큼 친절하다. (kind)
→ Hana is ＿＿＿＿＿＿＿＿＿＿ Jiho.

2 내 방은 남동생의 것만큼 깨끗하다. (clean)
→ My room is ＿＿＿＿＿＿＿＿＿＿ my brother's.

3 Eric은 Susan만큼 일찍 일어난다. (early)
→ Eric wakes up ＿＿＿＿＿＿＿＿＿＿ Susan.

4 봄은 겨울만큼 춥지 않다. (cold)
→ Spring is ＿＿＿＿＿＿＿＿＿＿ winter.

5 지나는 Sam만큼 피아노를 잘 친다. (well)
→ Jina plays the piano ＿＿＿＿＿＿＿＿＿＿ Sam.

6 이 자전거는 내 차만큼 비싸다. (expensive)
→ This bike is ＿＿＿＿＿＿＿＿＿＿ my car.

7 그 소년은 내 여동생만큼 나이가 많다. (old)
→ The boy is ＿＿＿＿＿＿＿＿＿＿ my sister.

8 Kate는 Ann만큼 바쁘지 않다. (busy)
→ Kate is ＿＿＿＿＿＿＿＿＿＿ Ann.

9 이 셔츠는 저것만큼 싸다. (cheap)
→ This shirt is ＿＿＿＿＿＿＿＿＿＿ that one.

10 거북이는 토끼만큼 빠르지 않다. (fast)
→ Turtles are ＿＿＿＿＿＿＿＿＿＿ rabbits.

틀리기 쉬운 내/신/포/인/트

'～만큼 …한'은 「as＋형용사의 원급＋as」로 써요.

빈칸에 들어갈 말로 알맞은 것은?

Mina's dress is as ＿＿＿＿＿＿ as mine.

① pretty
② prettier
③ the prettiest
④ more pretty

개 념 완 성 TEST

STEP 1 Map으로 개념 정리하기

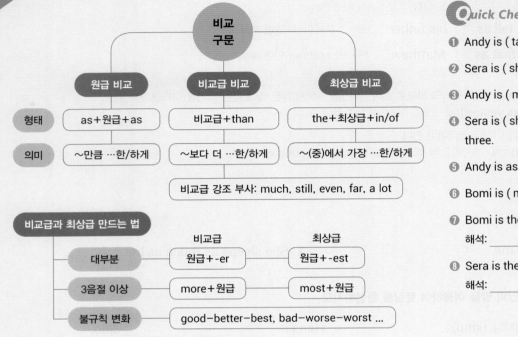

Quick Check

❶ Andy is (tall / taller) than Bomi.

❷ Sera is (short / shorter) than Bomi.

❸ Andy is (much / very) taller than Sera.

❹ Sera is (shorter / the shortest) of the three.

❺ Andy is as (old / older) as Sera.

❻ Bomi is (more / most) popular than Andy.

❼ Bomi is the youngest of the three.

해석: _____

❽ Sera is the most popular singer in Korea.

해석: _____

STEP 2 기본 다지기

빈칸완성

A 우리말과 일치하도록 빈칸에 알맞은 말을 넣어 문장을 완성하시오.

1 지우는 나보다 더 어리다. → Jiwoo is _____ _____ me.

2 미나는 우리 반에서 가장 친절한 사람이다. → Mina is _____ _____ person in my class.

3 Daniel은 넷 중에서 가장 빠른 주자이다. → Daniel is _____ _____ runner of the four.

4 이 문제가 저 문제보다 더 어렵다. → This question is _____ _____ than that one.

5 너는 항상 나보다 노래를 더 잘한다. → You always sing _____ _____ me.

6 지구는 태양보다 훨씬 더 작다. → The Earth is much _____ _____ the sun.

7 내 개는 너의 개만큼 귀엽다. → My dog is _____ _____ _____ yours.

8 과학은 수학보다 더 재미있다. → Science is _____ _____ _____ math.

9 오늘은 어제만큼 따뜻하다. → Today is _____ _____ _____ yesterday.

10 미라의 머리카락은 내 것만큼 짧다. → Mira's hair is _____ _____ _____ mine.

밑줄 친 부분이 어법상 바르면 〇라고 쓰고, 틀리면 바르게 고쳐 쓰시오.

1 This puzzle is <u>more easy</u> than that one. → _____

2 I am as <u>healthest</u> as my sister. → _____

3 August is usually the <u>hotter</u> month of the year. → _____

4 It is the <u>most tall</u> building in the world. → _____

5 This box is <u>a lot heavier</u> than that one. → _____

6 Kevin is <u>as busier</u> as his mother. → _____

7 Lisa is <u>much famous</u> than Nancy. → _____

주어진 문장을 읽고, 괄호 안의 말을 이용하여 비교하는 문장을 완성하시오.

1 Sangmin is 178 cm tall. Junsu is 170 cm tall.

→ Sangmin is _____ Junsu. (tall)

2 The red hat is $7. The blue hat is $10.

→ The red hat is _____ the blue one. (cheap)

3 This chair weighs 10 kg. That chair weighs 6 kg.

→ This chair is _____ that chair. (heavy)

4 It was −8℃ yesterday. It is also −8℃ today.

→ Today is _____ yesterday. (cold)

5 Mr. Smith is 38 years old. My uncle is 36 years old.

→ Mr. Smith is _____ my uncle. (old)

6 Sam wakes up early at 6:30 a.m. His brother and parents wake up at 7 a.m.

→ Sam wakes up _____ in his family. (early)

7 The math book is 4 cm thick. The science book is 2 cm thick.

→ The math book is _____ the science book. (thick)

8 Bobby's dog is as big as a wolf. Yuri's dog is as small as a rabbit.

→ Bobby's dog is _____ Yuri's dog. (big)

9 Jenny can jump up to 1 m high. Homin and Sera can jump up to 60 cm high.

→ Jenny can jump _____ of the three. (high)

STEP 3 서술형 따라잡기

그림이해
A 그림을 보고, 비교하는 문장을 완성하시오.

1
Yesterday   Today

2

3

1 Today is _____ _____ yesterday.

2 Suji is _____ _____ of the three runners.

3 The yellow ruler is _____ _____ _____ the blue one.

영작완성
B 우리말과 일치하도록 괄호 안의 말을 바르게 배열하여 문장을 쓰시오.

1 내 가방은 지나의 가방만큼 무겁다. (Jina's bag, as, is, heavy, my bag, as)

→ _____

2 Sam은 넷 중에서 가장 훌륭한 춤꾼이다. (the, dancer, of, best, Sam, is, four, the)

→ _____

3 이 컴퓨터는 그 가게에서 가장 비싸다. (in the store, most, this computer, expensive, the, is)

→ _____

4 이 책은 저 책보다 훨씬 더 두껍다. (than, much, is, this book, that book, thicker)

→ _____

문장영작
C 우리말과 일치하도록 괄호 안의 말을 이용하여 영작하시오.

1 나는 Lisa보다 수영을 잘할 수 있다. (can, swim, well)

→ _____

2 James는 학교에서 가장 유명한 사람이다. (famous, person, in the school)

→ _____

3 이번 겨울은 지난 겨울보다 훨씬 더 춥다. (winter, even, cold)

→ _____

4 Eric은 Tony만큼 늦게 집에 왔다. (come home, late)

→ _____

1 원급, 비교급, 최상급이 <u>잘못</u> 짝 지어진 것은?

① tall – taller – tallest

② old – older – oldest

③ bad – badder – baddest

④ good – better – best

⑤ happy – happier – happiest

5

> My computer is as _____ as Sojin's.

① old   ② new   ③ expensive

④ worse   ⑤ light

[2-3] 빈칸에 알맞은 말이 순서대로 짝 지어진 것을 고르시오.

2

> • My room is as large _____ Suho's.
> • Mijin is older _____ Lia.

① as – in   ② as – as   ③ as – than

④ than – as   ⑤ than – than

6 짝 지어진 단어의 관계가 나머지와 <u>다른</u> 하나는?

① deep – deeper   ② many – most

③ busy – busier   ④ young – younger

⑤ well – better

3

> • Sumin swam _____ than Jaemin.
> • The cheetah is the _____ animal in the world.

① fast – faster   ② fast – fastest

③ faster – faster   ④ faster – fast

⑤ faster – fastest

[7-8] 빈칸에 들어갈 말로 알맞은 것을 고르시오.

7

> Ryan eats _____ fruit than Andy.

① little   ② much   ③ most

④ less   ⑤ least

[4-5] 빈칸에 들어갈 말로 알맞지 <u>않은</u> 것을 고르시오.

4

> This year is _____ hotter than last year.

① even   ② a lot   ③ much

④ very   ⑤ far

8

> Bibimbap is the _____ dish in that restaurant.

① delicious   ② more delicious

③ deliciouser   ④ deliciousest

⑤ most delicious

9 빈칸에 들어갈 말이 나머지와 <u>다른</u> 하나는?

① Her hair is longer _____ mine.
② Today is hotter _____ yesterday.
③ Ron is the youngest _____ the four.
④ This shirt is cheaper _____ that one.
⑤ Time is more important _____ money.

10 ①~⑤ 중 **much**가 들어갈 위치로 알맞은 곳은?

China (①) is (②) bigger (③) than (④)
Korea (⑤).

11 표의 내용과 일치하는 것은?

Menu	Price
Pasta	$10
Pizza	$12
Hamburger	$8
Salad	$8
Hot dog	$5

① The pasta is more expensive than the pizza.
② The pizza is the most expensive dish.
③ The hamburger is cheaper than the salad.
④ The hamburger is as cheap as the hot dog.
⑤ The salad is the cheapest dish.

12 어법상 <u>틀린</u> 것끼리 짝 지어진 것은?

ⓐ Kate is the most pretty in my class.
ⓑ Today is the saddest day of his life.
ⓒ Russia is the largest country in the world.
ⓓ This room is far darker than that room.
ⓔ The tree is as taller as the building.

① ⓐ, ⓑ   ② ⓐ, ⓒ, ⓓ   ③ ⓐ, ⓔ
④ ⓑ, ⓒ, ⓓ   ⑤ ⓓ, ⓔ

13 우리말을 영어로 바르게 옮긴 것은?

그것은 정원에서 가장 키가 큰 나무이다.

① It is as tall as the tree in the garden.
② It is taller than the tree in the garden.
③ It is much taller than the tree in the garden.
④ It is the most tall tree in the garden.
⑤ It is the tallest tree in the garden.

14 빈칸 (A)~(C)에 들어갈 말이 바르게 짝 지어진 것은?

• Leon is ____(A)____ popular than Leonardo.
• Mike can speak Chinese ____(B)____ than his sister.
• Iron is ____(C)____ more useful than gold.

	(A)	(B)	(C)
①	more	well	more
②	more	better	very
③	more	better	much
④	much	better	very
⑤	much	well	much

[15-16] 밑줄 친 부분이 어법상 틀린 것을 고르시오.

15 ① Paul is <u>shorter</u> than Jim.
② My room is smaller than <u>you</u>.
③ Mira is as <u>friendly</u> as Ms. Lee.
④ This is the <u>longest</u> bridge in the world.
⑤ Somin is the <u>youngest</u> of the club members.

16 ① Jinho is as <u>smart</u> as Tom.
② Math is <u>more difficult</u> than English.
③ Canada is much <u>bigger</u> than Japan.
④ Thomas is the <u>heaviest</u> of the three.
⑤ The rabbit is <u>more faster</u> than the turtle.

17 두 문장을 비교하는 한 문장으로 바꿔 쓸 때, 빈칸에 들어갈 말로 알맞은 것은?

> Tony weighs 65 kilograms. Hansu weighs 58 kilograms.
> → Tony is _____ Hansu.

① more heavy
② more heavier than
③ much heavy than
④ heavier than
⑤ the heaviest

18 밑줄 친 부분을 잘못 고친 것은?

① Sam likes winter <u>much</u> than summer.
→ most
② I can jump <u>higher much</u> than you.
→ much higher
③ She is the best singer <u>in</u> all my friends.
→ of
④ Health is the <u>importantest</u> thing in my life.
→ most important
⑤ Lakes are <u>as not big as</u> oceans.
→ not as big as

19 우리말을 영어로 잘못 옮긴 것은?

① Tommy는 그의 남동생보다 더 말랐다.
→ Tommy is thinner than his brother.
② 그녀는 보라만큼 늦게 일어난다.
→ She gets up as late as Bora.
③ 미나는 학생들 중에서 가장 일찍 왔다.
→ Mina came the earlier of the students.
④ 그는 그 마을에서 가장 부자이다.
→ He is the richest person in the town.
⑤ 우리 아버지는 나보다 훨씬 더 힘이 세다.
→ My father is much stronger than me.

고난도
20 어법상 올바른 문장의 개수는?

> ⓐ The moon is small than the Earth.
> ⓑ Grapes are the sweetest than strawberries.
> ⓒ Yesterday was hotter than today.
> ⓓ Tom sings as well as Jinho.
> ⓔ This window is the widest of them all.

① 0개   ② 1개   ③ 2개
④ 3개   ⑤ 4개

21 다음 그림을 보고, 문장을 완성하시오.

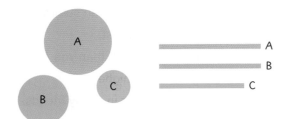

(1) Circle A is _____ of the three.

(2) Circle C is _____ of the three.

(3) Line A is _____ Line C.

(4) Line A is _____ Line B.

22 우리말과 일치하도록 괄호 안의 말을 이용하여 문장을 완성하시오.

(1) 오늘은 어제만큼 화창하다. (sunny)

→ Today is _____ yesterday.

(2) 수영은 요가보다 훨씬 더 재미있다.

(a lot, interesting)

→ Swimming is _____ yoga.

(3) 대왕고래는 세상에서 가장 큰 동물이다.

(large, animal)

→ The blue whale is _____ in the world.

고난도

23 어법상 틀린 부분을 찾아 바르게 고쳐 쓰시오.

(1) Health is far important than money.

_____ → _____

(2) Jeju-do is most large island in Korea.

_____ → _____

24 다음 표를 보고, 괄호 안의 말을 이용하여 문장을 완성하시오.

스마트폰	가격($)	무게(g)	인기도
A	420	130	★
B	300	150	★★★
C	420	100	★★

(1) Smartphone A is _____ Smartphone C. (heavy)

(2) Smartphone B is _____ of the three. (popular)

(3) Smartphone C is _____ Smartphone A. (expensive)

25 주어진 문장을 읽고, 괄호 안의 말을 이용하여 비교하는 문장을 완성하시오.

(1)
> I go to bed at 9 p.m. My little brother goes to bed at 10 p.m.

→ I go to bed _____.

(early)

(2)
> Hojin is 13 years old. Diana is 14 years old. Peter is 13 years old.

→ Diana is _____ the three.

(old)

C H A P T E R

14

접속사와 전치사

접속사는 단어와 단어, 절과 절 등을 이어주는 말이다.
전치사는 명사나 대명사 앞에 놓여 장소, 위치, 시간 등을 나타내는 말이다.

접속사: and, but, or, so

정답 및 해설 p.41

접속사 and, but, or, so는 등위 접속사로, 문법적으로 대등한 말들을 연결한다.

and	~과, 그리고 〈비슷한 내용을 연결〉	Eric **and** Ben are studying together. 단어　　　단어	Eric과 Ben은 함께 공부하고 있다.
but	그러나, ~이지만 〈상반되는 내용을 연결〉	Eric tried his best **but** failed the test. 구　　　　　　구	Eric은 최선을 다했**지만** 시험에서 떨어졌다.
or	~이나, 또는 〈둘 이상의 선택 사항을 연결〉	I can go to a concert **or** stay home. 구　　　　　구	나는 콘서트에 가**거나** 집에 머물 수 있다.
so	그래서 〈원인과 결과를 연결〉	I am tired, **so** I want to stay home. 절　　　　　절	나는 피곤**해서** 집에 머물고 싶다.

주의 등위 접속사 앞뒤로 대등한 요소가 온다.
It is *cold* **and** *rainy*. 춥고 비가 내린다.
→ cold와 rainy는 둘 다 형용사이다.

Tips and로 세 가지 이상을 연결할 경우, 「A, B, and C」로 쓴다.
I ate *an apple*, *a banana*, **and** *two strawberries*.
나는 사과 한 개와 바나나 한 개, 딸기 두 개를 먹었다.

궁금해요!
'구'와 '절'이 무엇인가요?

'구'는 두 개 이상의 단어 묶음으로 하나의 품사 역할을 하는 거예요.
'절'은 주어와 동사가 포함된 두 개 이상의 단어 묶음을 말해요.

 접속사 찾기

1 She is pretty and smart.　　**2** He was tired but happy.　　**3** Are you Japanese or Chinese?

기본연습 **A** 괄호 안에서 알맞은 것을 고르시오.

1 Peter (and / but) Subin are my friends.

2 He'll watch a movie (or / so) ride his bike.

3 They didn't invite me, (but / so) I didn't go.

4 Is he your father (and / or) your uncle?

5 It was sunny, (but / so) we went to the beach.

6 I want to buy a car, (but / or) it is very expensive.

7 The service was nice, (and / but) the food was good.

B 밑줄 친 접속사가 연결하는 단어나 구, 절에 ○로 표시하시오.

1 The box is small <u>but</u> heavy.

2 Would you like beef <u>or</u> chicken?

3 Do you go to school by bus <u>or</u> on foot?

4 I felt sick, <u>so</u> I took some medicine.

5 She likes reading books <u>and</u> playing the piano.

C 빈칸에 and, but, or, so 중 알맞은 것을 쓰시오.

1 Which do you want, coffee _____ tea?

2 He's feeling strong _____ healthy.

3 Is it Wednesday _____ Thursday today?

4 I was very tired, _____ I went to bed early.

5 It was a very difficult exam, _____ I passed it.

6 It is raining now, _____ you can't play outside.

7 Listen to the story _____ answer the questions.

8 Patrick likes history, _____ he doesn't like math.

D 두 문장을 한 문장으로 연결할 때, 빈칸에 알맞은 등위 접속사를 쓰시오.

1 Nancy is honest. She is also smart.
→ Nancy is honest _____ smart.

2 She called his name. He did not answer.
→ She called his name, _____ he did not answer.

3 Amy bought two croissants. She also bought a waffle.
→ Amy bought two croissants _____ a waffle.

4 Is Jane standing? Is she sitting on the bench?
→ Is Jane standing _____ sitting on the bench?

5 Betty usually comes home at 6. She arrived late tonight.
→ Betty usually comes home at 6, _____ she arrived late tonight.

6 The students forgot their homework. The teacher was disappointed.
→ The students forgot their homework, _____ the teacher was disappointed.

틀리기 쉬운
내/신/포/인/트

앞뒤에 연결되는 말들의
관계에 따라 사용해야
하는 접속사가 달라져요.

빈칸에 알맞은 말이 순서대로 짝 지어진 것은?

• I sent him an email, _____ he didn't read it.
• It was very warm, _____ we went swimming.

① and – but   ② and – so
③ but – so   ④ but – or

POINT 2 명령문＋and/or

「명령문, and ~」는 '…해라, 그러면 ~'의 의미이고, 「명령문, or ~」는 '…해라, 그렇지 않으면 ~'의 의미이다.
이때 접속사 and와 or 뒤에는 주어와 동사를 포함한 절이 온다.

명령문, and ~	…해라, 그러면 ~	Exercise,	and you'll be healthy.	운동해라, 그러면 건강해질 것이다.
명령문, or ~	…해라, 그렇지 않으면 ~	Hurry up,	or you'll be too late.	서둘러라, 그렇지 않으면 너무 늦을 것이다.

개념확인 옳은 해석 고르기

1 Smile, and you'll be happy.
　□ 그리고　□ 그러면

2 Get up and run.
　□ 그리고　□ 그러면

3 Have lunch, or you'll be hungry.
　□ 또는　□ 그렇지 않으면

기본연습 빈칸에 and와 or 중 알맞은 것을 쓰시오.

1 Wear a raincoat, ＿＿＿＿＿＿＿ you won't get wet.

2 Help me, ＿＿＿＿＿＿＿ I will buy you an ice cream.

3 Get some rest, ＿＿＿＿＿＿＿ you will feel better.

4 Pick up the box, ＿＿＿＿＿＿＿ it will block the way.

5 Stop talking, ＿＿＿＿＿＿＿ we can't listen to the song.

6 Open the window, ＿＿＿＿＿＿＿ fresh air will come in.

7 Cross the street, ＿＿＿＿＿＿＿ you will find the bank.

8 Tell me your phone number, ＿＿＿＿＿＿＿ I will call you.

9 Don't drive too fast, ＿＿＿＿＿＿＿ you will have an accident.

10 Turn down the music, ＿＿＿＿＿＿＿ you will wake up the baby.

11 Start doing your homework now, ＿＿＿＿＿＿＿ you won't finish it today.

틀리기 쉬운 내/신/포/인/트

접속사 앞뒤에 연결되는 절의 관계를 파악하여 and의 의미를 구별해요.

밑줄 친 부분의 의미가 나머지와 다른 하나는?

① Wear a scarf, and you will feel warm.
② Drink water, and you won't be thirsty.
③ Get up and get ready to go to school.
④ Study hard, and you will get good grades.

POINT 3 접속사: that

접속사 that은 '~라는 것'이라는 의미로 문장에서 주어, 보어, 목적어 역할을 하는 명사절을 이끈다.

가주어예요. → that이 이끄는 명사절이 진주어예요.

주어	**It** is not true	**that he is sick.**	그가 아프다는 것은 사실이 아니다.
보어	The problem is	**that he is sick.**	문제는 그가 아프다는 것이다.
목적어	I didn't know	**(that) he is sick.**	나는 그가 아프다는 것을 몰랐다.

→ that절이 목적어로 쓰이면 접속사 that을 생략할 수 있어요.

Tips that이 이끄는 명사절을 목적어로 취하는 동사에는 think, know, hear, find, say, hope, believe, feel 등이 있다.
I **heard (that)** Alice is your sister. 나는 Alice가 네 여동생이라고 들었다.
I don't **think (that)** this is a problem. 나는 이것이 문제라고 생각하지 않는다.

주의 접속사 that은 절과 함께 쓰고, 지시대명사 that은 단독으로 쓰며, 지시형용사 that은 명사와 함께 쓴다.
He said **that** *you have a cat*. 〈접속사〉 그는 네가 고양이를 기른다고 말했다.
That is Sujin's bike. 〈지시대명사〉 저것은 수진이의 자전거이다.
That *shirt* really suits you. 〈지시형용사〉 저 셔츠는 너에게 정말 잘 어울린다.

개념확인 that이 이끄는 명사절 찾기

1 I hope that you win.　　**2** It is true that he likes cats.　　**3** The truth is that I did my best.

기본연습 **A** 밑줄 친 that의 쓰임으로 알맞은 것을 고르시오.

1 Who is <u>that</u> girl over there?　　☐ 접속사　☐ 지시대명사　☐ 지시형용사

2 Is <u>that</u> your backpack?　　☐ 접속사　☐ 지시대명사　☐ 지시형용사

3 He said <u>that</u> the story was true.　　☐ 접속사　☐ 지시대명사　☐ 지시형용사

4 I felt <u>that</u> I made a big mistake.　　☐ 접속사　☐ 지시대명사　☐ 지시형용사

5 Look at <u>that</u> bird in the tree.　　☐ 접속사　☐ 지시대명사　☐ 지시형용사

6 Could you please say <u>that</u> again?　　☐ 접속사　☐ 지시대명사　☐ 지시형용사

7 It was surprising <u>that</u> they got married.　　☐ 접속사　☐ 지시대명사　☐ 지시형용사

8 The problem is <u>that</u> I am always busy.　　☐ 접속사　☐ 지시대명사　☐ 지시형용사

B 접속사 that이 들어갈 자리를 고르시오.

1 It (①) is (②) interesting (③) some animals (④) can use tools.

2 (①) I (②) hope (③) our team (④) wins the game.

3 The truth (①) is (②) the Earth (③) is (④) very sick.

4 Do (①) you (②) believe (③) we (④) can change the world?

5 You (①) know (②) we (③) don't have (④) any money.

C 밑줄 친 that이 이끄는 절의 역할로 알맞은 것을 고르시오.

1 Tom said <u>that</u> he didn't break the window. □ 주어 □ 보어 □ 목적어

2 It is not true <u>that</u> my father is dead. □ 주어 □ 보어 □ 목적어

3 I agree <u>that</u> the girl is very smart. □ 주어 □ 보어 □ 목적어

4 Her only hope is <u>that</u> her mother is okay. □ 주어 □ 보어 □ 목적어

5 We found <u>that</u> the children were sleeping. □ 주어 □ 보어 □ 목적어

6 She didn't know <u>that</u> the train was leaving. □ 주어 □ 보어 □ 목적어

7 It is a fact <u>that</u> he moved to Japan. □ 주어 □ 보어 □ 목적어

8 The problem is <u>that</u> he cannot drive a car. □ 주어 □ 보어 □ 목적어

D [보기]와 같이 접속사 that을 이용하여 두 문장을 한 문장으로 쓰시오.

> [보기] He wants to be a reporter. I know it.
> → <u>I know that he wants to be a reporter.</u>

1 He is a great soccer player. Everybody knows it.

→ _____

2 She didn't come back from Toronto. He heard this.

→ _____

3 They can go on a picnic this Friday. They hope this.

→ _____

4 Jane will be a doctor. I believe this.

→ _____

5 The two songs were too similar. She said this.

→ _____

틀/리/기 쉬운
내/신/포/인/트

접속사 that과 지시대명사
that을 구별하고 접속사의
특징을 기억해요.

밑줄 친 That(that) 중 생략할 수 있는 것은?

① <u>That</u> is my brother.
② Is <u>that</u> your computer?
③ He said <u>that</u> she was late.
④ Can you tell me about <u>that</u>?

접속사: when, before, after

정답 및 해설 p.41

접속사 when, before, after는 시간을 나타내는 부사절을 이끈다. 부사절은 문장에서 부사 역할을 하며, 문장의 앞과 뒤에 모두 올 수 있다.

when	~할 때	I was having lunch	when she came home.	그녀가 집에 왔을 때 나는 점심을 먹고 있었다.
before	~하기 전에	Wash your hands	before you have lunch.	네가 점심을 먹기 전에 손을 씻어라.
after	~한 후에	After he had lunch,	he did the dishes.	그는 점심을 먹은 후에 설거지를 했다.

↪ 부사절이 앞에 오면 부사절 뒤에 콤마(,)를 써야 해요.

주의 접속사 when은 '~할 때'라는 의미로 쓰이고, 의문사 when은 '언제'라는 의미로 쓰인다.
When you ride a bike, wear a helmet. 〈접속사〉 자전거를 탈 **때**, 헬멧을 써라.
When do you ride your bike? 〈의문사〉 너는 자전거를 **언제** 타니?

주의 시간의 부사절에서는 미래를 나타낼 때 현재시제로 쓴다.
I will visit you **when** I **go** to Rome. 내가 로마에 가면 너를 방문할게.

개념확인 **접속사 찾기**

1 I'll help you after I finish this.　**2** He met me before he left.　**3** When you arrive, call me.

기본연습 **A** 우리말과 일치하도록 빈칸에 알맞은 접속사를 쓰시오.

1 파스타를 먹은 후에 그는 설거지를 했다.
→ He washed the dishes _____ he ate pasta.

2 그녀는 잠자리에 들기 전에 샤워를 했다.
→ She took a shower _____ she went to bed.

3 영화가 끝난 후에 그들은 저녁을 먹었다.
→ They had dinner _____ the movie ended.

4 나는 기차에 탔을 때 그녀에게 전화를 했다.
→ I called her _____ I got on the train.

5 엄마가 돌아오시기 전에 나는 내 방을 청소했다.
→ I cleaned my room _____ my mom came back.

6 그가 지원이에게 꽃을 주었을 때, 그녀는 행복했다.
→ _____ he gave Jiwon a flower, she was happy.

7 그 남자가 들어갔을 때 그 개가 짖었다.
→ The dog barked _____ the man entered.

B 괄호 안에서 알맞은 것을 고르시오.

1 (Before / After) you leave, close the windows.

2 (When / Before) I raise my right arm, it hurts.

3 I lived in Seoul (before / after) I moved to Jeju-do.

4 (When / After) it rained for two days, the weather got cold.

5 (When / After) I was a little boy, I didn't eat onions.

6 Wash your hands (before / after) you touch dirty things.

C 밑줄 친 when의 쓰임으로 알맞은 것을 고르시오.

1 <u>When</u> did you watch the movie? ☐ 접속사 ☐ 의문사

2 My father cries <u>when</u> he watches sad movies. ☐ 접속사 ☐ 의문사

3 <u>When</u> does the science class start? ☐ 접속사 ☐ 의문사

4 He was seven years old <u>when</u> he learned to skate. ☐ 접속사 ☐ 의문사

D 보기 와 같이 괄호 안의 접속사를 이용하여 두 문장을 한 문장으로 쓰시오.

> 보기 Turn off the lights. You go out. (before)
> → Turn off the lights before you go out.

1 You can go out. You finish your homework. (after)

→ _____

2 He started playing the guitar. He was fifteen. (when)

→ _____

3 You should go to the restroom. The movie starts. (before)

→ _____

틀리기 쉬운
내/신/포/인/트

시간의 부사절을 이끄는
접속사들의 의미를 구별하여
기억해요.

빈칸에 공통으로 들어갈 말로 알맞은 것은?

- _____ she was young, she loved pop music.
- _____ I arrived, they were having dinner.

① That ② Before ③ After ④ When

POINT 5 접속사: because, if

접속사 because와 if는 각각 이유와 조건을 나타내는 부사절을 이끈다.

because	~ 때문에	I'll stay home	because it's cold.	춥기 때문에 나는 집에 머물 것이다.
if	(만약) ~한다면	If it is sunny,	I will take a walk.	날씨가 맑으면 나는 산책을 할 것이다.

↪ 조건의 부사절에서는 미래를 나타낼 때 현재시제로 써요.

주의 접속사 because 뒤에는 이유를 나타내는 절이 오고, 접속사 so 뒤에는 결과를 나타내는 절이 온다.
He was late **because** the bus didn't come. 버스가 오지 않았기 때문에 그는 늦었다.
The bus didn't come, **so** he was late. 버스가 오지 않아서 그는 늦었다.

주의 because of는 이유를 나타내는 전치사로 뒤에 명사(구)가 온다.
They had to stay home **because of** *the cold weather*. 그들은 추운 날씨 때문에 집에 머물러야 했다.

개념확인 부사절 찾기

1 I can't go because I'm busy.　　**2** If you find him, call me.　　**3** I cried because I lost my dog.

기본연습 **A** 우리말과 일치하도록 빈칸에 알맞은 접속사를 쓰시오.

1 네가 원하면, 너는 나와 함께 가도 된다.
→ _____ you want, you can go with me.

2 나는 늦게 일어나서 기차를 놓쳤다.
→ I missed the train _____ I got up late.

3 내일 비가 온다면 우리는 영화를 보러 갈 것이다.
→ We will go to a movie _____ it rains tomorrow.

4 그가 그녀의 생일을 잊어버려서 그녀는 슬펐다.
→ She was sad _____ he forgot her birthday.

5 네가 아프면, 너는 올 필요 없다.
→ _____ you are sick, you don't have to come.

B 괄호 안의 접속사가 들어갈 자리를 고르시오.

1 (if)　　(①) Anna studies hard, (②) she will pass the exam.

2 (if)　　(①) I'll be happy (②) he comes to my birthday party.

3 (because)　　(①) I can't eat the soup (②) it is too hot.

4 (because)　　(①) I ordered milk (②) I don't like coke.

5 (because)　　(①) Nick wanted to read some books, (②) he went to the library.

C 괄호 안에서 알맞은 것을 고르시오.

1 I'll leave tomorrow (if / when) it snows today.

2 (If / Before) you are tired, you can stay home.

3 (When / Because) I arrived, he was reading a book.

4 (If / Because) you have a question, you can ask me.

5 Ben couldn't come (after / because) he had to work.

6 (After / Because) I don't know her phone number, I can't call her.

7 We couldn't go hiking (before / because) the weather was bad.

8 She drank a cup of warm water (after / before) she went to bed.

D 보기 와 같이 괄호 안의 접속사를 이용하여 두 문장을 한 문장으로 쓰시오.

> 보기 It was very cold. He put on a jacket. (because)
> → Because it was very cold, he put on a jacket.

1 You know the answer. Raise your hand. (if)

→ _____

2 He won't buy the bike. It is too expensive. (if)

→ _____

3 You will miss the bus. You don't run. (if)

→ _____

4 He has a test tomorrow. He is studying hard. (because)

→ _____

5 My parents got angry. I fought with my brother. (because)

→ _____

6 We were late. We had to take a taxi. (because)

→ _____

틀 리 기 쉬 운
내/신/포/인/트

주절과 접속사가 이끄는 절의
의미 관계를 파악해요.

①~④ 중 접속사 If(if)가 들어갈 위치로 알맞은 곳은?

(①) I will (②) go to the beach (③) it is sunny (④).

전치사는 명사(구)나 대명사 앞에 쓰며, 전치사구는 문장에서 형용사 또는 부사 역할을 한다.

| 형용사 역할 | The cup **in the box** is mine. | 상자 안에 있는 컵은 내 것이다. |
| 부사 역할 | Let's meet **at the bus stop**. | 버스 정류장에서 만나자. |

다음 전치사는 장소를 나타낸다.

at ~에(서)	+좁은 장소, 특정 지점	**at** the bus stop 버스 정류장에	**at** home 집에	**at** the corner 모퉁이에
in ~ 안에, ~에(서)	+넓은 장소, 공간	**in** New York 뉴욕에	**in** the sky 하늘에	**in** the room 방 안에
on ~ 위에, ~에(서)	+표면	**on** the floor 바닥에	**on** the wall 벽에	**on** the street 거리에

Tips at은 행사나 모임 앞에 쓰기도 하고, on은 교통수단이나 통신 수단 앞에 쓰기도 한다.
at the party 파티에서　　**on** the phone 전화로

개념확인 전치사구 찾기

1 Turn right at the corner. **2** There is a picture on the wall. **3** Big Ben is in London.

기본연습 **A** 괄호 안에서 알맞은 것을 고르시오.

1 Be careful when you walk (in / on) the ice.

2 Patric will have dinner (at / on) Jimmy's house.

3 She put the apples (at / in) the yellow basket.

4 My family lived (at / in) Sydney two years ago.

5 Go straight two blocks and turn left (at / on) the church.

B 빈칸에 at, in, on 중 알맞은 것을 쓰시오.

1 I have some coins _____ my pocket.

2 There is a huge clock _____ the wall.

3 They made sandwiches _____ the kitchen.

4 Rosa will wait for him _____ the bus stop.

5 The yellow leaves started to fall _____ the ground.

다음 전치사는 위, 아래 등 위치를 나타낸다.

in ~ 안에		She put her pens **in** her pencil case. 그녀는 펜들을 필통에 넣었다.
on ~ 위에		Can you put this box **on** the table? 이 상자를 탁자 위에 올려 줄 수 있니?
under ~ 아래에		The kitten is sitting **under** the table. 아기 고양이가 탁자 아래에 앉아 있다.
in front of ~ 앞에		The black car is **in front of** the house. 검은색 차가 집 앞에 있다.
behind ~ 뒤에		The apple tree is **behind** the bench. 사과나무가 벤치 뒤에 있다.
next to ~ 옆에		The bakery is **next to** the bookstore. 제과점은 서점 옆에 있다.
between ~ 사이에		The boy sat down **between** the two girls. 소년은 두 소녀 사이에 앉았다.

Tips between *A* and *B*는 'A와 B 사이에'라는 뜻이다.
James is **between** *his mom* **and** *dad*. James는 그의 엄마와 아빠 사이에 있다.

개념확인 전치사구 찾기

1 He sat on the bench. **2** The hotel is next to the lake. **3** The sun is behind a cloud.

기본연습 **A** 우리말과 일치하도록 보기에서 알맞은 말을 골라 빈칸에 쓰시오. (중복 사용 가능)

| 보기 | in | on | under | in front of | behind | next to | between |

1 침대 아래에 → _____ the bed **2** 은행 옆에 → _____ the bank

3 책상 위에 → _____ the desk **4** 나무 아래에 → _____ the tree

5 의자 뒤에 → _____ the chair **6** 두 나무 사이에 → _____ two trees

7 책 옆에 → _____ the book **8** TV 앞에 → _____ the TV

9 그의 치아 사이에 → _____ his teeth **10** 빨간 차 안에 → _____ the red car

B 우리말과 일치하도록 괄호 안의 말과 알맞은 전치사를 이용하여 문장을 완성하시오.

1 그는 그의 스웨터 아래에 티셔츠를 입었다. (his sweater)

→ He wore a T-shirt _____.

2 탁자 위에 팔꿈치를 올리지 마라. (the table)

→ Don't put your elbows _____.

3 나는 두 명의 키가 큰 남자들 사이에 앉아 있었다. (two tall men)

→ I was sitting _____.

4 왕비는 거울 앞에 서 있었다. (the mirror)

→ The queen was standing _____.

5 호텔은 공항 바로 옆에 있었다. (the airport)

→ The hotel was right _____.

6 Gilbert는 소녀의 뒤에 앉아 그녀의 머리카락을 잡아당겼다. (the girl)

→ Gilbert sat _____ and pulled her hair.

C 그림을 보고, 빈칸에 알맞은 전치사를 써서 문장을 완성하시오.

1 There is a sofa _____ the two plants.

2 The girl is reading _____ the sofa.

3 The boy is hiding _____ the sofa.

4 A table and a box are _____ the sofa.

5 The cat is sleeping _____ the table.

6 The dog is sitting _____ the box.

전치사 at, on, in은 '~에'라는 뜻으로 시간을 나타낸다.

at	+시각, 특정 시점	~에	at 8 o'clock 8시에 at noon 정오에	at 4:20 p.m. 4시 20분에 at night 밤에
on	+요일, 날짜, 특정한 날		on Friday 금요일에 on May 20th 5월 20일에	on Christmas Day 크리스마스에 on my birthday 내 생일에
in	+연도, 월, 계절, 오전, 오후		in 2022 2022년에 in July 7월에	in summer 여름에 in the morning 아침에

전치사 for와 during은 '~ 동안'이라는 뜻으로 기간을 나타낸다.

for	+숫자를 포함한 구체적인 기간	~ 동안	for two weeks 2주 동안	for a month 한 달 동안
during	+특정 기간을 나타내는 명사구		during the exam 시험 동안	during the war 전쟁 동안

개념확인 시간 전치사구 찾기

1 Let's meet at 2 p.m.   **2** I'll go to Jeju-do in June.   **3** She will be there for 3 days.

기본연습 **A** 괄호 안에서 알맞은 것을 고르시오.

1 (at / in / on) 2021   **2** (at / in / on) night

3 (at / in / on) spring   **4** (at / in / on) November

5 (at / in / on) 9 o'clock   **6** (at / in / on) Saturday

7 (at / in / on) March 25th   **8** (at / in / on) Amy's birthday

9 (for / during) two hours   **10** (for / during) half an hour

11 (for / during) the meeting   **12** (for / during) summer vacation

B **보기** 에서 알맞은 말을 골라 문장을 완성하시오.

보기	at	on	in	for	during

1 The train will leave _____ 8:30 a.m.

2 Susan played the piano _____ 20 minutes.

3 I didn't have time to have breakfast _____ the morning.

4 Many people go to church _____ Christmas Eve.

5 I stayed at my grandmother's house _____ the vacation.

POINT 9 시간 전치사 (2)

다음 전치사는 시간의 전후, 기한, 계속, 시작 시점을 나타낸다.

before	~ 전에	Wash your hands **before** breakfast.	아침 식사 **전에** 손을 씻어라.
after	~ 후에	You can call her **after** 10 o'clock.	너는 10시 **이후에** 그녀에게 전화해도 된다.
by	〈기한〉 ~까지	I will finish the work **by** tomorrow.	나는 내일**까지** 그 일을 끝낼 것이다.
until	〈계속〉 ~까지	They played basketball **until** noon.	그들은 정오**까지** 농구를 했다.
from	〈시작 시점〉 ~부터	This store is open **from** 10 a.m.	이 가게는 오전 10시**부터** 문을 연다.

Tips from A to B는 'A부터 B까지'라는 뜻이다.
We go to school **from** *Monday* **to** *Friday*. 우리는 월요일부터 금요일까지 학교에 간다.

주의 before나 after 뒤에 명사(구)가 오면 전치사로 쓰인 것이고, 「주어+동사」의 절이 오면 접속사로 쓰인 것이다.
I'm going to study **after** dinner. 〈전치사〉 나는 저녁 식사 후에 공부할 것이다.
I'm going to study **after** I have dinner. 〈접속사〉 나는 저녁을 먹은 후에 공부할 것이다.

> until은 동작이 계속되는 시점을 나타내는 전치사로 stay, wait 등과 함께 쓰이고, by는 동작의 완료 기한을 나타내는 전치사로 finish, arrive 등과 함께 써요.

개념확인 옳은 해석 고르기

1 He'll be home by 7 p.m.

☐ 오후 7시까지   ☐ 오후 7시부터

2 I'll study hard from today.

☐ 오늘까지   ☐ 오늘부터

3 He left before breakfast.

☐ 아침 식사 전에   ☐ 아침 식사 후에

기본연습 A 우리말과 일치하도록 before, after, by, until, from 중 알맞은 것을 쓰시오.

1 저녁 식사 전에 아무것도 먹지 마라.

→ Don't eat anything ＿＿＿＿＿＿ dinner.

2 그는 아내의 죽음 이후 혼자서 살았다.

→ He lived alone ＿＿＿＿＿＿ his wife's death.

3 미나는 작년까지 맨체스터에 머물렀다.

→ Mina stayed in Manchester ＿＿＿＿＿＿ last year.

4 Linda는 아침 8시부터 일을 해야 한다.

→ Linda has to work ＿＿＿＿＿＿ 8 in the morning.

5 내일 아침까지 모든 것이 준비되어야 한다.

→ Everything should be ready ＿＿＿＿＿＿ tomorrow morning.

6 너는 여기서 2시까지 기다려야 해.

→ You should wait here ＿＿＿＿＿＿ 2 o'clock.

7 당신은 그 일을 정오까지 마칠 수 있나요?

→ Can you finish the work ＿＿＿＿＿＿ noon?

우리말과 일치하도록 괄호 안의 말과 알맞은 전치사를 이용하여 문장을 완성하시오.

1 그 식당은 내일까지 문을 열지 않을 것이다. (tomorrow)

→ The restaurant won't open _____.

2 그는 전쟁 후에 그의 나라로 돌아갔다. (the war)

→ He went back to his country _____.

3 너는 금요일까지 이 책을 읽는 것을 끝내야 한다. (Friday)

→ You must finish reading this book _____.

4 그녀는 오전 9시부터 오후 3시까지 학교에 있을 것이다. (9 a.m., 3 p.m.)

→ She will be at school _____.

5 그는 크리스마스 전에 그의 조부모님을 방문했다. (Christmas)

→ He visited his grandparents _____.

6 너는 포장지 위의 날짜 이후에 이 우유를 마실 수 없다. (the date)

→ You can't drink this milk _____ on the package.

7 6월 15일까지 제게 사진들을 보내주세요. (July 15th)

→ Please send me the photos _____.

C 밑줄 친 부분이 어법상 바르면 ○라고 쓰고, 틀리면 바르게 고쳐 쓰시오.

1 He promised to return <u>until</u> five o'clock. → _____

2 Sarah studied Spanish <u>from</u> April <u>by</u> June. → _____

3 They wanted to play board games <u>after</u> school. → _____

4 She usually washes her face <u>before</u> breakfast. → _____

5 My car broke down, so I can't drive it <u>by</u> next week. → _____

**틀 리 기 쉬 운
내/신/포/인/트**

by는 동작의 완료 기한을
나타내고, until은 동작의
계속을 나타내요.

빈칸에 by나 until을 쓸 때 나머지와 <u>다른</u> 하나는?

① They watched TV _____ midnight.
② She waited there _____ 4 p.m.
③ They will stay here _____ next week.
④ Can you finish the work _____ 6 o'clock?

POINT 10 도구·수단 전치사

전치사 with는 '~와 함께'라는 뜻 외에, 도구를 나타내는 말 앞에 쓰여 '~을 가지고'라는 의미로도 사용된다.
전치사 by는 '~까지'라는 뜻 외에, 수단을 나타내는 말 앞에 쓰여 '~을 타고, ~을 이용하여'라는 의미로도 사용된다.

with	+도구	~을 가지고	with a knife 칼로	with a hammer 망치로
by	+수단	~을 타고, ~을 이용하여	by subway 지하철을 타고	by mail 우편으로

Tips '걸어서'는 on foot으로 표현한다.
It takes five minutes **on foot**. 걸어서 5분 걸린다.

개념확인 옳은 해석 고르기

1 He lives <u>with</u> his parents.
☐ ~와 함께   ☐ ~을 가지고

2 They went there <u>by</u> bus.
☐ ~까지   ☐ ~을 타고

3 Cut the paper <u>with</u> scissors.
☐ ~와 함께   ☐ ~을 가지고

기본연습 빈칸에 with와 by 중 알맞은 것을 쓰시오.

1 We ate the food ＿＿＿＿＿＿ our fingers.

2 I will send you the data ＿＿＿＿＿＿ email.

3 He caught the fish ＿＿＿＿＿＿ a large net.

4 They went to the library ＿＿＿＿＿＿ bicycle.

5 You can go there ＿＿＿＿＿＿ bus or subway.

6 Slice the lemon ＿＿＿＿＿＿ a knife.

7 I want to pay ＿＿＿＿＿＿ credit card.

8 My father went to work ＿＿＿＿＿＿ subway yesterday.

9 I fixed the door ＿＿＿＿＿＿ a hammer.

10 You can write your answers ＿＿＿＿＿＿ this pen.

틀리기 쉬운 내/신/포/인/트

with는 '~와 함께'나 '~을 가지고'라는 뜻으로 쓰여요.

밑줄 친 부분의 의미가 나머지와 다른 하나는?

① Eat the eggs <u>with</u> a fork.
② I saw Bob in town <u>with</u> his sister.
③ She hit the nail <u>with</u> a hammer.
④ Join the two pieces together <u>with</u> glue.

개 | 념 | 완 | 성 TEST

정답 및 해설 p.43

STEP 1 Map으로 개념 정리하기

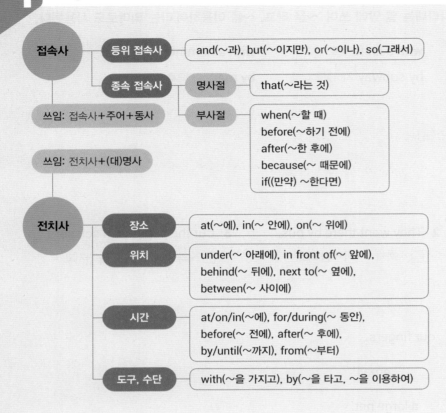

Quick Check

❶ It was sunny, (and / but) I didn't go out.

❷ Put your coat on, (and / or) you will catch a cold.

❸ I heard (that / when) it was very cold.

❹ We went out when it was sunny.
해석: _____

❺ I put my coat on because it was very cold.
해석: _____

❻ There was a lot of rain (at / in / on) Seoul.

❼ A raindrop fell (at / in / on) my face.

❽ It always rains (at / in / on) Sundays.

❾ We had a lot of rain (for / during) the vacation.

❿ The boy went to school (with / by) taxi.

STEP 2 기본 다지기

빈칸완성

A 우리말과 일치하도록 빈칸에 알맞은 말을 넣어 문장을 완성하시오.

1 나는 2시간 동안 영화를 봤다.
→ I watched a movie _____ two hours.

2 조용히 해라, 그렇지 않으면 아기가 깰 것이다.
→ Be quiet, _____ the baby will wake up.

3 너는 거기에 기차를 타고 가니?
→ Are you going there _____ train?

4 그 소년은 얼음 위에서 넘어졌다.
→ The boy fell down _____ the ice.

5 비가 오면, 나는 집에 머무를 것이다.
→ _____ it rains, I will stay home.

6 그는 그 이야기가 사실이라고 말했다.
→ He said _____ the story was true.

7 그녀는 저녁을 먹은 후 산책을 하러 갔다.
→ She went for a walk _____ she had dinner.

8 그 박물관 옆에 도서관이 있다.
→ There is a library _____ _____ the museum.

B 밑줄 친 부분이 어법상 바르면 ○라고 쓰고, 틀리면 바르게 고쳐 쓰시오.

1 Bears sleep <u>for</u> the winter. → _____

2 There are a lot of cars <u>on the road</u>. → _____

3 He wants to see you <u>before you go</u>. → _____

4 You should eat your food <u>by</u> a fork. → _____

5 <u>When</u> I got home, she was sleeping. → _____

6 There is a garden <u>in front</u> her house. → _____

7 There are four rooms <u>on</u> the house. → _____

8 I can't believe <u>it</u> he is only 10 years old. → _____

9 <u>Because of</u> it was too cold, he closed the door. → _____

10 He stayed in London <u>from Monday by Friday</u>. → _____

C 다음 문장을 괄호 안의 지시대로 바꿔 쓰시오.

1 The room was dark, so I couldn't see her face. (because를 문장의 첫 단어로 사용하여)

→ _____

2 If you take a taxi, you won't miss the train. (and를 사용하여)

→ _____

3 We could see stars because the sky was clear. (so를 사용하여)

→ _____

4 Everything will be okay. I believe this. (that을 사용하여 한 문장으로)

→ _____

5 He had a car accident. He was 7 years old. (when을 문장의 첫 단어로 사용하여 한 문장으로)

→ _____

6 If you don't wear a mask, you can catch flu. (or를 사용하여)

→ _____

7 Work hard. Your dream will come true. (if를 문장의 첫 단어로 사용하여 한 문장으로)

→ _____

STEP 3 서술형 따라잡기

그림이해

A 그림을 보고, 괄호 안의 말과 알맞은 전치사를 이용하여 문장을 완성하시오.

1 The bird is singing _____. (the branch)

2 There is a bench _____. (the trash can)

3 Tom is standing _____. (the bench)

4 Tom's dog is sitting _____. (the bench)

영작완성

B 우리말과 일치하도록 괄호 안의 말을 바르게 배열하여 문장을 쓰시오. (부사절을 앞에 쓸 것)

1 네가 원한다면, 여기에 머물러도 된다. (can, want, you, here, if, you, stay)

→ _____

2 경기가 시작되기 전에, 우리는 긴장했다. (the game, we, before, started, nervous, were)

→ _____

3 나는 어렸을 때, 초콜릿을 좋아했다. (I, chocolate, was, liked, I, when, young)

→ _____

4 나는 늦게 일어나서, 버스를 놓쳤다. (the bus, because, I, got up, I, missed, late)

→ _____

문장영작

C 우리말과 일치하도록 괄호 안의 말을 이용하여 영작하시오.

1 그는 두 시간 동안 그 책을 읽었다. (read, the book)

→ _____

2 그들은 점심 식사 후에 설거지를 했다. (wash the dishes, lunch)

→ _____

3 많은 사람들은 숫자 7이 운이 좋다고 믿는다. (believe, the number 7, lucky) (접속사를 생략하지 말 것)

→ _____

4 이 버튼을 눌러라, 그러면 문이 열릴 것이다. (press, this button, the door, open)

→ _____

[1-2] 빈칸에 들어갈 말로 알맞은 것을 고르시오.

1

> The bus didn't come, _____ he was late.

① or   ② so   ③ but

④ if   ⑤ that

2

> He fell, _____ he wasn't hurt.

① or   ② so   ③ but

④ when   ⑤ that

3 빈칸에 들어갈 말로 알맞지 않은 것은?

> Brad and Julie met in _____.

① 2019   ② May

③ spring   ④ Thursday

⑤ the evening

4 빈칸에 공통으로 들어갈 말로 알맞은 것은?

> • Is my answer right _____ wrong?
>
> • Close the window, _____ it'll get cold.

① or   ② so   ③ but

④ and   ⑤ before

5 빈칸에 알맞은 말이 순서대로 짝 지어진 것은?

> • He played soccer _____ an hour.
>
> • The books were lying _____ the floor.

① for − at   ② during − in

③ for − in   ④ during − on

⑤ for − on

6 밑줄 친 부분이 어법상 틀린 것은?

① I think that it will rain today.

② You can see the stars at night.

③ The story is funny but too long.

④ Brush your teeth after have dinner.

⑤ Please call me when you get home.

7 밑줄 친 부분의 우리말 뜻이 바르지 않은 것은?

① Don't kick the seat in front of you.

                   (네 앞의)

② Nick will stay there until next week.

                   (다음 주부터)

③ Who is sitting between them?

                   (그들 사이에)

④ She covered her mouth with her hand.

                   (그녀의 손으로)

⑤ Write the numbers under the picture.

                   (사진 아래에)

[8-9] 밑줄 친 부분의 쓰임이 나머지와 <u>다른</u> 하나를 고르시오.

8 ① I believe <u>that</u> he can be a champion.
② I thought <u>that</u> was a great plan.
③ She said <u>that</u> he gave up the race.
④ I hope <u>that</u> the weather will be fine.
⑤ He heard <u>that</u> Mary moved to New York.

9 ① <u>When</u> I hear that song, I feel sad.
② <u>When</u> she got there, he was working.
③ <u>When</u> are you going to leave for Seoul?
④ What were you doing <u>when</u> I called you?
⑤ He was four <u>when</u> he had a car accident.

10 빈칸에 들어갈 말이 보기와 같은 것은?

> 보기 Get some sleep, _____ you'll feel better.

① The actor is tall _____ handsome.
② Is your sister older _____ younger than you?
③ He took a taxi _____ he was late.
④ I'll wash my hands _____ I start to cook.
⑤ It was cold, _____ I turned on the heater.

[11-12] 두 문장이 같은 뜻이 되도록 할 때, 빈칸에 들어갈 말로 알맞은 것을 고르시오.

11
> The museum is behind the library.
> = The library is _____ the museum.

① in   ② under
③ between   ④ next to
⑤ in front of

12
> He arrived before the math exam began.
> = The math exam began _____ he arrived.

① and   ② but
③ when   ④ after
⑤ because

13 주어진 문장과 의미가 같은 것은?

> Bring your computer, and I will fix it.

① You will fix your computer for me.
② I will bring your computer to fix it.
③ I will bring your computer if you fix it.
④ If you bring your computer, I will fix it.
⑤ You should bring your computer for me.

14 우리말을 영어로 바르게 옮긴 것은?

> 점심시간은 오후 1시부터 2시까지이다.

① Lunch time is until 2 p.m.
② Lunch time is for 1 p.m. to 2 p.m.
③ Lunch time is at 1 p.m. and 2 p.m.
④ Lunch time is by 1 p.m. and 2 p.m.
⑤ Lunch time is from 1 p.m. to 2 p.m.

15 밑줄 친 부분을 생략할 수 <u>없는</u> 것은?

① I know that Mary is from Finland.
② Many people say that our team is the best.
③ It is not surprising that he said "no."
④ We believe that nothing is impossible.
⑤ Do you think that he is a good player?

16 어법상 <u>틀린</u> 부분을 바르게 고친 것은?

> Finish reading the book until 5 o'clock.

① Finish → To finish
② reading → to read
③ the를 생략
④ until → by
⑤ 5 o'clock → 5 o'clocks

17 대화의 빈칸에 들어갈 말로 알맞은 것은?

> A: How long did you sleep last night?
> B: _____

① I slept late at night.
② I slept for seven hours.
③ I usually go to bed early.
④ I slept well during the night.
⑤ I get up early in the morning.

고난도
18 밑줄 친 부분이 어법상 <u>틀린</u> 것의 개수는?

> ⓐ My favorite band is playing <u>on</u> the stage.
> ⓑ The sun went <u>behind</u> the clouds.
> ⓒ Kathy has a history class <u>in</u> 2 p.m.
> ⓓ The bookstore is <u>next to</u> the bakery.
> ⓔ She had dinner with her friends at <u>her</u> birthday.

① 1개　　　　② 2개　　　　③ 3개
④ 4개　　　　⑤ 5개

고난도
19 어법상 <u>틀린</u> 것끼리 짝 지어진 것은?

> ⓐ It was rainy and cold outside.
> ⓑ He picked up the coin at the street.
> ⓒ Dinner will be ready by seven o'clock.
> ⓓ I practiced dancing during two hours.
> ⓔ The post office is next the subway station.
> ⓕ You can play games or watching a movie.

① ⓐ, ⓒ　　　　　　② ⓐ, ⓑ, ⓔ
③ ⓑ, ⓒ, ⓔ　　　　④ ⓑ, ⓓ, ⓔ, ⓕ
⑤ ⓒ, ⓓ, ⓔ, ⓕ

고난도
20 빈칸 (A)~(C)에 들어갈 말이 바르게 짝 지어진 것은?

> • I believe ___(A)___ he will win first prize.
> • She usually goes to school ___(B)___ bus.
> • He wore a raincoat ___(C)___ it was raining.

	(A)	(B)	(C)
①	that	by	so
②	that	by	because
③	that	with	because
④	when	with	so
⑤	when	by	because

21 괄호 안의 접속사를 사용하여 두 문장을 한 문장으로 쓰시오.

(1) We needed more time. She agreed. (that)

→ _____

(2) Study hard. You will get good grades. (and)

→ _____

(3) I wake up. I take a shower. (after)

→ _____

22 어법상 틀린 부분을 바르게 고친 후, 틀린 이유를 쓰시오.

(1) Steve's birthday is in November 25th.

_____ → _____

틀린 이유: _____

(2) My family moved to this town at 2018.

_____ → _____

틀린 이유: _____

23 우리말과 일치하도록 조건 에 맞게 문장을 쓰시오.

(1) 조건 1. play, hour를 이용할 것
    2. 총 6단어로 쓸 것

그들은 두 시간 동안 농구를 했다.

→ _____

(2) 조건 1. cannot, the test를 이용할 것
    2. 총 6단어로 쓸 것

너는 시험 동안 말하면 안 된다.

→ _____

24 그림을 보고, 빈칸에 알맞은 전치사를 써서 방을 묘사하는 글을 완성하시오.

This is a picture of my room. There is a big box (1) _____ the desk. My cat is (2) _____ the box. My cat's ball is (3) _____ the desk. My dog is sleeping (4) _____ the chair.

고난도
25 Betty가 오늘 한 일을 나타낸 표와 내용이 일치하도록 조건 에 맞게 질문에 답하시오.

11:00 a.m.	clean my room
12:30 p.m.	have lunch
2:00 p.m.	go shopping
4:00 p.m.	watch a movie

조건 1. 전치사나 접속사를 반드시 포함할 것
    2. 완전한 문장으로 쓸 것

(1) What did Betty do before she had lunch?

→ _____

(2) What time did she go shopping?

→ _____

(3) What did she do after she went shopping?

→ _____

동아 (윤정미)

과		Chapter	Point	Page
1	be동사의 긍정문/부정문	1	1, 5	14, 18
1	일반동사의 긍정문/부정문	2	1, 2, 3	30, 31, 33
2	be동사의 의문문	1	5	18
2	일반동사의 의문문	2	4	34
2	의문사 의문문	7	3, 4	130, 132
2	현재진행형	5	6	93
3	명령문	10	1	172
3	조동사 can, will	6	4, 6	109, 112
4	be동사의 과거형	1	6	17
4	일반동사의 과거형	2	5, 6	36, 38
4	There is/are ~	10	5	178
5	동명사: 주어, 목적어, 보어	9	1, 2	158, 160
5	비인칭 주어 it	4	2	72
6	to부정사 명사적 용법: 목적어	8	3	146
6	감각동사+형용사	11	2	189
7	be going to	5	3, 4, 5	90, 91, 92
7	비교급/최상급 비교	13	3, 5	226, 229
8	접속사 that	14	3	243
8	접속사 when, before, after	14	4	245

동아 (이병민)

과		Chapter	Point	Page
1	be동사의 긍정문/부정문/의문문	1	1, 5, 6	14, 18, 20
1	일반동사의 긍정문/부정문	2	1, 2, 3	30, 31, 33
2	현재진행형	5	6	93
2	명령문	10	1	172
2	감탄문	10	3	174
3	조동사 can	6	4	109
3	일반동사의 의문문	2	4	34
3	의문사 의문문	7	1, 2, 3, 4	126, 128, 130, 132
4	be동사의 과거형	1	4	17
4	일반동사의 과거형	2	5, 6	36, 38
4	재귀대명사	4	4	75
5	조동사 will	6	6	112
5	수량형용사 a few, many	12	2, 3	206, 207
6	to부정사 명사적 용법: 목적어	8	3	146
6	접속사 when	14	4	245
7	4형식(수여동사)	11	3	191
7	조동사 have to, don't have to	6	8	114
8	동명사: 목적어	9	2	160
8	비교급 비교, 비교급 강조	13	3, 4	226, 228

1학년 교과서 문법 연계표

과	천재 (이재영)	Chapter	Point	Page
1	be동사의 긍정문	1	1	14
	be동사의 부정문/의문문	1	5, 6	18, 20
2	일반동사의 긍정문	2	1, 2	30, 31
	일반동사의 부정문/의문문	2	3, 4	33, 34
3	현재진행형	5	6	93
	조동사 will	6	6	112
4	There is/are ~	10	5	178
	조동사 can	6	4	109
5	be동사의 과거형	1	6	17
	일반동사의 과거형	2	5, 6	36, 38
	동명사: 주어, 목적어, 보어	9	1, 2	158, 160
6	to부정사 명사적 용법: 목적어	8	3	146
	조동사 should	6	9	116
7	to부정사 부사적 용법: 목적	8	5	148
	접속사 when	14	4	245
8	4형식(수여동사)	11	3	191
	비교급 비교	13	3	226

과	천재 (정사열)	Chapter	Point	Page
1	일반동사의 긍정문/부정문/의문문	2	1, 2, 3, 4	30, 31, 33, 34
	조동사 will	6	6	112
2	현재진행형	5	6	93
	to부정사 명사적 용법: 목적어	8	3	146
3	일반동사의 과거형	2	5, 6	36, 38
	부가의문문	10	4	176
4	4형식(수여동사)	11	3	191
	to부정사 부사적 용법: 목적	8	5	148
5	재귀대명사	4	4	75
	원급 비교	13	6	231
6	조동사 must	6	7	113
	동명사: 목적어	9	2	160
7	과거진행형	5	7	95
	최상급 비교	13	5	229
8	감탄문	10	3	174
	접속사 when	14	4	245

과	능률 (김성곤)	Chapter	Point	Page
1	be동사의 긍정문/부정문	1	1, 5	14, 18
1	일반동사의 긍정문/부정문	2	1, 2, 3	30, 31, 33
2	현재진행형	5	6	93
2	조동사 can, will	6	4, 6	109, 112
3	be동사의 과거형	1	6	17
3	일반동사의 과거형	2	5, 6	36, 38
3	동명사: 목적어	9	2	160
4	4형식(수여동사)	11	3	191
4	to부정사 명사적 용법: 목적어	8	3	146
5	비교급/최상급 비교	13	3, 5	226, 229
5	접속사 that	14	3	243
6	to부정사 부사적 용법: 목적	8	5	148
6	접속사 when	14	4	245
7	감탄문	10	3	174
7	5형식	11	5	195

과	능률 (양현권)	Chapter	Point	Page
1	동명사: 목적어	9	2	160
1	동격	3	9	61
2	be going to	5	3, 4, 5	90, 91, 92
2	to부정사 명사적 용법: 목적어	8	3	146
3	접속사 that	14	3	243
3	조동사 must	6	7	113
4	to부정사 부사적 용법: 목적	8	5	148
4	감탄문	10	3	174
5	접속사 and	14	1	240
5	접속사 when	14	4	245
6	부사 too	12	7	211
6	4형식(수여동사)	11	3	191
7	과거진행형	5	7	95
7	부가의문문	10	4	176
8	최상급 비교	13	5	229
8	부정대명사 one	4	5	77

1학년 교과서 문법 연계표

과	YBM (박준언)	Chapter	Point	Page
1	be동사의 긍정문	1	1	14
1	be동사의 부정문/의문문	1	5,6	18,20
2	일반동사의 긍정문	2	1,2	30,31
2	일반동사의 부정문/의문문	2	3,4	33,34
SL1	현재진행형	5	6	93
SL1	명령문	10	1	172
3	be동사의 과거형	1	6	17
3	일반동사의 과거형	2	5,6	36,38
3	감각동사+형용사	11	2	189
4	조동사 will	6	6	112
4	조동사 can	6	4	109
5	to부정사 명사적 용법: 목적어, 보어	8	2,3	145,146
5	감탄문	10	3	174
6	동명사: 목적어	9	2	160
6	비교급 비교	13	3	226
SL2	to부정사 부사적 용법: 목적	8	5	148
SL2	4형식(수여동사)	11	3	191
7	접속사 because	14	5	247
7	부가의문문	10	4	176
8	접속사 when	14	4	245
8	5형식	11	5	195

과	YBM (송미정)	Chapter	Point	Page
1	be동사의 긍정문	1	1	14
1	일반동사의 긍정문	2	1,2	30,31
1	be동사의 부정문/의문문	1	5,6	18,20
2	일반동사의 긍정문	2	1,2	30,31
2	일반동사의 부정문/의문문	2	3,4	33,34
3	There is/are ~	10	5	178
3	조동사 can	6	4	109
4	be동사의 과거형	1	6	17
4	일반동사의 과거형	2	5,6	36,38
4	조동사 will	6	6	112
5	현재진행형	5	6	93
5	감각동사+형용사	11	2	189
6	명령문	10	1	172
6	접속사 when	14	4	245
7	to부정사 명사적 용법: 목적어	8	3	146
7	동명사: 주어	9	1	158
8	비교급 비교	13	3	226
8	접속사 because	14	5	247
9	4형식(수여동사)	11	3	191
9	감탄문	10	3	174

과	미래엔 (최연희)	Chapter	Point	Page
1	be동사의 긍정문/부정문	1	1,5	14, 18
	일반동사의 긍정문/부정문	2	1,2,3	30, 31, 33
2	현재진행형	5	6	93
	조동사 can	6	4	109
3	동명사: 목적어	9	2	160
	감각동사+형용사	11	2	189
	There is/are ~	10	5	178
4	be동사의 과거형	1	6	17
	일반동사의 과거형	2	5,6	36, 38
	조동사 will	6	6	112
5	be going to	5	3,4,5	90, 91, 92
	to부정사 명사적 용법: 목적어, 보어	8	2,3	145, 146
6	접속사 that	14	3	243
	to부정사 부사적 용법: 목적	8	5	148
	4형식(수여동사)	11	3	191
7	조동사 have to	6	8	114
	조동사 should	6	9	116
	접속사 when	14	4	245
8	비교급 비교	13	3	226
	최상급 비교	13	5	229

과	비상 (김진완)	Chapter	Point	Page
1	be동사의 긍정문/부정문/의문문	1	1,5,6	14, 18, 20
	일반동사의 긍정문/부정문/의문문	2	1,2,3,4	30, 31, 33, 34
2	명령문	10	1	172
	현재진행형	5	6	93
3	be동사의 과거형	1	6	17
	일반동사의 과거형	2	5,6	36, 38
	감각동사+형용사	11	2	189
4	조동사 will	6	6	112
	4형식(수여동사)	11	3	191
5	비교급 비교	13	3	226
	최상급 비교	13	5	229
6	to부정사 명사적 용법: 목적어	8	3	146
	부가의문문	10	4	176
7	to부정사 부사적 용법: 목적	8	5	148
	접속사 that	14	3	243
8	동명사: 목적어	9	2	160
	접속사 when	14	4	245

1학년 교과서 문법 연계표

과	지학사 (민찬규)	Chapter	Point	Page
1	현재시제	5	1	86
	과거시제	5	2	88
	미래시제	5	3	90
2	현재진행형	5	6	93
	to부정사 명사적 용법: 목적어	8	3	146
3	to부정사 형용사적 용법	8	4	147
	동명사: 목적어	9	2	160
4	접속사 when	14	4	245
	조동사 should	6	9	116
5	to부정사 부사적 용법: 목적	8	5	148
	부가의문문	10	4	176
6	비교급 비교, 비교급 강조	13	3,4	226, 228
	최상급 비교	13	5	229
7	접속사 that	14	3	243
	4형식(수여동사)	11	3	191

과	금성 (최인철)	Chapter	Point	Page
1	일반동사의 긍정문/부정문	2	1,2,3	30, 31, 33
	일반동사의 의문문	2	4	34
2	현재진행형	5	6	93
	조동사 can/will/should	6	4,6,9	109, 112, 116
3	일반동사의 과거형	2	5,6	36, 38
	감탄문	10	3	174
4	감각동사+형용사	11	2	189
	접속사 when	14	4	245
5	to부정사 명사적 용법: 목적어	8	3	146
	빈도부사	12	9	214
6	접속사 that	14	3	243
	to부정사 부사적 용법: 목적	8	5	148
7	4형식(수여동사)	11	3	191
	5형식	11	5	195
8	동명사: 목적어	9	2	160
	비교급/최상급 비교	13	3,5	226, 229

문제로 쉬워지는 중학영문법

그래머
클라우드

3000제

문제로 쉬워지는 중학영문법

그래머 클라우드

3000제

정답 및 해설

LEVEL 1

동아출판

문제로 쉬워지는 중학영문법

그래머 클라우드

3000제

정답 및 해설   LEVEL 1

CHAPTER 1

be동사

POINT 1 be동사의 현재형   p. 14

개념확인 1 주어: I, be동사: am
2 주어: She, be동사: is
3 주어: They, be동사: are

기본연습

A
1 ~이다   2 (~에) 있다   3 (~에) 있다
4 ~이다   5 ~이다

B
1 is   2 am   3 are
4 is   5 are   6 are
7 is   8 are   9 is
10 am

POINT 2 인칭대명사와 be동사   p. 15

개념확인 1 He   2 We   3 It

기본연습 1 She, is   2 You, are   3 We, are
4 They, are   5 It, is   6 He, is

틀리기 쉬운 내신포인트

정답 ②

해설 Jisu and Suho는 3인칭이고 복수이므로 be동사는 are를 쓴다.

POINT 3 be동사 현재형의 줄임말   p. 16

개념확인 1 He is   2 They are   3 We are

기본연습

A
1 I'm   2 It's   3 You're
4 We're   5 She's   6 They're
7 He's   8 That's

B
1 I'm   2 It's   3 We're
4 He's   5 She's   6 They're
7 You're

POINT 4 be동사의 과거형   p. 17

개념확인 1 be동사: was, 과거 부사: yesterday
2 be동사: was, 과거 부사구: last night
3 be동사: were, 과거 부사구: in 2020

기본연습

A
1 was   2 is   3 was
4 are   5 were   6 were

B
1 was   2 was   3 were
4 were   5 are

틀리기 쉬운 내신포인트

정답 ③

해설 My sister가 3인칭 단수 주어이고 yesterday로 보아 과거의 일이므로 be동사의 과거형 was를 쓴다.

POINT 5 be동사의 부정문   p. 18

개념확인 1 I am **not** bored.
2 He was **not** late yesterday.
3 They are **not** in the mall.

기본연습

A
1 isn't   2 am not   3 is not
4 am not   5 aren't   6 is not
7 are not   8 is not   9 wasn't
10 wasn't   11 weren't   12 wasn't
13 were not   14 weren't

B
1 Harry wasn't   2 They're not 또는 They aren't
3 I'm not   4 Tina isn't   5 I wasn't
6 We weren't   7 The cookies weren't

C
1 I'm not   2 wasn't
3 She's not 또는 She isn't   4 is not
5 We're not 또는 We aren't   6 were not
7 was not   8 was not   9 are not
10 are not   11 were not   12 weren't

틀리기 쉬운 내신포인트

정답 ②

해설 am not은 amn't로 줄여 쓰지 않는다. (→ am not)

POINT 6 be동사의 의문문   p. 20

개념확인 1 be동사: Are, 주어: you
2 be동사: Was, 주어: John
3 be동사: Am, 주어: I

기본연습

A
1 Is it   2 Am   3 Is
4 Are   5 Was   6 Were

B
1 it is	**2** she isn't	**3** she wasn't
4 we aren't	**5** I'm not	**6** I am
7 they are	**8** it wasn't	**9** they were
10 he was	**11** they weren't	
12 I was 또는 we were		

C
1 Is it	**2** Was Jessica	**3** Is he
4 Were they	**5** Were you	**6** Are you
7 Am I		

개념완성 TEST

p. 22

STEP 1 Quick Check

① am   ② are   ③ was   ④ 나는 행복하다.
⑤ 그녀는 교실에 있다.   ⑥ aren't   ⑦ wasn't   ⑧ I am
⑨ he wasn't

STEP 2 기본 다지기

A
1 is	**2** are	**3** I'm not
4 were	**5** are not	**6** Is
7 He was	**8** was not	**9** Was she
10 Were they		

B
1 is	**2** are	**3** were
4 was	**5** are	**6** Was
7 Were		

C
1 We were very happy.
2 He was a famous actor.
3 Julia isn't(is not) in London now.
4 Were they in the office yesterday?
5 James and I aren't(are not) good singers.
6 Are Yujin and Sumi best friends now?
7 Her voice wasn't(was not) clear this morning.
8 The children weren't(were not) in the playground.
9 Was your room very clean?

STEP 3 서술형 따라잡기

A   **1** Yes, she is   **2** No, it wasn't

B   **1** Lucy and Eric are not soccer players.
2 Juwon was not busy last weekend.
3 Is your father in the garage now?
4 My brother and I were in the park yesterday.

C
1 Was Sally short last year?
2 I'm(I am) not a high school student.
3 Were you and Lisa in the library?
4 We're(We are) very hungry now.

학교 시험 실전 문제

p. 25

1 ②	**2** ②	**3** ④	**4** ⑤	**5** ③	**6** ④	**7** ①
8 ②	**9** ⑤	**10** ⑤	**11** ⑤	**12** ①	**13** ③	**14** ②
15 ④	**16** ②	**17** ④	**18** ④	**19** ④	**20** ④	

서술형
21 am, is, isn't, is, are, are
22 (1) Is your brother sleepy now?
　　(2) Were you hungry in the morning?
23 (1) No, they aren't
　　(2) Yes, I was
24 (1) Peter and Alice weren't(were not) in the museum an hour ago.
　　(2) Were Peter and Alice in the museum an hour ago?
25 (1) John and Eddie are friendly.
　　(2) Ken wasn't nervous yesterday.
　　(3) Ann and I were at the bookstore last night.
　　(4) Is your mother at home now?
　　(5) I'm very tired now.

1 Jihun and Hana는 복수 주어이고 현재 나이를 말하고 있으므로 be동사는 are를 쓴다.

2 I는 be동사로 am을 쓰고, Kate는 3인칭 단수 주어이고 현재를 말하고 있으므로 is를 쓴다.

3 ④ Mr. White가 3인칭 단수이므로 be동사는 is가 와야 한다.

4 ⑤ am not은 줄여 쓰지 않는다. (→ am not)

5 Are you ~?라고 물었고 뒤에 복수 명사가 나오므로 you는 2인칭 복수인 '너희들'을 가리킨다. 따라서 we로 답해야 한다.

6 Bill에 관해 물었으므로 대명사는 3인칭 단수 남성인 he로 바꾸고, 어제의 일에 대해 부정으로 답하는 것이므로 wasn't가 알맞다.

7 be동사가 과거형 were이므로 현재를 나타내는 부사 now는 쓸 수 없다.

8 be동사가 was이므로 2인칭 주어인 You는 쓸 수 없다.

9 ⑤는 be동사 뒤에 장소의 부사구가 와서 '(~에) 있다'라는 뜻이고, 나머지는 모두 '~이다'라는 뜻이다.

10 be동사의 부정문은 be동사 뒤에 not을 쓴다.

11 〈보기〉는 last weekend로 보아 복수 주어 They에 맞는 be동사의 과거형 were가 들어간다. ⑤는 two days ago로 보아 복수 주어 The pictures에 맞는 be동사의 과거형 were를 써야 한다. (①, ②, ④ was, ③ are)

12 be동사가 쓰인 문장의 부정문은 be동사 뒤에 not을 쓰고, be동사 is와 not은 줄여서 isn't로 쓸 수 있다.

13 ③ 1인칭 단수 주어 I에 맞는 be동사의 과거형은 was이다. (① → was not, ② → is, ④ → is, ⑤ → were)

14 ⓐ now로 보아 주어 I에 맞는 be동사는 am을 써야 한다. (→ am not)

15 ④ 과거의 일을 물었으므로 과거형으로 답해야 한다. (No, they aren't. → No, they weren't.)

16 복수 주어 Wendy and I에 맞는 be동사의 과거형은 were를 써야 한다.

17 ④는 now로 보아 복수 주어에 맞는 be동사 are를 쓰고, 나머지는 모두 be동사의 과거형 were를 쓴다.

18 과거형으로 답하고 있으므로 질문은 과거의 일을 물어야 하고, it으로 바꿀 수 있는 주어는 the musical이므로 ④가 알맞다.

19 ④ yesterday로 보아 be동사는 과거형이 와야 하므로 is를 was로 써야 한다.

20 ⓐ, ⓒ, ⓓ가 옳은 문장이다.
ⓑ 주어가 3인칭 복수이므로 be동사는 are를 쓴다. ⓔ 주어가 you이고 be동사는 과거형이 와야 하므로 Were를 쓴다.

21 I는 1인칭 단수 주어이므로 be동사는 am을 쓴다. 주어가 3인칭 단수일 경우 be동사는 is를 쓰고, 부정형은 isn't(is not)로 쓴다. 주어가 복수일 경우 be동사는 are를 쓴다.

22 be동사의 의문문은 「Be동사+주어 ~?」의 형태로 쓴다.

23 (1) '그들은 내 남동생들이야.'라고 했으므로, 부정의 대답을 해야 한다.
(2) '나는 병원에 있었어.'라고 했으므로, 긍정의 대답을 해야 한다.

24 (1) be동사의 부정문은 be동사 뒤에 not을 쓴다.
(2) be동사의 의문문은 「Be동사+주어 ~?」의 형태로 쓴다.

25 (1) John and Eddie는 복수 주어이므로 be동사는 are를 쓴다.
(2) Ken은 3인칭 단수 주어이므로 be동사의 과거형 was를 쓴다. was not은 wasn't로 줄여 쓸 수 있다.
(3) Ann and I는 복수 주어이므로 be동사의 과거형 were를 쓴다.
(4) be동사의 의문문은 「Be동사+주어 ~?」의 형태로 쓴다.
(5) I는 1인칭 단수 주어이므로 be동사는 am을 쓴다. I am은 I'm으로 줄여 쓸 수 있다.

POINT **1** 일반동사의 현재형   p. 30

개념확인 **1** be동사   **2** 일반동사   **3** 일반동사

기본연습

A
| **1** ⓓ | **2** ⓐ | **3** ⓔ |
| **4** ⓑ | **5** ⓒ | |

B
1 want	**2** watch	**3** sings
4 walk	**5** know	**6** drinks
7 play	**8** rides	

POINT **2** 일반동사의 3인칭 단수 현재형   p. 31

개념확인 **1** 주어: Jane, 동사: dances
2 주어: Tony, 동사: speaks
3 주어: Mina, 동사: studies

기본연습

A
1 smells	**2** does	**3** needs
4 closes	**5** fixes	**6** wants
7 stays	**8** takes	**9** sleeps
10 finishes	**11** sees	**12** tells
13 hurries	**14** washes	**15** learns
16 catches	**17** asks	**18** runs
19 makes	**20** tries	**21** passes
22 works	**23** enjoys	**24** flies
25 cries	**26** has	

B
1 misses	**2** wears	**3** like
4 drink	**5** comes	**6** writes
7 exercises	**8** has	**9** studies
10 teaches		

C
1 has	**2** speaks	**3** washes
4 play	**5** listen	**6** lives
7 reads	**8** goes	

틀리기 쉬운 내신포인트

정답 ④

해설 Yujin과 My mother는 둘 다 3인칭 단수 주어이므로 빈칸에는 각각 3인칭 단수 현재형인 brushes와 teaches를 써야 한다.

POINT 3 일반동사 현재형의 부정문   p. 33

개념확인 1 주어: Ann, 동사원형: have
         2 주어: They, 동사원형: eat
         3 주어: Eric, 동사원형: want

기본연습

A
1 don't   2 doesn't   3 don't
4 doesn't   5 don't   6 like
7 have

B
1 doesn't stop   2 don't get
3 doesn't take   4 don't live
5 don't play   6 doesn't teach

POINT 4 일반동사 현재형의 의문문   p. 34

개념확인 1 주어: you, 동사원형: play
         2 주어: she, 동사원형: like
         3 주어: they, 동사원형: use

기본연습

A
1 Do   2 Does   3 Do
4 Does   5 like   6 close
7 make   8 study

B
1 Do you like   2 Does she know
3 Do they need   4 Does he remember
5 Does Jessy play   6 Does Jimin make
7 Does Peter love   8 Do his dogs have
9 Does the baby cry   10 Do her parents sell

C
1 he does   2 he doesn't
3 I(we) do   4 it does
5 she doesn't   6 they don't
7 they do   8 she does
9 I(we) don't   10 we(you) don't

틀리기 쉬운 내신포인트

정답 ④

해설 의문문의 주어인 the show는 대답에서 3인칭 단수 it으로 받고, 내용상 부정의 대답이 들어가야 하므로 No, it doesn't. 로 답하는 것이 알맞다.

POINT 5 일반동사 과거형의 규칙 변화   p. 36

개념확인 1 studied   2 stopped   3 played

기본연습

A
1 cleaned   2 liked   3 walked
4 showed   5 loved   6 wanted
7 tried   8 helped   9 carried
10 visited   11 looked   12 talked
13 started   14 cried   15 dropped
16 danced   17 failed   18 enjoyed
19 opened   20 stopped   21 needed
22 closed   23 used   24 washed
25 worried   26 exercised   27 traveled
28 asked   29 finished   30 passed
31 arrived   32 wished   33 practiced
34 hurried

B
1 stayed   2 missed   3 played
4 cried   5 worked   6 planned

C
1 watched   2 studied   3 invited
4 cooked   5 moved   6 turned

틀리기 쉬운 내신포인트

정답 ④

해설 「단모음＋단자음」으로 끝나는 동사는 자음을 한 번 더 쓰고 -ed를 붙이므로, stop의 과거형은 stopped가 알맞다.

POINT 6 일반동사 과거형의 불규칙 변화   p. 38

개념확인 1 went   2 swam   3 hurt

기본연습

A
1 came   2 ate   3 caught
4 felt   5 did   6 made
7 saw   8 slept   9 wrote
10 set   11 broke   12 grew
13 lost   14 had   15 read
16 told   17 ran   18 taught
19 rode   20 found   21 put
22 sang   23 sat   24 spoke
25 sent   26 took   27 got
28 thought   29 fought   30 said
31 wore   32 gave   33 sold
34 stood   35 drank   36 flew
37 knew   38 left   39 heard
40 brought

B
1 met   2 fell   3 won
4 bought   5 spent

정답 ④

해설 ④ 동사 read(읽다)는 현재형과 과거형의 형태가 같으므로 과거형도 read로 써야 한다.

POINT 7 일반동사 과거형의 부정문 p. 40

개념확인 1 주어: I, 동사원형: watch
2 주어: He, 동사원형: like
3 주어: They, 동사원형: study

기본연습

A 1 did not   2 didn't   3 didn't
4 enjoy   5 have   6 turn
7 write   8 speak

B 1 didn't run   2 didn't agree   3 didn't do
4 didn't go   5 didn't bring   6 didn't lose
7 didn't read   8 didn't stop

POINT 8 일반동사 과거형의 의문문 p. 41

개념확인 1 주어: you, 동사원형: call
2 주어: he, 동사원형: meet
3 주어: they, 동사원형: sing

기본연습

A 1 Does, play   2 Do, know   3 Did, live
4 Did, listen   5 Did, join   6 Did, use

B 1 they didn't   2 she did   3 we did
4 he didn't

개념완성 T E S T p. 42

STEP 1 Quick Check

① drinks   ② don't   ③ Does, she does   ④ cooked
⑤ had   ⑥ didn't   ⑦ she did

STEP 2 기본 다지기

A 1 goes   2 exercise
3 doesn't teach   4 don't practice
5 Does, live   6 Do, speak
7 sang   8 arrived
9 didn't cry   10 Did, find

B 1 stopped   2 have   3 washes
4 doesn't   5 Did   6 watch

C 1 He has a headache.
2 My sister doesn't(does not) ride her bike every day.
3 Do they go to the movies on Saturdays?
4 Fred studies English in the library.
5 Does Sarah remember her first day at school?
6 He wrote a letter to Yumi.
7 My parents worked at a hospital.
8 Did Tom bring his lunch to school?
9 Minho and Gisu didn't(did not) do their homework last night.
10 My brother ate noodles for lunch yesterday.

STEP 3 서술형 따라잡기

A 1 Yes, she does
2 No, he didn't

B 1 He doesn't look well today.
2 Did you take the subway?
3 They didn't understand the math problem.
4 Does his cat have a small nose?

C 1 He eats two apples for breakfast.
2 She dropped her glasses yesterday.
3 My friends and I went to the museum yesterday.
4 Mark cleans his desk every day.

학교 시험 실전 문제 p. 45

1 ④   2 ④   3 ⑤   4 ⑤   5 ③   6 ③   7 ②
8 ④   9 ④   10 ③   11 ⑤   12 ④   13 ⑤   14 ⑤
15 ④   16 ②   17 ②   18 ②   19 ④   20 ③

서술형

21 (1) baked cookies
(2) didn't(did not) clean the living room
(3) went to Mina's birthday party

22 (1) No, he doesn't
(2) Yes, she did

23 (1) He didn't(did not) drop the cup.
(2) Did he drop the cup?

24 lives, has, goes, likes, watches, doesn't like

25 (1) Paul eats breakfast every day.
(2) Peter moved to Seoul last month.
(3) My father doesn't drive a car.
(4) Do you have a pen now?
(5) I didn't bring my watch yesterday.

1 「단모음＋단자음」으로 끝나는 동사는 자음을 한 번 더 쓰고 -ed를 붙이므로, plan의 과거형은 planned가 알맞다.

2 첫 번째 문장은 주어가 Steve로 3인칭 단수이므로 know의 3인칭 단수 현재형 knows가 알맞다. 두 번째 문장은 일반동사 현재형의 의문문으로, 「Do/Does＋주어＋동사원형 ～?」의 형태로 써야 하므로 동사원형 know가 알맞다.

3 last night(어젯밤)과 yesterday(어제)는 과거형과 함께 쓰이는 부사(구)이므로, 과거형의 의문문과 부정문에 쓰이는 Did(did)가 알맞다.

4 동사 plays는 play의 3인칭 단수 현재형이므로 복수 주어 Ann and Tim은 빈칸에 알맞지 않다.

5 주어 Bill이 3인칭 단수이므로 don't listen은 함께 쓸 수 없다.

6 뒤에 이어지는 대답으로 보아 긍정의 대답이 알맞다. 주어가 you인 일반동사 과거형의 의문문으로 물었으므로 대답은 Yes, I did.가 알맞다.

7 매일 아침에 우유를 마시냐는 물음에 우유를 좋아하지 않는다고 답하고 있으므로, 빈칸에는 부정의 대답이 알맞다. 주어(she)가 3인칭 단수이므로 대답은 No, she doesn't.가 알맞다.

8 ①, ② 일반동사의 의문문은 「Do/Does/Did＋주어＋동사원형 ～?」의 형태로 쓰므로, 동사원형 like와 open으로 써야 한다. ③ 부사 yesterday(어제)가 있으므로 동사는 과거형으로 써야 한다. (→ had) ⑤ 일반동사 과거형의 부정문은 「didn't＋동사원형」의 형태로 써야 한다. (→ live)

9 ④ Minho and I는 복수 주어이므로 일반동사 부정문은 「don't＋동사원형」으로 쓴다. 나머지는 모두 3인칭 단수 주어이므로 doesn't가 알맞다.

10 ③은 '하다'라는 뜻의 일반동사 do의 과거형이고, 나머지는 의문문이나 부정문을 만들기 위해 쓰인 조동사이다.

11 ⑤ 일반동사 과거형의 의문문으로 물었으므로, 부정의 대답은 「No, 주어＋didn't.」의 형태로 해야 한다. (No, they don't. → No, they didn't.)

12 ④ 주어(Hana)가 3인칭 단수인 일반동사 현재형의 의문문은 「Does＋주어＋동사원형 ～?」의 형태로 쓰므로, spoke는 동사원형 speak로 고쳐야 한다.

13 일반동사 과거형의 부정문은 「주어＋didn't(did not)＋동사원형 ～.」의 형태로 쓴다.

14 일반동사 과거형의 의문문은 「Did＋주어＋동사원형 ～?」의 형태로 쓴다. caught는 catch(잡다)의 과거형이다.

15 주어가 3인칭 단수(My uncle)인 일반동사 현재형의 부정문은 「주어＋doesn't(does not)＋동사원형 ～.」의 형태로 쓴다.

16 일반동사 과거형의 부정문은 「주어＋didn't(did not)＋동사원형 ～.」의 형태이다. 빈칸 뒤에 동사원형이 쓰인 문장은 ②이다.

17 (A) lose(잃어버리다)의 과거형은 lost이다.

(B) 일반동사 현재형의 의문문은 「Do/Does＋주어＋동사원형 ～?」의 형태로 쓰므로, 빈칸에는 동사원형 walk가 알맞다.

(C) last night(어젯밤)은 과거형 동사와 함께 쓰이므로, 과거형 동사의 부정형인 didn't practice가 알맞다.

18 Did you brush your teeth this morning?이라는 문장이 되므로, 세 번째로 오는 단어는 brush이다.

19 대답을 did로 했으므로 과거형 의문문으로 물어야 한다. 일반동사 과거형의 의문문은 「Did＋주어＋동사원형 ～?」의 형태로 쓰므로 ④가 알맞다.

20 ⓑ didn't 뒤에는 동사원형이 온다. (called → call) ⓒ cut (자르다)의 과거형은 cut이다. (cuted → cut) ⓓ 일반동사 과거형의 의문문은 「Did＋주어＋동사원형 ～?」의 형태로 쓴다. (finished → finish)

21 어제 한 일과 하지 않은 일이므로 동사를 과거형으로 쓴다.

22 (1) 태호가 파란색 셔츠를 입냐는 질문에 초록색 셔츠를 입는다고 했으므로, 빈칸에는 부정의 대답이 알맞다.
(2) Jenny가 Sam을 학교에서 만났냐는 질문에 함께 축구를 했다고 했으므로, 빈칸에는 긍정의 대답이 알맞다.

23 (1) 일반동사 과거형의 부정문은 「didn't(did not)＋동사원형」의 형태로 쓴다.
(2) 일반동사 과거형의 의문문은 「Did＋주어＋동사원형」의 형태로 쓴다.

24 주어가 3인칭 단수(Tom/He)로 바뀌므로, 동사도 모두 3인칭 단수 현재형으로 바꿔 쓴다. 주어가 3인칭 단수일 때 일반동사 현재형이 쓰인 부정문은 「doesn't＋동사원형」의 형태로 쓴다.

25 (1) 현재의 반복되는 일을 나타내도록 동사를 현재형으로 쓴다.
(2) 지난달의 일이므로 동사를 과거형으로 쓴다.
(3) 주어가 3인칭 단수일 때 일반동사 현재형이 쓰인 부정문은 「doesn't＋동사원형」으로 쓴다.
(4) 주어가 2인칭일 때 일반동사 현재형이 쓰인 의문문은 「Do you＋동사원형 ～?」으로 쓴다.
(5) 일반동사 과거형의 부정문은 「didn't＋동사원형」의 형태로 쓴다.

CHAPTER 3

명사와 관사

POINT 1 셀 수 있는 명사와 셀 수 없는 명사 p. 50

개념확인 1 students　2 club　3 tea

기본연습

A
1 ○	2 ×	3 ×
4 ○	5 ×	6 ○
7 ○	8 ×	9 ×
10 ×	11 ○	12 ○

B 1 Poland　2 Love　3 teams
4 boys

틀리기 쉬운 내신포인트

정답 ②

해설 앞에 a가 있으므로 셀 수 있는 명사가 들어가야 한다.

POINT 2 셀 수 있는 명사의 복수형: 규칙 변화 p. 51

개념확인 1 pencil　2 tomato　3 song

기본연습

A
1 buses	2 bags	3 foxes
4 brushes	5 glasses	6 watches
7 puppies	8 stories	9 wives
10 shelves	11 gloves	12 boxes
13 dishes	14 kisses	15 churches
16 crayons	17 flies	18 wolves
19 knives	20 parties	21 pianos
22 roofs	23 beaches	24 diaries

B
1 Cows	2 potatoes	3 coins
4 Monkeys	5 meat	6 candies
7 butter	8 sons	9 Leaves
10 money		

C
1 legs	2 snow
3 sugar	4 families
5 tomatoes	6 photos
7 benches	8 bookshelves
9 sandwiches	10 countries

틀리기 쉬운 내신포인트

정답 ③

해설 potato는 -o로 끝나는 명사이므로 -es를 붙여서 복수형을 만든다. (→ potatoes)

POINT 3 셀 수 있는 명사의 복수형: 불규칙 변화 p. 53

개념확인 1 man　2 fish　3 child

기본연습

A
1 men	2 deer	3 children
4 mice	5 geese	6 teeth
7 fish	8 matches	9 feet
10 sheep	11 boys	12 dresses

B
1 feet	2 children	3 deer
4 teeth	5 mice	6 Mathematics
7 stories	8 women	

C
1 Geese	2 feet	3 cities
4 teeth	5 children	6 sheep
7 women	8 fish	9 men
10 news	11 mice	

틀리기 쉬운 내신포인트

정답 ②

해설 첫 번째 빈칸 앞에는 a가 있으므로 단수 명사가 알맞고, 두 번째 빈칸 앞에는 two가 있으므로 복수 명사가 알맞다. goose의 복수형은 geese이다.

POINT 4 셀 수 없는 명사의 수량 표현 p. 55

개념확인 1 piece　2 bottle　3 glass

기본연습

A
1 cup	2 piece	3 spoonful
4 bottle	5 loaf	6 slice(piece)
7 glass	8 bowl	9 slice(piece)

B
1 cups of tea	2 pieces of cheese
3 bowls of fruit	4 spoonfuls of salt

C
1 cups	2 bottles	3 bottle
4 bowl	5 piece	6 glasses
7 loaf	8 spoonful	9 pieces
10 bowls		

D
1 a cup of water
2 a bowl of soup
3 two slices(pieces) of cake
4 three bottles of ink
5 two spoonfuls of sugar
6 a glass of milk
7 a piece of paper
8 three loaves of bread

정답 ④

해설 a piece of는 '한 조각의 ~'이라는 뜻으로 조각으로 나뉘는 것의 수량을 나타내는 표현이다. coffee의 수량은 a cup of로 나타낸다.

POINT 5 명사의 소유격 p. 57

개념확인 **1** Sam **2** my sister **3** the car

기본연습

A
1 the rabbit's tail
2 women's clothes
3 Daniel's uncle
4 the swan's feather
5 my parents' house
6 Dickens's(Dickens') novels

B
1 the wall of the house
2 the cover of the book
3 the top of the page
4 the name of the street
5 the roof of the building
6 the color of the shoes

POINT 6 부정관사 a/an p. 58

개념확인 **1** 부정관사: a, 명사: daughter
2 부정관사: an, 명사: oven
3 부정관사: an, 명사: iguana

기본연습

A
| 1 a | 2 an | 3 a |
| 4 a | 5 an | 6 an |

B
1 an	2 an	3 an
4 a	5 a	6 an
7 a	8 a	9 a
10 a	11 an	12 an

정답 ②

해설 an이 앞에 있으므로 첫소리가 모음으로 발음되는 명사가 와야 한다.

POINT 7 정관사 the p. 59

개념확인 **1** 정관사: The, 명사: sun
2 정관사: the, 명사: violin
3 정관사: the, 명사: door

기본연습
1 the	2 the	3 The
4 The	5 the	6 The
7 the	8 the	9 a, The
10 an, the		

정답 ③

해설 명사 뒤에 수식어구가 있을 때와 이미 언급한 명사를 다시 언급할 때는 정관사 the를 쓴다.

POINT 8 관사를 쓰지 않는 경우 p. 60

개념확인 **1** lunch **2** school **3** soccer

기본연습
1 ×	2 a	3 ×
4 ×	5 an	6 the
7 ×	8 ×, ×	

정답 ④

해설 과목 이름 앞에는 관사를 쓰지 않는다.

POINT 9 동격 p. 61

개념확인 **1** a famous writer **2** Minsu

기본연습
1 Paul Gauguin, a famous painter
2 Mr. Kim, my math teacher
3 Jane Goodall, an animal scientist
4 Justin Bieber, a good singer
5 Jude Law, a very popular actor
6 *Avatar*, my favorite movie

정답 ④

해설 빈칸에는 my favorite subject와 같은 대상인 과목명이 들어가야 한다.

STEP 1 Quick Check

① an, a   ② foxes, geese   ③ ○
④ 동물원의 이름은 Animals' Friends이다.
⑤ bottle   ⑥ bowls   ⑦ ○   ⑧ ✕

STEP 2 기본 다지기

A
1 an apple   2 five fish   3 by bus
4 the cello   5 The moon   6 the third
7 a glass of juice
8 two slices(pieces) of pizza
9 Mike, my uncle
10 Emily's mother

B
1 men   2 deer   3 is
4 pants   5 ○   6 cheese
7 cup   8 by car   9 ○

C
1 The girls ate cotton candies.
2 Look at the monkeys in this picture.
3 Five children played in the playground.
4 My baby brother has one tooth.
5 Rachel has a cute puppy.
6 William drank two glasses of water.
7 Kate's mother answered the phone.
8 Ms. Brown, my history teacher, loves her students.

STEP 3 서술형 따라잡기

A
two bottles of oil, three tomatoes, two fish, a loaf of bread

B
1 We have breakfast at 7 every day.
2 The cover of the book is thick.
3 My wish is my family's happiness.
4 Jane doesn't eat meat and tomatoes.

C
1 I go to school by subway.
2 We have two pigs and three sheep on our farm.
3 The vase with a handle is mine.
4 Anne Hathaway, his aunt, is a very famous actress.

---

1 ④	2 ⑤	3 ④	4 ③	5 ②	6 ⑤	7 ②
8 ②	9 ③	10 ③	11 ③	12 ④	13 ④	14 ④
15 ⑤	16 ③	17 ②	18 ②	19 ①	20 ④	

서술형

21 (1) ✕ (2) a (3) an (4) the
22 (1) moneys → money
    틀린 이유: money는 셀 수 없는 명사이므로 -s를 붙여서 복수형으로 쓸 수 없다.
   (2) foots → feet
    틀린 이유: foot의 복수형은 feet으로 써야 한다.
23 (1) a pair of gloves
   (2) two mice
   (3) two candies
24 (1) two glasses of juice
   (2) four pieces of pizza
   (3) a bowl of salad
25 (1) My dog's legs are very long.
   (2) The sun rises in the east.
   (3) Jess plays the piano every day.
   (4) Emily plays tennis once a week.

1 ④ foot의 복수형은 feet이다.

2 bag은 셀 수 있는 명사이고, 나머지는 모두 셀 수 없는 명사이다.

3 빈칸에는 셀 수 있는 명사의 복수형이 들어가야 한다. ant와 bird의 복수형은 ants와 birds로 쓰고, leaf는 leaves, woman은 women으로 쓴다. geese는 goose의 복수형이므로 빈칸에 알맞다.

4 빈칸에는 셀 수 있는 명사이면서 첫소리가 모음으로 발음되는 apple이 알맞다.

5 빈칸에는 셀 수 없는 명사이면서 a piece of를 사용하여 수량을 나타내는 paper가 알맞다.

6 ⑤ bread는 a loaf of(한 덩어리의 ~)나 a slice(piece) of(한 조각의 ~)를 사용하여 수량을 나타낸다.

7 카메라 한 대는 a를 써서 나타내고, 앞에 나온 카메라를 다시 가리킬 때는 the를 쓴다.

8 ② He's는 He is의 줄임말이고, 나머지는 모두 명사의 소유격을 나타내는 -'s이다.

9 콤마(,)를 사용하여 Mr. Lee와 my music teacher가 같은 대상임을 바르게 나타낸 것은 ③이다.

10 ③ 운동 경기를 나타내는 명사 앞에는 관사를 쓰지 않는다.

11 ③ elementary는 첫소리가 모음으로 발음되므로 an이 알맞고, 나머지는 모두 a가 알맞다.

12 빈칸에는 셀 수 있는 명사의 복수형이 들어가야 한다. salt는 셀 수 없는 명사이므로 복수형으로 쓸 수 없다.

13 a pair of 뒤에는 한 쌍으로 쓸 수 있는 대상이 와야 한다.

14 sheep은 단수형과 복수형의 형태가 같으므로 '양들'은 sheep으로 쓴다. 주어가 복수이므로 동사를 have로 쓴 ③이 바르게 옮긴 문장이다.

15 ①~④는 셀 수 없는 명사이고, ⑤의 fish는 셀 수 있는 명사이다.

16 ⓐ, ⓒ, ⓔ는 첫소리가 모음으로 발음되는 단어 앞이므로 an이 들어가야 하고, ⓑ, ⓓ는 첫소리가 자음으로 발음되는 단어 앞이므로 a가 들어가야 한다.

17 ② milk는 셀 수 없는 명사이므로 복수형으로 쓸 수 없다.
(→ two bottles of milk)

18 ② '잠자리에 들다'의 의미인 경우 bed 앞에 관사를 쓰지 않는다.
(→ bed)

19 ① 고유명사 앞에는 관사를 쓰지 않는다. (→ Amsterdam)

20 ⓒ, ⓓ, ⓔ가 옳은 문장이다.
ⓐ 사람의 소유격은 명사에 -'s를 붙이므로 men'은 men's로 써야 한다. ⓑ 셀 수 없는 명사(bread)의 복수는 단위를 복수형으로 써서 나타내므로 two slices of bread로 써야 한다.

21 (1) 고유명사 앞에는 관사를 쓰지 않는다.
(2) 첫소리가 자음으로 발음되는 단어 앞이므로 a를 쓴다.
(3) 첫소리가 모음으로 발음되는 단어 앞이므로 an을 쓴다.
(4) 명사 뒤에 수식어구(under the tree)가 있으므로 the를 쓴다.

22 (1) money는 셀 수 없는 명사이므로 moneys를 money로 고쳐 써야 한다.
(2) foot의 복수형은 feet이므로 foots를 feet으로 고쳐 써야 한다.

23 (1) '장갑 한 쌍'은 a pair of를 사용하여 나타낸다.
(2) mouse의 복수형은 mice로 쓴다.
(3) candy는 「자음+y」로 끝나는 명사이므로 y를 i로 바꾸고 -es를 붙여서 복수형을 만든다.

24 (1) 주스 두 잔이므로 two glasses of juice로 쓴다.
(2) 피자 네 조각이므로 four pieces of pizza로 쓴다.
(3) 샐러드 한 그릇이므로 a bowl of salad로 쓴다.

25 (1) 동물(dog)의 소유격은 명사에 -'s를 붙여서 나타낸다.
(2) 세상에서 유일한 것(sun)을 말할 때는 앞에 the를 쓴다.
(3) 악기 이름(piano)을 말할 때는 앞에 the를 쓴다.
(4) 운동 경기(tennis)를 말할 때는 the를 쓰지 않는다.

C H A P T E R **4**
대명사

POINT 1 인칭대명사   p. 70

개념확인 **1** 주격   **2** 소유격   **3** 목적격

기본연습

A **1** you   **2** Their   **3** her
    4 mine   **5** us   **6** Its

B **1** They   **2** her   **3** We
    4 He   **5** him   **6** It
    7 You   **8** us

C **1** your   **2** Their   **3** hers
    4 My   **5** her   **6** She
    7 you   **8** me   **9** They
    10 his

틀리기 쉬운 내신포인트

정답 ③

해설 첫 번째 빈칸 뒤에 friend라는 명사가 나오므로 소유격 인칭대명사 your가 알맞다. 두 번째 빈칸에는 주어가 들어가야 하는데, 뒤에 She라고 언급되어 있으므로 she가 알맞다.

POINT 2 비인칭 주어 it   p. 72

개념확인 **1** It   **2** It   **3** It

기본연습

A **1** ⓔ   **2** ⓐ   **3** ⓑ
    4 ⓒ   **5** ⓓ

B **1** 비인칭 주어   **2** 비인칭 주어   **3** 인칭대명사
    4 인칭대명사   **5** 비인칭 주어

C **1** It is cloudy   **2** It is 10(ten)
    3 It is February 2nd   **4** It is Monday

D **1** It is 3 km   **2** It is snowy
    3 It is Wednesday   **4** It is hot
    5 It is very cold   **6** It is winter
    7 It is summer   **8** It is twelve five
    9 Is it May 17th   **10** It is 200 meters

틀리기 쉬운 내신포인트

정답 ②

해설 ②는 '그것'이라는 뜻으로 가리키는 대상이 있는 인칭대명사이고, 나머지는 모두 비인칭 주어 It이다.

POINT 3 지시대명사   p. 74

개념확인   **1** These   **2** Those   **3** this

기본연습

A   **1** Those   **2** This   **3** these
     4 those   **5** That   **6** this
     7 That   **8** This

B   **1** These   **2** those   **3** Those
     4 That   **5** this   **6** these
     7 This

POINT 4 재귀대명사   p. 75

개념확인   **1** ourselves   **2** himself   **3** myself

기본연습

A   **1** itself   **2** themselves   **3** myself
     4 himself   **5** herself

B   **1** 강조 용법   **2** 강조 용법   **3** 재귀 용법
     4 재귀 용법

C   **1** (1) you (2) yourself
     2 (1) myself (2) me
     3 (1) ourselves (2) our
     4 (1) their (2) themselves
     5 (1) yourself (2) you

D   **1** himself   **2** myself   **3** themselves
     4 myself   **5** himself   **6** herself
     7 myself   **8** itself   **9** himself
     10 ourselves

틀리기 쉬운 내신포인트

정답 ③

해설 ③ 주어와 전치사의 목적어가 가리키는 대상이 같으므로 전치사의 목적어 자리에 재귀대명사인 myself를 써야 한다.

POINT 5 부정대명사 one   p. 77

개념확인   **1** 불특정한 연필   **2** 불특정한 모자

기본연습

A   **1** one   **2** it   **3** one
     4 one   **5** one   **6** ones

B   **1** one   **2** it   **3** one
     4 it

개념완성 **T E S T**   p. 78

STEP 1 Quick Check

① my ② me ③ this ④ these ⑤ himself
⑥ Sam은 자기 자신을 매우 사랑한다. ⑦ 밖에 비가 내린다.
⑧ one

STEP 2 기본 다지기

A   **1** It   **2** That   **3** these
     4 herself   **5** yourself   **6** it
     7 one   **8** They   **9** mine, yours
     10 his, He

B   **1** myself   **2** It   **3** hers
     4 It   **5** one   **6** These
     7 It

C   **1** They are in the closet.
     2 Did you help them?
     3 She gave some fruit to us.
     4 My mom bought a new purse. I don't like it.
     5 Susie looked at herself in the mirror.
     6 Simon himself always makes his own clothes.
     또는 Simon always makes his own clothes himself.
     7 It is Monday today.
     8 It is July 10th today.
     9 He broke his smartphone. He bought a new one.

STEP 3 서술형 따라잡기

A   **1** herself   **2** myself

B   **1** Is it Sunday today?
     2 I bought a nice present for myself.
     3 Andy is different from his brother.
     4 Those are my best friends.

C   **1** That jacket is not his.
     2 I don't like this movie genre.
     3 I grew these tomatoes myself.
     또는 I myself grew these tomatoes.
     4 It is 100 meters to the bus stop.

1 ③   2 ②   3 ④   4 ③   5 ①   6 ①   7 ②
8 ④   9 ④   10 ③   11 ①   12 ⑤   13 ③   14 ②
15 ②   16 ③   17 ③   18 ②   19 ③   20 ②

서술형

21 (1) It is August fourteenth(14th).
(2) It is Wednesday.
(3) It is 3 o'clock.
(4) It is rainy.

22 (1) These (2) This (3) Those (4) They

23 ⑤ one → it
틀린 이유: 앞에서 말한 수학 책을 가리키므로 인칭대명사
it으로 써야 한다.

24 He lives in Australia. His favorite sport is baseball.
He has two dogs. They love him a lot.

25 (1) We saw ourselves on TV.
(2) My father made dinner himself.
또는 My father himself made dinner.

1 앞에 나온 these flowers를 대신하는 인칭대명사 They가 알맞다.

2 '우리의'라는 뜻의 소유격 인칭대명사 our가 오는 것이 알맞다.

3 첫 번째 빈칸은 목적어 자리이므로 목적격 인칭대명사 him이 알맞다. 두 번째 빈칸은 '나의 것'이라는 뜻의 소유대명사 mine이 알맞다.

4 첫 번째 빈칸은 불특정한 것을 가리킬 때 쓰는 부정대명사 one이 알맞다. 두 번째 빈칸은 앞에서 말한 her new coat를 가리키는 인칭대명사 it이 알맞다.

5 빈칸에는 강조 용법으로 쓰인 재귀대명사 myself가 알맞다.

6 날짜와 날씨를 나타낼 때 쓰는 비인칭 주어 It이 들어가는 것이 알맞다.

7 가까운 곳에 있는 단수의 사물을 가리킬 때나 통화 시 자신을 소개할 때는 this를 쓴다.

8 ④ 거리를 나타낼 때 쓰는 비인칭 주어 It이 들어가는 것이 알맞다.

9 ④는 특정한 것을 가리키는 인칭대명사이고, 나머지는 모두 비인칭 주어이다.

10 cameras 앞에 소유격이 와야 하므로 hers를 소유격인 her로 고쳐야 한다고 말한 준수가 옳다.

11 〈보기〉의 재귀대명사는 동사의 목적어로 쓰인 재귀 용법이고, ① 의 재귀대명사는 전치사의 목적어로 쓰인 재귀 용법이다. 나머지 는 모두 강조 용법으로 쓰인 재귀대명사이다.

12 this book을 복수형으로 바꾸면 these books가 되고, 동사는 Are가 되어야 한다.

13 〈보기〉와 ③의 It은 거리를 나타내는 비인칭 주어이다.

14 ② 강조 용법으로 쓰인 재귀대명사는 생략할 수 있다.

15 ② '그녀의 것'이라는 소유대명사 hers가 되어야 한다.

16 ③ those로 물었으므로 대답은 they로 한다.
(No, it isn't. → No, they aren't.)

17 부정대명사 one은 불특정한 a pen을 가리킨다.

18 ⓐ 강조 용법으로 쓰인 재귀대명사 myself가 되어야 한다.

19 '이것들'은 these, '저것들'은 those로 표현한다.

20 ⓑ가 옳은 문장이다.
ⓐ 주어가 you이므로 목적어는 me가 되어야 한다. ⓒ him은 The teacher를 강조하는 재귀대명사 himself가 되어야 한다. ⓓ 시간을 나타내는 비인칭 주어 It으로 고쳐야 한다. ⓔ him을 '그의 것'이라는 뜻의 소유대명사 his로 고쳐야 한다.

21 비인칭 주어 It을 사용하여 날짜, 요일, 시간, 날씨를 나타내는 문장을 쓴다.

22 여러 사람을 말할 때는 these를 쓰고, 한 사람을 말할 때는 this 를 쓴다. 멀리 떨어져 있는 복수의 대상을 가리킬 때는 those를 쓰고, those나 these로 말한 것은 they로 받는다.

23 앞에서 언급한 것을 가리킬 때는 인칭대명사 it을 써야 한다.

24 Peter를 소개하는 글이므로 남자를 가리키는 3인칭 단수형 인칭대명사를 써서 글을 쓴다.

25 (1) 재귀대명사 ourselves를 목적어로 쓴다.
(2) 강조 용법으로 쓰이는 재귀대명사는 강조하는 말 바로 뒤나 문장의 끝에 쓸 수 있다.

CHAPTER 5

시제

POINT 1 현재시제   p. 86

개념확인 1 run, 달린다
2 likes, 좋아한다
3 wants, 원한다

기본연습
A 1 walks   2 are   3 has
4 flows

B 1 has   2 sleeps   3 clean
4 teaches   5 reads   6 is

C 1 have   2 live   3 wears
4 moves   5 opens

D 1 goes   2 rises   3 has
4 practice   5 writes   6 visits
7 makes

정답 ②

해설 반복되는 일을 나타낼 때는 현재시제를 쓴다. 주어가 3인칭 단수인 My brother이므로 ride에 -s를 붙인 rides가 알맞다.

POINT 2 과거시제   p. 88

개념확인 1 동사: was, 과거 부사: yesterday
2 동사: ate, 과거 부사구: last night
3 동사: moved, 과거 부사구: two days ago

기본연습
A 1 was   2 live   3 was
4 enjoyed   5 lost   6 went
7 visited

B 1 called   2 met   3 freezes
4 cleaned   5 rode   6 bought
7 saw

C 1 had   2 was   3 cooked
4 cried   5 arrived   6 reads
7 climbed   8 went   9 were
10 worked   11 go   12 invented

정답 ②

해설 첫 번째 문장은 every day가 쓰였으므로 현재시제가 알맞다. 주어가 3인칭 단수인 She이므로 has를 쓴다. 두 번째 문장에서 yesterday는 과거를 나타내는 부사이므로 과거형인 had가 알맞다.

POINT 3 미래시제   p. 90

개념확인 1 will, tomorrow
2 is going to, next week
3 will, soon

기본연습 1 take   2 lives   3 buy
4 are   5 to watch   6 cooked
7 is   8 are going to meet

정답 ④

해설 첫 번째 문장에서 will 뒤에는 항상 동사원형이 오므로, eat이 알맞다. 두 번째 문장에서 빈칸 뒤의 going to로 보아 be동사가 와야 하는데, 주어가 He이므로 is가 알맞다.

POINT 4 미래시제의 부정문   p. 91

개념확인 1 I will **not** wear the pants.
2 We are **not** going to swim.
3 He's **not** going to meet Jane.

기본연습
A 1 will not ride   2 won't start
3 am not going to be   4 are not going to meet

B 1 will not rain   2 won't walk
3 are not going to go   4 is not going to make

POINT 5 미래시제의 의문문   p. 92

개념확인 1 주어: you, 동사원형: call
2 주어: he, 동사원형: swim
3 주어: you, 동사원형: visit

기본연습
A 1 Will she visit
2 Will David like
3 Is he going to play
4 Are they going to watch

B **1** I will 또는 we will   **2** she isn't
     3 he won't   **4** they are
     5 I won't 또는 we won't   **6** I am 또는 we are

POINT 6 현재진행형   p. 93

개념확인 **1** be동사: are, 동사원형-ing: playing
         2 be동사: is, 동사원형-ing: singing
         3 be동사: am, 동사원형-ing: doing

기본연습

A
1 moving	**2** coming	**3** brushing
4 dancing	**5** telling	**6** standing
7 winning	**8** having	**9** sending
10 flying	**11** stopping	**12** taking
13 drawing	**14** sitting	**15** teaching
16 trying	**17** running	**18** cleaning
19 crying	**20** planning	**21** lying
22 visiting	**23** walking	**24** sleeping

B
1 is snowing	**2** is	**3** are
4 making	**5** is riding	

C
1 am watching	**2** is reading
3 are running	**4** is cooking
5 is washing	**6** is listening
7 are studying	**8** am writing
9 are swimming	

틀리기 쉬운 내신포인트

정답 ③

해설 '~하고 있다'라는 의미의 현재진행형은 「be동사+동사원형-ing」로 나타내며, 이때 be동사는 주어(He)에 맞춰 써야 하므로 is telling이 알맞다.

POINT 7 과거진행형   p. 95

개념확인 **1** 달리고 있었다
         2 수영하고 있었다
         3 보고 있었다

기본연습

A
1 was	**2** are	**3** were
4 was	**5** were	**6** was eating

B
1 was washing	**2** was watching
3 were making	**4** was using
5 were doing	**6** were looking

POINT 8 진행형의 부정문과 의문문   p. 96

개념확인 **1** 나는 울고 있지 않았다.
         2 너는 달리고 있니?
         3 그들은 자고 있지 않다.

기본연습

A
1 Are	**2** is not	**3** are not
4 waiting	**5** Are	**6** wasn't taking
7 having	**8** running	**9** Was
10 sitting	**11** Were	
12 were not writing		

B
1 are not playing	**2** Are, drawing
3 were not cleaning	**4** Was, doing
5 is not writing	**6** Were, cooking
7 was not sleeping	

C
1 are not dancing	**2** Is she eating
3 was not walking	**4** Were they running

틀리기 쉬운 내신포인트

정답 (1) She is not playing   (2) Was he riding

해설 (1) 진행형의 부정문은 「be동사+not+동사원형-ing」의 형태로 쓴다.
      (2) 진행형의 의문문은 「Be동사+주어+동사원형-ing ~?」의 형태로 쓴다.

개념완성 TEST   p. 98

STEP 1 Quick Check

① is   ② play   ③ was   ④ played   ⑤ will be
⑥ are going to play   ⑦ 우리는 지금 축구를 하고 있다.
⑧ 우리는 그때 축구를 하고 있었다.

STEP 2 기본 다지기

A
1 was	**2** eats	**3** teaches
4 left	**5** visited	**6** is lying
7 was writing	**8** were not listening	
9 will climb	**10** will not go	

B
1 were	**2** moves	**3** went
4 are	**5** come	**6** meet
7 stayed		

C 1 The store opened at 10 a.m.

2 My father is drinking coffee.

3 Mina and Jina were eating breakfast together.

4 Is she washing her hands?

5 They were not playing hockey.

6 Sally won't(will not) cook dinner.

7 Is he going to see a musical next week?

8 Was Sam brushing his teeth?

9 I am going to wear a red T-shirt today.

STEP 3 서술형 따라잡기

A 1 won't(will not) use paper cups

2 will plant trees

3 won't(will not) eat meat

4 will clean up the trash

B 1 Is she talking on the phone?

2 Are you going to meet Ann tomorrow?

3 He was not watching TV last night.

4 They are going to visit the museum next week.

C 1 He plays the violin every day.

2 They're(They are) swimming in the pool now.

3 We studied in the library yesterday.

4 I didn't(did not) watch the movie last weekend.

학교 시험 실전 문제
p. 101

1 ③	2 ②	3 ①	4 ④	5 ⑤	6 ④	7 ⑤
8 ①	9 ②	10 ③	11 ④	12 ③	13 ①	14 ③
15 ⑤	16 ③	17 ④	18 ⑤	19 ③	20 ④	

서술형

21 is building, is sleeping, are playing

22 (1) Amy and Tom are not running in the park.

(2) Will he buy a new smartphone?

(3) Was she watering the plants at that time?

(4) Kate was visiting her grandmother.

23 (1) made a cake

(2) played basketball

(3) is going to go shopping

24 (1) No, I won't

(2) Are you going to

25 (1) I practice yoga every day.

(2) She watched a movie last week.

(3) Are they cooking dinner now?

16 Chapter 5

---

1 ① running, ② lying, ④ raining, ⑤ studying으로 써야 한다.

2 부사 now(지금)가 있으므로 지금 하고 있는 일을 나타내는 현재진행형이 알맞다.

3 will을 포함하는 미래시제 의문문은 「Will+주어+동사원형 ~?」으로 쓴다.

4 visited는 과거형이므로 빈칸에는 과거를 나타내는 부사(구)가 알맞다. ④ next weekend(다음 주말)는 미래를 나타내는 부사구이다.

5 「be going to+동사원형」이 사용된 미래시제 문장이므로 빈칸에는 미래를 나타내는 부사(구)가 알맞다. ⑤ last night(어젯밤)은 과거를 나타내는 부사구이다.

6 첫 번째 문장의 yesterday는 과거를 나타내는 부사이므로 snow의 과거형인 snowed가 알맞다. 두 번째 문장은 일반적·과학적 사실을 나타내는 문장이므로 현재시제가 알맞다.

7 첫 번째 문장의 soon(곧)은 미래를 나타내는 부사이므로 미래시제가 알맞다. 두 번째 문장은 at that time(그때)으로 보아 과거에 진행 중이었던 일을 나타내는 과거진행형이 되도록 cleaning이 들어가는 것이 알맞다.

8 ① 주어가 I이므로 현재진행형의 be동사는 Am을 써야 한다. (→ Am)

9 ② 현재를 나타내는 부사 now가 있으므로 현재진행형 is not sleeping이 되어야 한다.

10 ③ 과거진행형으로 물었는데 미래시제로 답하는 것은 어색하다. (No, he won't. → No, he wasn't.)

11 ⓒ 과거를 나타내는 부사구(last week)가 있으므로 과거시제 의문문(Did+주어+동사원형 ~?)을 써야 한다. (Will → Did)

12 He is not going to ride his bike tomorrow.라는 문장이 되므로, 네 번째로 오는 단어는 going이다.

13 (A) 현재를 나타내는 부사 now가 있으므로 현재진행형이 되도록 Is가 알맞다.

(B) last week는 과거를 나타내는 부사구이므로 과거형 bought가 알맞다.

(C) tomorrow는 미래를 나타내는 부사이므로 미래시제의 부정을 나타내는 won't가 알맞다.

14 ③은 주어가 Ann and Peter로 복수이므로 빈칸에는 Are가 들어가고, 나머지 빈칸에는 모두 is(Is)가 들어간다.

15 ⑤ 일반적·과학적 사실은 현재시제로 나타내므로 have가 옳다. ① last night은 과거를 나타내는 부사구이므로 과거진행형으로 써야 한다. (is → was) ② 현재를 나타내는 부사 now가 있으므로 현재진행형으로 써야 한다. (Were → Are) ③ 미래를 나타내는 부사구 next week가 있으므로 미래시제로 써야 한다. (started → will start 또는 are going to start) ④ two minutes ago는 과거를 나타내는 부사구이므로 과거시제로 써야 한다. (arrives → arrived)

16 ⓒ 과거진행형 의문문인데 주어가 Danny and Tony로 복수이므로, be동사는 Were로 고쳐 써야 한다. (Was → Were) ⓓ 미래시제의 부정문은 「will not(won't)+동사원형」이나 「be동사+not+going to+동사원형」으로 써야 한다. (won't going to see → won't(will not) see 또는 am not going to see)

17 현재진행형 의문문에 대한 대답은 긍정일 때는 「Yes, 주어+be동사.」로 하고, 부정일 때는 「No, 주어+be동사+not.」으로 한다. TV를 보고 있는지 묻는 말에 음악을 듣고 있다고 답한 것으로 보아, 빈칸에는 부정의 대답이 들어가는 것이 알맞다.

18 과거진행형 의문문은 「Was/Were+주어+동사원형-ing ~?」의 형태로 쓰며, 주어가 you and Mike로 복수이므로 be동사는 Were가 알맞다.

19 ③은 be동사 is가 있으므로 현재진행형이 되도록 빈칸에 playing이 들어가고, 나머지 빈칸에는 모두 play가 들어간다.

20 ④ 미래시제의 의문문은 「Will+주어+동사원형 ~?」이나 「Be동사+주어+going to+동사원형 ~?」으로 써야 한다. (Did you buy → Will you buy 또는 Are you going to buy)

21 현재진행형은 「be동사의 현재형+동사원형-ing」의 형태로 쓰며, be동사는 주어에 따라 달라지는 것에 유의한다.

22 (1) 진행형의 부정문은 「be동사+not+동사원형-ing」의 형태로 쓴다.
(2) will의 의문문은 「Will+주어+동사원형 ~?」의 형태로 쓴다.
(3) 진행형의 의문문은 「Be동사+주어+동사원형-ing ~?」의 형태로 쓴다.
(4) 과거진행형은 「was/were+동사원형-ing」의 형태로 쓴다.

23 (1) 어제 한 일이므로 과거시제로 쓴다.
(2) 오늘 한 일을 말할 때는 과거시제로 쓴다.
(3) 미래에 할 일은 「be동사+going to+동사원형」의 형태로 쓴다.

24 (1) 미래 표현 will이 포함된 의문문의 답변은 부정일 때 「No, 주어+won't.」로 쓴다.
(2) B가 A의 물음에 부정의 답을 하며 be going to를 사용하여 말하고 있으므로, 빈칸에는 be going to를 이용한 의문문이 들어가야 한다. 이때 주어는 you를 쓰는 것에 유의한다.

25 (1) 매일 반복되는 일을 나타내므로 현재시제로 쓴다.
(2) 지난주의 일이므로 과거시제로 쓴다.
(3) 현재진행형의 의문문은 「Be동사+주어+동사원형-ing ~?」의 형태로 쓴다.

C H A P T E R

6

조동사

POINT **1** 조동사의 개념   p. 106

개념확인 **1** will   **2** must   **3** can

기본연습
A **1** be   **2** will meet   **3** should
4 may   **5** must keep

B **1** I can play   **2** Minho will go
3 You must recycle   **4** Mr. Brown may know

POINT **2** 조동사의 부정문   p. 107

개념확인 **1** cannot   **2** must not   **3** will not

기본연습 **1** My father cannot(can't) drive
2 Kevin may not be
3 You must not(mustn't) park
4 Sam should not(shouldn't) take
5 My family will not(won't) visit

틀리기 쉬운 내신포인트

정답 ③

해설 조동사의 부정문은 조동사 뒤에 not을 붙여 만들어야 하므로 ③은 may not take로 써야 한다.

POINT **3** 조동사의 의문문   p. 108

개념확인 **1** 조동사: Can, 동사원형: drive
2 조동사: Will, 동사원형: buy
3 조동사: Should, 동사원형: wear

기본연습
A **1** Can he speak   **2** Should we cancel
3 Must I call   **4** Will Mina go

B **1** you should   **2** she won't
3 he can't   **4** she will
5 she can   **6** you must
7 you shouldn't   **8** you may

POINT 4 can
p. 109

개념확인 1 ～할 수 있다   2 ～해 줄래?   3 ～하면 안 된다

기본연습

A
1 능력   2 요청   3 허가
4 요청   5 허가   6 요청
7 능력   8 허가   9 능력

B
1 Kate can use   2 You can visit
3 Can I eat   4 Can you post
5 Could you help   6 Can you turn on
7 Billy could not(couldn't) understand
8 You cannot(can't) make
9 She was able to cancel
10 I will be able to travel
11 He was not able to finish

틀리기 쉬운 내신포인트

정답 ③

해설 ③은 '～해 줄래?'라는 요청의 의미로 쓰였고, 나머지는 모두 '～해도 좋다'라는 허가의 의미로 쓰였다.

POINT 5 may
p. 111

개념확인 1 ～일지도 모른다
2 ～해도 될까요?
3 ～해도 좋다

기본연습

A
1 허가   2 허가   3 약한 추측
4 약한 추측   5 허가   6 약한 추측
7 허가   8 약한 추측

B
1 may   2 may   3 can
4 can   5 may   6 may

POINT 6 will, would
p. 112

개념확인 1 ～할 거니?   2 ～을 원하다   3 ～해 줄래요?

기본연습

A
1 I will be   2 He will not(won't) buy
3 Would you help   4 Would you come
5 Would you like to eat   6 She would like to go

POINT 7 must
p. 113

개념확인 1 ～해야 한다   2 ～임에 틀림없다
3 ～해서는 안 된다

기본연습

A
1 의무   2 추측   3 금지
4 추측

B
1 must   2 can   3 must
4 may   5 must

POINT 8 have to
p. 114

개념확인 1 ～해야 한다   2 ～할 필요가 없다

기본연습

A
1 의무   2 의무   3 금지
4 불필요

B
1 must(has to) water   2 don't have to worry
3 will have to go   4 had to do
5 must not(mustn't) smoke
6 had to work   7 must(have to) be
8 will have to wear
9 must not(mustn't) sleep
10 don't have to pay   11 had to finish
12 must(have to) change
13 doesn't have to clean

틀리기 쉬운 내신포인트

정답 ③

해설 첫 번째 문장은 주어가 3인칭 단수(Mary)이고 현재시제(these days)여야 하므로 has to를 써야 한다. 두 번째 문장은 주어가 I이고 과거시제(yesterday)여야 하므로 had to를 써야 한다.

POINT 9 should, had better
p. 116

개념확인 1 ～하지 말아야 한다   2 ～하는 게 좋겠다

기본연습

A
1 should see   2 should wear
3 should go back   4 should drink
5 should do
6 shouldn't(should not) stay up

B
1 had better go   2 had better not play
3 had better not eat   4 had better hurry
5 had better not sit   6 had better set

C
1 may 2 cannot
3 had better 4 don't have to
5 shouldn't

정답 ①

해설 '~해야 한다'라는 충고의 의미를 나타내는 should가 들어가야 한다.

C
1 You don't have to bring your lunch.
2 Would you like to play badminton?
3 Kate has to clean her room.
4 May I come in now?

개념완성 TEST

p. 118

STEP 1 Quick Check

① 능력 ② 허가 ③ 추측 ④ 추측 ⑤ 금지 ⑥ 불필요
⑦ 충고 ⑧ had to go ⑨ will have to go

STEP 2 기본 다지기

A
1 can 2 can(may) 3 won't
4 may 5 must(should) 6 have to
7 will 8 had better
9 must(should) not

B
1 can make 2 had better take
3 doesn't have to 4 had to walk
5 must wear 6 should have
7 Will you play

C
1 James was able to play the cello.
2 Students have to study hard.
3 He may not come to our party.
4 You must not(mustn't) use paper cups.
5 He cannot(can't) be tired.
6 I had to take the first train.
7 Julie will have to get up early tomorrow.
8 I couldn't believe the news. 또는
  I wasn't able to believe the news.
9 You will be able to get a taxi outside the station.

STEP 3 서술형 따라잡기

A
1 cannot(can't) read 2 can ride
3 can stand 4 cannot(can't) answer

B
1 I must go to the post office this afternoon.
2 You must not take photos in the museum.
3 We should not cross the street on a red light.
4 My sister may not like this skirt.

학교 시험 실전 문제

p. 121

1 ④ 2 ④ 3 ① 4 ② 5 ③ 6 ⑤ 7 ①
8 ② 9 ③ 10 ③ 11 ⑤ 12 ④ 13 ⑤ 14 ④
15 ② 16 ① 17 ③ 18 ③ 19 ⑤ 20 ②

서술형

21 (1) have to keep
  (2) is able to swim
22 (1) No, I won't
  (2) Yes, I can
23 (1) Can(Could) you move these books?
  (2) You can(may) borrow my notebook.
  (3) We should(must/have to) arrive at the station at 6.
  (4) You must(should) not open this box.
24 (1) I'd like to eat Chinese food.
  (2) You shouldn't(should not) be rude to people.
  (3) Minji has to study for the exam.
25 (1) You had better eat healthy food.
  (2) You had better see an eye doctor.
  (3) You had better write a letter to her.

1 주어가 3인칭 단수이므로 has to를 써야 한다.

2 Can Henry(= he) ~?로 묻는 말에는 Yes, he can. 또는 No, he can't.로 답할 수 있다.

3 Are you able to ~?로 묻는 말에는 Yes, I am. 또는 No, I'm not.으로 답할 수 있다.

4 '~해야 한다'라는 의미로 의무를 나타내는 have to는 조동사 must와 바꿔 쓸 수 있다.

5 ③은 '~해도 좋다'라는 허가의 의미를 나타내고, 나머지는 모두 '~일지도 모른다'라는 약한 추측의 의미를 나타낸다.

6 ⑤ 조동사 뒤에는 동사원형이 와야 한다. (→ Animals will talk with people.)

7 '~해야 한다'라는 뜻으로 약한 의무를 나타내는 조동사는 should이다.

8 '~해도 좋다'라는 뜻으로 허가를 나타내는 조동사는 may이다.

9 'Jake가 그 문제를 풀 수 있었다.'라는 과거의 능력을 나타내는 문장이다. 주어가 3인칭 단수이고 과거시제이므로 was able to로 바꿔 쓸 수 있다.

10 ① can의 부정은 cannot이나 can't로 쓴다. (→ cannot〔can't〕 climb)
② 조동사의 의문문은 「조동사+주어+동사원형 ~?」으로 쓴다. (→ Can I use)
④ 조동사 뒤에는 항상 동사원형이 온다. (→ can play)
⑤ 조동사는 주어의 인칭에 따라 형태가 변하지 않는다. (→ can name)

11 ⑤ must not은 '~해서는 안 된다'라는 뜻으로 금지를 나타내고, don't have to는 '~할 필요가 없다'라는 뜻으로 불필요를 나타낸다.

12 〈보기〉와 ④의 must는 '~임에 틀림없다'라는 뜻으로 강한 추측을 나타내고, 나머지는 모두 '~해야 한다'라는 뜻으로 의무를 나타낸다.

13 '~할 필요가 없다'라는 의미의 불필요를 나타낼 때는 don't have to를 쓰는데, 주어가 3인칭 단수이므로 doesn't로 쓴다.

14 ④ '~하고 싶다'라는 뜻으로 쓰이는 would like to 뒤에는 동사원형이 와야 한다. (buying → buy)

15 ② 사진을 찍어도 되는지 묻는 말에 허가해 놓고 사진을 찍지 말라고 금지하는 것은 어색하다. Yes, you can.을 No, you can't.로 고쳐야 자연스럽다.

16 '~할 필요가 없다'는 의미의 don't have to는 주어가 3인칭 단수일 때 doesn't have to로 쓴다.

17 ③은 '저를 위해 불을 좀 꺼 주시겠어요?'라는 요청의 말이 되어야 하므로 Can〔Could〕이 알맞다.

18 의무를 나타내는 must는 have to로 바꿔 쓸 수 있는데 주어가 3인칭 단수이므로 has to가 되어야 한다.

19 낚시를 하면 안 된다는 금지를 나타내는 표지판이다. ⑤ don't have to는 '~할 필요가 없다'라는 의미이므로 적절하지 않다.

20 ⓐ와 ⓔ가 옳은 문장이다.
ⓑ 조동사의 의문문은 「조동사+주어+동사원형 ~?」으로 쓴다. (→ Will you have some bread?)
ⓒ 주어가 복수이므로 has to가 아닌 have to로 써야 한다.
ⓓ 조동사는 두 개를 나란히 쓸 수 없으므로 미래의 능력을 나타낼 때는 will be able to로 써야 한다. (will can → will be able to)

21 (1) '~해야 한다'라는 의미로 의무를 나타내는 must는 have to와 바꿔 쓸 수 있다.
(2) '~할 수 있다'라는 의미로 능력을 나타내는 can은 be able to로 바꿔 쓸 수 있다.

22 (1) Amy를 만날 거냐는 물음에 가족들과 소풍을 갈 것이라고 했으므로 부정의 대답을 해야 한다.

(2) 문제를 풀 수 있냐는 물음에 답을 알려주고 있으므로 긍정의 대답을 해야 한다.

23 (1) 요청을 나타내는 can이나 could를 쓴다.
(2) 허가를 나타내는 can이나 may를 쓴다.
(3) 의무를 나타내는 must나 have to, should를 쓴다.
(4) 금지를 나타내는 must not이나 충고의 부정형인 should not을 쓴다.

24 (1) would like to 뒤에는 동사원형을 쓴다.
(2) should의 부정은 should 뒤에 not을 붙여 나타낸다.
(3) 주어(Minji)가 3인칭 단수이므로 의무를 나타내는 have to를 has to로 써야 한다.

25 '~하는 게 좋겠다'라는 강한 충고의 뜻으로 「had better+동사원형」의 형태로 문장을 쓴다.

CHAPTER 7 의문사

POINT 1 의문사 의문문   p. 126

개념확인   **1** Who   **2** What   **3** When

기본연습

A   **1** is   **2** do   **3** will
    4 likes   **5** can I   **6** did
    7 happened   **8** is Emma   **9** Mary come

B   **1** ⓑ   **2** ⓐ   **3** ⓓ
    4 ⓒ

C   **1** have   **2** made   **3** is
    4 were you

D   **1** Why are you angry?
    2 What does this word mean?
    3 Who is playing soccer?
    4 How did you meet him?
    5 Where can I find the book?

틀리기 쉬운 내신포인트

정답 ④

해설 일반동사가 있는 의문사 의문문은 「의문사+do/does/did +주어+동사원형 ~?」으로 쓴다.

POINT 2 who, whom, whose   p. 128

개념확인   **1** 누가   **2** 누구를   **3** 누구의

기본연습

A   **1** Whose   **2** Who   **3** Whose
    4 Who(m)   **5** Who

B   **1** Who   **2** Who   **3** Who
    4 Whose   **5** Whose   **6** Who
    7 Who   **8** Who

C   **1** ⓒ   **2** ⓑ   **3** ⓐ
    4 ⓔ   **5** ⓓ

D   **1** Who   **2** Whose   **3** Who
    4 Who(m)   **5** Whose   **6** Who(m)
    7 Whose   **8** Who(m)

틀리기 쉬운 내신포인트

정답 ③

해설 whose는 '누구의 ~'라는 뜻으로 소유를 묻는 의문사이므로, ③ '그녀는 Emma야.'라고 답하는 것은 어색하다.

POINT 3 what, which   p. 130

개념확인   **1** 무엇   **2** 누구를   **3** 어떤

기본연습

A   **1** What   **2** What   **3** Whose
    4 What   **5** Which   **6** What
    7 Who   **8** Which

B   **1** ⓑ   **2** ⓔ   **3** ⓒ
    4 ⓐ   **5** ⓓ   **6** ⓕ

C   **1** What   **2** Whose   **3** Who
    4 What   **5** Which   **6** What
    7 Which   **8** What   **9** Which
    10 Who(m)

D   **1** What does your brother need?
    2 What movie did you watch?
    3 What is that on the wall?
    4 Which color do you want, blue or black?
    5 Which drink will he choose, coffee or juice?

틀리기 쉬운 내신포인트

정답 ④

해설 축구와 야구 중 선택을 묻고 있으므로, '어떤 ~'이라는 의미의 Which가 알맞다.

POINT 4 where, when, why, how   p. 132

개념확인   **1** 언제   **2** 어디에   **3** 왜

기본연습

A   **1** Why   **2** When   **3** How
    4 Where   **5** How

B   **1** ⓒ   **2** ⓓ   **3** ⓐ
    4 ⓔ   **5** ⓑ

C   **1** Where   **2** How   **3** When
    4 Why   **5** Where   **6** When
    7 How   **8** Why   **9** When
    10 How   **11** Where   **12** Why

D   **1** Where is the bus stop?
    2 When should you leave?
    3 How did you know him?
    4 Why do you learn English?

틀리기 쉬운 내신포인트

정답 ②

해설 어디에서 옷을 사는지 묻는 말이 되어야 하므로, 장소를 묻는 의문사 Where이 알맞다.

개념확인 **1** 얼마나 먼　　**2** 얼마나 긴　　**3** 얼마나 키가 큰

기본연습

A
1 How old　　**2** How long　　**3** How tall
4 How much　　**5** How often　　**6** How many
7 How far

B
1 ⓒ　　**2** ⓐ　　**3** ⓑ
4 ⓓ　　**5** ⓕ　　**6** ⓔ
7 ⓗ　　**8** ⓖ

C
1 How old　　**2** How often　　**3** How tall
4 How long　　**5** How much　　**6** How long
7 How many　　**8** How much　　**9** How many
10 How far

틀리기 쉬운 내신포인트

정답 ②

해설 How much ~?는 셀 수 없는 명사의 양을 묻는 표현이다.
comic books는 셀 수 있는 명사이므로 How many ~?
로 고쳐야 한다.

개념 완성 T E S T　　　　　　p. 136

STEP 1 Quick Check

① Who　② Whose　③ What　④ When　⑤ Where
⑥ Why　⑦ 너는 어떻게 그녀를 만났니?
⑧ 너는 얼마나 자주 그녀를 만나니?

STEP 2 기본 다지기

A
1 Who likes　　**2** Whose bag
3 Where did, find　　**4** When will, visit
5 What can, do　　**6** Why is, learning
7 Why do, think　　**8** How does, go
9 How much time　　**10** How many books

B
1 Whom → Who　　**2** know → knows
3 What → Which　　**4** much → many
5 does → do

C
1 Who　　**2** Whose pen
3 How tall　　**4** What will, order
5 When did, buy　　**6** Where did, go
7 How does, speak　　**8** Why do, read

STEP 3 서술형 따라잡기

A
1 What color　　**2** How much, ten(10)
3 How many, six(6)

B
1 Why do you like Junsu?
2 Who are you looking for?
3 How long do you sleep at night?
4 Which do you need, a pen or a pencil?

C
1 How tall is that giraffe?
2 When did you buy the new shirt?
3 Where does your uncle teach math?
4 Whose smartphone is that on the desk?

학교 시험 실전 문제　　　　　　p. 139

1 ①　**2** ②　**3** ③　**4** ③　**5** ④　**6** ②　**7** ①
8 ③　**9** ⑤　**10** ③　**11** ②　**12** ④　**13** ③　**14** ④
15 ②　**16** ⑤　**17** ⑤　**18** ⑤　**19** ④　**20** ③

서술형

21 (1) When did Sujin come back?
(2) How often does Sam watch movies?

22 (1) Who entered the classroom?
(2) Whose cup is this?
(3) What can Mina make?

23 (1) What is your name?
(2) How old are you?
(3) When is your birthday?

24 (1) Where
(2) How
(3) Who(m)
(4) What time

25 (1) Why did Mike go home early?
(2) How long is your winter vacation?
(3) How many tickets do you need?
(4) How much milk did you drink?

1 B가 자신의 부모님이라고 대답하는 것으로 보아, '누구'라는 뜻
으로 사람에 대해 묻는 의문사 Who가 알맞다.

2 B가 생선을 더 좋아한다고 대답하는 것으로 보아, '어느 것'이라
는 뜻으로 여러 개 중 선택을 묻는 의문사 Which가 알맞다.

3 B가 장소로 대답하는 것으로 보아, '어디에'라는 뜻으로 장소를
묻는 의문사 Where가 알맞다.

4 ③ 가장 친한 친구에 대해 묻고 있으므로 '누구'라는 뜻의 의문사
Who가 알맞다.

5 왜, 어디서, 언제, 얼마나 자주 운동을 하는지 묻는 것은 자연스럽지만, '누구를'이라는 뜻의 Whom이 들어가는 것은 어색하다.

6 How many ~?는 '얼마나 많은 ~'이라는 뜻으로 수를 묻는 말이므로, ② '31일이 있어.'라고 답하는 것이 알맞다.

7 Whose ~는 '누구의 ~'라는 뜻으로 소유를 묻는 의문사이므로, ① '그것들은 내 거야.'라고 답하는 것이 알맞다.

8 ③ 유미가 어디에 사는지는 알 수 없다.

9 첫 번째 문장은 '얼마나 자주'를 묻는 How often ~?이 알맞고, 두 번째 문장은 '얼마 동안'을 묻는 How long ~?이 알맞다.

10 대답에서 때를 말하고 있으므로, '언제'라는 뜻의 의문사 when을 사용하여 질문하는 것이 알맞다.

11 Who did you invite for the party?가 되어야 하므로, 네 번째로 오는 단어는 invite이다.

12 Who teaches music in your school?이 되어야 하므로, 쓰이지 않는 단어는 does이다.

13 ③ 가격을 묻는 질문에 길이가 얼마나 되는지 답하는 것은 어색하다.

14 ④에는 때를 묻는 When이 들어가는 것이 알맞다.

15 의문사가 있는 be동사 의문문은 「의문사+be동사+주어 ~?」의 어순으로 써야 한다.

16 ⑤ 누가 문을 열었는지 묻는 말이 되어야 하므로 Whom을 Who로 고쳐야 한다.

17 ⑤에는 '누구의 ~'라는 뜻으로 쓰이는 Whose가 들어가고, 나머지는 모두 What이 들어가야 한다.

18 every day는 빈도를 나타내므로 How often ~?으로 얼마나 자주 피아노를 치는지 묻는 것이 알맞다.

19 ⓐ 장소를 묻는 Where, ⓑ 때를 묻는 When, ⓒ, ⓔ '어떤 ~'이라는 뜻으로 쓰이는 Which, ⓓ 상태를 묻는 How가 알맞다.

20 How much 다음에는 셀 수 없는 명사가 오고, How many 다음에는 셀 수 있는 명사의 복수형이 와야 한다. (ⓑ How much → How many, ⓓ How many → How much)

21 (1) B가 때를 말하고 있으므로 의문사 when을 사용하여 과거시제로 질문을 쓴다.
(2) B가 빈도를 말하고 있으므로 how often을 사용하여 질문을 쓴다.

22 (1) '누가'라는 뜻으로 사람에 대해 물을 때는 who, (2) '누구의 ~'라는 뜻으로 소유를 물을 때는 whose, (3) '무엇'이라는 뜻으로 사물에 대해 물을 때는 what을 쓴다.

23 (1) 이름을 묻는 질문이 알맞다.
(2) 나이를 묻는 질문이 알맞다.
(3) 생일을 묻는 질문이 알맞다.

24 (1) 장소를 물을 때는 where, (2) 방법을 물을 때는 how, (3) 사람에 대해 물을 때는 who(m), (4) 구체적인 시각을 물을 때는

what time을 쓴다.

25 (1) 이유는 why로 묻는다.
(2) '얼마 동안'인지 물을 때는 how long을 사용하여 묻는다.
(3) 셀 수 있는 명사의 수는 how many로 묻는다.
(4) 셀 수 없는 명사의 양은 how much로 묻는다.

CHAPTER 8
to부정사

POINT 1   to부정사의 형태와 쓰임   p. 144

개념확인 1 to play   2 to read   3 to study

기본연습
A   1 to learn   2 to help   3 to be
    4 to take   5 to study

B   1 to read   2 to watch   3 to become
    4 to live   5 to buy

틀리기 쉬운 내신포인트

정답 ③

해설 '~하는 것을'이라는 뜻으로 명사 역할을 하는 「to+동사원형」 형태의 to부정사가 알맞다.

POINT 2   명사적 용법: 주어, 보어 역할   p. 145

개념확인 1 주어   2 보어

기본연습 1 to be   2 to watch   3 to travel
    4 to keep   5 to jog   6 to write
    7 to become

POINT 3   명사적 용법: 목적어 역할   p. 146

개념확인 1 목적어   2 보어

기본연습 1 expected to pass   2 need to read
    3 hopes to live   4 agreed to buy
    5 promised not to open

틀리기 쉬운 내신포인트

정답 ③

해설 want는 to부정사를 목적어로 쓰는 동사이다.

POINT 4   형용사적 용법   p. 147

개념확인 1 a hat   2 time   3 homework

기본연습
A   1 to write   2 to exercise
    3 work to do   4 snacks to eat
    5 to drink

B   1 a newspaper to read
    2 a jacket to wear
    3 some money to buy a bag
    4 time to practice the dance
    5 someone to fix her car
    6 an umbrella to use

POINT 5   부사적 용법   p. 148

개념확인 1 너와 이야기를 나눠서   2 옷을 사기 위해

기본연습
A   1 감정의 원인   2 결과   3 목적
    4 감정의 원인   5 목적

B   1 to see me   2 ran to catch
    3 sad to hear   4 disappointed to lose
    5 to stay healthy   6 to study music
    7 grew up to be   8 to ask a question
    9 to pass the exam   10 to be 100 years old

C   1 명사   2 명사   3 부사
    4 형용사   5 부사   6 형용사
    7 명사   8 부사   9 부사
    10 명사

틀리기 쉬운 내신포인트

정답 ③

해설 〈보기〉와 ③은 to부정사의 부사적 용법이고, 나머지는 명사적 용법이다.

개념완성 TEST   p. 150

STEP 1 Quick Check

① It   ② to cook   ③ to drink   ④ to eat
⑤ 나는 빵을 좀 사기 위해 빵집에 갔다.
⑥ 나는 요리사가 되어서 기뻤다.
⑦ 그녀는 자라서 요리사가 되었다.

STEP 2 기본 다지기

A   1 to wash   2 to learn   3 to read
    4 to do   5 to meet(see)   6 to buy
    7 to save   8 to hear   9 to be(become)
    10 It, to speak   11 to see(watch)

B   1 not to go   2 to write   3 to take
    4 It   5 to study   6 to meet
    7 to teach   8 to be   9 ○

C **1** decided not to take a taxi
2 chose not to go to Tokyo
3 not to watch a horror movie
4 rude to talk loudly in a library
5 to climb the mountain
6 to sell concert tickets
7 to visit his grandparents
8 to stay in Singapore for two months

STEP 3 서술형 따라잡기

A **1** to go camping
2 to practice soccer
3 to watch a movie
4 to meet Mike at the library

B **1** I want to learn French this winter.
2 Can I have something to drink?
3 He went to the park to walk his dog.
4 It is very hard to run in the marathon.

C **1** I hope to become a doctor.
2 Ann promised to come to my birthday party.
3 Mike uses his smartphone to play games.
4 Tony needs a book to read on the train.
5 It is dangerous to swim in a deep river.

학교 시험 실전 문제   p. 153

1 ④	2 ①	3 ④	4 ②	5 ⑤	6 ⑤	7 ④
8 ④	9 ⑤	10 ②	11 ③	12 ⑤	13 ③	14 ④
15 ①	16 ③	17 ②	18 ①	19 ②	20 ③	

[서술형]

21 (1) wants to watch an art movie
(2) plans to borrow a book from the library
(3) hopes to play tennis with Mina
22 (1) It is not easy to finish the project today.
(2) It is very important to study English.
23 (1) time to do
(2) homework to do
24 (1) to play basketball
(2) to take pictures
25 (1) My plan is to grow yellow tulips.
(2) Kevin wants to visit his grandparents.
(3) Cindy needs something to drink.
(4) I'm happy to hear the news.

1 want는 to부정사를 목적어로 취하는 동사이므로 to go가 알맞다.

2 to부정사 주어(to watch football games)가 뒤에 왔으므로 가주어 It이 알맞다.

3 her clothes를 수식하는 형용사적 용법의 to부정사가 알맞다.

4 to부정사의 부정은 to부정사 앞에 not을 써서 나타낸다.

5 첫 번째 빈칸에는 감정의 원인을 나타내는 to부정사가 들어가야 하고, 두 번째 빈칸에는 결과를 나타내는 to부정사가 들어가야 한다.

6 〈보기〉와 ⑤는 명사적 용법으로 쓰였다.
(①, ④ 부사적 용법 ②, ③ 형용사적 용법)

7 〈보기〉와 ④는 부사적 용법으로 쓰였다.
(①, ⑤ 형용사적 용법 ②, ③ 명사적 용법)

8 주어 역할을 하는 to부정사구(to+동사원형)의 형태가 알맞다.

9 형용사적 용법의 to부정사(to take a taxi)가 명사(money)를 뒤에서 수식하는 형태가 알맞다.

10 감정을 나타내는 형용사(happy) 뒤에 '~해서'라는 뜻으로 감정의 원인을 나타내는 to부정사가 오는 것이 알맞다.

11 가주어 it을 사용하여 It is fun to make friends.가 되어야 하므로, 네 번째로 오는 단어는 to이다.

12 ⑤ '~하는 것(이다)'라는 뜻의 보어로 쓰이는 to부정사가 되어야 하므로, win은 to win으로 써야 한다.

13 promise는 to부정사를 목적어로 쓰고, to부정사는 「to+동사원형」의 형태로 쓴다.

14 주어로 쓰인 to부정사구는 단수 취급한다.

15 진주어 to부정사구(to save energy)를 대신하는 가주어 It으로 써야 한다.

16 ③ want는 to부정사를 목적어로 취하므로 study는 to study가 되어야 한다.

17 ② '잡기 위해'라는 뜻으로 목적을 나타내는 부사적 용법의 to부정사는 「to+동사원형」의 형태로 써야 하므로, to catches는 to catch가 되어야 한다.

18 모두 옳은 문장이다.
(ⓐ, ⓑ, ⓓ 명사적 용법 ⓒ 부사적 용법 ⓔ 형용사적 용법)

19 ② someone을 꾸며 주는 형용사적 용법의 to부정사가 되어야 하므로 to help로 써야 한다.

20 모두 목적의 의미로 쓰인 부사적 용법의 to부정사가 쓰인 문장이다. to부정사는 「to+동사원형」으로 써야 한다.
(ⓑ to took → to take, ⓓ to are → to be)

21 want, plan, hope는 to부정사를 목적어로 쓰는 동사들이다. 각 동사 뒤에 「to+동사원형」 형태의 to부정사를 써서 문장을 완성한다.

22 to부정사구가 주어로 쓰일 때는 주어 자리에 가주어 It을 쓰고 to부정사구는 문장 뒤로 보낼 수 있다.

23 '~할'이라는 의미로 명사를 뒤에서 꾸며 주는 형용사적 용법의 to부정사를 쓴다.

24 행동의 목적을 나타내는 부사적 용법의 to부정사를 쓴다. Tim은 '농구를 하기 위해서', Jack은 '사진을 찍기 위해서'가 알맞다.

25 (1) 보어로 쓰인 명사적 용법의 to부정사를 쓴다.
(2) want의 목적어로 쓰인 명사적 용법의 to부정사를 쓴다.
(3) something을 꾸며 주는 형용사적 용법의 to부정사를 쓴다.
(4) 감정의 원인을 나타내는 부사적 용법의 to부정사를 쓴다.

C H A P T E R 9
동명사

POINT 1 동명사의 형태와 쓰임 p. 158

개념확인 1 Dancing　2 riding　3 singing

기본연습

A
1 running　2 going　3 sitting
4 lying　5 exercising　6 playing
7 becoming　8 waiting

B
1 going　2 Getting　3 not taking
4 is　5 was

C
1 주어　2 전치사의 목적어
3 동사의 목적어　4 주어
5 보어　6 동사의 목적어
7 전치사의 목적어　8 보어

D
1 Singing　2 collecting　3 being
4 eating　5 studying　6 worrying
7 Taking　8 swimming

틀리기 쉬운 내신포인트

정답 ④

해설 〈보기〉와 ④는 동사의 목적어로 쓰였고, ①은 보어, ②와 ③은 주어로 쓰였다.

POINT 2 동명사를 목적어로 쓰는 동사 p. 160

개념확인 1 동사: kept, 목적어: laughing
2 동사: likes, 목적어: swimming
3 동사: enjoy, 목적어: dancing

기본연습

A
1 to play　2 opening　3 to buy
4 doing　5 waiting　6 driving
7 playing　8 to get up　9 to paint
10 watching

B
1 finish cleaning　2 stopped snowing
3 enjoy traveling　4 practices singing
5 kept talking　6 mind waiting
7 gave up reading

C
1 going(to go)　2 learning
3 to speak　4 cooking
5 talking(to talk)　6 looking
7 watching(to watch)　8 writing

해설 목적어로 to부정사가 왔으므로 동명사를 목적어로 쓰는 enjoy는 빈칸에 들어갈 수 없다. begin, like, love는 목적어로 동명사와 to부정사를 모두 쓴다.

POINT 3 동명사 vs. 진행형   p. 162

개념확인 1 쓰는 중이다   2 굽는 것이다   3 도망치는 중이다

기본연습
1 ⓐ   2 ⓑ   3 ⓐ
4 ⓐ   5 ⓑ   6 ⓑ
7 ⓐ   8 ⓑ   9 ⓑ
10 ⓐ

정답 ④

해설 ④는 진행형으로 쓰인 「동사원형+-ing」이고, 나머지는 모두 동명사이다.

POINT 4 동명사의 관용 표현   p. 163

개념확인 1 수영하러 가다   2 만나는 게 어때
3 청소하느라 바쁘다

기본연습
1 spent, practicing   2 go camping
3 How(What) about crossing
4 spends, buying   5 is good at using
6 is interested in joining

개념완성 TEST   p. 164

STEP 1 Quick Check

① is   ② making   ③ 나는 쿠키 만드는 것을 즐긴다.
④ making   ⑤ 나는 쿠키를 만들고 있다.
⑥ 나는 쿠키를 만들고 싶다.   ⑦ 나는 쿠키를 만드느라 바쁘다.

STEP 2 기본 다지기

A
1 writing(to write)   2 Planning
3 raining   4 looking   5 talking
6 listening   7 fixing   8 working
9 studying   10 traveling   11 is sleeping

B
1 meeting   2 to pass   3 playing
4 is   5 going   6 taking
7 ○

C
1 Tina likes going to the zoo in summer.
2 Harry loves listening to K-pop music.
3 Jessy enjoyed watching a sci-fi movie.
4 Mike practices playing the piano every day.
5 Jack finished reading the book last night.
6 Sarah is busy washing her dog.
7 I'm good at drawing flowers.
8 Choosing a gift is difficult.
9 Heating a big house is expensive.

STEP 3 서술형 따라잡기

A
1 enjoys dancing   2 finish eating
3 is busy watering

B
1 His job is driving a taxi.
2 They gave up waiting for the bus.
3 Swimming in the sea is not easy.
4 Jina and I were playing basketball in the park.

C
1 I'm interested in playing the piano.
2 My mother practices taking pictures.
3 Ben spent time working in his garden.
4 Did you go skiing with your friends last weekend?

학교 시험 실전 문제   p. 167

1 ⑤   2 ④   3 ⑤   4 ④   5 ①   6 ⑤   7 ②
8 ④   9 ③   10 ④   11 ③   12 ①   13 ②, ④
14 ④   15 ⑤   16 ④   17 ②   18 ③   19 ③   20 ③

서술형
21 (1) to travel → traveling
    (2) are → is
22 (1) stopped running
    (2) felt like sitting
23 (1) is good at dancing
    (2) enjoys listening to K-pop
    (3) began learning(to learn) Korean
24 (1) mind opening
    (2) taking off
25 (1) practiced playing the guitar
    (2) enjoyed fishing in the river
    (3) was busy doing her homework
    (4) spent, making model planes

1 문장의 주어로 쓸 수 있는 것은 동명사와 to부정사이므로 Driving이 알맞다.

2 문장의 보어로 쓸 수 있는 것은 동명사와 to부정사이므로 inventing이 알맞다.

3 목적어 자리에 동명사가 왔으므로 to부정사를 목적어로 취하는 동사 wants는 알맞지 않다.

4 첫 번째 문장의 finish는 목적어로 동명사를 취하고, 두 번째 문장에는 be busy -ing 표현이 쓰였으므로 공통으로 동명사 washing이 알맞다.

5 ① start는 목적어로 동명사와 to부정사 모두를 취하는 동사이므로 to rain은 옳다.
② 현재진행형이 되도록 sending으로 써야 한다.
③ How about -ing?의 표현이 되도록 동명사 raising으로 써야 한다.
④ stop은 목적어로 동명사를 취하는 동사이므로 crying으로 써야 한다.
⑤ 전치사의 목적어 자리이므로 동명사 eating으로 써야 한다.

6 ⑤는 보어로 쓰인 동명사이고, 나머지는 모두 동사의 목적어로 쓰인 동명사이다.

7 ② watching은 진행형으로 쓰인 「동사원형+-ing」이고, 나머지는 모두 동명사이다.

8 첫 번째 문장은 be good at -ing 표현이 쓰였으므로 동명사 playing이 와야 한다. 두 번째 문장의 mind는 동명사를 목적어로 취하므로 waiting이 와야 한다.

9 〈보기〉와 ③은 동명사이고, 나머지는 모두 진행형으로 쓰인 「동사원형+-ing」이다.

10 keep은 동명사를 목적어로 취하는 동사이고, 의미상 미래시제가 와야 한다.

11 전치사 without 뒤에는 동명사가 와야 한다.

12 모두 옳은 문장이다.
ⓐ Cooking은 문장의 주어로 쓰인 동명사이다.
ⓑ feel like -ing의 표현이 쓰인 문장이다.
ⓒ to read는 begin의 목적어로 쓰인 to부정사이다. begin은 목적어로 to부정사와 동명사를 모두 쓸 수 있다.
ⓓ 주어로 쓰인 동명사는 항상 단수 취급하므로 is는 옳다.

13 ① 전치사 for의 목적어는 동명사 being으로 써야 한다.
③ mind는 목적어로 동명사를 취하므로 eating으로 써야 한다.
⑤ hope는 목적어로 to부정사를 취하므로 to meet으로 써야 한다.

14 ④ want는 to부정사를 목적어로 취하므로 to ride가 들어가야 한다.

15 '~하기 위해 멈추다'라는 뜻은 부사적 용법의 to부정사를 써서 나타낸다.

16 주어로 쓰인 동명사는 항상 단수 취급하므로, are는 is로 고쳐야 한다.

17 ② feel like -ing는 '~하고 싶다'라는 뜻의 표현이므로, '그녀는 일찍 잠자리에 들고 싶었다.'라는 의미이다.

18 A의 말에서 finish는 목적어로 동명사를 취하고, B의 말에서 be busy -ing는 관용 표현으로 '~하느라 바쁘다'라는 뜻이므로, 빈칸에는 모두 동명사가 알맞다.

19 (A) give up은 목적어로 동명사를 취하므로 learning이 알맞다.
(B) continue는 목적어로 동명사와 to부정사를 모두 쓸 수 있으므로 looking for나 to look for가 알맞다.
(C) practice는 목적어로 동명사를 취하므로 singing이 알맞다.

20 ⓐ 전치사 for 뒤에 동명사 coming이 와야 한다.
ⓒ need는 목적어로 to부정사를 취하므로 to eat이 와야 한다.
ⓔ enjoy는 목적어로 동명사를 취하므로 meeting이 와야 한다.

21 (1) give up은 목적어로 동명사를 취하므로 to travel을 traveling으로 고쳐야 한다.
(2) 주어로 쓰인 동명사는 항상 단수 취급하므로 are는 is로 고쳐야 한다.

22 (1) stop은 '~을 멈추다'라는 의미로 쓰일 때는 목적어로 동명사를 쓴다.
(2) '~하고 싶다'는 feel like -ing로 쓴다.

23 (1) '~하는 것을 잘하다'는 be good at -ing로 쓴다.
(2) '즐기다'라는 뜻의 enjoy는 목적어로 동명사를 쓴다.
(3) '시작하다'라는 뜻의 begin은 목적어로 동명사와 to부정사를 모두 쓸 수 있다.

24 (1) 보라가 더워하고 있으므로 창문을 열어도 되는지 묻는 것이 알맞다. mind는 동명사를 목적어로 취하므로 opening으로 쓴다.
(2) '~하는 게 어때?'는 How about -ing?로 쓴다.

25 (1), (2) practice와 enjoy는 동명사를 목적어로 취한다.
(3) '~하느라 바쁘다'는 be busy -ing로 쓴다.
(4) '~하는 데 시간을 보내다'는 「spend +시간+-ing」로 쓴다.

CHAPTER 10

문장의 종류

POINT 1 명령문   p. 172

개념확인 1 Be   2 Come   3 Wash

기본연습
A 1 Be   2 talk   3 sit
   4 Open   5 Be   6 Don't
   7 Don't   8 Don't be

B 1 Be quiet   2 Don't swim   3 Don't cross
   4 Don't be late

틀리기 쉬운 내신포인트

정답 ③

해설 부정 명령문은 동사원형 앞에 **Don't**를 쓴다.

POINT 2 제안문   p. 173

개념확인 1 가자   2 먹자   3 주문하지 말자

기본연습
A 1 Let's   2 be   3 drink
   4 not   5 not eat   6 walk
   7 let's not   8 let's

B 1 Let's be   2 Let's have 3 Let's not buy
   4 Let's not go

POINT 3 감탄문   p. 174

개념확인 1 day   2 birds   3 terrible

기본연습
A 1 What   2 How   3 How
   4 What   5 How   6 How
   7 What   8 How   9 What

B 1 How bright   2 How fast
   3 How quickly   4 What big feet
   5 What a huge whale   6 What a great

C 1 How clever   2 How warm
   3 How hard   4 How well
   5 What an interesting novel
   6 What an exciting show
   7 What lovely flowers

틀리기 쉬운 내신포인트

정답 ④

해설 빈칸 뒤에 pretty dolls가 있으므로 「What+(a/an)+형용사+명사+주어+동사!」 형태의 감탄문이 알맞다.

POINT 4 부가의문문   p. 176

개념확인 1 isn't he?   2 can you?   3 didn't she?

기본연습
A 1 isn't   2 will   3 doesn't
   4 shall   5 could   6 were

B 1 doesn't she   2 won't she
   3 could you   4 isn't he
   5 will you   6 did you
   7 aren't they   8 does he
   9 isn't it   10 shall we
   11 didn't he

C 1 No, they can't   2 Yes, I do
   3 No, it isn't   4 Yes, she does
   5 No, it wasn't   6 Yes, he did

틀리기 쉬운 내신포인트

정답 ③

해설 두 문장 모두 일반동사의 과거형이 쓰인 부정문이므로 부가의문문은 did를 사용하여 긍정문으로 쓴다.

POINT 5 There is/are ~   p. 178

개념확인 1 a cat   2 two ducks   3 dust

기본연습
A 1 There is   2 There isn't
   3 There were   4 There are
   5 Is there   6 There are
   7 There weren't   8 Are there
   9 Is there   10 There were

B 1 There aren't any students
   2 There is some cheese
   3 There are twelve months
   4 Is there a giraffe
   5 There was a beautiful picture
   6 There weren't many trees

C
 1 There are(There're) seven colors
 2 There was a big television
 3 There wasn't(was not) any money
 4 Is there a library
 5 Was there any sugar

틀리기 쉬운 내신포인트

정답 ②

해설 첫 번째 문장의 food는 셀 수 없는 명사이므로 is가 알맞다.
두 번째 문장의 31 days는 복수 명사이므로 are가 알맞다.

개념완성 T E S T
p. 180

STEP 1 Quick Check

① Push ② run ③ close ④ Let's not ⑤ How
⑥ 정말 아름다운 날씨구나! ⑦ isn't ⑧ is ⑨ are

STEP 2 기본 다지기

A **1** Be   **2** How   **3** What
   4 isn't it   **5** There isn't **6** did she
   7 Let's write **8** Don't play   **9** There were

B **1** What   **2** ○   **3** There are
   4 ○   **5** How   **6** can't he
   7 Don't fight **8** Is there   **9** shall we

C **1** How tall this building is!
   2 What a beautiful smile your sister has!
   3 Order a book on the Internet.
   4 Don't park your car here.
   5 Steve and Lucy are from Canada, aren't they?
   6 It isn't hot in Seoul now, is it?
   7 They played basketball last Saturday, didn't they?
   8 There is a new bookstore on the first floor.

STEP 3 서술형 따라잡기

A **1** are two cats   **2** is a dog

B **1** Don't touch your nose.
   2 Let's find out about street food.
   3 What a nice teacher!
   4 You will visit the museum, won't you?

C **1** How wide the river is!
   2 Let's not swim in this lake.
   3 James didn't invite you, did he?
   4 Be nice to your friends.

학교 시험 실전 문제
p. 183

1 ② **2** ⑤ **3** ③ **4** ⑤ **5** ③ **6** ② **7** ③
8 ③ **9** ② **10** ② **11** ② **12** ② **13** ③ **14** ⑤
15 ⑤ **16** ④ **17** ③ **18** ③ **19** ③ **20** ①

서술형

21 (1) What a great player (2) How delicious
22 (1) There are five apples and a bottle of milk
    (2) Let's buy two eggs and three oranges
23 ③ doesn't he → isn't he
    틀린 이유: 앞 문장의 동사가 is sleeping이므로 부가의문
    문은 be동사를 써서 isn't he로 써야 한다.
24 (1) Don't bring (2) Throw (3) Don't shout
25 (1) Let's watch (2) doesn't it (3) it does (4) How

1 명령문은 동사원형으로 시작하는데 뒤에 형용사 quiet이 왔으므
로 be가 알맞다.

2 주어가 Sally이고 조동사 can이 쓰였으므로 부가의문문은 can't
she가 알맞다.

3 There is ~. 구문의 의문문으로, 동사가 is이므로 주어로 단수
명사나 셀 수 없는 명사가 와야 한다. children은 복수 명사이다.

4 ⑤는 빈칸 뒤에 형용사 careful이 있으므로 Be 또는 Let's be
를 써야 한다.

5 첫 번째 문장은 형용사 strong을 강조하는 감탄문이므로 「How
+형용사+주어+동사」로 쓴다. 두 번째 문장은 명사 coat를 강
조하는 감탄문이므로 「What+a/an+형용사+명사+주어+
동사」로 쓴다.

6 부가의문문에 대한 대답은 대답의 내용이 부정이면 No로 한다.
No, I didn't.로 답했으므로 ② '나는 너에게 전화하지 않았어.'
라는 뜻이다.

7 ③ 소풍을 가자고 제안하는 말에 Yes라고 긍정적으로 답한 후,
집에 머물자고 하는 것은 어색하다.

8 〈보기〉는 '~이 있다'라는 뜻의 There is/are ~. 구문의 There
로, ③과 쓰임이 같다. 나머지는 모두 '거기에, 저기에'라는 뜻의
부사이다.

9 주어진 문장을 감탄문으로 바꾸면 What a beautiful garden
this house has!이다.

10 '~하지 말자'라는 뜻의 문장은 「Let's not+동사원형 ~.」으로
쓴다.

11 ②는 「How+부사+주어+동사!」 형태의 감탄문이므로 How를
써야 하고, 나머지는 모두 「What+(a/an)+형용사+명사+주어
+동사!」 형태의 감탄문이므로 What을 써야 한다.

12 ③ 남자아이는 강아지 한 마리와 함께 있으므로 There is a dog
with a boy.가 되어야 한다.

13 ③ 제안문은 「Let's+동사원형 ~.」의 형태로 쓴다.

① turns → turn ② What → How ④ didn't → didn't they
⑤ There is → There are)

14 〈보기〉의 빈칸 뒤에 복수 명사 members가 쓰였으므로 are가
들어가야 한다. ⑤ 앞 문장의 동사가 aren't이므로 부가의문문에
는 are가 알맞다. (① be ② weren't ③, ④ is/was)

15 앞 문장을 영어로 옮기면 He is wearing a blue T-shirt이고,
뒤에 부가의문문으로 isn't he?를 붙이는 것이 알맞다.

16 감탄문으로 써야 하므로 「How+형용사/부사+주어+동사!」 형
태인 How interesting the game is! 또는 「What+(a/an)+
형용사+명사+주어+동사!」 형태인 What an interesting
game (it is)!가 알맞다.

17 ⓐ 「How+형용사+주어+동사!」 형태의 감탄문이므로 How를
써야 한다. (What → How) ⓒ '~하자'라는 의미로 제안하는 문
장은 Let's로 시작해야 한다. (Let → Let's) ⓔ 명령문은 동사원
형으로 시작해야 한다. (Checks → Check)

18 ③ Let's 뒤에 동사원형을 써야 한다. (→ Let's play)

19 ⓑ 「What+(a/an)+형용사+명사+주어+동사!」 형태의 감탄문
이므로 How를 What으로 고쳐야 한다. ⓓ 앞 문장의 동사가 일반
동사의 과거시제이므로 부가의문문은 didn't they?로 써야 한다.

20 (A) 앞 문장에 can't가 쓰였으므로 부가의문문에는 can을 써야
한다.
(B) 「What+(a/an)+형용사+명사+주어+동사!」 형태의 감탄
문이므로 What을 써야 한다.
(C) 뒤에 오는 주어가 복수(three eggs)이므로 복수형 be동사
are가 알맞다.

21 (1) What 감탄문은 「What+(a/an)+형용사+명사+주어+
동사!」 형태로 쓴다.
(2) How 감탄문은 「How+형용사/부사+주어+동사!」 형태로
쓴다.

22 (1) '~이 있다'는 There is/are ~.로 나타내고, 뒤에 오는 명사
가 복수이므로 be동사는 복수형인 are를 쓴다.
(2) '~하자'는 「Let's+동사원형 ~.」으로 쓴다.

23 ③ 앞 문장의 동사가 is sleeping이므로 부가의문문은 isn't
he?로 써야 한다.

24 명령문은 동사원형으로 시작하고, 부정 명령문은 「Don't+동사
원형 ~.」으로 쓴다.
(1) 반려견을 데려오지 말라는 내용의 부정 명령문을 쓴다.
(2) 쓰레기통에 쓰레기를 버리라는 내용의 긍정 명령문을 쓴다.
(3) 동물에게 소리 지르지 말라는 내용의 부정 명령문을 쓴다.

25 (1) '~하자'는 「Let's+동사원형 ~.」으로 쓴다.
(2) 앞 문장이 일반동사 현재형의 긍정문이므로 부가의문문은
doesn't it이 알맞다.
(3) Yes로 답했으므로 it does가 알맞다.
(4) 뒤에 형용사가 왔으므로 How 감탄문이 알맞다.

C H A P T E R **11**
문장의 구조

POINT 1 1형식, 2형식   p. 188

개념확인 **1** became   **2** is   **3** cried

기본연습
1 1형식	**2** 1형식	**3** 2형식
4 1형식	**5** 1형식	**6** 2형식
7 2형식	**8** 1형식	**9** 1형식
10 2형식	**11** 2형식	**12** 2형식

POINT 2 2형식: 감각동사   p. 189

개념확인 **1** soft   **2** sweet   **3** sad

기본연습

A
1 sad	**2** wonderful	**3** delicious
4 romantic	**5** fresh	**6** looks like

B
1 sounds	**2** feels	**3** tastes
4 smells	**5** looks	

C
1 beautiful	**2** looks like	**3** felt like
4 taste	**5** ○	

D
1 This drink tastes like strawberries.
2 The baby's skin feels so soft.
3 You look like a gentleman.
4 This flower smells sweet.
5 She looks beautiful in this photo.
6 His voice sounds pleasant.
7 Why does this soup taste strange?

틀리기 쉬운 내신포인트

정답 ④

해설 2형식 문장에서 감각동사(look)의 주격 보어로는 형용사가
와야 하며 부사는 올 수 없다.

POINT 3 3형식, 4형식   p. 191

개념확인 **1** opened   **2** taught   **3** sent

기본연습

A
1 They / have / a piano.
    주어   동사   목적어

2 He / showed / me / his photos.
    주어   동사   간접목적어   직접목적어

3 She / sent / her cousin / a text.
　　주어　동사　간접목적어　직접목적어

4 Adam / writes / children's books.
　　주어　　동사　　목적어

5 My brother / broke / his arm.
　　주어　　　동사　　목적어

6 She / didn't leave / him / any messages.
　　주어　　동사　　간접목적어　직접목적어

B **1** bought　**2** entered　**3** met
　　4 wrote　**5** gave

C **1** They bought some clothes at the store.
　　2 He sent me a Christmas card.
　　3 She gave us some delicious snacks.
　　4 Jake asked me a question.
　　5 My mom read us an interesting story.
　　6 Do you need any help?
　　7 Can you lend me your car this evening?

정답 ①

해설 수여동사 give는 뒤에 「간접목적어(~에게)+직접목적어 (~을)」를 취한다.

POINT **4** 4형식을 3형식으로 바꾸는 법　p. 193

개념확인 **1** 간접목적어: me, 직접목적어: her camera
　　2 간접목적어: his son, 직접목적어: a watch
　　3 간접목적어: him, 직접목적어: a question

기본연습

A **1** for　　**2** to　　**3** to
　　4 to　　**5** for　　**6** for
　　7 for　　**8** to　　**9** to
　　10 for　　**11** of

B **1** brings good luck to him
　　2 cooked some dishes for his friends
　　3 gave a gold ring to Susan
　　4 bought a cap for him on his birthday
　　5 made a warm sweater for me
　　6 showed the painting to the visitors

C **1** me English　　**2** him an email
　　3 her my address　**4** a flower for him
　　5 your book to me　**6** me a difficult question
　　7 me my coat

정답 ③

해설 4형식 문장을 3형식 문장으로 바꿀 때, send, bring, give 는 전치사 to를 사용하고 buy는 for를 사용한다.

POINT **5** 5형식　p. 195

개념확인 **1** makes　　**2** call　　**3** found

기본연습 **1** My family / calls / Judy / a tomboy.
　　　　주어　　동사　목적어　목적격 보어

2 This blanket / will keep / you / warm.
　　주어　　　　동사　　목적어　목적격 보어

3 The news / made / people / angry.
　　주어　　동사　　목적어　목적격 보어

4 She / found / the science exam / difficult.
　　주어　　동사　　목적어　　　목적격 보어

5 The movie / made / him / famous.
　　주어　　　동사　　목적어　목적격 보어

6 Ms. Wilson / keeps / her room / clean.
　　주어　　　동사　　목적어　목적격 보어

정답 ③

해설 「주어+동사+목적어+목적격 보어」의 5형식 문장으로, 빈 칸에는 목적격 보어로 형용사가 알맞다.

개 념 완 성 **T E S T**　p. 196

STEP 1 **Q**uick Check

① 1형식　② 2형식　③ 3형식　④ 4형식　⑤ to
⑥ clean　⑦ smells like
⑧ 나는 그를 Einstein이라고 불렀다.
⑨ 나는 그를 행복하게 했다.

STEP 2 기본 다지기

A **1** sleep　　**2** smelled　　**3** made
　　4 bought　　**5** to　　　**6** cleaned
　　7 called　　**8** show　　**9** for
　　10 made　　**11** for

B **1** heavily　　**2** difficult　　**3** soft
　　4 me a new song 또는 a new song to me
　　5 a bag　　**6** the kid　　**7** warm

C **1** The young girl looks like an angel.

2 He cooked dinner for me.

3 May I ask a favor of you?

4 I made a new cat tower for my cat.

5 I gave some carrots to my horse.

6 Mr. Kim sends some flowers to his wife every day.

7 She teaches us Spanish.

8 Tom bought his brother comic books.

9 Can you get me a hotcake?

STEP 3 서술형 따라잡기

A **1** me a (birthday) cake   **2** a book for me

3 me a card   **4** a robot to me

B **1** The sofa looks comfortable.

2 Do you enjoy taking pictures?

3 We are going to call him Peter Pan.

4 He told me a detective story.

C **1** I feel cold now.

2 The soap smells like roses.

3 I showed Danny my drawings.
또는 I showed my drawings to Danny.

4 I found the window open.

학교 시험 실전 문제

p. 199

1 ④	2 ②	3 ④	4 ③	5 ④	6 ⑤	7 ④
8 ②	9 ②	10 ④	11 ①	12 ⑤	13 ②	14 ③
15 ④	16 ③	17 ③	18 ④	19 ④	20 ③	

[서술형]

21 (1) bought Jane a teddy bear

(2) bought a teddy bear for Jane

22 (1) You look like a model today.

(2) Your new gloves look warm.

23 (1) We plan to learn French this year.

(2) I'll show you my new shoes.

(3) People call Bach the father of music.

24 ⓑ careful → carefully
틀린 이유: 「주어+동사+목적어」로 이루어진 3형식 문장이므로 수식어는 부사로 써야 한다.

25 (1) The machine kept the water clean.

(2) The fan made the boy cool.

(3) The boy called his dad Bike Master.

1 ④는 「주어(I)+동사(will send)+목적어(my photos)」로 이루어진 3형식 문장이다. to my parents는 문장의 형식에 영향을 주지 않는 수식어구이다.

2 감각동사 뒤에 명사가 오는 경우에는 「감각동사+like+명사」의 형태로 쓴다. 구름이 토끼 같아 보인다고 해야 자연스러우므로 동사는 look이 알맞다.

3 동사 뒤에 목적어(James)와 형용사 목적격 보어(angry)가 왔으므로 5형식 문장에 쓰이는 made가 알맞다. found는 문맥상 알맞지 않다.

4 감각동사의 주격 보어로는 형용사가 와야 하며 부사는 올 수 없다.

5 get은 3형식 문장으로 쓸 때 간접목적어 앞에 전치사 for를 쓰므로 알맞지 않다.

6 ask는 3형식 문장으로 쓸 때 간접목적어 앞에 전치사 of를 쓰는 동사이다.

7 주어진 문장과 ④는 「주어+동사+간접목적어+직접목적어」로 이루어진 4형식 문장이다. (① 5형식 ②, ③, ⑤ 3형식)

8 주어진 문장과 ②는 「주어+동사+목적어+목적격 보어」로 이루어진 5형식 문장이다. (①, ③ 4형식 ④ 2형식 ⑤ 3형식)

9 동사 give, teach, send, show는 3형식 문장을 쓸 때 간접목적어 앞에 전치사 to를 쓰고, make는 간접목적어 앞에 전치사 for를 쓴다.

10 ④의 very fast는 1형식 문장에 쓰인 부사구이고, 나머지는 모두 주격 보어이다.

11 '~을 …하게 유지하다'는 「keep+목적어+목적격 보어(형용사)」의 5형식 문장으로 써야 한다.

12 ⑤는 1형식 문장으로 wonderful을 부사 wonderfully로 써야 한다.

13 buy와 make는 3형식 문장으로 쓸 때 간접목적어 앞에 전치사 for를 쓴다.

14 taste와 look과 같은 감각동사 뒤에 명사가 오는 경우에는 「감각동사+like+명사」의 형태로 쓴다.

15 salty(짠)는 '맛'에 해당하므로 감각동사 taste가 자연스럽고, soft(부드러운)는 '촉각'에 해당하므로 감각동사 feel이 자연스럽다. touch는 '만지다, 손을 대다'라는 뜻으로 뒤에 목적어가 와야 한다.

16 ③ 「주어+동사+주격 보어(형용사)」로 이루어진 2형식 문장이다. (① careful → carefully, ② normal → normally, ④ quietly → quiet, ⑤ badly → bad)

17 「buy+간접목적어+직접목적어」는 「buy+직접목적어+for+간접목적어」로 바꿔 쓸 수 있다.

18 ④는 간접목적어와 직접목적어를 갖는 4형식 문장이다. 나머지는 모두 목적어와 목적격 보어를 갖는 5형식 문장이다.

19 ④ make는 3형식 문장으로 쓸 때 간접목적어 앞에 전치사 for 를 쓴다. (to me → for me)

20 ⓒ 감각동사 look 다음에 형용사가 오므로 like를 삭제해야 한다.
ⓓ 5형식 문장은 「주어+동사+목적어+목적격 보어」의 어순으로 쓴다. (very interesting this book → this book very interesting)

21 '~에게 …을 사 주다'는 「주어+buy+간접목적어+직접목적어」 나 「주어+buy+직접목적어+for+간접목적어」의 형태로 쓴다.

22 (1) 「감각동사(look)+like+명사」의 형태가 되도록 쓴다.
(2) 「감각동사+주격 보어(형용사)」 형태의 문장을 쓴다.

23 (1) 「주어+동사+목적어」 형태의 3형식 문장을 쓴다.
(2) 「주어+동사+간접목적어+직접목적어」 형태의 4형식 문장을 쓴다.
(3) 「주어+동사+목적어+목적격 보어」 형태의 5형식 문장을 쓴다.

24 3형식 문장의 수식어는 부사로 써야 하므로 careful을 carefully 로 고쳐야 한다.

25 keep, make, call을 이용하여 「주어+동사+목적어+목적격 보어」의 5형식 문장을 쓴다.

POINT 1 형용사의 쓰임   p. 204

개념확인 1 short   **2** green   **3** beautiful

기본연습

A
1 old   **2** hungry   **3** clean
4 small   **5** black   **6** fast
7 young   **8** funny   **9** long
10 white   **11** sad   **12** kind
13 blue   **14** tall   **15** yellow
16 beautiful   **17** red   **18** short

B
1 보어   **2** 명사 수식   **3** 보어
4 명사 수식   **5** 명사 수식   **6** 보어
7 명사 수식   **8** 보어   **9** 명사 수식
10 보어

C
1 my close friend   **2** ○
3 Her yellow bag
4 these difficult questions
5 a long skirt   **6** that high mountain
7 two clean glasses   **8** ten fresh oranges
9 ○   **10** that old man

틀리기 쉬운 내신포인트

정답 ①

해설 명사를 수식하거나 보어 역할을 할 수 있는 것은 형용사이다.

POINT 2 수량형용사: many, much, a lot of   p. 206

개념확인 1 형용사: many, 명사: books
2 형용사: much, 명사: money
3 형용사: many, 명사: bottles

기본연습

A
1 much   **2** much   **3** many
4 many   **5** a lot of   **6** lots of

B
1 much / a lot of / lots of
2 many / a lot of / lots of
3 many / a lot of / lots of
4 a lot of desks / lots of desks / many desks

틀리기 쉬운 내신포인트

정답 ②

해설 flowers는 셀 수 있는 명사이므로 앞에 many나 a lot of (lots of)가 와야 한다.

POINT 3 수량형용사: (a) few, (a) little   p. 207

개념확인 **1** 약간의   **2** 거의 없는   **3** 거의 없는

기본연습
A **1** few   **2** a little   **3** a little
  4 a few   **5** little   **6** a few
B **1** few   **2** little   **3** a little
  4 a few   **5** little

틀리기 쉬운 내신포인트
정답 ③
해설 문맥상 '거의 없는'이라는 뜻이 되어야 한다. friend는 셀 수 있는 명사이므로 few가 알맞다.

POINT 4 수량형용사: some, any   p. 208

개념확인 **1** I have **some** sugar.
  2 I can't find **any** stamps.
  3 He didn't buy **any** clothes.

기본연습
A **1** some   **2** any   **3** some
  4 some   **5** any
B **1** some   **2** some   **3** any
  4 some   **5** any

틀리기 쉬운 내신포인트
정답 ①
해설 첫 번째 문장은 긍정문이므로 some이 알맞고, 두 번째 문장은 부정문이므로 any가 알맞다.

POINT 5 감정 형용사   p. 209

개념확인 **1** 흥미로운   **2** 지루해하는   **3** 신나게 하는

기본연습
A **1** interested   **2** interesting   **3** bored
  4 boring   **5** surprising   **6** surprised
  7 excited   **8** exciting
B **1** excited   **2** interesting   **3** surprising
  4 bored

POINT 6 부사의 쓰임   p. 210

개념확인 **1** quickly   **2** really   **3** joyfully

기본연습
1 fast   **2** lived   **3** speaks
4 hard   **5** opened   **6** runs
7 difficult   **8** talked   **9** kind
10 listen   **11** good   **12** much
13 he agreed right away   **14** likes
15 happy   **16** think   **17** famous

POINT 7 부사의 형태   p. 211

개념확인 **1** 빨리   **2** 느리게   **3** 아름답게

기본연습
A **1** really   **2** happily   **3** quietly
  4 clearly   **5** well   **6** nicely
  7 badly   **8** angrily   **9** sadly
  10 possibly   **11** usefully   **12** deeply
  13 comfortably   **14** seriously   **15** strangely
  16 sweetly   **17** simply   **18** safely
  19 kindly   **20** perfectly   **21** lightly
  22 similarly
B **1** brightly   **2** well   **3** suddenly
  4 wise   **5** heavily   **6** beautiful
C **1** Luckily   **2** easily   **3** terribly
  4 different   **5** carefully   **6** kind
  7 gently   **8** dangerous
D **1** well   **2** carefully

틀리기 쉬운 내신포인트
정답 ③
해설 〈보기〉와 ①, ②, ④는 형용사와 부사의 관계이고, ③은 명사와 형용사의 관계이다.

POINT 8 형용사와 형태가 같은 부사   p. 213

개념확인 **1** 높이   **2** 빠른   **3** 일찍

기본연습
1 형용사   **2** 형용사   **3** 형용사
4 부사   **5** 부사   **6** 형용사
7 부사   **8** 부사   **9** 형용사
10 부사   **11** 부사   **12** 형용사

POINT 9 빈도부사 p. 214

개념확인 1 sometimes 2 always 3 never

기본연습

A 1 always 2 sometimes 3 often
4 never 5 always 6 sometimes
7 never 8 often 9 usually
10 usually 11 sometimes 12 often
13 usually

B 1 ① 2 ② 3 ②
4 ② 5 ② 6 ①
7 ① 8 ① 9 ②
10 ①

C 1 never 2 always 3 often
4 sometimes

틀리기 쉬운 내신포인트

정답 ④

해설 빈도부사는 주로 be동사와 조동사의 뒤, 일반동사의 앞에
오므로, ④ always는 is 뒤에 써야 한다.

개념완성 T E S T p. 216

STEP 1 Quick Check

① many ② a little ③ some ④ surprised ⑤ sweet
⑥ fast ⑦ always ⑧ never

STEP 2 기본 다지기

A 1 cute 2 interesting 3 early
4 usually 5 any 6 few
7 a little 8 a lot of

B 1 much 2 easily 3 little
4 A few 5 too slowly 6 fast
7 some 8 three yellow 9 normally

C 1 그는 그 오래된 차를 쉽게 고쳤다.
2 Lisa는 보통 학교에 걸어서 간다.
3 John은 가끔 그의 친구들과 야구를 한다.
4 그들은 시험을 위해 열심히 공부했다.
5 그녀는 긴 검은 머리카락을 가졌다.
6 나는 주머니에서 약간의 동전을 발견했다.
7 많은 학생들이 스마트폰을 가지고 있다.
8 그들은 우유를 조금도 원하지 않는다.

STEP 3 서술형 따라잡기

A 1 lots of, a little 2 many, a few

B 1 We will always remember you.
2 Hajun needs some onions and carrots.
3 Jiho exercised hard to lose weight.
4 There were few people in the library.

C 1 We walked quietly in the hall.
2 Alice bought too much furniture for the living room.
3 Ron never cleans his room.
4 Amy put a little(some) honey in her tea.

학교 시험 실전 문제 p. 219

1 ② 2 ⑤ 3 ④ 4 ② 5 ③ 6 ③ 7 ①
8 ④ 9 ④ 10 ③ 11 ③ 12 ⑤ 13 ③ 14 ②
15 ④ 16 ④ 17 ⑤ 18 ③ 19 ② 20 ⑤

서술형

21 (1) suddenly
(2) expensive shirt
22 (1) safely (2) easily (3) late
23 (1) lots of (2) a little (3) any
24 (1) beautiful your dress → your beautiful dress
(2) any → some
(3) excited → exciting
(4) highly → high
25 (1) always gets up
(2) sometimes goes jogging
(3) never walks

1 ②는 명사와 형용사의 관계이고, 나머지는 모두 형용사와 부사의
관계이다.

2 빈칸에는 주어를 보충 설명해 주는 형용사가 와야 알맞다. well
은 '잘, 좋게'라는 뜻의 부사이므로 빈칸에 올 수 없다.

3 빈칸에는 동사 eat(먹다)을 수식하는 부사가 와야 알맞다.
friendly는 '친절한'이라는 뜻의 형용사이다.

4 ugly는 '못생긴'이라는 뜻의 형용사이고, 나머지는 모두 부사이
다.

5 첫 번째 문장은 부정문이므로 any를 써야 하고, 두 번째 문장은
긍정문이므로 some을 써야 한다.

6 homework는 셀 수 없는 명사이고 friends는 셀 수 있는 명사
인데, 둘 다와 함께 쓸 수 있는 것은 a lot of이다.

7 첫 번째 문장에는 '열심히'라는 뜻의 부사 hard가 들어가고, 두 번째 문장에는 '어려운'이라는 뜻의 형용사 hard가 들어가야 알맞다.

8 첫 번째 문장에는 '빨리'라는 뜻의 부사 fast가 들어가고, 두 번째 문장에는 '빠른'이라는 뜻의 형용사 fast가 들어가야 알맞다.

9 ④ food는 셀 수 없는 명사이므로 much가 쓰인 것이 알맞다. (① → a little, ② → some, ③ → much, ⑤ → many)

10 첫 번째 빈칸에는 '얼마나 자주'라는 뜻으로 빈도를 묻는 표현이 되도록 often이 알맞다. 두 번째 빈칸에는 아침을 매일 먹는다고 했으므로, '나는 아침을 결코 거르지 않는다.'는 문장이 되도록 never가 알맞다.

11 ③ two와 같이 수를 나타내는 말은 형용사 앞에 써야 한다. (cute two → two cute)

12 a lot of는 '많은'이라는 뜻이고, 뒤에 셀 수 있는 명사가 위치하므로 many로 바꿔 쓸 수 있다.

13 ③의 late는 '늦은'이라는 뜻의 형용사이고, 나머지는 모두 '늦게'라는 뜻의 부사이다.

14 ⓐ picture는 셀 수 있는 명사이므로 a little을 a few로 고쳐야 한다.
ⓒ 부정문이므로 some을 any로 고쳐야 한다.

15 ④ 동사 helped를 수식하는 부사 kindly로 고쳐야 한다.

16 ④ 그녀를 거기에서 본 것이 감정을 느끼게 하는 것이므로 surprising으로 고쳐야 한다.

17 snow와 coffee는 셀 수 없는 명사이므로 (A)와 (B)에는 각각 little과 much가 알맞고, 세 번째 문장은 긍정문이므로 (C)에는 some이 알맞다.

18 ③ 미라는 일주일에 두 번 책을 읽으므로, Mira sometimes reads books.가 옳다.

19 ② fast는 형용사와 부사의 형태가 같다. (→ fast)

20 모두 옳은 문장이다.

21 (1) 형용사 sudden의 부사형은 suddenly이다.
(2) 보어 역할의 형용사 expensive를 명사를 수식하는 형태로 바꾼다.

22 동사인 (1) arrived, (2) scare, (3) came을 꾸미는 부사가 와야 하므로, 각각 safely, easily, late로 써야 한다. late는 형용사와 부사의 형태가 같다.

23 (1) 책상 위에 책이 많이 있고, book은 셀 수 있는 명사이므로 lots of를 써야 한다.
(2) 컵에 오렌지 주스가 약간 있고, orange juice는 셀 수 없는 명사이므로 a little을 써야 한다.
(3) 책상 위에는 연필이 없으므로 부정문에 쓸 수 있는 any를 쓴다.

24 (1) 인칭대명사는 형용사 앞에 써야 한다.

(2) 권유문에서는 some을 써야 한다.
(3) 경기가 감정을 느끼게 하는 대상이므로 -ing 형용사를 써야 한다.
(4) high는 형용사와 부사의 형태가 같으므로 high로 써야 한다.

25 (1) 수지는 매일 아침 일찍 일어난다고 했으므로 always를 써야 한다.
(2) 수지는 월요일과 금요일에 조깅을 한다고 했으므로 sometimes를 써야 자연스럽다.
(3) 학교가 가깝지 않아서 걸어가지 않는다고 했으므로 never를 써야 한다.

CHAPTER 13

비교 구문

POINT 1 비교급과 최상급: 규칙 변화   p. 224

개념확인 1 longest   2 colder   3 more useful

기본연습
1 faster – fastest
2 bigger – biggest
3 louder – loudest
4 taller – tallest
5 higher – highest
6 happier – happiest
7 larger – largest
8 thinner – thinnest
9 cuter – cutest
10 stronger – strongest
11 more difficult – most difficult
12 easier – easiest
13 nicer – nicest
14 busier – busiest
15 harder – hardest
16 more exciting – most exciting
17 shorter – shortest
18 smaller – smallest
19 hotter – hottest
20 cheaper – cheapest
21 younger – youngest
22 more delicious – most delicious
23 more beautiful – most beautiful
24 heavier – heaviest

POINT 2 비교급과 최상급: 불규칙 변화   p. 225

개념확인 1 better   2 least   3 worse

기본연습
1 less – least
2 brighter – brightest
3 thicker – thickest
4 better – best
5 slower – slowest
6 prettier – prettiest
7 worse – worst
8 more – most
9 more active – most active
10 tastier – tastiest
11 colder – coldest
12 more famous – most famous
13 longer – longest
14 darker – darkest
15 more – most
16 dirtier – dirtiest
17 better – best
18 earlier – earliest
19 sweeter – sweetest
20 weaker – weakest
21 more expensive – most expensive
22 more interesting – most interesting

틀리기 쉬운 내신포인트

정답 ②

해설 good의 비교급은 better이고 최상급은 best이다.

POINT 3 비교급을 이용한 비교   p. 226

개념확인 1 younger   2 faster   3 better

기본연습

A
1 smaller   2 harder   3 sweeter
4 yours   5 than

B
1 bigger than   2 older than   3 lighter than
4 earlier than   5 better than   6 taller than
7 more important than
8 more carefully than
9 more popular than

C
1 shorter than   2 faster than
3 heavier than   4 thicker than
5 cheaper than   6 higher than

틀리기 쉬운 내신포인트

정답 ④

해설 빈칸 뒤에 than이 있는 것으로 보아 비교급이 와야 한다.

POINT 4 비교급 강조   p. 228

개념확인 1 much   2 even

기본연습
1 much faster than   2 even longer than
3 still worse than   4 a lot better than
5 far more delicious than
6 much more expensive than

틀리기 쉬운 내신포인트

정답 ④

해설 '훨씬'이라는 의미로 비교급을 강조할 때는 much, even, far 등의 부사를 쓴다. very는 원급을 강조한다.

POINT 5 최상급을 이용한 비교   p. 229

개념확인 1 smartest   2 strongest

기본연습

A
1 shortest   2 most difficult
3 nicest   4 the most interesting
5 the worst   6 the oldest
7 the tallest   8 bigger
9 the highest   10 more expensive

B
1 the saddest   2 the biggest
3 the longest   4 the most delicious

5 the brightest   **6** the coldest

7 the hottest   **8** the loudest

9 the most difficult   **10** the most important

11 the youngest   **12** the most famous

C   **1** the fastest   **2** the oldest

3 the heaviest   **4** the tallest

틀리기 쉬운 내신포인트

정답 ④

해설 '~에서 가장 …한'은 「the+최상급+in ~」으로 써야 한다. popular는 3음절인 형용사이므로 최상급은 most popular 로 쓴다.

POINT 6   **원급을 이용한 비교**   p. 231

개념확인   **1** old   **2** much

기본연습   **1** as kind as   **2** as clean as

3 as early as   **4** not as(so) cold as

5 as well as   **6** as expensive as

7 as old as   **8** not as(so) busy as

9 as cheap as   **10** not as(so) fast as

틀리기 쉬운 내신포인트

정답 ①

해설 '~만큼 …한'은 「as+형용사의 원급+as」로 쓰므로 형용사 pretty가 알맞다.

개념완성 **TEST**   p. 232

STEP 1 Quick Check

① taller   ② shorter   ③ much   ④ the shortest   ⑤ old

⑥ more   ⑦ 보미는 셋 중에서 가장 어리다.

⑧ Sera는 한국에서 가장 인기 있는 가수이다.

STEP 2 기본 다지기

A   **1** younger than   **2** the kindest

3 the fastest   **4** more difficult

5 better than   **6** smaller than

7 as cute as   **8** more interesting than

9 as warm as   **10** as short as

B   **1** easier   **2** healthy as   **3** hottest

4 tallest   **5** ○   **6** as busy

7 more famous / much more famous

C   **1** taller than   **2** cheaper than   **3** heavier than

4 as cold as   **5** older than   **6** the earliest

7 thicker than   **8** bigger than   **9** the highest

STEP 3 서술형 따라잡기

A   **1** hotter than   **2** the fastest   **3** as long as

B   **1** My bag is as heavy as Jina's bag.

2 Sam is the best dancer of the four.

3 This computer is the most expensive in the store.

4 This book is much thicker than that book.

C   **1** I can swim better than Lisa.

2 James is the most famous person in the school.

3 This winter is even colder than last winter.

4 Eric came home as late as Tony.

학교 시험 실전 문제   p. 235

1 ③   **2** ③   **3** ⑤   **4** ④   **5** ④   **6** ②   **7** ④

8 ⑤   **9** ③   **10** ②   **11** ②   **12** ③   **13** ⑤   **14** ③

15 ②   **16** ⑤   **17** ④   **18** ①   **19** ③   **20** ④

서술형

21 (1) the largest(biggest)

(2) the smallest

(3) longer than

(4) as long as

22 (1) as sunny as

(2) a lot more interesting than

(3) the largest animal

23 (1) important → more important

(2) most large → the largest

24 (1) heavier than

(2) the most popular

(3) as expensive as

25 (1) earlier than my little brother

(2) the oldest of

1 bad의 비교급은 worse이고 최상급은 worst이다.

2 첫 번째 문장은 '~만큼 …한'이 되도록 「as+원급+as」가 쓰이는 것이 알맞다. 두 번째 문장은 '~보다 …한'이 되도록 「비교급+than」이 쓰이는 것이 알맞다.

3 첫 번째 빈칸에는 뒤에 than이 있으므로 비교급 faster가 알맞다. 두 번째 문장은 '~에서 가장 …한'이 되도록 「the+최상급+in ~」이 쓰이는 것이 알맞다. fast의 최상급은 fastest이다.

4 '훨씬'이라는 뜻으로 비교급을 강조할 때는 부사 even, a lot, much, far 등을 쓴다. very는 원급을 강조한다.

5 as와 as 사이에는 형용사나 부사의 원급이 들어간다. bad의 비교급인 worse는 알맞지 않다.

6 ② many와 most는 '원급-최상급'의 관계이다. 나머지는 모두 '원급-비교급'의 관계이다.

7 「비교급+than」이 되도록 형용사 little의 비교급 less가 알맞다.

8 「the+최상급+in ~」이 되도록 delicious의 최상급 most delicious가 알맞다.

9 ③ 최상급 비교에서 '~ 중에서'를 뜻하는 of가 알맞다. 나머지는 모두 비교급 문장이므로 than이 알맞다.

10 비교급을 강조하는 부사 much는 비교급 앞에 쓴다.

11 피자가 12달러로 가장 비싼 요리이므로 ②가 표의 내용과 일치한다.

12 ⓐ pretty는 최상급을 y를 i로 바꾸고 -est를 붙여 만드므로, prettiest로 써야 한다. (most pretty → prettiest) ⓔ 원급 비교는 「as+원급+as」로 써야 하므로 taller는 tall로 고쳐야 한다.

13 '~에서 가장 ⋯한'이라는 뜻의 최상급 비교 문장이므로 「the+최상급+in ~」의 형태로 쓴다.

14 (A) popular의 비교급은 단어 앞에 more를 붙여 쓴다.
(B) well의 비교급은 better로 써야 한다.
(C) 비교급을 강조할 때는 비교급 앞에 much, still, even, far, a lot 등을 써서 표현한다.

15 ② 비교하는 대상은 같은 형태여야 하므로 you가 아닌 your room 혹은 yours가 알맞다.

16 ⑤ fast의 비교급은 faster로 쓴다. more과 -(e)r은 함께 쓸 수 없다.

17 비교급 구문이므로 「비교급+than」 형태가 들어가야 알맞다.

18 ① than이 있으므로 형용사 much의 비교급 more로 고쳐야 한다.

19 ③ '~ 중에서 가장 ⋯하게'이므로 부사 early의 최상급 earliest로 고쳐야 한다.

20 ⓐ, ⓑ than이 있고 두 대상을 비교하고 있으므로 비교급으로 고쳐야 한다. (ⓐ small → smaller, ⓑ the sweetest → sweeter)

21 (1), (2) 셋 이상의 대상을 비교하여 '가장 ~한'이라는 뜻을 나타낼 때는 최상급을 쓴다.
(3) 두 대상을 비교하여 '~보다 더 ⋯한'이라는 뜻을 나타낼 때는 비교급을 쓴다.
(4) '~만큼 ⋯한'이라는 뜻을 나타낼 때는 「as+원급+as」를 쓴다.

22 (1) '~만큼 ⋯한'은 「as+원급+as」로 나타낸다.

(2) '~보다 훨씬 더 ⋯한'은 「a lot+비교급+than」으로 나타낸다.
(3) 「the+최상급+of/in」 형태가 되도록 large의 최상급 largest를 쓴다.

23 (1) 3음절 이상인 단어의 비교급은 원급 앞에 more를 붙여 쓴다.
(2) 「the+최상급+(명사)+in」 형태의 최상급 비교 문장이 되어야 하므로 most 앞에 the를 붙이고, large의 최상급인 largest로 쓴다.

24 (1) A가 C보다 무거우므로 「비교급+than」으로 나타낸다.
(2) B가 가장 인기가 있으므로 「the+최상급」으로 나타낸다.
(3) C와 A의 가격이 같으므로 「as+원급+as」로 나타낸다.

25 (1) 나는 남동생보다 일찍 잠자리에 드므로 early의 비교급 earlier를 이용하여 쓴다.
(2) Diana가 셋 중에 나이가 가장 많으므로 최상급 oldest를 이용하여 쓴다.

CHAPTER 14
접속사와 전치사

POINT 1 접속사: and, but, or, so   p. 240

개념확인 1 and   2 but   3 or

기본연습

A 1 and   2 or   3 so
4 or   5 so   6 but
7 and

B 1 small, heavy   2 beef, chicken
3 by bus, on foot
4 I felt sick, I took some medicine
5 reading books, playing the piano

C 1 or   2 and   3 or
4 so   5 but   6 so
7 and   8 but

D 1 and   2 but   3 and
4 or   5 but   6 so

틀리기 쉬운 내신포인트

정답 ③

해설 첫 번째 문장은 상반되는 내용을 연결하는 but이 들어가고, 두 번째 문장은 원인과 결과를 연결하는 so가 들어가는 것이 알맞다.

POINT 2 명령문+and/or   p. 242

개념확인 1 그러면   2 그리고   3 그렇지 않으면

기본연습 1 and   2 and   3 and
4 or   5 or   6 and
7 and   8 and   9 or
10 or   11 or

틀리기 쉬운 내신포인트

정답 ③

해설 ③은 '그리고'의 의미이고, 나머지는 모두 '(…해라,) 그러면 ~'의 의미이다.

POINT 3 접속사: that   p. 243

개념확인 1 that you win   2 that he likes cats
3 that I did my best

기본연습

A 1 지시형용사   2 지시대명사   3 접속사
4 접속사   5 지시형용사   6 지시대명사
7 접속사   8 접속사

B 1 ③   2 ③   3 ②
4 ③   5 ②

C 1 목적어   2 주어   3 목적어
4 보어   5 목적어   6 목적어
7 주어   8 보어

D 1 Everybody knows that he is a great soccer player.
2 He heard that she didn't come back from Toronto.
3 They hope that they can go on a picnic this Friday.
4 I believe that Jane will be a doctor.
5 She said that the two songs were too similar.

틀리기 쉬운 내신포인트

정답 ③

해설 ③ 동사(said)의 목적어인 명사절을 이끄는 접속사 that은 생략할 수 있다. 나머지는 모두 지시대명사이다.

POINT 4 접속사: when, before, after   p. 245

개념확인 1 after   2 before   3 When

기본연습

A 1 after   2 before   3 after
4 when   5 before   6 When
7 when

B 1 Before   2 When   3 before
4 After   5 When   6 after

C 1 의문사   2 접속사   3 의문사
4 접속사

D 1 You can go out after you finish your homework.
2 He started playing the guitar when he was fifteen.
3 You should go to the restroom before the movie starts.

틀리기 쉬운 내신포인트

정답 ④

해설 '~할 때'라는 의미로 시간을 나타내는 부사절을 이끄는 접속사 When이 알맞다.

POINT 5 접속사: because, if p. 247

p. 247

개념확인 1 because I'm busy 2 If you find him
3 because I lost my dog

기본연습

A 1 If 2 because 3 if
4 because 5 If

B 1 ① 2 ② 3 ②
4 ② 5 ①

C 1 if 2 If 3 When
4 If 5 because 6 Because
7 because 8 before

D 1 If you know the answer, raise your hand.
2 He won't buy the bike if it is too expensive.
3 You will miss the bus if you don't run.
4 Because he has a test tomorrow, he is studying hard.
5 My parents got angry because I fought with my brother.
6 Because we were late, we had to take a taxi.

틀리기 쉬운 내신포인트

정답 ③

해설 if는 '(만약) ~한다면'의 뜻으로 조건의 부사절을 이끄므로, ③에 들어가는 것이 알맞다.

POINT 6 장소 전치사 p. 249

개념확인 1 at the corner 2 on the wall
3 in London

기본연습

A 1 on 2 at 3 in
4 in 5 at

B 1 in 2 on 3 in
4 at 5 on

POINT 7 위치 전치사 p. 250

개념확인 1 on the bench 2 next to the lake
3 behind a cloud

A 1 under 2 next to 3 on
4 under 5 behind 6 between
7 next to 8 in front of 9 between
10 in

B 1 under his sweater
2 on the table
3 between two tall men
4 in front of the mirror
5 next to the airport
6 behind the girl

C 1 between 2 on 3 behind
4 in front of 5 under 6 in

POINT 8 시간 전치사 (1) p. 252

개념확인 1 at 2 p.m. 2 in June 3 for 3 days

기본연습

A 1 in 2 at 3 in
4 in 5 at 6 on
7 on 8 on 9 for
10 for 11 during 12 during

B 1 at 2 for 3 in
4 on 5 during

POINT 9 시간 전치사 (2) p. 253

개념확인 1 오후 7시까지 2 오늘부터 3 아침 식사 전에

기본연습

A 1 before 2 after 3 until
4 from 5 by 6 until
7 by

B 1 until tomorrow 2 after the war
3 by Friday 4 from 9 a.m. to 3 p.m
5 before Christmas 6 after the date
7 by July 15th

C 1 by five o'clock 2 from April to June
3 ○ 4 ○
5 until next week

틀리기 쉬운 내신포인트

정답 ④

해설 ④는 동작의 완료 기한을 나타내는 by가 알맞다. 나머지는 모두 동작의 계속을 나타내는 until이 알맞다.

도구 · 수단 전치사　　　　　p. 255

개념확인　1 ~와 함께　　　2 ~을 타고　　　3 ~을 가지고

기본연습　1 with　　　　2 by　　　　3 with
　　　　　4 by　　　　　5 by　　　　6 with
　　　　　7 by　　　　　8 by　　　　9 with
　　　　　10 with

틀리기 쉬운 내신포인트

정답　②

해설　②는 '~와 함께'라는 뜻이고, 나머지는 모두 '~을 가지고'라는 뜻이다.

개념완성 T E S T　　　　　p. 256

STEP 1 Quick Check

① but　② or　③ that
④ 날씨가 맑았을 때 우리는 밖에 나갔다.
⑤ 날씨가 너무 추워서 나는 코트를 입었다.
⑥ in　⑦ on　⑧ on　⑨ during　⑩ by

STEP 2 기본 다지기

A　1 for　　　　2 or　　　　3 by
　　4 on　　　　5 If　　　　6 that
　　7 after　　　8 next to

B　1 during　　2 ○　　　　3 ○
　　4 with　　　5 ○　　　　6 in front of
　　7 in　　　　8 that　　　9 Because
　　10 from Monday to Friday

C　1 Because the room was dark, I couldn't see her face.
　　2 Take a taxi, and you won't miss the train.
　　3 The sky was clear, so we could see stars.
　　4 I believe that everything will be okay.
　　5 When he was 7 years old, he had a car accident.
　　　또는 When he had a car accident, he was 7 years old.
　　6 Wear a mask, or you can catch flu.
　　7 If you work hard, your dream will come true.

STEP 3 서술형 따라잡기

A　1 on the branch　　　2 next to the trash can
　　3 behind the bench　　4 under the bench

B　1 If you want, you can stay here.
　　2 Before the game started, we were nervous.
　　3 When I was young, I liked chocolate.
　　4 Because I got up late, I missed the bus.

C　1 He read the book for two hours.
　　2 They washed the dishes after lunch.
　　3 Many people believe that the number 7 is lucky.
　　4 Press this button, and the door will open.

학교 시험 실전 문제　　　　　p. 259

1 ②　2 ③　3 ④　4 ①　5 ⑤　6 ④　7 ②
8 ②　9 ③　10 ①　11 ⑤　12 ④　13 ④　14 ⑤
15 ③　16 ④　17 ②　18 ②　19 ④　20 ②

서술형

21 (1) She agreed that we needed more time.
　　(2) Study hard, and you will get good grades.
　　(3) I take a shower after I wake up.
　　　또는 After I wake up, I take a shower.
22 (1) in → on
　　　틀린 이유: 날짜 앞에는 전치사 on을 써야 한다.
　　(2) at → in
　　　틀린 이유: 연도 앞에는 전치사 in을 써야 한다.
23 (1) They played basketball for two hours.
　　(2) You cannot talk during the test.
24 (1) next to (2) in (3) on (4) under
25 (1) She cleaned her room before she had lunch.
　　(2) She went shopping at 2 p.m.
　　(3) She watched a movie after she went shopping.

1　뒤에 결과가 이어지므로 접속사 so(그래서)가 알맞다.

2　뒤에 대조되는 내용이 이어지므로 접속사 but(~이지만)이 알맞다.

3　시간의 전치사 in 뒤에는 연도, 월, 계절, 오전, 오후 등이 올 수 있다. 요일 앞에 쓰는 전치사는 on이다.

4　첫 번째 빈칸에는 선택을 나타내는 접속사 or(~이나)가 알맞다. 두 번째 문장은 '…해라, 그렇지 않으면 ~'의 의미를 나타내도록 접속사 or가 알맞다.

5　첫 번째 빈칸에는 구체적인 기간 앞에 와서 '~ 동안'의 의미를 나타내는 전치사 for가 알맞다. 두 번째 빈칸에는 표면을 나타내는 말 앞에 와서 '~ 위에'라는 의미를 나타내는 전치사 on이 알맞다.

6　④ '~한 후에'라는 의미의 접속사 after 뒤에는 「주어+동사」가 있는 절이 와야 하므로 after you have dinner가 되어야 한다.

7 ② until next week는 '다음 주까지'라는 뜻이다.

8 ②는 '저것'이라는 의미의 지시대명사이다. 나머지는 모두 동사의 목적어 역할을 하는 명사절을 이끄는 접속사이다.

9 ③은 '언제'라는 의미의 의문사이다. 나머지는 모두 '~할 때'라는 의미의 접속사이다.

10 〈보기〉는 '…해라, 그러면 ~'의 의미의 문장으로 접속사 and가 알맞다. ①에는 tall과 handsome을 연결하는 접속사 and가 알맞다. (② or, ③ because나 but, ④ before, ⑤ so)

11 박물관은 도서관 뒤에(behind) 있으므로 도서관은 박물관 앞에 (in front of) 있다고 할 수 있다.

12 수학 시험이 시작되기 전에(before) 그가 도착했으므로 수학 시험은 그가 도착한 후에(after) 시작되었다고 할 수 있다.

13 주어진 문장은 '…해라, 그러면 ~'이라는 뜻의 「명령문, and ~」가 쓰였으므로, '네가 컴퓨터를 가져오면, 내가 그것을 고쳐줄 것이다.'라는 ④와 의미가 같다.

14 'A부터 B까지'는 from *A* to *B*로 쓴다.

15 ③의 that은 주어로 쓰인 명사절을 이끄는 접속사이며 생략할 수 없다. 나머지는 모두 that이 목적어로 쓰인 명사절을 이끄는 접속사이므로 생략할 수 있다.

16 해야 하는 일의 완료 기한을 나타낼 때는 '~까지'라는 의미의 전치사 by를 써야 한다.

17 How long ~?으로 얼마나 오래 잤는지(기간)를 물었으므로, '~ 동안'이라는 의미의 전치사 for를 사용하여 답한 ②가 알맞다.

18 ⓒ 시각 앞에는 전치사 at을 쓴다.
ⓔ 특정한 날 앞에는 전치사 on을 쓴다.

19 ⓑ 표면을 나타낼 때는 전치사 on을 쓴다. (at → on)
ⓓ 숫자를 포함한 구체적인 기간을 나타낼 때는 전치사 for를 쓴다. (during → for)
ⓔ '~ 옆에'는 next to로 쓴다. (next → next to)
ⓕ or는 등위접속사로 앞뒤에 연결되는 말이 같은 형태여야 한다. (watching → watch)

20 (A) 동사 believe의 목적어 역할을 하는 명사절을 이끄는 접속사 that이 알맞다.
(B) '~을 타고'라는 의미로 수단을 나타내는 전치사 by가 알맞다.
(C) 이유를 나타내는 절을 이끄는 접속사 because가 알맞다.

21 (1) 접속사 that을 사용하여 첫 번째 문장을 동사 agreed의 목적어 역할을 하는 명사절로 쓴다.
(2) 「명령문, and ~」 구문을 사용하여 '…해라, 그러면 ~'의 의미를 나타내는 문장으로 연결한다.
(3) 일어난 후에 샤워를 한다는 내용으로 접속사 after(~ 후에)를 사용하여 문장을 연결한다. 부사절이 앞에 올 때는 부사절 뒤에 콤마(,)를 쓴다.

22 날짜 앞에는 전치사 on을 쓰고, 연도 앞에는 전치사 in을 쓴다.

23 (1) 숫자를 포함한 구체적인 기간을 나타낼 때는 전치사 for를 쓴다. 운동 경기 앞에는 the를 쓰지 않는 것에 유의한다.
(2) 특정 기간을 나타내는 명사구는 전치사 during과 함께 쓴다.

24 (1) next to: ~ 옆에
(2) in: ~ 안에
(3) on: ~ 위에
(4) under: ~ 아래에

25 (1) Betty는 점심을 먹기 전에 방을 청소를 했다.
(2) Betty는 2시에 쇼핑을 하러 갔다. 시각 앞에는 전치사 at을 쓴다.
(3) Betty는 쇼핑을 하러 간 후에 영화를 봤다.